The Internationalization of the Firm:
A Reader

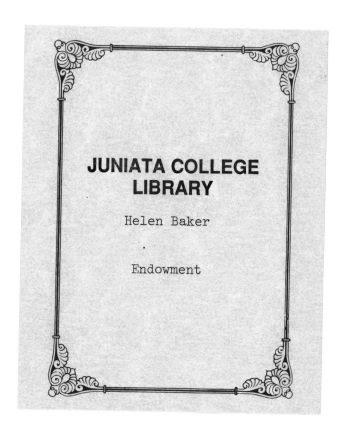

The Internationalization of the Firm:
A Reader

Edited by

Peter J Buckley and Pervez N Ghauri

Academic Press
Harcourt Brace Jovanich, Publishers
London   San Diego   New York   Boston
Sydney   Tokyo   Toronto

ACADEMIC PRESS LIMITED
24/28 Oval Road,
London NW1 7DX

United States Edition published by
ACADEMIC PRESS, INC.
San Diego, CA 92101

A catalogue record for this book is available from the British Library
ISBN 0–12–139161–2

Typeset by Latimer Trend & Co. Ltd, Plymouth, Devon
Printed in Great Britain at the University Press, Cambridge

Contents

PART V: SCANDINAVIAN APPLICATIONS

Introduction and Overview

Peter J. Buckley and Pervez N. Ghauri

The internationalization of the firm has been a key issue in international business research right from the outset. Internationalizing means changing state and thus implies dynamic change. The growth of the firm is the background to internationalization and to some degree the distinction between internationalization and growth is false. The crossing of national boundaries in the process of growth may be argued to be a meaningless threshold (Buckley, 1990a). However, there are features which are unique to internationalization, or, at least, there are significant degrees of difference between growth at home and internationalization. This volume seeks to explore these differences.

The rate and direction of internationalization have been the subject of many studies, some of which are represented here. Moreover, this area has not been without controversy. Do firms internationalize by a gradual, incremental process going through a number of definite stages? Is this stage of internationalization model valid for established multinational firms or only for naïve, small firms with little international experience? How far can firms use their experience (learning) to miss out stages in this process and move directly to a deep form of involvement in the foreign market? On how many fronts can a firm pursue internationalization? Should it proceed step by step, going first to nearby countries in terms of physical and cultural distance? Do established multinational firms need to obey any such rules? These and other questions were in the minds of the researchers who undertook the studies which follow and their efforts have illuminated our understanding of the forces at work. Naturally, definitive conclusions have not always been reached.

The relationship between internationalization and forms of foreign market servicing is a close one. The conditions under which a firm will choose exporting, licensing or foreign investment interact with internationalization. The management and control of the activities and organization of the multinational firm are also a crucial part of the conceptualization of internationalization.

A considerable amount of the important work on internationalization has been carried out in the Nordic countries. It is therefore appropriate not only that the key works should be reproduced here but that empirical examples should be drawn largely from these countries.

This collection then covers: key works (introducing the product cycle, internalization and stages of development models), methods of foreign market servicing, studies of the internationalization process, work on the organization of multinational firms and applications to Scandinavia.

1. ANTECEDENTS

The first section of this collection covers key articles introducing basic concepts which have had a fundamental effect on subsequent research and writing.

The volume opens with a work which can justly claim the epithet 'seminal', Raymond Vernon's 1966 article 'International investment and international trade in the product cycle'. The argument of this paper is that firms are highly stimulated by their local environment and are more likely to innovate when their immediate surroundings are more conducive to the creation of (particular) new techniques or products. For internationalization to occur these innovations must be transferable to other economies. In adapting to its market, the firm moves through stages from innovation to standardization and maturity according to the developing forces of supply and demand for its product. This model of sequential decision making has had a great influence on internationalization theory. The model was originally developed to explain US investment in Europe and also in cheap labour countries. Its usefulness goes beyond Vernon's reappraisal of efficacy under changed world conditions (1979) or the sting of its critics (e.g. Giddy, 1978). Its relevance arises from the fact that the dynamic of the model lies in the interaction of the evolving forces of demand (taste) patterns and production possibilities. In some ways, its powerful, yet simple, dynamic resting on the changing equilibria of demand and supply over time, has never been bettered. The twin rationales of cost imperatives and market pull are simply explained in Vernon's model. Its programmatic nature may have straightjacketed later analyses into a unilinear internationalization path. Although its validity for the explanation of the behaviour modern multinationals may be questioned, this article spawned much of the empirical literature on international marketing.

The second article has been the focus of ideas for many subsequent researchers. Johanson and Wiedersheim-Paul examine the internationalization of four Swedish firms. For this admittedly small sample they find a regular process of gradual incremental change. The firm progresses from no regular exports to export through independent representatives and the establishment of sales subsidiaries to the establishment of production facilities. Flows of information between the firm and the market are (as in Vernon's model) crucial in this process and the cultural distance between spatially separated units of the firm is termed psychic distance. The establishment profiles of the four firms are mapped across a number of countries in time and the gradualist pattern is confirmed. This path-breaking article gave rise to considerable controversy centred on the general applicability of the findings and the underlying theory. Suggestions have been made that experienced firms can 'jump' stages and transfer learning from one market to another without having to go through each stage in each separate foreign market. The knowledge collection and planning processes of large multinationals can, some authors feel, obviate the need for incremental learning. Some empirical findings suggest a less gradualist and one directional expansion path. The theory has also been questioned in its classification of stages or stages of involvement ranked in order of 'depth'. Is a licensing deal a deeper form of involvement than a foreign agency agreement? Methodologically, looking back in time in a successful firm eliminates firms which have failed at an earlier stage, i.e. it induces a bias towards longer routes of establishment (see Hedlund and Kverneland (1984), Reading 8 in this volume). More carefully designed experiments are required to establish the conditions under which stages approaches are valid. Nevertheless, the article reprinted here is a classic piece of empirical research with wide implications for internationalization.

It was followed, in 1977, by the piece by Johanson and Vahlne, reproduced here as Reading 3. This article examines the internationalization process by investigating the development of knowledge and the building of a commitment within the firm to foreign markets. The twin notions of increasing knowledge about foreign markets as a means of reducing uncertainty and the creation of a commitment to foreign ventures had been examined in a key study by Aharoni (1966) and the authors here tie these notions to the framework of the behavioural theory of the firm. Internationalization is again envisaged as the product of a series of incremental decisions. Decisions taken at a point in time affect subsequent steps in the process. Psychic distance is invoked and is defined as 'the sum of the factors preventing the flow of information from and to the market'. The decision-making process is dependent on the firm's previous experience. Again, the empirical evidence is based on a very small number of companies. Four Swedish companies are examined from Reading 2, a case study of the Swedish pharmaceutical firm Pharmacia is introduced and other Uppsala industry studies are quoted (special steel, pulp and paper and nine further cases). Casual empirical evidence from other countries is also adduced. The two notions of market commitment and market knowledge entered the literature as key elements of internationalization.

The dominant paradigm in research on the multinational firm is the internalization approach. Reading 4 is an early summary of the theoretical work in this tradition by Buckley and Casson whose book the *Future of the Multinational Enterprise* (1976) was a basic contribution. This paper attempts to explain the division of national markets (and therefore of the world market) between domestic firms and foreign multinationals. It does so by reference to two effects: the location effect and the ownership effect. The location effect determines where value adding activities take place and the ownership effect explains who owns and controls those activities. The concepts of least cost location and growth by internalization of markets are thus introduced to internationalization theory. Firms grow by replacing the (imperfect) external market and earn a return from so doing until the point at which the benefits of further internalization are outweighed by the costs. The types of benefit and cost of growth by internalization are listed and it is suggested that certain types of market are more likely to be internalized than others, given the configuration of the world economy. These ideas were expanded in Buckley and Casson (1985), Casson (1987) and Buckley (1988, 1989, 1990b). Thus the direction of internationalization can be predicted by predicting changes in cost and market conditions. These factors are classified as industry specific, region specific, firm specific and nation specific.

2. METHODS OF FOREIGN MARKET SERVICING

There are three generic methods by which a firm can penetrate a particular foreign market: exporting, licensing or direct investment. Each of these methods has a variety of subtypes and the interaction between the methods are, in practice, very important. The readings here are representative of a huge literature on each of exporting, licensing, joint ventures and foreign direct investment. For a review of this literature see Young et al (1989).

Exporting may be regarded as the most straightforward way of selling in a foreign market, avoiding, as it does, most of the costs of doing business abroad. It is separated from the other two main forms of foreign market servicing by the location factor in that the bulk of the value adding activities take place in the home (not the foreign) market. Exporting may attract tax advantages and the associated risks are low because usually little capital is involved. However, the fixed costs of exporting (including making contact, negotiating prices, arranging shipping, adaptation of product and promotion) mean that a small volume of export sales can be uneconomic. Costs of product adaptation, tariff and non-tariff barriers and transport costs may dictate local operations rather than exporting.

A number of studies investigate export behaviour of all types of firms. The first reading (Reading 5) in this section (Cavusgil, 1984) utilizes an alternative approach and attempts to delineate differences among exporting firms when firms are classified by their degree of internationalization. It identifies three types of exporter; experimental exporters, active exporters and committed exporters. These firms are then compared with each other in respect of measurable company characteristics. These characteristics include domestic environment, nature of international business involvement, marketing policy aspects, and export market research practices. The data base for the investigation is a series of interviews with 70 systematically selected American firms. The study builds upon the sequential nature of internationalization (see Reading 2) and associates this sequential exporting with the three stages of internationalization identified. The reading reveals significant differences among the three types of exporters and provides further insight into the export marketing behaviour of firms. It provides a useful background for designing a more comprehensive investigation of the issues and suggests that future investigations may also consider classifying firms by alternative criteria in addition to stages of internationalization.

International licensing appears to combine the best of both worlds—the advantage in technology and skills of the licensing multinational plus the local knowledge of the licensee. However licensing accounts for only 7% of the total foreign sales of British companies (Buckley and Prescott, 1989) and approximately the same proportion in the other major trading nations. The reasons lie in the costs and difficulties of designing and maintaining contractual arrangements. These transaction costs centre on the identifi-ability of the advantage, policing costs (constraining the licensee from using the knowledge in 'ways which have not been paid for'), the danger of creating a competitor, problems in the market for licences (including the buyer uncertainty problem; that the buyer does not know what to pay for the knowledge until he has it, when he has it he has no need to pay for it!) and the search costs in bringing buyer and seller together (Buckley and Davies, 1981). In other instances, the market structure may militate in favour of licensing as a form of market entry—cross licensing in oligopolistic industries may be preferable to head-to-head competition. Licensing may also be a second best choice when exporting or direct investment are ruled out by government policy, intra-firm scarcities or risk profiles. Licensing may also be useful to extend the life of an idea or technology or to reach small or difficult foreign markets. In the theory of international business, the choice between licensing and direct investment is crucial in illustrating the choice between a market (external) solution—licensing, and an internal solution—direct investment (Buckley and Casson, 1976; 1985).

The article by Welch (Reading 6) is unusual in that it attempts to quantify the costs of licensing and therefore captures the importance and magnitude of transaction costs. This piece is important not only for its insights into the licensing process but also for its meticulous interrogation of some valuable primary data. This data is suggestive of a number of interesting hypotheses but it also provides one of the few extant attempts to measure cost magnitudes. The survey of literature provides a useful backdrop to the empirical issues related to the importance of patents, know-how and other forms of proprietary knowledge and the difficulties for firms in appropriating benefits from the international exploitation of technological advances. It also covers the search costs of finding a licensee, the negotiation costs and pulls these together (in the important Table 8). Licensing is also compared and contrasted to foreign direct investment. Licensing is shown to be a potentially important part of the international operations of companies.

The foreign investment decision is a crucial step in internationalization. In fact foreign direct investment is often treated as if it were synonymous with internationalization. Just as there are many forms of contractual arrangements for conducting international business, of which licensing is just one (Buckley, 1989) so there are many forms of foreign direct investment. The major motives for conducting foreign direct investment are market orientated, cost orientated and for control of key inputs. Readings 7 to 10 examine direct investment in a number of contexts. Reading 7 examines the direct investment behaviour by small and medium-sized enterprises. It gives the theoretical background to the analysis of such investment from a number of viewpoints, both theoretical and empirical. The special factors influencing foreign direct investment by smaller firms are drawn out and key constraints are found to be the relationship between firm and market, shortages of capital and management time and the role of uncertainty. In passing, the evolutionary approach to internationalization is discussed. Reading 8 takes the criticism of inter-nationalization further by stages. In examining Swedish investment in Japan, the degree of international experience of companies is found to be an influence on foreign investment entry into the Japanese market. The relevance of the slow learning approach is questioned for a large and increasing number of firms. However, Japan is such a special case (as Hedlund and Kverneland acknowledge) that further research is required to establish definitive conclusions.

Joint ventures are an important form of foreign direct investment and are currently subject to a great deal of theoretical and empirical scrutiny (Contractor and Lorange, 1988). They are an important means of entry into markets which are difficult for foreign firms to penetrate because of legal, regulatory or cultural barriers. Japan is a case in point. Buckley, Mirza and Sparkes (1985) in Reading 9 examine joint ventures for a sample of European firms (almost certainly a sample which overlaps with that in Reading 8!). This article also notes the strategic importance of penetrating certain large foreign markets. It enables learning to occur which can be transferred to all parts of the company (including home operations), it enables competition to be met head-on and it closes down an opportunity for competitors to have a free ride in one market (the home market in the case of Japanese firms). Thus foreign direct investment and joint ventures must be seen as part of a global competitive game.

Reading 10 (Harrigan, 1984) relates joint venture activity to global strategies and proposes a framework for predicting whether firms will co-operate in forming joint venture or other forms of interfirm co-operation. It also suggests which factors/forces destabilize co-operative joint ventures and suggests that under certain conditions joint ventures are most appropriate for strategic needs. Joint ventures are considered to be a better way to internationalize and may be used as pre-emptive manoeuvres to ensure that access to distribution channels, suppliers and technology in promising industries are not foreclosed. They are also ways of ensuring that potential entrants do not team up with competitors.

3. THE INTERNATIONALIZATION PROCESS

We have already introduced a pioneer study of the internationalization process in 'antecedents' (Reading 2). Over the period from the late fifties, there has been growing interest in the internationalization process of firms. This is exemplified by the readings in this volume where we can see the gradual development of research in this area. Starting from Dunning (1958), Vernon (1966), Servan-Schreiber (1967) and Horst (1972), through Readings 2 and 3, and Loustarinen (1979) we have seen how the focus has shifted from the decision to export to a more longitudinal approach, namely, the international-ization process. Reading 11 is a good example of this development. This reading points out that although widely used, the term internationalization has not been clearly defined. It should, according to the reading, be broadened to include both the inward and outward aspects of the process. As well as the longitudinal character of the research, the study also draws our attention to other aspects such as the impact of individuals and the evolution of communication patterns. It seems that more research is necessary both on the process and the analysis of the decision and that these should be integrated. Reading 11 by Welch and Luostarinen surveys this literature. This reading presents a strong defence of the concept of internationalization as a sequential process. It adduces evidence from Luostarinen's study of Finnish firms (1979) and alludes to studies of Japanese companies and those from business history (a source mostly neglected by the Readings in this volume) to support evidence of sequential development. It also suggests *contra* Hedlund and Kverneland (Reading 8) that jumps in the stage pattern in *any one foreign market* may result from learning across the firm, i.e. from other foreign markets. Thus overall foreign knowledge may diffuse through the firm and allow more rapid penetration of foreign markets tackled at a later date.

Reading 12 (Turnbull, 1987) challenges the gradual stages theory of internationaliza-tion. Turnbull argues forcefully that an 'orderly and progressive sequence' cannot be observed in many cases of internationalization. This sequential process is contrasted with a contingency approach (Reid, 1983) where 'reversal' of stages can occur and where the 'stage' of internationalization is largely determined by the operating environment, industry structure and marketing strategy of the firm. The measurement of international-ization is felt to be conceptually difficult, particularly in multi-product, multi-divisional firms where export dependence, number of export markets served and export structure varies across and among business units. These criticisms are backed up by empirical results derived from British data on 24 companies from three industries (marine diesel engines, motor vehicle components and telecommunication equipment). The results do not support an evolutionary path in international expansion. Industry factors are important and companies often use experimental means of reaching foreign markets. The strategy followed by the company is a major determinant of export structure so that firm and market specific factors play an important role *at any one point of time* in determining export form.

John Stopford (Reading 13) emphasizes the importance of organizational structures and the vital role it plays in a firm's international activities. The author also points out that it is important because structural changes take place in firms which are most active internationally and in those firms which go abroad for the first time. After going abroad these firms realize that the structure based on their local activities is not sufficient or appropriate in the new environment. Moreover, the changing strategies of the firms also force them to match the structure to new strategies and to changing management styles. This Reading is of particular interest because it compares American and European practices in managing foreign operations. It also speculates about the changes which are expected to occur. Although the author admits that it is not fair to generalize across Europe in terms of one management style, there is evidence that European firms, as a whole, are changing and they are coming to resemble American firms. At the same time American-based multinationals are facing difficulties in managing multi-product, multi-culture operations in different countries. The author poses a question on the possible convergence of management practices between United States and European-based international firms. He also discusses the constraints as well as pressures towards this convergence. The important message is, however, that firms involved in international activities, whether they are Europe based or United States based, can learn from each others' experience. Jesper Strandskov (Reading 14) presents a new approach to study the internationalization process of the firm, where he considers export engagement in the context of a process taking place as a result of successive decisions made by management over a period of time. With support from the experience of a Danish company during a 30-year period, the author presents a stage-of-growth model for export activities. The model consists of stages characterized as (1) sporadic export involvement, (2) experimental export involvement, (3) foreign market expansion, (4) development of overseas sales branches, and (5) foreign market consolidation. Although it is accepted that the export development process is firm specific because particular contingency factors and circumstances vary from firm to firm and situation to situation, the stage-of-growth model points out some common features and regularities in the export development of firms.

Reading 15 by Bruce Kogut considers foreign direct investment as a sequential process. It argues that the multinational enterprise has the ability to exploit three uniquely international distortions in markets. These are: (1) the ability to arbitrage institutional restrictions, (2) informational externalities which are captured by the firm in the conduct of international business (learning cost externalities) and (3) cost savings gained by joint production in marketing and manufacturing. Kogut argues that the operational flexibility of a multinational system is undervalued because there is a tendency to view foreign direct investment as a decision made at a moment in time. The excessive concentration on the transfer of resources has meant that the fact that such investments are sequential decisions has been ignored. This series of sequential decisions determines the value and direction of these transferred resources. Although the argument is not fully articulated, Kogut's contribution draws attention to the process aspects of foreign direct investment and puts the history of the firm centre-stage. Investment decisions should not be entirely disembodied from the firm in real time in Kogut's view.

4. ORGANIZING THE MULTINATIONAL FIRM

A number of studies are available on the organization and management of the multinational firm. Studies such as 'Strategic Management in Multinational Companies' (Doz, 1986), 'Managing the Multinational Subsidiary' (Hulbert and Brandt, 1980) and Hedlund and Aman (1984) are worth mentioning. In this section, however, we have selected a number of readings which have been particularly innovative.

The first reading in this section (Reading 16) by Prahalad and Doz (1981) deals with the problems of maintaining strategic control over subsidiaries in a multinational firm. The authors argue that the nature of control in this relationship changes over time (see also Ghauri in this volume). As resources such as capital, technology and management are invested in the subsidiary, the head office, over time, cannot control these resources by influencing the subsidiary. The authors present a conceptual framework to define organizational context, and argue that it can be used as a means of control. They also classify MNCs in four categories: (1) fragmented, (2) dependent, (3) autonomous, and (4) integrated. However, the conclusion is that HQ's ability to control cannot be taken for granted.

The next reading (Bartlett, 1981) is by now considered seminal in its analysis of organizational forms of MNCs. It illustrates a fundamental methodological problem and looks beyond organizational structure to find that MNCs meet the demands of their multicultural environment. The author deals with the strategic challenges faced by MNCs through five US health care companies, and examines the way in which these firms deal with the pressures from local government and global competitors. He examines the means by which those firms which retain their simple international division structures, maintain stability in their formal organizations and at the same time deal with changes in people, relationships and processes through more informal means. These companies developed a flexible multidimensional decision process that their international environment demanded.

The next contribution on the management of Headquarters–subsidiary relationships in Swedish multinationals questions the existing literature on Foreign Direct Investment (FDI) which deals with the global competition with a traditional marketing or/and product life cycle approach (see e.g. Vernon, 1966; Buckley and Casson, 1979, and Prahalad and Doz 1981, in this collection). The study introduces recent developments in internationalization using a network approach (see Johanson and Mattsson (1988), Reading 21). It deals with an evolutionary phenomenon where foreign operations become more influential and independent from the parent firm. The article assumes that a foreign subsidiary has a three-dimensional relationship, i.e. with the head office, local authorities and with the local network. It presents empirical evidence from Swedish firms and their subsidiaries from South-East Asia: Thailand, Philippines and Indonesia. The author has interviewed the population of Swedish firms and their subsidiaries which have manufacturing facilities in these countries. These empirical investigations support the assumption that a new relationship pattern is emerging where the foreign subsidiaries become more influential than the parent firms and make their own decisions as regards purchasing of raw material and components, products and production decisions, relationship with other actors in their network and with the local authorities. Moreover, the emergence of 'centre-to-centre' relationships are also observed, where some regional subsidiaries communicate directly with others around them—often without the consent of their Head Office.

Reading 19 (Buckley, Pass and Prescott, 1990) is an attempt to integrate approaches to the foreign market servicing decisions of multinational firms. Foreign market servicing decisions concern the choice of which production or service facility should cover which particular foreign market and the means by which this should be performed. Thus the mode of servicing (exporting, licensing, investment) and the channel decisions need to be integrated. The article deals with a wider range of functions than is usual and presents some strong propositions on the form and development of foreign market servicing channels, focusing on the key choices of location and of internal versus external control systems. The simple choice of exporting, licensing or investment is too crude a division because it ignores the crucial issues of channel management and the flows of information within the firm. The management of information and choice of form link this theoretical piece with the internationalization approach and provide testable propositions for empirical work.

5. SCANDINAVIAN STUDIES

It will be obvious that many of the key studies of internationalization have been carried out in Scandinavia, often using samples from these countries. (See also Hornell and Vahlne, 1986, Swedenborg, 1979, Juul and Walters, 1987 and Luostarinen, 1979.) This section includes five articles which have special relevance beyond their Scandinavian origins. They elucidate key concepts and show the importance of the interaction between theory and empirical work.

Reading 20 (Hallén and Wiedersheim-Paul, 1979) deals with psychic distance and buyer–seller interaction. The authors claim that the gap between buyers and sellers is two-dimensional. Firstly, the 'hard' dimension such as the physical distance and secondly, the soft dimension connected with differences in attitudes and perceptions caused for instance, by differences in cultural environments (in a wide sense) between buyers and sellers. Although the reading addresses buyers and sellers, the approach is wide-ranging and can be applied to comparative management and management in multinational firms. The 'soft' dimension of distance is of particular importance in international marketing and management. As inter-firm relationships (such as that between head office and subsidiary) develop, mutual understanding between the units reduces this psychic gap.

More recently the internationalization of industrial firms has been explained through networks and relationships between firms. The network model has been largely developed at Uppsala (Hagg and Johanson, 1982, Johanson and Mattsson, 1985, Thorelli, 1986, and Ghauri, 1989). According to this approach firms internationalize because other firms in their national network internationalize. The industrial system is composed of firms engaged in production, distribution and use of goods and services. The relationships between the firms are described as a network. The firms within the network are dependent on each other, and their activities therefore need to be co-ordinated. These networks are stable or/are changing but the transactions take place within the framework of these established relationships. In the process however, some new relationships are developed and some old ones are disrupted because of the competitive activities of different actors.

Thus, although there are competitive relationships, interdependences are stressed in the network approach. The firms have to develop and maintain relationships with other firms in the network. This process of developing and maintaining relationships is of a cumulative nature and the firms are striving to establish a prominent position in their networks. At each point the firm has a position in the network which explains its relationship to the other firms. Here one basic assumption is that the firm is dependent on external resources controlled by other firms. Therefore, it is dependent on its network in foreign markets while internationalizing. The firm thus has to work for international integration. The network approach also influences the internationalization of the market—for example a production net can be more or less internationalized. A higher degree of internationalization means that there are strong relationships between different national networks. These relationships developed by the firm are thus considered as market investments. Moreover, the firms which are highly internationalized would prefer to have a number of activities performed externally by sub-contractors and can still have the desired control due to these relationships.

The article by Johanson and Mattsson (Reading 21) is a good example of the network approach, where a general description of market as network is provided with several examples. The article also deals with internationalization according to the network approach. While analysing the network approach the authors characterize firms as the early starter, the lonely international, the late starter and the international, among others. This article is particularly interesting as it compares the network approach with two other models, the theory of internalization (Buckley and Casson, 1976 and Rugman, 1982) which is widely accepted as a theory explaining multinational enterprise, and the internationalization model developed at Uppsala (see Readings 2 and 3) which is described as a gradual step-by-step commitment in a foreign market. The article claims that the model which aims to explain multinational enterprise is not sufficient to explain or analyse further internationalization. It also claims that the internalization models fail in situations where both the firm and market are highly internationalized. It suggests that the internalization model is more valid for the early starter stage and not for other stages of internationalization.

The third contribution in this section, by Hyder and Ghauri, is a longitudinal study of joint venture relationships between Swedish firms and firms from developing countries. This is an empirical study which analyses two joint venture relationships between Swedish and Indian partners. A model is developed based on exchange of resources, which takes place during the operational period of the joint venture. The relationship is considered to change over time as the interplay between control and co-operation/conflict varies from time to time. An attempt is made to measure performance, which is then used to explain interests of the partners, why they entered the joint venture, what benefits they derive, the kind of conflicts which arise during the relationship and how these are solved. Expectations of the partners as regards the resource exchange are also considered important, and are compared with the actual contribution of the partners over time. Co-operation and conflict depend upon the ability to fulfil each other's requirements and expectations. One of the main conclusions of the study has been that conflicts emerge when partners have difficulties in agreeing on the choice of major policies. The importance of recruiting local employees on the basis of efficiency and competence and not on loyalty and relationship is emphasized. The article is interesting in the sense that it provides us with longitudinal evidence about how the partners handle joint venture relationships.

Forsgren and Holm (Reading 23) analyse relationships between the internationalization of divisional management and the existence of multi-culture structures in 22 Swedish firms. The authors claim that there is no doubt that the parent company (the 'centre') designs the organization and controls the subsidiaries (the 'periphery'), but this perspective is dependent on the stage of the internationalization process. Consistent with Reading 18 (Ghauri), this paper also suggests that in the later stages of the internationalization process the periphery becomes stronger and plays a more important and dominant role in the group's total operations with power over a particular product or function area. Moreover, the subsidiaries start extending their operations outside their local market. This leads to the situation where the firm as a whole consists of several centres located in different geographical areas and the 'centre'–'periphery' structure fades away. The authors present this as a 'multi-centre' structure. They also imply that the larger a unit share of a division's operations the more likely it is that the unit's local critical resources influence its activities.

Their conclusion is that the development of the firm into a multi-centre structure leads to a number of foreign bases with substantial resources on the operational level. These bases, because of their control of a significant amount of resources, influence the formal structure of organization. The theoretical conclusion of their study is the higher the significance of multi-centre structures the higher the probability of an internationalization of the management and consequently a gradual relocalization of the governance structure in the firm. This leads to the fact that the power balance changes from top management to divisional management.

The final paper in this volume (Reading 24) is a study of the international strategy of Norwegian companies by Pat Joynt. The framework used is an attempt to integrate Porter's model of competitive advantage (1985) with Scandinavian approaches to internationalization. Joynt examines internationalization along six axes: production methods, sales objectives, organization structure, market servicing methods, markets and personnel. Thus internationalization must be placed in the context of the value chain and the nature of international competition. As other authors have emphasized, learning is a key element in the internationalization process and Joynt explores the 'action learning' methodology in his analysis of Norwegian data. The small size of most Norwegian firms on the world market means that niche strategies have to be sought but Joynt identifies several general areas of competitive strength for success in international markets.

6. SUMMARY

The analysis of internationalization has been a vital driving force in international business research. Seemingly disparate pieces of research based on product cycle models (Vernon, 1966: Reading 1), stages of internationalization (Johanson and Wiedersheim-Paul, 1975: Reading 2, Johanson and Vahlne, 1977: Reading 3), studies of small firm or first-time foreign investors (Buckley, Newbould and Thurwell, 1988, first edition, 1978; Buckley, Berkova and Newbould, 1983, Reading 6 in this volume), network approaches to internationalization (Johanson and Mattsson, 1986: Reading 19), internalization theory (Buckley and Casson, 1976; 1985), the international marketing and purchasing approach

(Paliwoda and Turnbull, 1986; Turnbull and Valla, 1989) and studies critical of stages theories (Readings 8 and 12) are now being crystallized into a coherent view of internationalization. Such a view has evolutionary stages elements as part of its make up. But these stages are now much more circumscribed in context and flexible in nature than the extrapolation of early studies would suggest. For naïve, first time investors or internationally inexperienced larger firms, a strategy of creeping incrementalism may still be valid. However, for larger, diversified multinationals, a global planning horizon is now much nearer as several readings above demonstrate. The choice of methods of doing business abroad is now much wider than even 20 years ago and choices can be tailored to the precise needs of internationalizing firms. This flexibility (often gained through experience) may well, in many cases, obviate the need for incremental learning and feedback through stages. We should not, however, underestimate the importance of gradual learning, even for the most experienced and internationally diversified firms.

REFERENCES

Aharoni, Y. (1966) *The Foreign Investment Decision Process.* Graduate School of Business Administration, Harvard University: Boston, MA.

Buckley, P. J. (1983) New Forms of International Industrial Cooperation: A Survey of the Literature. *Aussenwirtschaft* **38**(2): 195–222. Reprinted in Buckley and Casson (1985).

Buckley, P. J. (1988) The Limits of Explanation: Testing the Internalization Theory of the Multinational Enterprise. *Journal of International Business Studies* **XIX**(2): 181–193.

Buckley, P. J. (1989) *The Multinational Enterprise: Theory and Applications.* Macmillan: London.

Buckley, P. J. (1990a) Barriers to the Internationalization Process of Firms: paper presented at the Conference on Strategic Change, University of Venice, Venice, Italy.

Buckley, P. J. (1990b) Problems and Developments in the Core Theory of International Business. *Journal of International Business* **XXI**(4): 657–665.

Buckley, P. J., Berkova, Z., Newbould, G. D. (1983) *Direct Investment in the UK by Smaller European Firms* Macmillan: London.

Buckley, P. J., Casson, M. (1976) *The Future of the Multinational Enterprise.* Macmillan: London.

Buckley, P. J., Casson, M. (1985) *The Economic Theory of the Multinational Enterprise.* Macmillan: London.

Buckley, P. J., Davies, H. (1981) Foreign Licensing in Overseas Operations: Theory and Evidence from the UK. In Hawkins, R. G., Prasad, A. J. (eds) *Technology Transfer and Economic Development.* JAI Press Inc.: Greenwich, CT.

Buckley, P. J., Newbould, G. D., Thurwell, J. (1988) *Foreign Direct Investment by Smaller UK Firms.* Macmillan: London (previously published in 1978 as *Going International: The Experiences of Smaller Firms Overseas*).

Buckley, P. J., Prescott, K. (1989) The Structure of British Industry's Sales in Foreign Markets. *Managerial and Decision Economics* **10**(3): 189–208.

Casson, M. (1987) *The Firm and the Market.* Basil Blackwell: Oxford.

Contractor, F., Lorange, P. (eds) (1988) *Cooperative Strategies in International Business.* Lexington Books, D. C. Heath & Co.: Lexington, MA.

Doz, Y. (1986) *Strategic Management in Multinational Companies.* Pergamon Press: Oxford.

Dunning, J. H. (1958) *American Investment in British Manufacturing Industry.* George Allen & Unwin: London.

Ghauri, P. N. (1989). Global Marketing Strategies: Swedish Firms in South-East Asia. In Kaynak, E., Lee, K. M. (eds) *Global Business, Asia-Pacific Dimensions.* Routledge: London.

Giddy, I. H. (1978) The Demise of the Product Cycle Model in International Business Theory. *Columbia Journal of World Business,* **13**: 90–97.

Hagg, I., Johanson, J. (1982) *Foretag i natverk, ny syn pa Konkurrenskraft.* SNS: Stockholm.

Hedlund, G., Kverneland, A. Are Establishments and Growth Strategies for Foreign Market Changing?: paper presented at the 9th European International Business Association Conference, Oslo, 18–20 December 1983.

Hedlund, G., Aman, P. (1984) *Managing Relationships with Foreign Subsidiaries*. Sveriges Mekan Forbund: Vastervik.

Hornell, E., Vahlne, J.-E. (1986) *Multinationals—The Swedish Case*. Croom Helm: London.

Horst, T. O. (1972) Firm and Industry Determinants of the Decision to Investment Abroad: An Empirical Study. *Review of Economics and Statistics* **54:** 258–66.

Hulbert, J. M., Brandt, W. K. (1980) *Managing the Multinational Subsidiary*. Holt Reinhart and Winston: New York.

Johanson, J., Vahlne, J.-E. (1990) The Mechanism of Internationalization. *International Marketing Review*, **7(4):** 11–24.

Joynt, P. (1989) International Strategy: A Study of Norwegian Companies. In Prasad, S. B. *Advances in International Corporative Management* **4:** 131–146. JAI Press Inc.: Greenwich, CT.

Juul, M., Walters, P. G. P. (1987) The internationalisation of Norwegian Firms: A study of the UK experience. *Management International Review*, **27(1):** 13–21.

Luostarinen, R. (1979) *The Internationalization of the Firm*. Acta Academia Oeconomica Helsingiensis: Helsinki.

Paliwoda, S. J., Turnbull, P. W. (eds) (1986) *Research in International Marketing*. Croom Helm: London.

Reid, S. (1983) Firm Internationalization, Transaction Costs and Strategic Choice. *International Marketing Review* **1(2):** 44–56.

Rugman, A. M. (1982) *Inside the Multinationals*. Croom Helm: London.

Servan-Schreiber, J. J. (1969) *The American Challenge*. Pelican: Harmondworth.

Swedenborg, B. (1979) *Multinational Operations of Swedish Firms*. Almquist & Wicksell: Stockholm.

Thorelli, H. (1986) Networks: Between Markets and Hierarchies. *Strategic Management Journal* **7:** 37–51.

Turnbull, P. and Valla, J. P. (eds) (1989) *Strategies for International Industrial Marketing*. Croom Helm: London.

Vernon, R. (1979) The Product Cycle Hypothesis in a New International Environment *Oxford Bulletin of Economics and Statistics* **41:** 255–67.

Young, S. et al. (1989) *International Market Entry and Development: Strategies and Management*. Harvester Wheatsheaf: Hemel Hempstead.

Part I

Antecedents

CONTENTS

1

International Investment and International Trade in the Product Cycle

Raymond Vernon

Anyone who has sought to understand the shifts in international trade and international investment over the past twenty years has chafed from time to time under an acute sense of the inadequacy of the available analytical tools. While the comparative cost concept and other basic concepts have rarely failed to provide some help, they have usually carried the analyst only a very little way toward adequate understanding. For the most part, it has been necessary to formulate new concepts in order to explore issues such as the strengths and limitations of import substitution in the development process, the implications of common market arrangements for trade and investment, the underlying reasons for the Leontief paradox, and other critical issues of the day.

As theorists have groped for some more efficient tools, there has been a flowering in international trade and capital theory. But the very proliferation of theory has increased the urgency of the search for unifying concepts. It is doubtful that we shall find many propositions that can match the simplicity, power, and universality of application of the theory of comparative advantage and the international equilibrating mechanism; but unless the search for better tools goes on, the usefulness of economic theory for the solution of problems in international trade and capital movements will probably decline.

The present paper deals with one promising line of generalization and synthesis which seems to me to have been somewhat neglected by the main stream of trade theory. It puts less emphasis upon comparative cost doctrine and more upon the timing of innovation, the effects of scale economies, and the roles of ignorance and uncertainty in influencing trade patterns. It is an approach with respectable sponsorship, deriving bits and pieces of its inspiration from the writings of such persons as Williams, Kindleberger, MacDougall, Hoffmeyer, and Burenstam-Linder.[1]

Emphases of this sort seem first to have appeared when economists were searching for an explanation of what looked like a persistent, structural shortage of dollars in the world. When the shortage proved ephemeral in the late 1950s, many of the ideas which the shortage had stimulated were tossed overboard as prima facie wrong.[2] Nevertheless, one cannot be exposed to the main currents of international trade for very long without feeling that any theory which neglected the roles of innovation, scale, ignorance and uncertainty would be incomplete.

Reprinted from *Quarterly Journal of Economics*, Vol 80; R. Vernon, 'International investment and international trade in the product cycle'

LOCATION OF NEW PRODUCTS

We begin with the assumption that the enterprises in any one of the advanced countries of the world are not distinguishably different from those in any other advanced country, in terms of their access to scientific knowledge and their capacity to comprehend scientific principles.[3] All of them, we may safely assume, can secure access to the knowledge that exists in the physical, chemical and biological sciences. These sciences at times may be difficult, but they are rarely occult.

It is a mistake to assume, however, that equal access to scientific principles in all the advanced countries means equal probability of the application of these principles in the generation of new products. There is ordinarily a large gap between the knowledge of a scientific principle and the embodiment of the principle in a marketable product. An entrepreneur usually has to intervene to accept the risks involved in testing whether the gap can be bridged.

If all entrepreneurs, wherever located, could be presumed to be equally conscious of and equally responsive to all entrepreneurial opportunities, wherever they arose, the classical view of the dominant role of price in resource allocation might be highly relevant. There is good reason to believe, however, that the entrepreneur's consciousness of and responsiveness to opportunity are a function of ease of communication; and further, that ease of communication is a function of geographical proximity.[4] Accordingly, we abandon the powerful simplifying notion that knowledge is a universal free good, and introduce it as an independent variable in the decision to trade or to invest.

The fact that the search for knowledge is an inseparable part of the decision-making process and that relative ease of access to knowledge can profoundly affect the outcome are now reasonably well established through empirical research.[5] One implication of that fact is that producers in any market are more likely to be aware of the possibility of introducing new products in that market than producers located elsewhere would be.

The United States market offers certain unique kinds of opportunities to those who are in a position to be aware of them.

First, the United States market consists of consumers with an average income which is higher (except for a few anomalies like Kuwait) than that in any other national market—twice as high as that of Western Europe, for instance. Wherever there was a chance to offer a new product responsive to wants at high levels of income, this chance would presumably first be apparent to someone in a position to observe the United States market.

Second, the United States market is characterized by high unit labour costs and relatively unrationed capital compared with practically all other markets. This is a fact which conditions the demand for both consumer goods and industrial products. In the case of consumer goods, for instance, the high cost of laundresses contributes to the origins of the drip-dry shirt and the home washing machine. In the case of industrial goods, high labour cost leads to the early development and use of the conveyor belt, the fork-lift truck and the automatic control system. It seems to follow that wherever there was a chance successfully to sell a new product responsive to the need to conserve labour, this chance would be apparent first to those in a position to observe the United States market.

Assume, then, that entrepreneurs in the United States are first aware of opportunities to satisfy new wants associated with high income levels or high unit labour costs. Assume further that the evidence of an unfilled need and the hope of some kind of monopoly windfall for the early starter both are sufficiently strong to justify the initial investment that is usually involved in converting an abstract idea into a marketable product. Here we have a reason for expecting a consistently higher rate of expenditure on product development to be undertaken by United States producers than by producers in other countries, at least in lines which promise to substitute capital for labour or which promise to satisfy high-income wants. Therefore, if United States firms spend more than their foreign counterparts on new product development (often misleadingly labelled 're-search'), this may be due not to some obscure sociological drive for innovation but to more effective communication between the potential market and the potential supplier of the market. This sort of explanation is consistent with the pioneer appearance in the United States (conflicting claims of the Soviet Union notwithstanding) of the sewing machine, the typewriter, the tractor, etc.

At this point in the exposition, it is important once more to emphasize that the discussion so far relates only to innovation in certain kinds of products, namely to those associated with high income and those which substitute capital for labour. Our hypothesis says nothing about industrial innovation in general; this is a larger subject than we have tackled here. There are very few countries that have failed to introduce at least a few products; and there are some, such as Germany and Japan, which have been responsible for a considerable number of such introductions. Germany's outstanding successes in the development and use of plastics may have been due, for instance, to a traditional concern with her lack of a raw materials base, and a recognition that a market might exist in Germany for synthetic substitutes.[6]

Our hypothesis asserts that United States producers are likely to be the first to spy an opportunity for high-income or labour-saving new products.[7] But it goes on to assert that the first producing facilities for such products will be located in the United States. This is not a self-evident proposition. Under the calculus of least cost, production need not automatically take place at a location close to the market, unless the product can be produced and delivered from that location at lowest cost. Besides, now that most major United States companies control facilities situated in one or more locations outside of the United States, the possibility of considering a non-United States location is even more plausible than it might once have been.

Of course, if prospective producers were to make their locational choices on the basis of least-cost considerations, the United States would not always be ruled out. The costs of international transport and United States import duties, for instance, might be so high as to argue for such a location. My guess is, however, that the early producers of a new product intended for the United States market are attracted to a United States location by forces which are far stronger than relative factor-cost and transport considerations. For the reasoning on this point, one has to take a long detour away from comparative cost analysis into areas which fall under the rubrics of communication and external economies.

By now, a considerable amount of empirical work has been done on the factors affecting the location of industry.[8] Many of these studies try to explain observed locational patterns in conventional cost-minimizing terms, by implicit or explicit reference to labour cost and transportation cost. But some explicitly introduce problems of communication and external economies as powerful locational forces. These factors were given special emphasis in the analyses which were a part of the New York Metropolitan

Region Study of the 1950s. At the risk of oversimplifying, I shall try to summarize what these studies suggested.[9]

In the early stages of introduction of a new product, producers were usually confronted with a number of critical, albeit transitory, conditions. For one thing, the product itself may be quite unstandardized for a time; its inputs, its processing, and its final specifications may cover a wide range. Contrast the great variety of automobiles produced and marketed before 1910 with the thoroughly standardized product of the 1930s, or the variegated radio designs of the 1920s with the uniform models of the 1930s. The unstandardized nature of the design at this early stage carries with it a number of locational implications.

First, producers at this stage are particularly concerned with the degree of freedom they have in changing their inputs. Of course, the cost of the inputs is also relevant. But as long as the nature of these inputs cannot be fixed in advance with assurance, the calculation of cost must take into account the general need for flexibility in any locational choice.[10]

Second, the price elasticity of demand for the output of individual firms is comparatively low. This follows from the high degree of production differentiation, or the existence of monopoly in the early stages.[11] One result is, of course, that small cost differences count less in the calculations of the entrepreneur than they are likely to count later on.

Third, the need for swift and effective communication on the part of the producer with customers, suppliers, and even competitors is especially high at this stage. This is a corollary of the fact that a considerable amount of uncertainty remains regarding the ultimate dimensions of the market, the efforts of rivals to pre-empt that market, the specifications of the inputs needed for production, and the specifications of the products likely to be most successful in the effort.

All of these considerations tend to argue for a location in which communication between the market and the executives directly concerned with the new product is swift and easy, and in which a wide variety of potential types of input that might be needed by the production unit are easily come by. In brief, the producer who sees a market for some new product in the United States may be led to select a United States location for production on the basis of national locational considerations which extend well beyond simple factor cost analysis plus transport considerations.

THE MATURING PRODUCT[12]

As the demand for a product expands, a certain degree of standardization usually takes place. This is not to say that efforts at product differentiation come to an end. On the contrary; such efforts may even intensify, as competitors try to avoid the full brunt of price competition. Moreover, variety may appear as a result of specialization. Radios, for instance, ultimately acquired such specialized forms as clock radios, automobile radios, portable radios, and so on. Nevertheless, though the subcategories may multiply and the efforts at product differentiation increase, a growing acceptance of certain general standards seems to be typical.

Once again, the change has locational implications. First of all, the need for flexibility declines. A commitment to some set of product standards opens up technical possibilities for achieving economies of scale through mass output, and encourages long-term commitments to some given process and some fixed set of facilities. Second, concern about production cost begins to take the place of concern about product characteristics. Even if increased price competition is not yet present, the reduction of the uncertainties surrounding the operation enhances the usefulness of cost projections and increases the attention devoted to cost.

The empirical studies to which I referred earlier suggest that, at this stage in an industry's development, there is likely to be considerable shift in the location of production facilities at least as far as internal United States locations are concerned. The empirical materials on international locational shifts simply have not yet been analysed sufficiently to tell us very much. A little speculation, however, indicates some hypotheses worth testing.

Picture an industry engaged in the manufacture of the high-income or labour-saving products that are the focus of our discussion. Assume that the industry has begun to settle down in the United States to some degree of large-scale production. Although the first mass market may be located in the United States, some demand for the product begins almost at once to appear elsewhere. For instance, although heavy fork-lift trucks in general may have a comparatively small market in Spain because of the relative cheapness of unskilled labour in that country, some limited demand for the product will appear there almost as soon as the existence of the product is known.

If the product has a high income elasticity of demand or if it is a satisfactory substitute for high-cost labour, the demand in time will begin to grow quite rapidly in relatively advanced countries such as those of Western Europe. Once the market expands in such an advanced country, entrepreneurs will begin to ask themselves whether the time has come to take the risk of setting up a local producing facility.[13]

How long does it take to reach this stage? An adequate answer must surely be a complex one. Producers located in the United States, weighing the wisdom of setting up a new production facility in the importing country, will feel obliged to balance a number of complex considerations. As long as the marginal production cost plus the transport cost of the goods exported from the United States is lower than the average cost of prospective production in the market of import, United States producers will presumably prefer to avoid an investment. But that calculation depends on the producer's ability to project the cost of production in a market in which factor costs and the appropriate technology differ from those at home.

Now and again, the locational force which determined some particular overseas investment is so simple and so powerful that one has little difficulty in identifying it. Otis Elevator's early proliferation of production facilities abroad was quite patently a function of the high cost of shipping assembled elevator cabins to distant locations and the limited scale advantages involved in manufacturing elevator cabins at a single location.[14] Singer's decision to invest in Scotland as early as 1867 was also based on considerations of a sort sympathetic with our hypothesis.[15] It is not unlikely that the overseas demand for its highly standardized product was already sufficiently large at that time to exhaust the obvious scale advantages of manufacturing in a single location, especially if that location was one of high labour cost.

In an area as complex and 'imperfect' as international trade and investment, however, one ought not anticipate that any hypothesis will have more than a limited explanatory power. United States airplane manufacturers surely respond to many 'non-economic' locational forces, such as the desire to play safe in problems of military security. Producers in the United States who have a protected patent position overseas presumably take that fact into account in deciding whether or when to produce abroad. And other producers often are motivated by considerations too complex to reconstruct readily, such as the fortuitous timing of a threat of new competition in the country of import, the level of tariff protection anticipated for the future, the political situation in the country of prospective investment and so on.

We arrive, then, at the stage at which United States producers have come around to the establishment of production units in the advanced countries. Now a new group of forces is set in train. In an idealized form, Figure 1 suggests what may be anticipated next.

As far as individual United States producers are concerned, the local markets thenceforth will be filled from local production units set up abroad. Once these facilities are in operation, however, more ambitious possibilities for their use may be suggested. When comparing a United States producing facility and a facility in another advanced country, the obvious production-cost differences between the rival producing areas are usually differences due to scale and differences due to labour costs. If the producer is an international firm with producing locations in several countries, its costs of financing capital at the different locations may not be sufficiently different to matter very much. If economies of scale are being fully exploited, the principal differences between any two locations are likely to be labour costs.[16] Accordingly, it may prove wise for the international firm to begin servicing third-country markets from the new location. And if labour cost differences are large enough to offset transport costs, then exports back to the United States may become a possibility as well.

Any hypotheses based on the assumption that the United States entrepreneur will react rationally when offered the possibility of a lower-cost location abroad is, of course, somewhat suspect. The decision-making sequence that is used in connection with international investments, according to various empirical studies, is not a model of the rational process.[17] But there is one theme that emerges again and again in such studies. Any threat to the established position of an enterprise is a powerful galvanizing force to action; in fact, if I interpret the empirical work correctly, threat in general is a more reliable stimulus to action than opportunity is likely to be.

In the international investment field, threats appear in various forms once a large-scale export business in manufactured products has developed. Local entrepreneurs located in the countries which are the targets of these exports grow restive at the opportunities they are missing. Local governments concerned with generating employment or promoting growth or balancing their trade accounts begin thinking of ways and means to replace the imports. An international investment by the exporter, therefore, becomes a prudent means of forestalling the loss of a market. In this case, the yield on the investment is seen largely as the avoidance of a loss of income to the system.

The notion that a threat to the status quo is a powerful galvanizing force for international investment also seems to explain what happens after the initial investment. Once such an investment is made by a United States producer, other major producers in the United States sometimes see it as a threat to the status quo. They see themselves as losing position relative to the investing company, with vague intimations of further losses to come. Their 'share of the market' is imperilled, viewing 'share of the market' in global terms. At the same time, their ability to estimate the production-cost structure of their competitors, operating far away in an unfamiliar foreign area, is impaired; this is a particularly unsettling state because it conjures up the possibility of a return flow of

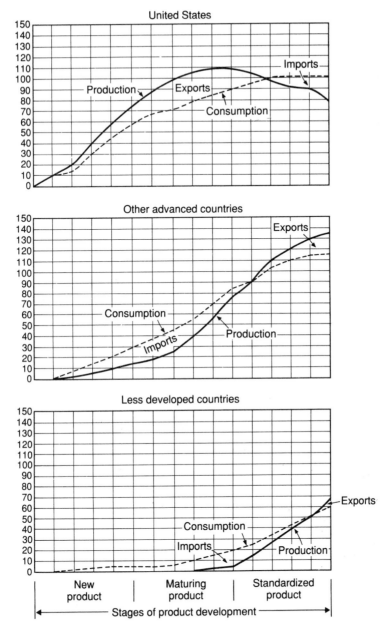

Fig. 1. Development of Production Units.

products to the United States and a new source of price competition, based on cost differences of unknown magnitude. The uncertainty can be reduced by emulating the pathfinding investor and by investing in the same area; this may not be an optimizing investment pattern and it may be costly, but it is least disturbing to the status quo.

Pieces of this hypothetical pattern are subject to empirical tests of a sort. So far, at any rate, the empirical tests have been reassuring. The office machinery industry, for instance, has seen repeatedly the phenomenon of the introduction of a new product in the United States, followed by United States exports,[18] followed still later by United States imports. (We have still to test whether the timing of the commencement of overseas production by United States subsidiaries fits into the expected pattern.) In the electrical and electronic products industry, those elements in the pattern which can be measured show up nicely.[19] A broader effort is now under way to test the United States trade patterns of a group of products with high income elasticities; and, here too, the preliminary results are encouraging.[20] On a much more general basis, it is reassuring for our hypotheses to observe that the foreign manufacturing subsidiaries of United States firms have been increasing their exports to third countries.

It will have occurred to the reader by now that the pattern envisaged here also may shed some light on the Leontief paradox.[21] Leontief, it will be recalled, seemed to confound comparative cost theory by establishing the fact that the ratio of capital to labour in United States exports was lower, not higher, than the like ratio in the United States production which had been displaced by competitive imports. The hypothesis suggested in this paper would have the United States exporting high-income and labour-saving products in the early stages of their existence, and importing them later on.[22] In the early stages, the value-added contribution of industries engaged in producing these items probably contains an unusually high proportion of labour cost. This is not so much because the labour is particularly skilled, as is so often suggested. More likely, it is due to a quite different phenomenon. At this stage, the standardization of the manufacturing process has not got very far; that is to come later, when the volume of output is high enough and the degree of uncertainty low enough to justify investment in relatively inflexible, capital-intensive facilities. As a result, the production process relies relatively heavily on labour inputs at a time when the United States commands an export position; and the process relies more heavily on capital at a time when imports become important.

This, of course, is an hypothesis which has not yet been subjected to any really rigorous test. But it does open up a line of inquiry into the structure of United States trade which is well worth pursuing.

THE STANDARDIZED PRODUCT

Figure 1, the reader will have observed, carries a panel which suggests that, at an advanced stage in the standardization of some products, the less-developed countries may offer competitive advantages as a production location.

This is a bold projection, which seems on first blush to be wholly at variance with the Heckscher-Ohlin theorem. According to that theorem, one presumably ought to anticipate that the exports of the less-developed countries would tend to be relatively labour-intensive products.

One of the difficulties with the theorem, however, is that it leaves marketing considerations out of account. One reason for the omission is evident. As long as knowledge is regarded as a free good, instantaneously available, and as long as individual producers are regarded as atomistic contributors to the total supply, marketing problems cannot be expected to find much of a place in economic theory. In projecting the patterns of export from less-developed areas, however, we cannot afford to disregard the fact that information comes at a cost; and that entrepreneurs are not readily disposed to pay the price of investigating overseas markets of unknown dimensions and unknown promise. Neither are they eager to venture into situations which they know will demand a constant flow of reliable marketing information from remote sources.

If we can assume that highly standardized products tend to have a well-articulated, easily accessible international market and to sell largely on the basis of price (an assumption inherent in the definition), then it follows that such products will not pose the problem of market information quite so acutely for the less-developed countries. This establishes a necessary if not a sufficient condition for investment in such industries.

Of course, foreign investors seeking an optimum location for a captive facility may not have to concern themselves too much with questions of market information; presumably, they are thoroughly familiar with the marketing end of the business and are looking for a low-cost captive source of supply. In that case, the low cost of labour may be the initial attraction drawing the investor to less-developed areas. But other limitations in such areas, according to our hypothesis, will bias such captive operations toward the production of standardized items. The reasons in this case turn on the part played in the production process by external economies. Manufacturing processes which receive significant inputs from the local economy, such as skilled labour, repairmen, reliable power, spare parts, industrial materials processed according to exacting specification, and so on, are less appropriate to the less-developed areas than those that do not have such requirements. Unhappily, most industrial processes require one or another ingredient of this difficult sort. My guess is, however, that the industries which produce a standardized product are in the best position to avoid the problem, by producing on a vertically-integrated self-sustaining basis.

In speculating about future industrial exports from the less-developed areas, therefore, we are led to think of products with a fairly clear-cut set of economic characteristics.[23] Their production function is such as to require significant inputs of labour; otherwise there is no reason to expect a lower production cost in less-developed countries. At the same time, they are products with a high price elasticity of demand for the output of individual firms; otherwise, there is no strong incentive to take the risks of pioneering with production in a new area. In addition, products whose production process did not rely heavily upon external economies would be more obvious candidates than those which required a more elaborate industrial environment. The implications of remoteness also would be critical; products which could be precisely described by standardized specifications and which could be produced for inventory without fear of obsolescence would be more relevant than those which had less precise specifications and which could not easily be ordered from remote locations. Moreover, high-value items capable of absorbing significant freight costs would be more likely to appear than bulky items low in value by weight. Standardized textile products are, of course, the illustration par excellence of the sort of product that meets the criteria. But other products come to mind such as crude steel, simple fertilizers, newsprint, and so on.

Speculation of this sort draws some support from various interregional experiences in industrial location. In the United States, for example, the 'export' industries which moved to the low-wage south in search of lower costs tended to be industries which had no great need for a sophisticated industrial environment and which produced fairly standardized products. In the textile industry, it was the grey goods, cotton sheetings and men's shirt plants that went south; producers of high-style dresses or other unstandardized items were far more reluctant to move. In the electronics industry, it was the mass producers of tubes, resistors and other standardized high-volume components that showed the greatest disposition to move south; custom-built and research-oriented production remained closer to markets and to the main industrial complexes. A similar pattern could be discerned in printing and in chemicals production.[24]

In other countries, a like pattern is suggested by the impressionistic evidence. The underdeveloped south of Italy and the laggard north of Britain and Ireland both seem to be attracting industry with standardized output and self-sufficient process.[25]

Once we begin to look for relevant evidence of such investment patterns in the less-developed countries proper, however, only the barest shreds of corroboratory information can be found. One would have difficulty in thinking of many cases in which manufacturers of standardized products in the more advanced countries had made significant investments in the less-developed countries with a view of exporting such products from those countries. To be sure, other types of foreign investment are not uncommon in the less-developed countries, such as investments in import-replacing industries which were made in the face of a threat of import restriction. But there are only a few export-oriented cases similar to that of Taiwan's foreign-owned electronics plants and Argentina's new producing facility, set up to manufacture and export standard sorting equipment for computers.

If we look to foreign trade patterns, rather than foreign investment patterns, to learn something about the competitive advantage of the less-developed countries, the possibility that they are an attractive locus for the output of standardized products gains slightly more support. The Taiwanese and Japanese trade performances are perhaps the most telling ones in support of the projected pattern; both countries have managed to develop significant overseas markets for standardized manufactured products. According to one major study of the subject (a study stimulated by the Leontief paradox), Japanese exports are more capital-intensive than is the Japanese production which is displaced by imports;[26] this is what one might expect if the hypothetical patterns suggested by Figure 1 were operational. Apart from these cases, however, all that one sees are a few provocative successes such as some sporadic sales of newsprint from Pakistan, the successful export of sewing machines from India, and so on. Even in these cases, one cannot be sure that they are consistent with the hypothesis unless he has done a good deal more empirical investigation.

The reason why so few relevant cases come to mind may be that the process has not yet advanced far enough. Or it may be that such factors as extensive export constraints and overvalued exchange rates are combining to prevent the investment and exports that otherwise would occur.

If there is one respect in which this discussion may deviate from classical expectations, it is in the view that the overall scarcity of capital in the less-developed countries will not prevent investment in facilities for the production of standardized products.

There are two reasons why capital costs may not prove a barrier to such investment.

First, according to our hypotheses, the investment will occur in industries which require some significant labour inputs in the production process; but they will be concentrated in that subsector of the industry which produces highly standardized products capable of self-contained production establishments. The net of these specifications is indeterminate so far as capital-intensiveness is concerned. A standardized textile item may be more or less capital-intensive than a plant for unstandardized petro-chemicals.

Besides, even if the capital requirements for a particular plant are heavy, the cost of the capital need not prove a bar. The assumption that capital costs come high in the less-developed countries requires a number of fundamental qualifications. The reality, to the extent that it is known, is more complex.

One reason for this complexity is the role played by the international investor. Producers of chemical fertilizers, when considering whether to invest in a given country, may be less concerned with the going rate for capital in that country than with their opportunity costs as they see such costs. For such investors the alternatives to be weighed are not the full range of possibilities calling for capital but only a very restricted range of alternatives, such as the possibilities offered by chemical fertilizer investment elsewhere. The relevant capital cost for a chemical fertilizer plant, therefore, may be fairly low if the investor is an international entrepreneur.

Moreover, the assumption that finance capital is scarce and that interest rates are high in a less-developed country may prove inapplicable to the class of investors who concern us here.[27] The capital markets of the less-developed countries typically consist of a series of water-tight, insulated, submarkets in which wholly different rates prevail and between which arbitrage opportunities are limited. In some countries, the going figures may vary from 5 to 40 per cent, on grounds which seem to have little relation to issuer risk or term of loan. (In some economies, where inflation is endemic, interest rates which in effect represent a negative real cost are not uncommon.)

These internal differences in interest rates may be due to a number of factors: the fact that funds generated inside the firm usually are exposed to a different yield test than external borrowings; the fact that government loans are often floated by mandatory levies on banks and other intermediaries; and the fact that funds borrowed by governments from international sources are often re-loaned in domestic markets at rates which are linked closely to the international borrowing rate, however irrelevant that may be. Moreover, one has to reckon with the fact that public international lenders tend to lend at near-uniform rates, irrespective of the identity of the borrower and the going interest rate in his country. Access to capital on the part of underdeveloped countries, therefore, becomes a direct function of the country's capacity to propose plausible projects to public international lenders. If a project can plausibly be shown to 'pay its own way' in balance-of-payment and output terms at 'reasonable' interest rates, the largest single obstacle to obtaining capital at such rates has usually been overcome.

Accordingly, one may say that from the entrepreneur's viewpoint certain systematic and predictable 'imperfections' of the capital markets may reduce or eliminate the capital-shortage handicap which is characteristic of the less-developed countries; and, further, that as a result of the reduction or elimination such countries may find themselves in a position to compete effectively in the export of certain standardized capital-intensive goods. This is not the statement of another paradox; it is not the same as to say that the capital-poor countries will develop capital-intensive economies. All we are concerned with here is a modest fraction of the industry of such countries, which in turn is a minor fraction of their total economic activity. It may be that the anomalies such industries represent are systematic enough to be included in our normal expectations regarding conditions in the less-developed countries.

Like the other observations which have preceded, these views about the likely patterns of exports by the less-developed countries are attempts to relax some of the constraints imposed by purer and simpler models. Here and there, the hypotheses take on plausibility because they jibe with the record of past events. But, for the most part, they are still speculative in nature, having been subjected to tests of a very low order of rigorousness. What is needed, obviously, is continued probing to determine whether the 'imperfections' stressed so strongly in these pages deserve to be elevated out of the footnotes into the main text of economic theory.

NOTES

The preparation of this article was financed in part by a grant from the Ford Foundation to the Harvard Business School to support a study of the implications of United States foreign direct investment. This paper is a by-product of the hypothesis-building stage of the study.

1. J. H. Williams, 'The Theory of International Trade Reconsidered,' reprinted as Chap. 2 in his *Postwar Monetary Plans and Other Essays.* (Oxford: Basil Blackwell, 1947); C. P. Kindleberger, *The Dollar Shortage* (New York: Wiley, 1950); Erik Hoffmeyer, *Dollar Shortage.* (Amsterdam: North-Holland, 1958); Sir Donald MacDougall, *The World Dollar Problem.* (London: Macmillan, 1957); Staffan Burenstam-Linder, *An Essay on Trade and Transformation* (Uppsala: Almqvist & Wicksells, 1961).

2. The best summary of the state of trade theory that has come to my attention in recent years is J. Bhagwati, 'The Pure Theory of International Trade,' *Economic Journal,* LXXIV (Mar. 1964), 1–84. Bhagwati refers obliquely to some of the theories which concern us here; but they receive much less attention than I think they deserve.

3. Some of the account that follows will be found in greatly truncated form in my 'The Trade Expansion Act in Perspective,' in *Emerging Concepts in Marketing,* Proceedings of the American Marketing Association, December 1962, pp. 384–89. The elaboration here owes a good deal to the perceptive work of Se'ev Hirsch, summarized in his unpublished doctoral thesis, 'Location of Industry and International Competitiveness,' Harvard Business School, 1965.

4. Note C. P. Kindleberger's reference to the 'horizon' of the decision-maker, and the view that he can only be rational within that horizon; see his *Foreign Trade and The National Economy* (New Haven: Yale University Press, 1962), p. 15 *passim.*

5. See, for instance, Richard M. Cyert and James G. March, *A Behavioral Theory of the Firm* (Englewood Cliffs, N.J.: Prentice-Hall, 1963), esp. Chap. 6; and Yair Aharoni, *The Foreign Investment Decision Process,* to be published by the Division of Research of the Harvard Business School, 1966.

6. See two excellent studies: C. Freeman, 'The Plastics Industry: A Comparative Study of Research and Innovation,' in *National Institute Economic Review,* No. 26 (Nov. 1963), p. 22 *et seq.*; G. C. Hufbauer, *Synthetic Materials and the Theory of International Trade* (London: Gerald Duckworth, 1965). A number of links in the Hufbauer arguments are remarkably similar to some in this paper; but he was not aware of my writings nor I of his until after both had been completed.

7. There is a kind of first-cousin relationship between this simple notion and the 'entrained want' concept defined by H. G. Barnett in *Innovation: The Basis of Cultural Change* (New York: McGraw-Hill, 1953), p. 148. Albert O. Hirschman, *The Strategy of Economic Development* (New Haven: Yale University Press, 1958), p. 68, also finds the concept helpful in his effort to explain certain aspects of economic development.

8. For a summary of such work, together with a useful bibliography, see John Meyer, 'Regional Economics: A Survey,' in the *American Economic Review,* LIII (Mar. 1963), 19–54.

9. The points that follow are dealt with at length in the following publications: Raymond Vernon, *Metropolis, 1985* (Cambridge: Harvard University Press, 1960), pp. 38–85; Max Hall (ed.), *Made in New York* (Cambridge: Harvard University Press, 1959), pp. 3–18, 19 *passim*; Robert M. Lichtenberg, *One-Tenth of a Nation* (Cambridge: Harvard University Press, 1960), pp. 31–70.

10. This is, of course, a familiar point elaborated in George F. Stigler, 'Production and Distribution in the Short Run,' *Journal of Political Economy,* XLVII (June 1939), 305, *et seq.*

11. Hufbauer, *op. cit.,* suggests that the low price elasticity of demand in the first stage may be due simply to the fact that the first market may be a 'captive market' unresponsive to price changes; but that later, in order to expand the use of the new product, other markets may be brought in which are more price responsive.

12. Both Hirsch, *op. cit.,* and Freeman, *op. cit.,* make use of a three-stage product classification of the sort used here.

13. M. V. Posner, 'International Trade and Technical Change,' *Oxford Economic Papers,* Vol. 13 (Oct. 1961), p. 323, *et seq.* presents a stimulating model purporting to explain such familiar trade phenomena as the exchange

of machine tools between the United Kingdom and Germany. In the process he offers some particularly helpful notions concerning the size of the 'imitation lag' in the responses of competing nations.

14. Dudley M. Phelps, *Migration of Industry to South America* (New York: McGraw-Hill, 1963), p. 4.

15. John H. Dunning, *American Investment in British Manufacturing Industry* (London: George Allen & Unwin, 1958), p. 18. The Dunning book is filled with observations that lend casual support to the main hypotheses of this paper.

16. Note the interesting finding of Mordecai Kreinin in his 'The Leontief Scarce-Factor Paradox,' *The American Economic Review*, LV (Mar. 1965), 131–39. Kreinin finds that the higher cost of labour in the United States is not explained by a higher rate of labour productivity in this country.

17. Aharoni, *op. cit.*, provides an excellent summary and exhaustive bibliography of the evidence on this point.

18. Reported in U.S. Senate, Interstate and Foreign Commerce Committee, *Hearings on Foreign Commerce*, 1960, pp. 130–39.

19. See Hirsch, *op. cit.*

20. These are to appear in a forthcoming doctoral thesis at the Harvard Business School by Louis T. Wells, tentatively entitled 'International Trade and Business Policy'.

21. See Wassily Leontief, 'Domestic Production and Foreign Trade: The American Capital Position Re-examined,' *Proceedings of the American Philosophical Society*, Vol. 97 (Sept. 1953), and 'Factor Proportions and the Structure of American Trade: Further Theoretical and Empirical Analysis,' *Review of Economics and Statistics*, XXXVIII (Nov. 1956).

22. Of course, if there were some systematic trend in the inputs of new products—for example, if the new products which appeared in the 1960s were more capital-intensive than the new products which appeared in the 1950s—then the tendencies suggested by our hypotheses might be swamped by such a trend. As long as we do not posit offsetting systematic patterns of this sort, however, the Leontief findings and the hypotheses offered here seem consistent.

23. The concepts sketched out here are presented in more detail in my 'Problems and Prospects in the Export of Manufactured Products from the Less-developed Countries,' U.N. Conference on Trade and Development, Dec. 16, 1963 (mimeo.).

24. This conclusion derives largely from the industry studies conducted in connection with the New York Metropolitan Region study. There have been some excellent more general analyses of shifts in industrial location among the regions of the United States. See e.g., Victor R. Fuchs, *Changes in the Location of Manufacturing in the United States Since 1929* (New Haven: Yale University Press, 1962). Unfortunately, however, none has been designed, so far as I know, to test hypotheses relating locational shifts to product characteristics such as price elasticity of demand and degree of standardization.

25. This statement, too, is based on only impressionistic materials. Among the more suggestive, illustrative of the best of the available evidence, see J. N. Toothill, *Inquiry into the Scottish Economy* (Edinburgh: Scottish Council, 1962).

26. M. Tatemoto and S. Ichimura, 'Factor Proportions and Foreign Trade: the Case of Japan,' *Review of Economics and Statistics*, XLI (Nov. 1959), 442–46.

27. See George Rosen, *Industrial Change in India* (Glencoe, Ill.: Free Press, 1958). Rosen finds that in the period studied from 1937 to 1953, 'there was no serious shortage of capital for the largest firms in India.' Gustav F. Papanek makes a similar finding for Pakistan for the period from 1950 to 1964 in a book about to be published.

2

The Internationalization of the Firm—Four Swedish Cases[1]

Jan Johanson and Finn Wiedersheim-Paul

INTRODUCTION

The widespread interest in multinational firms has given rise to many articles and books on various aspects of the international strategies of firms. Research has been concentrated on the large corporations, particularly the American.

Many firms, however, start international operations when they are still comparatively small and gradually develop their operations abroad. From our studies of international business at the University of Uppsala we have several observations indicating that this gradual internationalization, rather than large, spectacular foreign investments, is characteristic of the internationalization process of most Swedish firms. It seems reasonable to believe that the same holds true for many firms from other countries with small domestic markets. A related observation is that the type of development during the early stages is of importance for the following pattern. Similar observations have also been made about US firms and have been used as an argument in discussions of foreign investments and international marketing.[2]

In this paper we describe and analyse the internationalization of four Swedish firms—Sandvik, Atlas Copco, Facit and Volvo. All of them sell more than two-thirds of their turnover abroad and have production facilities in more than one foreign country. In Sweden[3] they are often used as examples and patterns in discussions of international operations. Usually such discussions only treat the operations of the firms during later years when they have already become large and international. Here we adopt a more longitudinal approach, describing and discussing the whole development which has led to their present international position.

Before the case descriptions we give an account of our view of the internationalization process, on which these descriptions are based, and discuss some patterns which follow from this view. In the concluding section we discuss some similarities and differences between the firms with respect to the internationalization.

Reprinted with permission from *Journal of Management Studies*, October 1975, pp 305–322
Copyright © 1975 Basil Blackwell Limited

THE INTERNATIONALIZATION PROCESS

The term international usually refers to either an attitude of the firm towards foreign activities or to the actual carrying out of activities abroad.[4] Of course there is a close relationship between attitudes and actual behaviour. The attitudes are the basis for decisions to undertake international ventures and the experiences from international activities influence these attitudes. In the case descriptions we have to concentrate on those aspects of the internationalization that are easy to observe, that is the international activities. We consider, however, these attitudes as interesting and important and the discussion of the internationalization process is basically an account of the interaction between attitudes and actual behaviour.

Our basic assumption is that the firm first develops in the domestic market[5] and that the internationalization is the consequence of a series of incremental decisions. We also assume that the most important obstacles to internationalization are lack of knowledge and resources. These obstacles are reduced through incremental decision-making and learning about the foreign markets and operations. The perceived risk of market investments decreases and the continued internationalization is stimulated by the increased need to control sales and the increased exposure to offers and demands to extend the operations. We are not trying to explain why firms start exporting[6] but assume that, because of lack of knowledge about foreign countries and a propensity to avoid uncertainty, the firm starts exporting to neighbouring countries or countries that are comparatively well-known and similar with regard to business practices etc. We also believe that the firm starts selling abroad via independent representatives, as this means a smaller resource commitment than the establishment of a sales subsidiary.[7]

Considering the development of operations in individual countries we expect a stepwise extension of operations. Of course it is possible to identify different types of steps and a different number of stages. We have chosen to distinguish between four different stages. They are:

1. no regular export activities
2. export via independent representatives (agent)
3. sales subsidiary and
4. production/manufacturing

We think these stages are important because

(a) they are different with regard to the degree of involvement of the firm in the market
(b) they are often referred to by people in business.

There are two aspects about the degree of involvement. The four stages mean successively larger resource commitments and they also lead to quite different market experiences and information for the firm. The first means that the firm has made no commitment of resources to the market and that it lacks any regular information channel to and from the market. The second means that the firm has a channel to the market through which it gets fairly regular information about sales influencing factors. It also means a certain commitment to the market. The third means a controlled information channel to the market, giving the firm ability to direct the type and amount of information flowing from the market to the firm. During this stage the firm also gets direct experience of resource influencing factors. The fourth stage means a still larger resource commitment.

We call the sequence of stages, mentioned above, the *establishment chain*.[8] We have, of course, simplified the matter somewhat by exaggerating the differences between the four steps. It is not always obvious whether a firm has established relations with an agent or not, while a joint venture with an earlier representative can be placed in the second or the third stage, etc.

Of course we do not expect the development always to follow the whole chain. First, several markets are not large enough for the resource demanding stages. Second, we could expect jumps in the establishment chain in firms with extensive experience from other foreign markets.

Considering the extension of activities to new markets, it is possible that the concept of psychic distance may prove useful.[9] This concept is defined as factors preventing or disturbing the flows of information between firms and market. Examples of such factors are differences in language, culture, political systems, level of education, level of industrial development, etc. For obvious reasons, psychic distance is correlated with geographic distance. But exceptions are easy to find. Some countries in the British Commonwealth are far apart geographically, e.g. England and Australia, but for different reasons they are near to each other in terms of psychic distance. The USA and Cuba are near to each other geographically, but, for political reasons, far apart with regard to psychic distance. As these examples indicate, psychic distance is not constant. It changes because of the development of the communication system, trade and other kinds of social exchange. In general we expect most changes to take place rather slowly.[10]

Psychic distance, however, is of course not the only important factor for international operations. In most textbooks about international business the size of the potential market is considered the most important factor for international operations. 'The first activity phase of export planning then, is identifying and measuring market opportunity.'[11] Thus we should expect that market size influences decisions in the internationalization process. We could expect either that the firm first starts operations in countries with large markets or that they prefer to start in smaller markets. In the latter case the argument may be that small markets are more similar to the domestic Swedish market and require a smaller initial resource commitment or have less competitive domestic industries.

But there are reasons to expect that the patterns of agency establishment differ from those of sales subsidiary establishments with respect to the two factors. The agency establishments, according to our view, are made primarily during the early stages of internationalization, which means that they could be expected to be more closely related to psychic distance than to the size of the market. The sales subsidiary establishments— and still more production—could be expected to be influenced primarily by the market size as it generally requires a larger minimum resource commitment than an independent representative. The production establishments are influenced by different forces; on one hand, by psychic distance, on the other, by factors such as, e.g. tariffs, non-tariff barriers and transport costs. As a result it is hard to observe any correlation between psychic distance and production establishments.

A third pattern which could be expected is that after the establishment of the first agency a phase follows when agencies are established in several markets. In the same way we could expect a separate phase dominated by the establishment of sales subsidiaries in several markets. Last, a phase with the establishment of production in several markets will follow. We assume that the three different phases in the internationalization of the firm are dependent on the development of the activity knowledge and the organizational structure of the firm. During the agent phase the firm builds an export department with the capability and responsibility for the establishment and maintenance of agencies. Establishment of sales subsidiaries means that units for the control of subsidiaries are organized. In the last phase, units for coordination of production and marketing in different countries are developed.

It should be noted that the discussion so far has dealt exclusively with the development of the marketing side of the firm. We do not regard this as a serious limitation. Marketing operations in this sense are predominant among the international activities of at least the Swedish firms.[12] Furthermore it has been shown that the marketing side is often a determining factor in the development of the firm.[13] Last, a similar development is likely when internationalization takes place on the purchasing side of the firm.[14]

THE INTERNATIONALIZATION PROCESS—FOUR CASES

Here we describe the internationalization of the four firms Sandvik, Atlas Copco, Facit and Volvo. The descriptions are based on various types of published data[15] about the firms which have been checked and supplemented by interviews with the firms. As we said before, we have chosen to use the moments when a firm establishes agencies, a sales subsidiary and production facilities as key factors in the process of internationalization. It has been possible to identify these moments with fairly high accuracy in most cases.

In order to help the reader we have constructed diagrams illustrating the 'establishment profiles' of the firms. These profiles show when the firm has started operations in twenty national markets. To standardize the case descriptions the countries are the same for all cases.

The analysis of the establishment patterns is based on a ranking of countries according to psychic distance.[16] As mentioned above, we believe that the psychic distance changes very slowly. Thus the rank order of countries according to the present psychic distance from Sweden, which is given in the 'establishment profiles' with a few exceptions, reflects the psychic distance fairly accurately even when the internationalization has taken a long time, as in our cases.

In order to compare the relations between establishments and the two kinds of market characteristics, we used a very crude indicator of market size, GNP 1960. As it is only used for the ranking of countries we do not think this crudeness is of much importance. Most market size indicators are fairly well correlated with GNP which also changes rather slowly.

Sandvik AB

Steel production in Sandviken started in 1862 in order to exploit the Bessemer process. During the first years the product line consisted mainly of industrial raw material: pig iron, ingot and blanks. These products became successively less important and were replaced by more manufactured special steel products, like cold-rolled strips, wire, tubes and saws; product groups that are still very important for Sandvik. In 1910 production of steel conveyors was started and in the 1940s hard metal products were introduced. The latter have been of great significance for the development of the firm during the last decades. At present about 40 per cent of the turnover comes from this product group and Sandvik is one of the biggest producers of hard metal products in the world. Another type of product which has been introduced during the 1960s is alloys used in nuclear reactors.

Of the four firms described Sandvik is the oldest and also the one which first started its internationalization course. The first contacts with representatives were established in the 1860s. Sandvik's early start with representatives in foreign countries was an innovation at that time. Until then the Swedish iron and steel exporting had mainly been undertaken by trading firms. A probable explanation of these early foreign representatives is that the founder of Sandvik, G. F. Göransson, had earlier been general manager in a trading firm with extensive connections abroad.

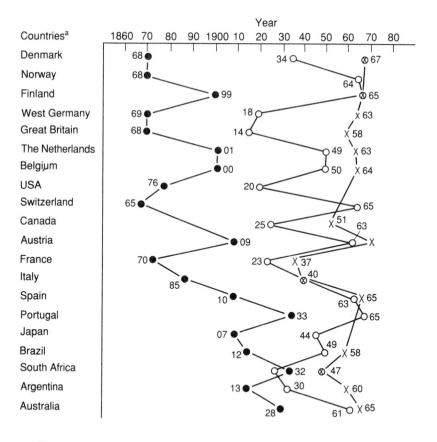

^aRanked according to psychic distance from Sweden.

● agent   X manufacturing subsidiary
○ sales subsidiary   ⊗ sales and manufacturing subsidiary

Fig. 1. Profiles of Establishments, Sandvik.

As can be seen from the profile for agency establishments they were set up in successively more distant markets. We computed the Spearman rank correlation coefficient between the time order of establishments and the order of psychic distance and market size respectively (see Table 1). Obviously there is high correlation between the order of agency establishments and distance. The coefficient of the market size factor should be interpreted with care as most of the establishments took place a long time ago. But it is remarkably low.

The same distance-related behaviour, as for the agencies, cannot be observed in the establishments of sales subsidiaries. As the profile shows, Sandvik did not establish the first subsidiaries in the nearest markets, the Nordic countries, but in the large industrial markets like Germany, Great Britain and the USA.

The reason for not establishing trading links in the Nordic countries and the big import markets like Switzerland and the Netherlands was probably that Sandvik had access to efficient representatives, in these markets, with well developed channels to the customers.

Establishments after 1940 have mainly been made in important markets where Sandvik until then lacked sales subsidiaries, e.g. the Nordic countries and EEC countries. During the 1950s Sandvik developed a policy to use subsidiaries in foreign marketing and, when entering new markets during the 1960s, sales subsidiaries were used from the beginning.

Table 1 also shows that the sales subsidiary establishments do not follow the same time pattern as the agency establishments. In this case the market size factor's highest correlation is with the order of establishments. This is in accordance with our expectations.

The patterns for the manufacturing subsidiaries is quite different from the other kinds of establishment. The first production establishments were made in distant markets. They were saw production in France, Finland and Italy and drill production in South Africa and Canada. There is no correlation at all between the order of production establishments and the factors of distance and size.

According to the establishment chain, described above, firms first make contacts with an independent representative in the foreign market. Later they set up sales subsidiaries and after that, in some cases, production. At the same time there is also a broadening to other markets. The internationalization course of Sandvik is well in accordance with this picture. On practically all markets, independent representatives have been the first connections. Then, after a considerable period of time, they have been replaced by sales subsidiaries. Canada is the only country where a subsidiary was not preceded by a

Table 1. Rank correlation (Spearman) between the order of Sandvik foreign establishments and psychic distance and market size

	Psychic distance[b]	Market size[b]
Agents	0.79 (0.001)[a]	0.24 (0.181)
Sales subsidiaries	0.16 (0.227)	0.66 (0.002)
Production	−0.01 (0.496)	0.06 (0.386)

[a] In this and all tables that follow, the probability of getting the coefficient or a more extreme value is shown in brackets after each coefficient. It is done in order to give the reader an indication of the 'strength' of the coefficients.

[b] The correlation between the measures of distance and size is only 0.06.

representative. The reason was that Sandvik's representative in the USA and, later, the subsidiary there, performed the marketing in Canada as well.

In 1971, 85 per cent of the total turnover of around 1800 million Swedish kronor came from abroad. The main part of sales is made by the subsidiaries and the independent representatives are nowadays of little significance. The number of independent representatives reached its maximum about 1950 but, since then, has radically diminished.

Two new patterns can be seen in Sandvik's establishments during the last few years. First, Sandvik has developed a new organization of subsidiaries, especially intended to handle the marketing of conveyor bands. The head office of this group is situated in Stuttgart in West Germany and the manufacturing units are in the USA and West Germany. Second, several establishments during the last five years have been made as joint ventures. The products involved are those used in the nuclear industry in France, the USA and West Germany. One reason for these joint ventures is that a 'national connection' is very important as projects in this area are often characterized by 'buy national' behaviour. Another reason is that Sandvik alone cannot afford the heavy investments needed.

Atlas Copco

The firm started in 1873. At the beginning the production was railway material of various kinds. Soon, other products were added; steam engines for ships and machine tools. Production of pneumatic tools started in the 1890s and already at the turn of the century the marketing of rock drills was started. In 1905 Atlas produced the first air compressor of their own design. In 1917 the company was merged with another firm, producing diesel engines.

As early as in 1880 exports were substantial. Diesel engines were the dominant export products until some years after 1930, while the compressed air products were sold mostly on the domestic market. After World War II the selling of pneumatic products soon dominated and the diesel motor production was sold in 1948.

During the first years after the war the selling efforts were concentrated on 'the Swedish method'—lightweight rock drill equipment combined with Sandvik's rock drills. At the end of the 1950s the production and selling were changed towards heavier equipment, stationary compressors and pneumatic tools.

Atlas Copco is five years younger than Sandvik but started the internationalization process considerably later. The successive establishment of contacts with representatives on more and more distant markets, which the model predicts, is evident also for Atlas Copco but less clear than for Sandvik (see Figure 2).

The establishment of sales and production subsidiaries was not common until after World War II, when Atlas Copco sold off its production of diesel motors and concentrated on pneumatic products. During the first few years of the 1950s twenty-three sales subsidiaries were established. By concentrating on 'the Swedish method', Atlas Copco also concentrated on an active marketing strategy, including well developed sales organizations, storing and technical service in the local markets. Sales subsidiaries were considered necessary for this strategy.

The first manufacturing subsidiary abroad was started in Great Britain in 1939. Most important was the acquisition in 1956 of Arpic in Belgium. This firm was an important competitor of Atlas Copco. During the 1960s several establishments were made in more

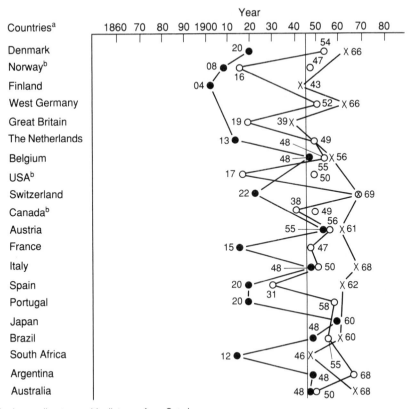

Fig. 2. Profiles of Establishments, Atlas Copco.

aRanked according to psychic distance from Sweden.
bIn Norway, USA and Canada we have marked two sales subsidiary establishments. The first one sold diesel products, the second pneumatic equipment.

● agent   X manufacturing subsidiary
○ sales subsidiary   ⊗ sales and manufacturing subsidiary

distant countries. The reasons for this expansion were mostly to overcome various barriers to trade.

The pattern of establishment is similar to Sandvik's but less pronounced. The agency establishments are correlated with the distance factor and the sales subsidiary establishments with the market size factor. The production establishments are correlated with neither.

Table 2. Rank correlation (Spearman) between the order of Atlas Copco foreign establishments and psychic distance and market size

	Psychic distance	Market size
Agents	0.40 (0.041)	−0.26 (0.123)
Sales subsidiaries	0.33 (0.072)	0.48 (0.018)
Production	0.16 (0.242)	−0.11 (0.312)

The development in individual markets is illustrated in Figure 2. In most cases representatives have been used before subsidiaries. But many of these representatives were used in the marketing of diesel products. The selling of pneumatic products, being more method than product oriented, was from the start performed by subsidiaries in the important markets. Four of the sales subsidiaries were not preceded by representatives. Two of these were failures in so far as they soon had to close down (the USA and Canada).

One of them was not established until 1952 (West Germany). The late establishment in the German market was due to the fact that Atlas Copco met its strongest competition in this market, and it was considered too tough for selling. The first regular export to Germany did not occur until 1951, when the selling of the recently developed pneumatic equipment for mines started.

Selling abroad as a ratio of total turnover 1922 (1900 million Swedish kronor) was nearly 90 per cent. The majority of this selling is made by about thirty-five foreign subsidiaries, but Atlas Copco has representatives in more than 100 countries. There are manufacturing units in ten countries.

Facit

This firm was formed in a reconstruction in 1922. The new enterprise took over the production of a calculating machine from a bankrupt firm, AB Facit. In the beginning of the 1930s a new version of this machine was developed. The new product started Facit's expansion on foreign markets. Some figures of turnover illustrate this. During the period 1923–33 the turnover was constant, 2.5 million Swedish kronor. Until 1939 there was an increase to 10 million Swedish kronor. In 1939 the export ratio was 80–85 per cent and the number of export markets was about seventy.

The expansion also continued with the buying of other firms; viz. in 1939 a manufacturer of typing machines, in 1942 a manufacturer of calculating machines and in 1966 a manufacturer of accounting and calculating machines. In 1972, after a financial crisis, Facit merged with a well-known Swedish multinational firm, Electrolux.

The internationalization process in Facit is unlike Sandvik's and Atlas Copco's. About ten years after the reconstruction in 1922, contacts were established with independent representatives on a large number of markets at the same time. There was no tendency to start on neighbouring markets.

There was, however, a high negative correlation with the market size, indicating that Facit first established agency relations in small countries (see Table 3).

Table 3. Rank correlation (Spearman) between the order of Facit foreign establishments and psychic distance and market size

	Psychic distance	Market size
Agents	0.25[a] (0.200)	−0.53[a] (0.040)
Sales subsidiaries	0.60 (0.004)	0.21 (0.179)

[a] Only fourteen observations were used due to difficulties in dating some agent establishments.

The establishment of subsidiaries, which started at the end of the 1940s, is less confined to a certain time period. They are highly correlated with the distance factor but not with market size. The reasons for substituting subsidiaries for representatives are numerous. For one thing, it became a policy for Facit to use sales subsidiaries. For specific markets reasons, such as better control, the reinforcement of the selling organization and dissatisfaction with the representative were mentioned.

The motives for setting up manufacturing subsidiaries abroad have been mostly defensive in character. The foremost reasons for these establishments have been barriers to exporting to the markets concerned. This is also the case of those markets where licensing has been used. The general policy of Facit has not been to decentralize production geographically, but to export from Sweden.

In one case Facit has sold a sales subsidiary to the former representative on the market. This is the only example of a backward move in the 'establishment chain'. In all other cases the establishments have followed the 'chain' pattern.

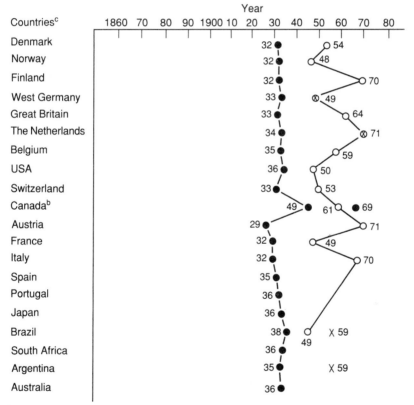

[a]Establishments of manufacturing subsidiaries are so few that they cannot be connected by a line.
[b]The subsidiary started in 1961, but in 1968 was sold to the former agent on the market.
[c]Ranked according to psychic distance from Sweden.

● agent   X   manufacturing subsidiary
O sales subsidiary   ⊗   sales and manufacturing subsidiary

Fig. 3. Profiles of Establishments, Facit[a].

In 1971 the turnover was about 950 million Swedish kronor. Forty-nine per cent of this turnover was sold through subsidiaries, 17 per cent through independent foreign representatives. The total export ratio was 66 per cent. The number of foreign subsidiaries was twenty, distributed among fourteen countries. Three of these were manufacturing units, two both manufacturing and sales and 15 sales.

A new development, considered of great importance, is various agreements with foreign companies, often Japanese, on development and production of new products.

Volvo[17]

The company started its activities in 1927, but the first product, a car, was already finished the year before. The production of cars appeared to be rather sensitive to seasonal variations and in 1928 Volvo started producing trucks as well, the sales of which were more evenly distributed throughout the year.

Export selling was a part of the first production plans and shortly after the start Volvo began establishing representatives abroad.

This was first done on neighbouring markets, Denmark and Norway and on less industrialized distant ones like Argentina, Brazil, Spain and Portugal. No attempt was made to sell to the large European markets until the 1950s. One reason for this behaviour was the hard competition from the domestic industries on these markets. From the start Volvo's policy was to not use its own affiliates or subsidiaries. However, early on Volvo had to break with its policy and establish selling subsidiaries in Finland and Norway, due to difficulties in finding retailers on these markets. A wave of establishments followed in the 1950s when Volvo started up new selling subsidiaries in most European countries, and in the USA and Canada.

This establishment pattern is very similar to Facit's with a high correlation between subsidiary establishments and distance and a negative correlation between agent establishments and market size.

The establishment of manufacturing units on most markets has not occurred before that of sales subsidiaries and the strategy has been to keep production in Sweden as long as possible. Establishments are said to be caused mainly by barriers to trade. Volvo has in such cases used assembly plants to avoid tariffs, import fees and other barriers. In Canada and Australia those plants were preceded by sales subsidiaries. This was not the case in Belgium. This plant was intended to produce for the EEC market. Besides the markets studied, Volvo also has its own assembly plants in Peru and Malaysia. As can be seen, assembly plants are often situated in distant countries.

The model's assumption that a firm starts selling to markets through representatives is correct for all countries except Finland. The two other very early establishments, in Norway and Argentina, were soon shut down, in Norway due to World War II and, in Argentina, because of barriers to import. A number of years thereafter the distribution was run by agents. When the markets again became important Volvo established new subsidiaries.

Special circumstances were at hand in the USA, West Germany and Switzerland. In the USA, Volvo had an agent for part of the market before establishing a subsidiary for the other parts. For a couple of years, an agency and a subsidiary were used side by side. Volvo thereafter took over and used a single subsidiary for the whole market. Also, in Switzerland, an agent was first used. After some years a subsidiary took over part of the

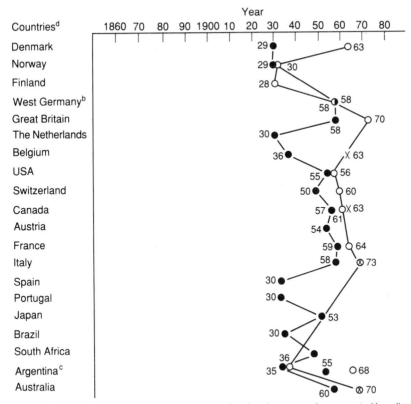

Year

| Countries[d] | 1860 70 80 90 1900 10 20 30 40 50 60 70 80 |

[a]Establishments of manufacturing subsidiaries are so few that they cannot be connected by a line.
[b]Establishment of agent and subsidiary in the same year.
[c]The subsidiary, which started in 1936, was closed down and substituted by an agent in 1955.
[d]Ranked according to psychic distance from Sweden.

  ● agent   X manufacturing subsidiary
  ○ sales subsidiary   ⊗ sales and manufacturing subsidiary

Fig. 4. Profiles of Establishments, Volvo[a].

market, but an agency is still used for the other parts. In West Germany two different local agents appeared, but their sales were of minor importance. Volvo therefore started a subsidiary in order to cover the whole market.

In 1973 Volvo has more than 100 export markets and the export ratio exceeds 70 per cent of the total turnover of about 7000 million Swedish kronor. In 1973 Volvo had manufacturing subsidiaries in five countries and sales subsidiaries in twelve. A new tendency in Volvo's international development in the last few years is a number of

Table 4. Rank correlation (Spearman) between the order of Volvo foreign establishments and psychic distance and market size

	Psychic distance	Market size
Agents	0.23 (0.076)	−0.70 (0.001)
Sales subsidiaries	0.47 (0.021)	0.06 (0.386)

cooperation agreements and 'joint ventures' with various foreign companies regarding the construction and production of engines, gear boxes etc.

THE INTERNATIONALIZATION COURSE—SOME CONCLUDING REMARKS

First, compared to their present sizes the four firms were small when they started internationalization. Of course we have to be careful comparing sizes over so long a time period. However, they were not small in comparison with other Swedish firms in their respective industries at that time. Sandvik had 300 employees and a sales value of 1 million Swedish kronor in 1870. Atlas Copco was of similar size when it started exporting in the 1880s. Facit and Volvo had sales values of 2–3 million Swedish kronor when they started exporting forty years later.

Two of the firms—Sandvik and Volvo—had export in mind when they were established. It is interesting to note that the founders of both these firms—Göransson and Gabrielsson—had long experience of selling abroad. Göransson had been general manager of a trading firm. Gabrielsson was a sales manager in SKF and had been employed at the SKF subsidiary in Paris.

The internationalization process was much faster in the firms that started latest. Sandvik, which established its first agency contact in 1868, needed sixty-five years to get agents in all twenty markets investigated. Atlas Copco, that established its first contact in 1904, needed fifty-five years, Volvo started in 1929 and needed thirty years and Facit, finally, with its first contacts in 1929 needed twenty years.

We expected to find a negative relationship between psychic distance and the establishments. At least we expected that agency relations should be established first in neighbouring and similar countries. To a certain extent we expected the establishment of sales subsidiaries to occur in the same order. Both kinds of establishments were expected to be influenced by the size of the market. In that case, however, we expected the relationship to be stronger with the sales subsidiary establishments.

To a certain extent the establishments have followed this course. However, there are obvious differences between the firms as shown in the following table (Table 5).

All the coefficients of distance have the expected sign and some of them are significant at the 0.05 level. But the differences between the firms are so large that there is reason to

Table 5. Rank correlation (Spearman) between agency establishments and psychic distance and respective market size

	Sandvik	Atlas Copco	Facit	Volvo
Psychic distance	0.79 (0.001)	0.40 (0.041)	0.25[a] (0.200)	0.23 (0.076)
Size	0.24 (0.181)	−0.26 (0.123)	−0.53[a] (0.040)	−0.70 (0.001)

[a] Based on only fourteen observations due to lack of information on establishing years of agents.

believe that they have followed different strategies of internationalization. This impression is strengthened when looking at the size of the coefficients which are rather low, with the exception of Volvo and Facit, which have significant negative coefficients. Whereas Sandvik and, to a certain extent, Atlas Copco could be described as having followed a course of establishing agency contacts in successively more distant countries, Volvo and Facit have started in the smaller countries and later extended to large countries. Atlas Copco has not followed any pronounced course with respect to the two country characteristics. This is not surprising as the product on which Atlas Copco based its main internationalization, drill equipment, has markets in countries with certain resources which need not be correlated with any of the above mentioned characteristics.

Looking at the sales subsidiary establishments the pattern is quite different (Table 6). It should be noted that the correlations between agency and sales subsidiary establishments are all lower than 0.30. The distance factor seems to have influenced Facit's and possibly Volvo's subsidiary establishments, whereas Sandvik's and Atlas Copco's are correlated with the market size. It seems reasonable to draw the conclusion that the firms have followed different internationalization strategies with respect to the two variables.

To a certain extent the establishing behaviour is similar within two groups, Sandvik and Atlas Copco in one and Facit and Volvo in the other one. A possible explanation of the difference between the two groups is that the members of the first group had started their internationalization process already at the end of the nineteenth century, while the two other firms did not start establishing until the late 1920s and the effects of the two factors may very well have changed during this long time period.

Another possible explanation of the difference between the two groups is that Sandvik and Atlas Copco manufacture and market more unique products than Facit and Volvo. The latter firms, according to that explanation, have had to avoid the domestic competitive situation in the big industrial countries, whereas the former have found gaps in those markets.

We may conclude that in order to be able to understand the patterns of different firms we have to develop some conditional model of internationalization. At the present stage we cannot formulate any such model, but we consider this a primary objective of our future research.

It should also be noted that the manufacturing establishments of Sandvik and Atlas Copco—the others have set up so few of such establishments—are not at all correlated with the two factors (-0.01 and 0.06 for Sandvik and 0.16 and -0.11 for Atlas Copco).

The establishment chain—no regular export, independent representative (an agent), sales subsidiary, manufacturing—seems to be a correct description of the order of the

Table 6. Rank correlation (Spearman) between subsidiary establishments and psychic distance and respective market size

	Sandvik	Atlas Copco	Facit	Volvo
Psychic distance	0.16 (0.227)	0.33 (0.072)	0.60 (0.004)	0.47 (0.021)
Size	0.66 (0.002)	0.48 (0.018)	0.21 (0.179)	0.06 (0.386)

development of operations of the firms in individual countries. This is illustrated in Table 7. Of sixty-three sales subsidiaries, fifty-six were preceded by agents and this pattern is the same for all the firms. With regard to the manufacturing establishments there is a difference between Sandvik and Atlas Copco on one hand, where twenty-two out of twenty-seven establishments were preceded by sales subsidiaries, and Facit and Volvo on the other, where five out of seven occurred without the firm having any sales subsidiary in the country. However, in no case has a firm started production in a country without having sold in the country via an agency or sales subsidiary before.

In all firms there have been periods of agency establishments, sales subsidiary establishments and, in the case of Sandvik and Atlas Copco, of manufacturing establishments. In two of the firms—Sandvik and Volvo—there has followed a period of international joint ventures for special purposes.

Considering the first establishment of sales subsidiaries it does not seem to have been a step in a conscious and goal directed strategy of internationalization—at least not in the case of Sandvik, Atlas Copco and Volvo. For various reasons they had to take over representatives or start subsidiaries. Gradually, when they had gained experience of setting up and managing subsidiaries they developed policies of marketing through subsidiaries in some of the firms. It should be noted that the firm Atlas Copco, which most consistently used subsidiaries for export marketing, did that when it got a new general manager, the former manager of a department store.

The manufacturing subsidiaries almost all manufacture for local or, in some cases, regional markets. They have finishing, assembly or component production which could be called marketing production. The only exception is Atlas Copco's factory in Belgium making stationary pneumatic equipment.

Generally the development of the firms seems to be in accordance with the incremental internationalization view discussed. In a few cases, notably Atlas Copco after World War II and Facit's agency establishments, the direction and velocity of internationalization has, however, been influenced heavily by strategic decisions.[18]

Table 7. Establishment patterns for the investigated firms

	Pattern					
	Sales subsidiary			Production subsidiary		
	n	a		n	a	s
Firm	↓	↓		↓	↓	↓
	s	s		p	p	p
Sandvik	2	18		0	2	13
Atlas Copco	3	14		0	3	9
Facit	0	14		0	2	3
Volvo	2	10		0	2	3
Total	7	56		0	9	28

n   no regular export activity
a   export via an agent
s   sales subsidiary
p   production subsidiary
An arrow denotes change from one state to another

NOTES

1. This study has been financially supported by the Swedish Council for Social Science Research and the Svenska Handelsbanken Foundation for Social Science Research. Appreciation is expressed to our colleagues in the international business research programme for their valuable comments.

2. See Gruber, W., Mehta, R. and Vernon, R., 'The R and D Factor in International Trade and International Investment of The United States,' *Journal of Political Economy*, Vol. 75, No. 1, February 1967, pp. 20–37, and Caves, R. E., 'International Corporations: The Industrial Economics of Foreign Investment', *Economica*, Vol. 38, No. 149, 1971, pp. 1–27, in discussions of foreign direct investments; also Terpstra, V., *International Marketing*, New York: McGraw-Hill, 1972.

3. Since its crisis in 1971, Facit is not quoted as an example any longer.

4. These two aspects of the international process are discussed in Kindleberger, C. P., *American Business Abroad*, Boston: Yale University Press, 1969.

5. Cf. Vernon, R., 'International Investment and International Trade in the Product Cycle', *Quarterly Journal of Economics*, Vol. 80, pp. 190–207, 1966, May and Burenstam-Linder, S., *An Essay on Trade and Transformation*, Stockholm: Almqvist & Wicksell, 1961. Market and country are used interchangeably in this paper.

6. This question is investigated in a research project by F. Wiedersheim-Paul entitled 'Export Propensity of the Firm'.

7. A more detailed discussion of the internationalization process is given in Johanson, J. and Vahlne, J. E., 'The Internationalization Process of the Firm', *Mimeographed Working Paper*, Department of Business Administration, 1974.

8. Similar discussions of a stepwise extension of activities in individual countries can be found in, for example, Gruber, W., Mehta, R., Vernon, R., op. cit., and Caves, R. E., op. cit.

9. 'Psychic Distance' has been used by, for example Beckermann, W., 'Distance and the Pattern of Intra-European Trade', *Review of Economics and Statistics*, Vol. 28, 1956, Linnemann, H., *An Econometric Study of International Trade Flows*, Amsterdam: North-Holland, 1966, and Wiedersheim-Paul, F., *Uncertainty and Economic Distance—Studies in International Business*, Uppsala: Almqvist and Wicksell, 1972. Here we use the concept with the same meaning as in Wiedersheim-Paul, op. cit., 1972.

10. Of course, changes due to political decisions can be very fast, e.g. USA–Cuba.

11. Root, F. R., *Strategic Planning for Export Marketing*, Copenhagen: Elhar Hareks Forlag, 1964, p. 11.

12. See, information from 'A File of Swedish Subsidiaries Abroad', Centre for International Business Studies, Department of Business Administration, University of Uppsala.

13. Chandler, A. D., *Strategy and Structure*, Cambridge, Mass.: MIT Press, 1962.

14. Håkansson, H. and Wootz, B., 'Internationalization of the Purchasing Function of the Firm', *Mimeographed Working Paper*, Department of Business Administration, Uppsala, 1974.

15. Carlson, S., *Ett Halvsekels Affärer, in Ett Svenskt Jernverk (A Swedish Steel Mill)*, Sandviken, 1937, Gärdlund, T., Janelid, I. and Ramström, D., *Atlas Copco, 1873–1973*, Stockholm: 1973, and *Mimeographed Research Papers* by students at the Department of Business Administration, Uppsala.

16. The ranking, with minor modifications, is taken from Hörnell, E., Vahlne, J.-E. and Wiedersheim-Paul, F., *Export och Utlands-Etableringar (Export and Foreign Establishment)*, Stockholm, 1973.

17. The discussion below relates exclusively to the automobile manufacturing part of the company.

18. Three of the firms, after a period of international operation, changed their names to adapt to the international market. The only exception is Volvo.

3

The Internationalization Process of the Firm—a Model of Knowledge Development and Increasing Foreign Market Commitments

Jan Johanson* and Jan-Erik Vahlne*

INTRODUCTION

Several studies of international business have indicated that internationalization of the firms is a process in which the firms gradually increase their international involvement. It seems reasonable to assume that within the frame of economic and business factors, the characteristics of this process influence the pattern and pace of internationalization of firms. In this paper we develop a model of the internationalization process of the firm that focuses on the development of the individual firm and particularly on its gradual acquisition, integration, and use of knowledge about foreign markets and operations and on its successively increasing commitment to foreign markets. The basic assumptions of the model are that lack of such knowledge is an important obstacle to the development of international operations and that the necessary knowledge can be acquired mainly through operations abroad. This holds for the two directions of internationalization we distinguish, increasing involvement of the firm in the individual foreign country and successive establishment of operations in new countries. In this paper we will, however, concentrate on the extension of operations in individual markets.

We have incorporated in our model some results of previous empirical studies of the development of international operations, seeking theoretical explanation through the behavioural theory of the firm (Cyert and March, 1963). Specifically we believe that internationalization is the product of a series of incremental decisions. Our aim is to identify elements shared in common by the successive decision situations and to develop thereby a model of the internationalization process which will have explanatory value. Because we, for the time being, disregard the decision style of the decision-maker himself,

*Jan Johanson is a member of the faculty of the Center for International Business Studies at the University of Uppsala, Sweden. Jan-Erik Vahlne is on the faculty of the Institute of International Business, Stockholm School of Economics, Stockholm, Sweden. The authors are indebted to their colleagues at the Center for International Business Studies, Department of Business Administration, University of Uppsala for valuable comments and to David Baker for careful criticism of content and language. Financial support has been given by the Svenska Handelsbanken Foundation for Social Science Research.

Reprinted with permission from *Journal of International Business Studies*, Vol 8, No 1, pp 23–32 and, to a certain extent, the specific properties of the various decision situations, our model has only limited predictive value. We believe, however, that all the decisions that, taken together, constitute the internationalization process—decisions to start exporting to a country, to establish export channels, to start a selling subsidiary, and so forth—have some common characteristics which are also very important to the subsequent internationalization. Our model focuses on these common traits.

We hope that the model will contribute to conceptualization in the field of internationalization of the firm and thus increase understanding of the development of international operations as described in the empirical studies. We hope, too, that it can serve as a frame of reference for future studies in the problem area and may also be useful as a tool in the analysis of the effects of various factors on the pattern and pace of internationalization of the firm.

In the first section we describe the empirical background of our study. Next we outline the model of the internationalization process defining the main variables and the interaction among them. We then sum up by discussing some implications of the model and suggesting some problems for future research.

EMPIRICAL BACKGROUND

The model is based on empirical observations from our studies in international business at the University of Uppsala that show that Swedish firms often develop their international operations in small steps rather than by making large foreign production investments at single points in time. Typically firms start exporting to a country via an agent, later establish a sales subsidiary, and eventually, in some cases, begin production in the host country.

We have also observed a similar successive establishment of operations in new countries. Of particular interest in the present context is that the time order of such establishments seems to be related to the psychic distance between the home and the import/host countries (Hörnell, Vahlne and Wiedersheim-Paul, 1972, Johanson and Wiedersheim-Paul, 1974). The psychic distance is defined as the sum of factors preventing the flow of information from and to the market. Examples are differences in language, education, business practices, culture and industrial development.

Studies of the export organization of the Swedish special steel firms (Johanson, 1966) and of the Swedish pulp and paper industry (Forsgren and Kinch, 1970) have shown that almost all sales subsidiaries of Swedish steel companies and pulp and paper companies have been established through acquisition of the former agent or have been organized around some person employed by the agent. Most of the establishments were occasioned by various kinds of economic crises in the agent firms. Sales to a market by the agent had preceded establishment of a sales subsidiary in each of nine cases investigated by Hörnell and Vahlne (1972). Further case studies of the development of international activities by Swedish firms have allowed us to generalize our observations. Sales subsidiaries are preceded in virtually all cases by selling via an agent; similarly, local production is generally preceded by sales subsidiaries.

A summary of the results we reached in two studies follows. They are by no means meant to be statistically representative, but the results are typical of studies we know. The first example is a case study of the internationalization process of the second largest

Swedish pharmaceutical firm, Pharmacia. At the time of the case study (1972) Pharmacia had organizations of its own in nine countries, of which three were performing manufacturing activities. In eight of these cases the development pattern was as follows. The firm received orders from the foreign market and after some time made an agreement with an agent (or sold licences regarding some parts of the product line). After a few years Pharmacia established sales subsidiaries in seven of those countries (and in the eighth they bought a manufacturing company bearing the same name, Pharmacia, that had previously served as an agent). Two of the seven sales subsidiaries further increased their involvement by starting manufacturing activities. It is interesting to note that even this production decision was incremental, the new production units began with the least complicated manufacturing activities and later successively added more complicated ones.

In the ninth country Pharmacia started a sales subsidiary almost immediately when demand from the market was discovered. But the company did not totally lack experience even in this case. The decision-maker had received parts of his education in the country in question, and before the decision he had become acquainted with the representative of another pharmaceutical firm who was later made the head of the subsidiary (Hörnell, Vahlne, and Wiedersheim-Paul, 1973).

In another study we investigated the internationalization of four Swedish engineering firms. Below we quote some of the conclusions of the study (Johanson and Wiedersheim-Paul, 1975).

The establishment chain—no regular export, independent representative (agent), sales subsidiary, production—seems to be a correct description of the order of the development operations of the firms in individual countries. This is illustrated in Table 1. Of sixty-three sales subsidiaries fifty-six were preceded by agents; this pattern holds for all the firms. With regard to the production establishments there is a difference between Sandvik and Atlas Copco on one hand, where twenty-two out of twenty-seven establishments were preceded by sales subsidiaries, and Facit and Volvo on the other, where five out of seven occurred without the firm having any sales subsidiary in the country. However, in no case has a firm started

Table 1. Establishment patterns for the investigated firms

Firm	Pattern	Sales subsidiary		Production subsidiary		
		n ↓ s	a ↓ s	n ↓ p	a ↓ p	s ↓ p
Sandvik		2	18	0	2	13
Atlas Copco		3	14	0	3	9
Facit		0	14	0	2	3
Volvo		2	10	0	2	3
Total		7	56	0	9	28

n   no regular export activity
a   selling via agent
s   sales subsidiary
p   production subsidiary
An arrow denotes change from one state to another

production in a country without having sold in the country via an agency or a sales subsidiary before.

Regarding the first establishment of sales subsidiaries, they do not seem to have been a step in a conscious and goal directed internationalization—at least not in Sandvik, Atlas Copco, and Volvo. For various reasons they had to take over representatives or start subsidiaries. As they gradually have gained experience in starting and managing subsidiaries, they have developed policies of marketing through subsidiaries in some of the firms. It should be noted that the firm Atlas Copco which most consistently used subsidiaries for export marketing did so when it acquired a new general manager, a former manager of a department store.

The producing subsidiaries almost all produce for local or in some cases regional markets. Their activity embraces finishing assembly or component works which could be called marketing production. The only exception is Atlas Copco's factory in Belgium making stationary pneumatic equipment.

Generally the development of the firm seems to be in accordance with the incremental internationalization view discussed.

This gradual internationalization is not exclusively a Swedish phenomenon, as the following quotations demonstrate.

On its part exporting is a means also of reducing costs of market development. Even if investment is necessary in the future, exporting helps to determine the nature and size of the market. As the market develops, warehouse facilities are established, later sales branches and subsidiaries (Singer, National Cash Register, United Show Machinery). The record of company development indicates that the use of selling subsidiaries at an early stage reduced the later risks of manufacturing abroad. These selling affiliates permitted the slow development of manufacturing from repairing, to packaging, to mixing, to finishing, to processing or assembling operations, and finally to full manufacture (Behrman, 1969, p. 3).

Within countries there is often a pattern of exports from the United States, followed by the establishment of an assembly or packaging plant, followed by progressively more integrated manufacturing activities (Vaupel, 1971, p. 42).

Without reference to any specific empirical observations Gruber, Mehta, and Vernon (1967) mention that 'one way of looking at the overseas direct investments of US producers of manufacturers is that they are the final step in a process which begins with the involvement of such producers in export trade'. Knickerbocker (1972) also refers to this process and explicitly distinguishes agents and sales subsidiaries as separate steps in the process. Lipsey and Weiss (1969, 1972) refer to a 'market cycle' model with similar characteristics. However, in none of these cases have the dynamics of this process been investigated. It has only been used as an argument in the discussion of related problems.

Specification of the problem

If internationalization indeed follows the pattern described above, how can we explain it? We do not believe tht it is the result of a strategy for optimum allocation of resources to different countries where alternative ways of exploiting foreign markets are compared and evaluated. We see it rather as the consequence of a process of incremental adjustments to changing conditions of the firm and its environment (cf. Aharoni, 1966).

Changes in the firm and its environment expose new problems and opportunities. Lacking routines for the solution of such sporadic problems, the concern's management 'searches in the area of the problem' (Cyert and March, 1963). Each new discontinuity is regarded as an essentially unprecedented and unparalleled case, the problems and opportunities presented are handled in their contexts. Thus commitments to other markets are not explicitly taken into consideration, resource allocations do not compete with each other.

Another constraint on the problem solution is the lack of, and difficulty of obtaining market knowledge in international operations. That internationalization decisions have an incremental character is, we feel, largely due to this lack of market information and the uncertainty occasioned thereby (Hörnell, Vahlne and Wiedersheim-Paul, 1972, Johanson, 1970). We believe that lack of knowledge due to differences between countries with regard to, for example, language and culture, is an important obstacle to decision making connected with the development of international operations. We would even say that these differences constitute the main characteristic of international as distinct from domestic operations. By market knowledge we mean information about markets and operations in those markets, which is somehow stored and reasonably retrievable—in the mind of individuals, in computer memories and in written reports. In our model we consider knowledge to be vested in the decision-making system, we do not deal explicitly with the individual decision-maker.

THE INTERNATIONALIZATION MODEL

As indicated in the introduction a model in which the same basic mechanism can be used to explain all steps in the internationalization would be useful. We also think that a dynamic model would be suitable. In such a model the outcome of one decision—or more generally one cycle of events—constitutes the input of the next. The main structure is given by the distinction between the state and change aspects of internationalization variables. To clarify we can say that the present state of internationalization is one important factor explaining the course of following internationalization as in expression (1) below

$$\Delta I = f(?)$$

where

I = state of internationalization

The state aspects we consider are the resource commitment to the foreign markets—market commitment—and knowledge about foreign markets and operations. The change aspects are decisions to commit resources and the performance of current business activities. The basic mechanism is illustrated schematically in Figure 1.

Market knowledge and market commitment are assumed to affect both commitment decisions and the way current activities are performed. These in turn change knowledge and commitment (cf. Aharoni, 1966).

In the model, it is assumed that the firm strives to increase its long-term profit, which is assumed to be equivalent to growth (Williamson, 1966). The firm is also striving to keep risk-taking at a low level. These strivings are assumed to characterize decision-making on all levels of the firm. Given these premises and the state of the economic and business factors which constitute the frame in which a decision is taken, the model assumes that the state of internationalization affects perceived opportunities and risks which in turn influence commitment decisions and current activities. We will discuss the mechanism in detail in the following sections.

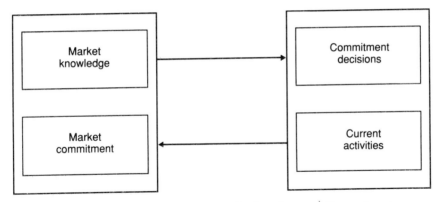

Fig. 1. The Basic Mechanism of Internationalization—State and Change Aspects.

State aspects

The two state aspects are resources committed to foreign markets—market commitment—and knowledge about foreign markets possessed by the firm at a given point of time. The reason for considering the market commitment is that we assume that the commitment to a market affects the firm's perceived opportunities and risk.

Market commitment

Let us first take a look at the market commitment concept. To begin with we assume that it is composed of two factors—the amount of resources committed and the degree of commitment, that is, the difficulty of finding an alternative use for the resources and transferring them to it. Resources located in a particular market area can often be considered a commitment to that market. However, in some cases such resources can be sold and the financial resources can easily be used for other purposes. The degree of commitment is higher the more the resources in question are integrated with other parts of the firm and their value is derived from these integrated activities. Thus, as a rule, vertical integration means a higher degree of commitment than a conglomerative foreign investment. An example of resources that cannot easily be directed to another market or used for other purposes is a marketing organization that is specialized around the products of the firm and has established integrated customer relations. However, resources located in the home country and employed in development and production of products for a separate market also constitute a commitment to that market. The more specialized the resources are to the specific market the greater is the degree of commitment. And even if such resources can easily be directed to development and production for other markets, as for example engineers in a central engineering department, they cannot always be profitably used there. Consider Volvo—the Swedish car manufacturer—with a large part of its production capacity employed in production of cars for the US market. Even if that capacity is not highly committed to the US production, it is not easy, at least in the short run, to use it for production for other markets. And although the engineers employed in adapting the car to the US requirements can probably be used for another purpose, it is not certain that they can be profitably employed there. On the whole, it seems reasonable to assume that the resources that are located in the particular market are most committed to that market, but we shall not disregard the commitment that follows from employing parts of the domestic capacity for a particular market.

The other part of market commitment—the amount of resources committed—is easy to grasp. It is close to the size of the investment in the market, using this concept in a broad sense, including investment in marketing, organization, personnel, and other areas.

Market knowledge

In our model, knowledge is of interest because commitment decisions are based on several kinds of knowledge. First, knowledge of opportunities or problems is assumed to initiate decisions. Second, evaluation of alternatives is based on some knowledge about relevant parts of the market environment and about performance of various activities. Very generally, the knowledge 'relates to present and future demand and supply, to competition and to channels for distribution, to payment conditions and the transferability of money, and those things vary from country to country and from time to time' (Carlson, 1974).

A classification of knowledge which is useful for us is based on the way in which knowledge is acquired (Penrose, 1966, p. 53). One type, objective knowledge, can be taught, the other, experience or experiential knowledge, can only be learned through personal experience. With experiential knowledge, emphasis is placed on the change in the services the human resources can supply which arises from their activity (ibid. p. 53), and '. . . experience itself can never be transmitted, it produces a change—frequently a subtle change—in individuals and cannot be separated from them' (ibid. p. 53) 'Much of the experience of businessmen is frequently so closely associated with a particular set of circumstances that a large part of a man's most valuable services may be available only under these circumstances' (ibid. p. 53).

We believe that this experiential knowledge is the critical kind of knowledge in the present context. It is critical because it cannot be so easily acquired as objective knowledge. In domestic operations we can to a large extent rely on lifelong basic experiences to which we can add the specific experiences of individuals, organizations and markets in foreign operations; however, we have no such basic experiential knowledge to start with. It must be gained successively during the operations in the country.

We believe that the less structured and well defined the activities and the required knowledge are, the more important is experiential knowledge. We think it is particularly important in connection with activities that are based on relations to other individuals. Managerial work and marketing are examples of such activities. Especially in the marketing of complex and soft-ware-intensive products, experiential knowledge is crucial.

An important aspect of experiential knowledge is that it provides the framework for perceiving and formulating opportunities. On the basis of objective market knowledge it is possible to formulate only theoretical opportunities, experiential knowledge makes it possible to perceive 'concrete' opportunities—to have a 'feeling' about how they fit into the present and future activities.

We can also distinguish between general knowledge and market-specific knowledge. General knowledge concerns, in the present context, marketing methods and common characteristics of certain types of customers, irrespective of their geographical location, depending, for example, in the case of industrial customers, on similarities in the production process. The market-specific knowledge is knowledge about characteristics of the specific national market—its business climate, cultural patterns, structure of the market system, and, most importantly, characteristics of the individual customer firms and their personnel.

Establishment and performance of a certain kind of operation or activity in a country require both general knowledge and market-specific knowledge. Market-specific knowledge can be gained mainly through experience in the market, whereas knowledge of the operation can often be transferred from one country to another country. It is the diffusion of this general knowledge which facilitates lateral growth, that is, the establishment of technically similar activities in dissimilar business environments.

There is a direct relation between market knowledge and market commitment. Knowledge can be considered a resource (or, perhaps preferably, a dimension of the human resources), and consequently the better the knowledge about a market, the more valuable are the resources and the stronger is the commitment to the market. This is especially true of experiential knowledge, which is usually associated with the particular conditions on the market in question and thus cannot be transferred to other individuals or other markets.

Change aspects

The change aspects we have considered are current activities and decisions to commit resources to foreign operations.

Current business activities

There is, to begin with, a lag between most current activities and their consequences. Those consequences may, in fact, not be realized unless the activities are repeated more or less continuously. Consider, for example, marketing activities, which generally do not result in sales unless they are repeated for some time. In many cases the time lag is considerable, and the marketing investment represents an important and ever-increasing commitment to the market. The longer the lag, the higher the commitment of the firm mounts. It seems reasonable to assume that the more complicated and the more differentiated the product is, the larger the total commitment as a consequence of current activities will come to be.

Current activities are also the prime source of experience. It could be argued that exprience could be gained alternatively through the hiring of personnel with experience, or through advice from persons with experience. To clarify the roles of these alternative ways of integrating experience into the firm in the internationalization process, we distinguish between firm experience and market experience, both of which are essential. Persons working on the boundary between the firm and its market must be able to interpret information from inside the firm and from the market. The interpretation of one kind of information is possible only for one who has experience with the other part. We conclude that, for the performance of marketing activities, both kinds of experience are required; and in this area it is difficult to substitute personnel or advice from outside for current activities. The more the activities are production-oriented, or the less interaction is required between the firm and its market environment, the easier it will be to substitute hired personnel or advice for current activities, and consequently the easier it will be to start new operations that are not incremental additions to the former operations. It should be remembered, however, that even production activities are dependent on the general business climate, which cannot easily be assessed in ways other than performance of business activities.

To some extent it may be possible to hire personnel with market experience and to use them profitably after some time in the marketing activities. The delay is occasioned by the need for the new personnel to gain the necessary experience in the firm. But if the new personnel have already worked as representatives for the exporter, the delay may approach zero. Thus, the best way to quickly obtain and use market experience is to hire a sales manager or a salesman of a representative or to buy the whole or a part of the firm. In many cases this kind of experience is not for sale; at the time of entry to a market the experience may not even exist. It has to be acquired through a long learning process in connection with current activities. This factor is an important reason why the internationalization process often proceeds slowly.

Commitment decisions

The second change aspect is decisions to commit resources to foreign operations. We assume that such decisions depend on what decision alternatives are raised and how they are chosen. Regarding the first part we assume that decisions are made in response to perceived problems and/or opportunities on the market. Problems and opportunities— that is awareness of need and possibilities for business actions—are assumed to be dependent on experience. Like Penrose, we might even say that opportunities—and problems—are part of that experience. Firm experience, as well as market experience, is relevant. Problems are mainly discovered by those parts of the organization that are responsible for operations on the market and primarily by those who are working there. For them, the natural solution to problems will be the extension of the operations on the market to complementing operations. In any case we assume the solutions to market operations problems are searched for in the neighbourhood of the problem symptoms, that is in the market activities (Cyert and March, 1963). In the same way opportunities will be perceived mainly by those who are working on the market, and such opportunities will also lead to extension of the operations on the market. They will be related to those parts of the environment that the firm is interacting with (Pfeffer, 1974). Thus, whether decision alternatives are raised in response to problems or in response to opportunities, they will be related to the operations currently performed on the market. Alternative solutions will generally consist of activities that mean an extension of the boundaries of the organization and an increase in commitment to the market. We could speak of an opportunity horizon that—given the operations performed—describes the kind of activities that are likely to be suggested by those responsible for operations.

But opportunities are also seen by individuals in organizations with which the firm is interacting; these individuals may propose alternative solutions to the firm in the form of offers or demands. The probability that the firm is offered opportunities from outside is dependent on the scale and type of operations it is performing; that is, on its commitment to the market.

We distinguish between an economic effect and an uncertainty effect of each additional commitment. We assume that the economic effect is associated primarily with increases in the scale of operations on the market, and that the uncertainty effect concerns the market uncertainty, that is the decision-makers' perceived lack of ability to estimate the present and future market and market-influencing factors. We mean that this market uncertainty is reduced through increases in interaction and integration with the market environment—steps such as increases in communication with customers, establishment of new service activities or, in the extreme case, the take-over of customers.

Our thinking on this point is further illustrated by the system of relationships below:

R^* = maximum tolerable market (market i) risk = f (firm's resource position, firm's risk approach)

R = existing market risk situation = $C_i \cdot U$

where C = existing market commitment

U = existing market uncertainty

ΔR = incremental risk implied by an incremental addition to operations on market i

Scale increasing decisions are assumed to affect the size of C but not the size of U so that

$$\Delta R = U \cdot \Delta C_i > 0$$

Uncertainty reducing decisions are assumed to affect U, primarily so that

$$\Delta R = \Delta U (C + \Delta C) + \Delta C_i \cdot U_i < 0$$

Using this framework we say that scale-increasing decisions will be taken when $R < R^*$. The firm will incrementally extend its scale of existing operations on the market—in expectation of large returns—until its tolerable risk frontier (R^*) is met. Scale-increasing commitments may, for example, be occasioned by a decline in uncertainty about the market (U_i) incidental to gaining market knowledge acquired with experience. Such a decline in market uncertainty can be expected when the market conditions are fairly stable and heterogeneous. If market conditions are very unstable, experience cannot be expected to lead to decreased uncertainty. And, if market conditions are very homogeneous, experience is probably not a necessary requirement for market knowledge. Under such market conditions an optimal scale of operations can be chosen from the beginning. Market uncertainty can also decline as a consequence of a competitive—or political—stabilization of market conditions. Scale-increasing commitments may also follow a rise of the maximum tolerable risk level due to an increase in the total resources of the firm or a more aggressive approach toward risk. We can in any event say that large increases in the scale of operations in the market will only take place in firms with large total resources or in firms which feel little uncertainty about the market.

Uncertainty-reducing commitments on the other hand will be made when $R > R^*$. The firm will respond to this imbalance by taking steps to increase interactions and integration with the market environment. Such an imbalance may be the result of a decrease in the maximum tolerable market risk (R^*) or an increase in the existing risk situation on the market (R_i). The latter case may, in its turn, be occasioned by an increase in market commitment (C_i) or market uncertainty (U_i). Market commitments that increase risk are, according to our assumptions, those that increase the scale of existing operations on the market. Such increases are likely to be associated with current activities in an expanding market but can also be a consequence of the scale-increasing decisions discussed in the previous paragraph. Note that increases in the scale of operations on the market can be expected to lead to uncertainty-reducing commitments, that is increased interaction and integration with the market environment. Market uncertainty (U_i) can be expected to rise as a consequence of experience in a dynamic market environment, showing that the original perception of the market was too simple. It may also rise because of a structural change in market conditions, for example, in connection with the entrance of new competitors on the market or introduction of new techniques. A typical example of the former is the change of the market situation of Swedish pulp and paper firms due to the entrance of North American producers on the European market (Kinch, 1974). However, increases in market uncertainty due to political changes cannot be expected to lead to the uncertainty-reducing commitments discussed here since such commitments cannot be expected to affect the political situation.

This discussion requires some further comments. First, it is very partial since we do not take into account how various factors other than scale may affect the economy of the market operations. The technology of the firm probably has a great impact on the economy of different types of market operations. Secondly, the variable 'firm's approach to market risk' is a very complicated factor. We can, for example, distinguish between three different strategies with respect to this factor. One may be that a high risk level on one market is compensated by a low risk level on other markets. Another is that the tolerable risk level is the same on all markets. A third is that risk taking on the market is delegated to those working on the market as long as decisions do not require additional resources from the firm.

We conclude this discussion of commitment decisions by observing that additional commitments will be made in small steps unless the firm has very large resources and/or market conditions are stable and homogeneous, or the firm has much experience from other markets with similar conditions. If not, market experience will lead to a step-wise increase in the scale of the operations and of the integration with the market environment where steps will be taken to correct imbalance with respect to the risk situation on the market. Market growth will speed up this process.

Empirical verification

We think that the general characteristics of the model fit nicely with empirical observations given earlier. In order to validate it empirically we intend to make two kinds of empirical studies. Firstly, we shall make one or two intensive case studies to see if the mechanism can be used for explanation in empirical situations. In those case studies, we shall try to measure the internationalization variables, market commitment and market knowledge, and investigate how they develop during the internationalization of the firm.

Secondly, we intend to make comparative studies of the internationalization courses of different firms. Assuming that such factors as firm size, technology, product line, home country, etc., via the mechanism discussed affect the character of the internationalization in different ways, we will investigate whether firms that differ with respect to those factors also differ with respect to the patterns of internationalization. Such studies will require more systematic discussions of the expected influence of the factors. The present model will constitute the framework of such discussions.

Possible applications

In many countries various programmes to affect foreign trade and operations are designed and carried out. Still more are discussed. Usually such programmes are based on models in which prices of factors and products in different countries are the only explaining factors. We think that our model can help in giving such discussions and programmes a better base. An evaluation of a Swedish export stimulation programme showed that the 'export stimulation measures affect firms' export behaviour in different ways due to differences in their degrees of previous export experience' (Olson, 1975). Our model indicates how such experience can be expected to affect the export behaviour. It also makes it possible to develop a better understanding of foreign investment behaviour.

We also think that the model can be useful in planning and decision making in the firm with regard to international operations. Many firms consider internationalization a promising strategy. There are, however, numerous examples of firms which have started international operations without success. We think that the importance of the experience factor is often overlooked. The model indicates how it is related to other internationalization variables thus giving a better base for planning and executing the internationalization process.

And finally we hope, as do other students in the field, that our way of reasoning will add something to the understanding of the process by which firms become international or even multinational. Thus, many studies of international trade and investment have shown that oligopolistic industries have the greatest international engagement. Such features as high R&D intensity, advertising intensity and efforts at product differentiation characterized these industries (Gruber, Mehta, Vernon, 1967; Hymer, 1960; Kindleberger, 1969; Caves, 1971; Vaupel, 1971). Oligopolistic competition, however, lacks explanatory value at the firm level; we have to look for other features to explain variations in the level of international involvement among the several firms in a given oligopolistic industry (Horst, 1972, Knickerbocker, 1973). Perhaps our model of the internationalization process can help in providing a part of this explanation by stressing the importance of some factors affecting the decision-making process.

REFERENCES

Aharoni, Y. *The Foreign Investment Decision Process.* Boston, 1966.

Behrman, J. *Some Patterns in the Rise of the Multinational Enterprise.* Chapel Hill, 1969.

Carlson, S. *Investment in Knowledge and the Cost of Information.* Acta Academiae Regiae Scientiarum Upsaliensis, Uppsala, 1974.

Caves, R. E. 'International Corporations: The Industrial Economics of Foreign Investment', *Economics* (1971) vol. 38.

Cyert, R. M., March, J. G. *A Behavioral Theory of the Firm.* Englewood Cliffs, 1963.

Forsgren, M., Kinch, N. *Foretagets anpassning till forandringar i omgivande system.* En studie av massa- och pappersindustrin. Uppsala, 1970.

Gruber, W., Menta, R., Vernon, R. 'The R&D Factor in International Trade and International Investment of the United States'. *Journal of Political Economy.* February 1967.

Horst, T. O. 'Firm and Industry Determinants of the Decision to Invest Abroad: An Empirical Study'. *Review of Economics and Statistics.* 1972.

Hymer, S. 'The International Operations of National Firms. A Study of Direct Investment.' Doctoral dissertation, Mass. Institute of Technology. 1960.

Haakansson, F., Wootz, B. 'Supplier Selection in an International Environment—An Experimental Study,' *Journal of Marketing Research.* February 1975.

Hörnell, E., Vahlne, J.-E., Wiedersheim-Paul, F. *Export och utlandsetableringar.* Stockholm, 1973.

Johanson, J. (ed.) *Exportstrategiska problem.* Stockholm, 1972.

Johanson, J. 'Svenskt kvalitetsstål på utländska marknader.' Mimeographed licentiate dissertation. Dept. of Business Administration, Uppsala, 1966.

Johanson, J., Wiedersheim-Paul, F. 'The Internationalization of the Firm—Four Swedish Cases'. *Journal of Management Studies.* 1975.

Kinch, N. 'Utlandsetableringar inom massa-och pappers-industrin' In *Företagsekonomisk forskning kring internationellt foretagande,* ed. by Jan-Erik Vahlne. Stockholm, 1974.

Kindleberger, C. P., *American Business Abroad.* New Haven, 1969.

Knickerbocker, F. T. *Oligopolistic Reaction and Multinational Enterprise.* Boston, 1973.

Lipsey, R. E., Weiss, M. Y. 'The Relation of US Manufacturing Abroad to US Exports. A Framework for Analysis', *Business and Economics Section Proceedings.* American Statistical Association, 1969.

Lipsey, R. E., Weiss, M. Y. 'Analyzing Direct Investment and Trade at the Company Level.' *Business and Economic Section Proceedings.* American Statistical Association, 1972.

Olson, H. C. *Studies in Export Promotion Attempts to Evaluate Export Stimulation Measures for the Swedish Textile and Clothing Industries.* Uppsala, 1975.

Penrose, E., *The Theory of the Growth of the Firm.* Oxford, 1966.

Pfeffer, J. 'Merger as a Response to Organizational Interdependence'. *Administrative Science Quarterly* 6 (1972).

Vaupel, J. V. 'Characteristics and Motivations of the US Corporations that Manufacture Abroad'. Mimeographed, Boston, 1971.

Williamson, J. 'Profit Growth and Sales Maximization'. *Economica* 33 (1966).

4

A Theory of International Operations

Peter J. Buckley and Mark Casson

This chapter provides a theoretical framework for the explanation and prediction of the methods of market servicing (or 'sourcing policies') of multinational enterprises (MNEs).

1. THE DIVISION OF NATIONAL MARKETS

A national market for a final product can be served in four main ways: by indigenous firms, by subsidiaries of MNEs located in the market, by exports to the market from foreign locally owned firms and by exports from foreign plants owned by MNEs. The first two methods are distinguished from the second two by the 'location effect': the market is served by local production rather than export. The first method is distinguished from the second and the third method from the fourth by the 'ownership effect': production is owned and controlled by domestic nationals rather than by a foreign-owned international corporation.

Final goods markets cannot, however, be considered in isolation from the markets for the intermediate goods involved in the production process. Intermediate goods too are subject to ownership and location effects. In order to service a final product market it may be advantageous to locate different stages of production in different locations. Also the ownership of 'the good' may change as we move through the process—an example of this is licensing where essential proprietary knowledge to produce the final good is licensed from one producer to another.

In order to examine these factors in detail the following sections deal firstly with location effects and then with ownership effects.

2. THE LOCATION OF PRODUCTION FACILITIES

Production in a multi-stage process can be characterized as a sequence of distinct activities linked by the transport of semi-processed materials. The orthodox theory of location assumes constant returns to scale, freely available and therefore standardized technology and that firms are price takers in all factor markets. Given such assumptions, a firm chooses its optimal location for each stage of production by evaluating regional production costs and choosing the set of locations for which the overall average cost of production is minimized. Regional production costs vary only according to regional differentials in non-tradeable goods (the price of tradeables is standardized by trade), the relative prices of tradeables and non-tradeables and elasticities of substitution between pairs of non-tradeables and between tradeables and non-tradeables. Overall average production costs are minimized by the correct choice of the least cost 'route' from the location of raw materials through to the final destination.[1]

This location strategy is complicated in practice by a number of factors.

First, there are increasing returns to scale in many activities. Where only one destination is to be serviced, increasing returns means that location strategy may change in response to a change in the size of market. Where more than one destination is to be serviced, increasing returns in either production or transportation create an incentive to concentrate each stage of production at just a few locations. Increasing returns at any one stage of production or in the transport of any one semi-processed material may be diffused through the entire process, leading to the relocation of plants involved in quite remote stages of production, and to the reorganization of the entire network of trade.

The second major factor is that modern businesses perform many activities other than routine production. Such activities require different inputs from production, but need to be integrated with the production process. They have a twofold influence on location: their own least cost location will differ from that of routine production because of their differing input requirements and secondly they will exercise a locational 'pull' on routine production. Two important non-production activities are marketing and research and development (R&D).[2] Both these functions represent an integral set of activities. Marketing has three main constituents: stockholding, distribution and advertising. The location of stockholding depends on the interplay between the better quality of service provided by decentralized stockholding and the declining costs of large, centralized warehouses. Only above a certain market size is local stockholding efficient. Routine advertising and distribution are generally located in the final market. The location of R&D will depend largely on the regional differentials in the price of the most important non-traded input—skilled labour. However, this will be modified by information costs which play the same role as transport costs in routine production. Where a firm relies on the creation and internal use of productive knowledge from its own R&D department, there are strong reasons for centralizing this creative function and integrating it closely with the more creative aspects of marketing and production.[3] Constant reworking of ideas through teamwork is necessary for least cost innovation and the importance of information flows will encourage the centralization of these activities. However, the more routine 'development' work may be much more diffused: the communications problem is not so great and local knowledge and inputs are more important. We conclude that the location strategy of a firm which integrates production marketing and R&D is highly complex. The activities are normally interdependent and information flows as well as transport costs must be considered. Information costs which increase with distance encourage the centralization of activities where exchanges of knowledge through teamwork are of the essence. Such activities are the 'high level' ones of basic research, innovative production and the development marketing strategy; they require large inputs of skilled labour, and the availability of skilled labour will therefore exert a significant influence on the location strategy of such firms.[4]

The third factor which complicates the location strategies of firms is that in practice they operate largely in imperfectly competitive markets. This means that, in many cases, MNEs cannot be considered as price takers in intermediate and factor markets. Consequently, a firm which can force down input or factor prices in a particular region will tend to concentrate the production processes which are intensive in these inputs in that region. It has been argued that the explanation of monopsony power may also exert a significant influence on a firm's choice of production technique in a particular region.[5]

The fourth factor is government intervention. The influence of taxes and tariffs and other regulations such as preferential duties has been shown by many analysts to affect location[6] and it is unnecessary to elaborate on this here.

Finally, location decisions will be influenced by the ownership effect, or the extent to which the internalization of markets in the firm modify the above considerations. This is examined in detail in the following section.

To sum up, the location decisions of firms in the international economy will in practice differ considerably from the predictions of the theory of the location of production under ideal competitive conditions where transport costs are the only barrier to trade. The possibilities of economies of scale in certain activities, the complexities of the activities, the extent of their integration, the type of market structure and the extent of government intervention will all influence location strategy. We now examine ownership effects and the extent to which location strategy is dependent on the replacement of external markets by internal markets within the firm.

3. THE OWNERSHIP OF PRODUCTION

Having considered location effects in some detail, we can now turn our attention to the ownership of production, considering production locations unchanged. A strong case can be made for the contention that the major dynamic of the world economy is changing *ownership* effects which influence the pattern of distribution of production between MNEs and national firms. Resource endowments are to a large extent geographically fixed: copper, bauxite and oil reserves for instance. The question at issue is why US-owned copper companies, US and Canadian aluminium producers and US and UK oil companies should dominate their markets. We argue here that the essence of the ownership effect can be explained in terms of the internalization of key intermediate goods markets within firms of particular nationalities.

In a situation where firms are attempting to maximize profits in a world of imperfect markets, there will often exist an incentive to bypass imperfect markets in intermediate products. Their activities which were previously linked by the market mechanism are brought under common ownership and control in a 'market' internal to the firm. Where markets are internalized across national boundaries, MNEs are created.[7]

Benefits of internalization arise from the avoidance of imperfections in the external market, but there are also costs. The optimum size of firm is set where the costs and benefits of further internalization are equalized at the margin. We now go on to examine these costs and benefits and to consider how they apply in practice.

Benefits from 'internalization' arise from five main types of market imperfection. Firstly, production takes time. Often activities linked by the market involve significant time lags and the relevant futures markets required for their co-ordination are inadequate or completely lacking. This creates a strong incentive for the creation of an internal future market. Secondly, the efficient explanation of market power may require discriminating pricing of a type not feasible in an external market—this will encourage the monopolist to integrate forward and the monopsonist to integrate backwards. Thirdly, internal markets remove—or prevent the growth of—bilateral concentrations of market power, and thus reduce the likelihood of unstable bargaining situations. The fourth type of imperfection occurs where there is inequality between buyer and seller with respect to the evaluation of a product. 'Buyer uncertainty' is prevalent where the product in question is a type of knowledge, which cannot be properly valued unless the valuer is in full possession of it. Buyer uncertainty is eliminated when buyer and seller are part of the same organization. Fifth, internalization may be a way of avoiding government intervention. Prices reported in an organization are much more difficult to monitor than those in an external market. Consequently government evaluation of tax and tariff payments and its enforcement of exchange control regulations becomes difficult, and the firm is able to exploit this through transfer pricing.

There are also costs of internalization which may offset the benefits. Firstly, some of the costs of operating a market—whether internal or external—are fixed independently of the volume of transactions, so that if a single external market is split up and internalized within a number of distinct firms the costs of market organization for each firm will tend to rise. Secondly, when a single external market is replaced by several internal ones it may be necessary for firms to adjust the scales of the activities linked by the markets to make them compatible; this may mean that some activities have to be operated on a less efficient scale than would be possible with a larger external market. Thirdly, there may be increased communication costs. In an external market only price and quantity information is exchanged, but the demands of an internal market are normally greater because of the additional flows of accounting and control information. Finally, internalization costs have an international dimension arising from problems associated with foreign ownership and control. It should be noted that such problems can, in varying degrees, be reduced or eliminated by *partially* internalizing a market; for instance disposing of excess output on the open market or subcontracting outside the firm.

Having set out the general theory of the costs and benefits of internalizing markets, we now turn to the application of the theory. It can be argued that the benefits of internalization are particularly large in two cases. Firstly in industries where firms need to receive future supplies of vital raw materials and secondly in industries where flows of technical and marketing knowledge are important. The first phase of the growth of MNEs (up to the end of World War I) was concerned with maintaining and developing raw material supplies through vertical integration. However the major force in the world economy at the present time arises from the special advantages of internalizing flows of knowledge. It is this factor to which we look to account for the continued strength of the ownership effect.

The production of knowledge (through R&D) is a lengthy process which requires careful synchronization with other activities within the firm. Knowledge is a (temporary) 'natural monopoly' which is best exploited through discriminatory pricing. The buyers of knowledge are in many cases monopsonists, by virtue of control of regional distribution outlets, and so bilateral monopoly is likely if knowledge is licensed through an external market. Buyer uncertainty applies with particular force, for knowledge cannot be valued until it is in full possession of the valuer. Finally, because of difficulties of evaluation, knowledge flows provide an excellent basis for transfer pricing.

Internalization across national boundaries of markets in knowledge-based products is clearly of great importance in accounting for overseas production by MNEs. Subsidiaries of MNEs are likely to be successful in taking a large share of foreign markets because of the 'branch plant effect' arising from subsidiary unit's access to the internal markets of MNEs. This access gives it a great advantage over those firms which have access only to (often inadequate) external markets. The greater the market imperfections, the more disadvantaged are 'national' firms in competing with MNEs.

Branch plant effect—the fact that subsidiaries of MNEs can out-perform national firms arise not from multinationality but from access to internal markets. This has two main aspects. Firstly, subsidiaries can obtain inputs which are simply not available in external markets. Most important among such inputs are proprietary knowledge (the output of past R&D), marketing know-how (arising from a worldwide intelligence system) and production experience. Secondly, branch plants can often obtain inputs more cheaply within the firm than their competitors can on the open market. This price differential arises, not from plant economies, but from access to the firm's internal futures markets, and from tax savings arising from transfer pricing.

Ownership effects may impinge on the location policies of MNEs. Firstly, efficient transfer pricing normally involves giving the highest mark-up to operations in the lowest tax area. This policy may imply a complete change of location strategy within the scheme of section 2. Secondly, internalization involves increased communication costs in the form of accounting and control information. As communication costs increase with geographical, social and linguistic 'distance', this will bias the location of internally co-ordinated activities towards a central region.

4. THE DIVISION OF NATIONAL MARKETS EXPLAINED

Combining both ownership and location effects allows us to give the reasons for the division of particular markets between domestic producers, local subsidiaries of MNEs, exports from foreign-owned plants and exports from MNEs. The division between exports and local servicing is largely the result of the economics of location. Least cost location, influenced by regional price differentials and by barriers to trade largely governs the proportion of a market serviced by exports. This however is modified by the economics of internalizing a market, for not only can this affect the least cost location of any stage of production but the strategy of a MNE after having internalized a market may differ from that which external market forces would dictate. Consequently, the question of servicing a final market is inextricably bound up with the nature and ownership of internal markets—which will be dictated by the costs of benefits of internalization.

In order to predict the division of national markets between the above groups we must have information relating to the following variables.

(1) *Industry specific factors*: the nature of the product, the structure of the external market and the relation between the optimal scales of the activities linked by the market;

(2) *Region specific factors*: factor costs in different regions, intermediate and raw material availability, the geographical and social distance between the regions involved:

(3) *Nation specific factors*: the political and fiscal structures particularly of the nations involved;

(4) *Firm specific-factors*: in particular the ability of management to communicate internally across national boundaries, and to cope with the legal and accounting complexities of international ownership.

From the above, the strategy of MNEs can be explained by combining our knowledge of locational influences with the opportunities of internalizing markets profitably. Location and ownership effects are interdependent for the least cost location of an activity is at least partly determined by the ownership of the activities integrated with it.

NOTES

1. For a full exposition see Peter J. Buckley and Mark Casson *The Future of the Multinatinal Enterprise*, Macmillan, London 1976. Chapter II, Section 3.

2. R&D includes the innovative aspects of advertising.

3. Note the similarity of this argument with Raymond Vernon 'International Investment and International Trade in the Product Cycle', *Journal of Economics*, Vol. 80 (1966), pp. 190–207.

4. This agrees with Hymer's 'Law of Uneven Development': the centralization of 'higher order activities' in the parent. See S. Hymer 'The Multinational Corporation and the Law of Uneven Development' in J. N. Bhagwati (ed.), *Economics and World Order*, Macmillan, 1972.

5. See e.g. D. E. de Meza, Multinationals' Choice of Technique, *mimeo*, Reading, 1975.

6. Notably T. Horst, 'The Theory of the Multinational Firm: Optimal Behaviour under Different Tariff and Tax Rates', *Journal of Political Economy*, Vol. 79, (1971), pp. 1059–1072.

7. Note the similarity of this argument with Stephen H. Hymer, *The International Operations of National Firms*, MIT Press, Cambridge, Mass., 1976.

Part II

Methods of Foreign Market Servicing

CONTENTS

5

Differences Among Exporting Firms Based on Their Degree of Internationalization

S. Tamer Cavusgil

Too many studies of export marketing behaviour have averaged results from all types of firms in a sample, when insight would require classifying them into some meaningful groups and then comparing average group responses (1). The present discussion illustrates the use of the latter strategy in analysing data; firms are first grouped by their degree of internationalization and then analysed for significant differences among them. Three categories of exporting firms (experimental, active, and committed) are contrasted with respect to measurable company characteristics, domestic market environment, nature of the company's international business involvement, marketing policy aspects, and foreign market research practices. The findings provide partial support for the stages of internationalization framework and generate insights into the export marketing practices of firms which would not be possible from a study which aggregated all firms into one large sample.

METHOD

Data collection procedures

The data base for this investigation is derived from a series of personal interviews with 70 manufacturing companies from Wisconsin and Illinois. These firms were selected systematically from the directories of the Milwaukee World Trade Club and Chicago World Trade Club. Initally, a larger number of firms were identified and contacted in order to gain their cooperation. Through an advance letter typed on the University of Wisconsin–Whitewater letterhead, those executives principally responsible for international marketing were asked to participate in a study of exporting. Those companies that indicated a willingness to participate were then contacted by phone in order to schedule an interview with a key executive.

Personal interviews took place during the latter part of 1981. In all cases, the respondent was the executive principally responsible for international business activities of the firm. The interviews lasted from one to two hours and covered a variety of topics including past history of international involvement, current international activity, international market research activities, background company characteristics, and other issues. A semistructured data collection instrument was used to guide the interviews, all of which were tape-recorded for later analysis.

Stages of internationalization framework

Most scholars now agree that firms tend to exhibit an evolutionary process in the way they become involved in international business (3, 4, 6, 7, 9, 10, 11). Several stages can be identified along this gradual involvement process, including preinvolvement, reactive involvement, limited experimental involvement, active involvement, and committed involvement (3, 5). Clearly, not all firms will travel the entire internationalization path. Many firms, for example, find it desirable to restrict their international involvement to an opportunistic strategy by responding primarily to unsolicited orders from foreign customers or distributors.

The sequential nature of the internationalization process can be attributed to greater perceived risk associated with international business decisions, tentative nature of managerial expectations, and greater genuine uncertainty. These circumstances generate a very cautious type of management, one that makes incremental rather than total commitments for taking advantage of export market opportunities. As the firm gains more international experience, management may develop higher expectations, more rational and comprehensive policies concerning international business, as well as new organizational procedures for handling the new tasks.

In the present study we focus on only three stages of the internationalization process. These are experimental involvement, active involvement, and committed involvement. *Experimental involvement* characterizes the behaviour of those managements who exert little commitment to overseas market development. Entry into exporting is typically prompted by unsolicited inquiries. The company responds to these inquiries in a passive (reactive) manner and treats international business as marginal business. Export sales in many of these firms may not account for more than 10% of total business. Often a few foreign markets (customers) are involved. Furthermore, experimenting exporters will often employ product and pricing strategies that are a simple extension of the domestic marketing mix. They will allocate managerial and financial resources and production capacity to export markets with some degree of reluctance. Short-term objectives will prevail over long-term goals.

Active involvement occurs when management recognizes the important contributions international business can make toward accomplishing corporate goals. Managers are now willing to make a long-term commitment to cultivating export markets. International business opportunities and problems now capture the attention of those decision makers higher up in the organization. Unused capacity may be allocated to only export orders. Products are designed to meet the specific needs of overseas customers; pricing policies are revised to secure effective penetration of foreign markets. In the active involvement stage, firms will have expanded their exporting activity to a number of key markets. Export activity is no longer considered to be marginal business, and it is conducted on a regular basis rather than sporadically. An export marketing department may be formed, usually as a spin-off of the domestic marketing/sales department.

Committed involvement represents the final stage firms may reach in the evolutionary process of internationalization. A committed exporter searches for business opportunities worldwide, not restricting itself to the traditional markets. The distinction between domestic and foreign sales may now appear artificial. This ultimate stage in the internationalization process usually brings about other types of international involvement, such as direct investment in overseas production facilities, sales subsidiaries, worldwide sourcing arrangements, and so on. An overseas division will usually be set up to assume responsibility over these operations. In the committed involvement stage, it is not unreasonable to find a company assessing opportunities in the global market much more systematically than before.

Procedure for classifying firms

The procedure for classifying the 70 firms into experimental, active, and committed involvement stages was primarily judgemental. A group of 25 graduate business students along with the principal researcher classified each firm into one of the three categories after considering *all* available information about the company, and in light of the conceptual framework of internationalization stages discussed above. A consensus had to be reached in the group before a firm was classified as an experimental, active, or committed exporter. Also, the judges refrained from using a single criterion (such as firm size or export sales/total sales ratio) to classify the firms. The classification was based on a multitude of characteristics in harmony with the conceptual framework. This was done in order to shed light on the validity of the internationalization hypothesis. To the extent that such a classificatory framework produces significant differences among the three groups of firms, we would have evidence pointing to the usefulness of the framework. Such an approach is also consistent with previous research efforts that attemtped to validate the internationalization hypothesis (2, 5, 8).

Using the above procedure, the judges characterized 28 of the firms as experimental exporters, 18 firms as active exporters, and the remaining 24 firms as committed exporters. A greater proportion of the experimental and committed exporters turned out to be industrial goods manufacturers, whereas the majority of active exporters were primarily consumer goods producers.

FINDINGS

Relating the stages of internationalization to measurable company characteristics

Is progression through the internationalization process a function of company size? Do committed exporters tend to be larger than experimental and active exporters? The findings in this respect were not consistent. When firm size was measured by the number of full-time employees and related to internationalization stages, no statistically significant relationship emerged. When firm size was measured by annual sales, however, there was a statistically significant relationship at the 0.00 level (see Table 1). In particular, experimental firms were more likely to have annual sales of less than $10 million;

Table 1. Test of significant relationship between company sales and degree of internationalization

	Number of firms in each stage		
Annual company sales	Experimental	Active	Committed
Less than $10 million	13	4	3
$10 million to $100 million	6	10	5
More than $100 million	5	4	13

Chi-square test statistic, $\chi^2 = 18.09$, with 4 degrees of freedom is significant at the 0.00 level.
Index of predictive association, $\lambda = 0.31$, with company sales as the predictor variable.

committed exporters sales in excess of $100 million; and active exporters somewhere in between. The strength of the relationship is moderate at best, however, as implied by lambda of 0.31 (index of predictive association has an upper limit of 1.00). A tentative conclusion to be drawn from these results is that there is a tendency for larger-volume companies to have progressed more along the internationalization process. This relationship does not appear to be strong, however, implying that a company's internationalization is not greatly influenced by its size, especially when the latter is measured by number of employees. The direction of causality is also subject to speculation.

When the company's length of experience in exporting is cross-tabulated with its internationalization stage, a weak level of association is found (see Table 2). Although there are directional tendencies for experimental firms to have less than 20 years of export experience and for committed exporters to have more than 20 years of experience, export experience is not a strong predictor of internationalization. This finding implies that a 'natural' progress over time from experimental to active to committed stages is not necessarily a certainty. Many firms may find it desirable to maintain their involvement at the experimental level, despite greater experience gained over the years. Lack of top management interest or the presence of accessible sales potentials domestically may be responsible for the firm's less than full commitment to exploiting foreign market potentials.

The data in Table 3 suggest a weak-to-moderate relationship between export intensity of the firm, as measured by exports/total sales ratio, and the stages of internationalism. Again, there is a tendency for experimental exporters to export less than 10% of their

Table 2. Cross-tabulation of company's export experience with degree of internationalization

	Number of firms in each stage		
Length of company experience in exporting	Experimental	Active	Committed
Less than 10 years	12	4	2
10 to 20 years	5	5	5
21 to 40 years	4	4	7
More than 40 years	6	2	8

Index of predictive association is $\lambda = 0.14$, with export experience as the predictor.

Table 3. Cross-tabulation of export intensity with degree of internationalization

Export sales as a percentage of total company sales	Number of firms in each stage		
	Experimental	Active	Committed
Less than 10%	16	7	3
10% to 19%	4	6	5
20% to 39%	4	4	6
More than 40%	1	1	10

Index of predictive association is $\lambda = 0.31$, with export intensity as the predictor.

output and for committed exporters to export more than 40% of total output. Export intensity, however, fails to emerge as a perfect correlate of internationalization. One may argue that true internationalization cannot be measured by a single dimension such as export intensity; perhaps it is the result of other concomitant changes in the organization, including certain attitudinal changes among management personnel.

There seems to be a stronger relationship between export profits as a percentage of total company profits and the stage of internationalization (Table 4). Here export profits emerge as a moderately strong predictor of a company's internationalization. More than two-thirds of experimental exporters generate less than 10% of their profits from foreign sales. In contrast, almost one-half of the committed exporters derive more than 40% of their profits from overseas sales. It appears that progression over the experimental/active/ committed exporter stages is enhanced by greater degree of reliance in foreign markets as a source of profits. In addition, the latter variable appears to be a better predictor of internationalization than export intensity.

The degree of internationalization was related to one additional company character-istic—the scope of the domestic market for the company. Previous research had suggested that having already established a broad-based domestic market, a company might find it easier to expand into international markets (10). The expectation is that with 'extra-regional expansion' or 'internationalization at home', the firm will be in a better state of readiness to penetrate foreign markets. We were not able to confirm this expectation since almost all of the experimental, active, and committed exporters were found to be actively marketing in the entire US market. The scope of the domestic market was not necessarily narrower in the case of experimental or active exporters.

Table 4. Cross-tabulation of export profits with degree of internationalization

Profits derived from exporting as a percentage of total company profits	Number of firms in each stage		
	Experimental	Active	Committed
Less than 10%	17	6	2
10% to 19%	3	7	2
20% to 39%	4	4	8
More than 40%	—	1	11

Index of predictive association is $\lambda = 0.46$, with export profits as the predictor.

Domestic market environment of the firms

Firms in the sample were questioned as to the nature and extent of their competition in the US market as a way of understanding their motivations for being interested in international market opportunities. The majority of the firms indicated that they encountered 'moderate competition' in the home market (see Table 5). This response was consistent across the three groups of firms. Of the firms that had a 'below average level of competition', most were in the experimental exporting stage. This may be reasonable because the firms in the experimental involvement stage tended to be smaller firms who had carved a specific niche in the market with their products, and therefore encountered less competition for their specific products.

Firms in the experimental involvement stage identified 'growing home markets' as their key opportunity in the immediate future. Exporting to world markets and using additional distributors were also mentioned. A significant proportion of committed exporters (47%), on the other hand, singled out export markets as their best opportunity. This reflects a greater awareness of foreign market opportunities and a greater significance attached to foreign markets. In addition, saturation of the domestic market is a driving factor for committed exporters in seeking additional foreign markets. Many of the executives of committed exporters were blunt about the fact that their domestic market was mature or declining, and that exporting was their only source of real growth. Consequently, they appeared eager to develop an aggressive exporting, licensing, and investment stance.

Nature of international business involvement

Needless to say, firms in different internationalization stages had different types of international involvement. For 79% of *all* firms, the principal international activity was

Table 5. Domestic market environment of the firms

Characteristics of domestic market	Percentage of firms in each stage		
	Experimental	Active	Committed
Intensity of competition in the US			
Low level of competition	31	13	14
Moderate competition	65	73	76
Substantial competition	4	14	10
Major opportunity facing the firm			
Growing market at home	29	12	21
Growing market abroad	24	25	47
Expansion of product lines	18	25	21
Acquiring new foreign distributors	18	—	—
Other	11	38	11
Major challenge encountered domestically			
Pressures on price/profit margins	50	36	43
Maturing industry	7	7	22
Threats posed by larger competitors	29	29	7
High interest rates	14	14	21
Unfavourable aspects of demand	—	14	7

exporting, but this varied among the firms (see Table 6). This is in line with the expectation that exporting is the initial strategy to penetrate foreign markets. As the firm travels the internationalization path, it will also become involved in licensing and foreign production.

When asked how the firm had its *initial* involvement in exporting, the answers varied depending upon the internationalization stages. Firms in the experimental and active involvement stages indicated that they simply responded to unsolicited foreign orders (40% and 25% respectively). Firms in the committed involvement stage suggest that they actively sought out foreign orders as their first international involvement. An explanation for this discrepancy may be that firms in the committed involvement stage have been exporting for a long time (usually more than 20 years) and, therefore, really cannot recall their initial international involvement. It would probably be safe to say that even these committed firms had their interest piqued by unsolicited orders or inquiries, or by a chance meeting of foreign buyers.

Both the desire for profits and the desire to achieve sales growth were cited as the major motivation for initial involvement in exporting by the majority of firms. Staying competitive, diversification as a way of achieving stability, and using excess manufacturing capacity accounted for the remaining responses. After the firms had become more involved in exporting, however, they appeared to be more interested in seeking profits and less interested in fulfilling other objectives. This may be a logical pattern for companies to take. As a firm begins its involvement with exporting, it knows it will take a few years to get established and to recover its original costs; hence one of the major motivations is sales growth and market share. Then, as the firm progresses into the higher exporting categories, it will want to see some of the efforts pay off, and will become more conscious of profits. This is especially true among committed exporters.

For firms experimenting with exporting, the most pressing problem is working with foreign distributors. At this stage of internationalization, these firms have not committed

Table 6. The nature of company's international business involvement

Facets of international involvement	Percentage of firms in each stage		
	Experimental	Active	Committed
Primary form of involvement is exporting	92	81	68
Initial exporting was prompted by unsolicited orders	48	36	14
Initial motivation for export start was primarily profit-related	50	19	42
Major motivation *now* for exporting is profits	50	50	58
The most troublesome problem in exporting is:			
Working with foreign distributors	42	7	17
Exchange rate risks	25	53	59
Cultural and economic differences	16	—	12
Political instability, etc.	—	13	12
Redtape, regulatory restrictions, etc.	8	7	—
Other	9	20	—

sufficient resources to provide for a wide distribution network abroad. Therefore, finding, selecting, and training a distributor in large part determines the amount of sales they receive from foreign markets. In a sense, these firms are helpless without the commitment of the distributor. The most significant exporting problem for both active and committed exporters, on the other hand, is fluctuations in the value of foreign currencies. This is natural as these firms derive a higher percentage of company revenues from foreign sales. Therefore, an unfavourable currency fluctuation affects their bottom line more than it would a firm with a relatively small share of profits from exporting.

Marketing policy aspects of international involvement

Sixty-two per cent of the exported products were considered 'not unique' by company executives. A greater proportion of active exporters classified their products as unique when compared to competition (see Table 7). When asked to describe their principal export product, one-third of all executives indicated that their products were of high quality. Twenty-two per cent stated that they produced a 'traditional product that gave good value for the money'. Twenty-one per cent described their product as highly technical, but this included such products as bull semen and diesel engines which may not be characterized as highly complex by others. The interviews seem to suggest that, regardless of internationalization stage, a company does not need a stupendous new product to be successful in exporting. Typically, a high-quality product seems to be sufficient.

With respect to choice of export markets, no differences emerged among the three types of exporters. For all firms, Western Europe was the primary export market, followed by

Table 7. Marketing policy aspects of international involvement

Features of marketing policy	Percentage of firms in each stage		
	Experimental	Active	Committed
Principal export product is the same product sold domestically	80	69	67
Principal export product is 'unique'	36	50	26
Principal export market is Canada/Mexico/Western Europe	51	70	61
Organizational arrangement used for exports is a special export division	58	68	73
Major export channel includes a foreign distributor	56	47	50
Face-to-face contacts with foreign distributors take place:			
Once every 2 years or less frequently	37	12	8
Once a year	36	50	8
Twice a year or more often	27	38	84
Support provided for distributors includes:			
Sales aids	41	29	15
Initial sales and technical training	29	36	45
A formal sales and payment policy exists	11	40	75
A formal payment policy exists	44	60	79

Canada/Mexico, Latin America, Far East, and Australia/New Zealand. This is in contrast to initial expectations that the experimental and active exporters would concentrate on 'psychologically close' countries such as Canada, and that the committed exporters would exhibit a greater propensity to venture into non-traditional markets. This expectation was not confirmed, as we found no differences among the firms with respect to foreign market preferences.

In considering the types of organizational arrangement firms developed for export operations, we do find that a firm is more likely to have a special export division the greater is its degree of internationalization. Furthermore, firms appear to develop additional policies concerning exporting as they progress through internationalization, and they tend to formalize them to a greater degree. It is also evident that top executives of experimental exporters become more directly involved in exporting decisions than the executives of active and committed exporters.

With respect to relationships with foreign distributors, it was found that the experimental firms have face-to-face contact with their distributors least often and provide primarily sales aids. Active exporters and committed exporters visit overseas distributors more often and provide sales and technical training as well for their distributors. In addition, market research assistance, volume discounts, and temporary personnel for starting up a new operation may also be provided.

Foreign market research practices

As the firms progressed through the internationalization stages, foreign market research became much more important to them, as evidenced by the commitment of financial and managerial resources to the tasks involved. The percentage of executives who stated that the analysis of foreign market potentials is 'at least as important' as the domestic marketing research varied substantially for the three types of exporters (see Table 8). As the commitment of the company for foreign markets increased, a more thorough analysis of potentials was required. In addition, management took time more frequently to assess foreign market potentials.

As a company progresses through the internationalization stages, it becomes more likely to use a *variety* of informational sources in foreign market research. It was found that dependence on a limited number of sources was replaced by a tendency to utilize a multitude of information sources. In the experimental and active exporting stages, the most important source of data for export market research was perceived to be industry/business publications and contacts made at trade shows. Information obtained from other firms in the industry was the second most helpful source for experimenting and active exporters, and the most helpful for committed exporters. Information obtained from the US Department of Commerce, although it appears to be helpful to experimenting exporters, becomes less useful during the active and committed involvement stages. This is probably because of the nature of the information assistance provided by the US Department of Commerce. Its 'broad' and 'basic' nature serves the needs of the experimental firms well. Information needs become much more specific, however, with passage into the active and committed stages. The company now finds it necessary to develop an internal 'information system' for foreign market research purposes. It can also be expected that, with greater experience, managers become more proficient in searching for and maintaining satisfactory sources of information.

Table 8. Foreign market research practices of companies

Foreign market research practices	Percentage of firms in each stage		
	Experimental	Active	Committed
Foreign market research is perceived to be equally as important as domestic marketing research	17	63	77
Analysing foreign market opportunities is a frequent task (conducted several times a year)	14	17	57
Foreign market opportunity analysis is a fairly formalized process with written reports	—	7	30
The task is perceived to be complex and requires a high level of data analysis	4	14	26
Computerized data bases are regularly used in foreign market opportunity analysis	13	29	42
The most important source of data used in foreign market research is:			
Government (US Dept. of Commerce, etc.)	24	13	13
Industry/business publications and reports	36	34	22
Other firms	32	27	30
Internal company sources	8	13	17
Other	—	13	18
The most important problem associated with foreign market data:			
Too broad to be useful	25	30	18
Not reliable; biased	25	50	41
Out of date	8	10	—

CONCLUSION

This study attempted to reveal differences among exporting firms at varying levels of internationalization. The results suggest that experimenting, active, and committed exporters can be distinguished in terms of measurable characteristics: company size as measured by sales and the per cent of profits derived from exporting. Beyond that, significant differences exist among the three types of exporters in terms of their domestic market environment, the nature of international business involvement, policy aspects of international marketing, and foreign market research practices.

The present study represents a useful background for designing a more comprehensive investigation of the issues using a cross section of firms. Future investigators may also consider classifying firms by alternative criteria in addition to stages of internationalization. These criteria may include SIC codes, international orientation of company management, choice of foreign markets, and other meaningful dimensions. Such specific investigations of exporting are bound to generate richer insights than otherwise possible.

The findings do offer some implications for public policy concerning stimulation of export activity among firms. Most significantly, there is a need to view exporting firms as a heterogeneous rather than a homogeneous group. Depending upon the degree of internationalization, companies differ in terms of intensity of export activity, interest and commitment in pursuing international opportunities, information and assistance needs, and most importantly, their export potential. Therefore, if an immediate and substantial increase is desired in the level of US exports, it would be best to focus promotional and assistance efforts on the active and committed exporters rather than on experimental exporters. This research delineated ways in which active and committed exporters differ from experimental exporters. Such an understanding is imperative for designing promotional and assistance efforts in exporting.

The author wishes to acknowledge the financial support of this research through a State Research Grant from the University of Wisconsin System. Thanks are expressed to Professor Warren J. Bilkey and John R. Nevin of the University of Wisconsin–Madison for their valuable comments on an earlier draft of this article.

REFERENCES

1. Bilkey, Warren J. An attemped integration of the literature on the export behavior of firms. *Journal of International Business Studies* **9**: 33–46 (Spring/Summer 1978).

2. Bilkey, Warren J., Tesar, George. The export behavior of smaller sized Wisconsin manufacturing firms. *Journal of International Business Studies* **8**: 93–98 (Spring/Summer 1977).

3. Cavusgil, S. Tamer. On the internationalization process of firms. *European Research* **8**: 273–281 (November 1980).

4. Cavusgil, S. Tamer. On the nature of decision making for export marketing. In: Hunt, S. D., Bush, R., eds, *Marketing Theory: Philosophy of Science Perspectives.* American Marketing Association (1982) pp. 177–180.

5. Cavusgil, S. Tamer. Some observations on the relevance of critical variables for internationalization stages. In: Czinkota, M. R., Tesar, G., eds, *Export Management.* New York: Praeger (1982) pp. 276–286.

6. Cavusgil, S. Tamer, Nevin, John R. Internal determinants of export marketing behavior: An empirical investigation. *Journal of Marketing Research* **28**: 114–119.

7. Chisnall, Peter M. Challenging opportunities of international marketing. *European Research* **5**: 12–34 (February 1977).

8. Czinkota, Michael R., Johnston, Wesley J. Segmenting U.S. firms for export development. *Journal of Business Research* **9**: 353–365 (December 1981).

9. Johanson, J., Vahlne, J. The internationalization process of the firm—A model of knowledge development and increasing foreign commitments. *Journal of International Business Studies* **8**: 23–32 (Spring/Summer 1977).

10. Welch, Lawrence S., Wiedersheim-Paul, Finn. Domestic expansion: Internationalization at home. *Essays in International Business*, No. 2. Center for International Business Studies, University of South Carolina (December 1980).

11. Wiedersheim-Paul, Finn, Olson, Hans C., Welch, Lawrence S. Pre-export activity: the first Step in internationalization. *Journal of International Business Studies* **9**: 47–58 (Spring/Summer 1978).

6

Outward Foreign Licensing by Australian Companies

Lawrence S. Welch

1. INTRODUCTION

There has been limited study of outward foreign licensing by Australian firms as a method for developing international operations. Two recent empirical studies have provided some aggregate statistics on outward licensing as a component of technology transfer. As part of an investigation of technology flows and foreign firms, Parry and Watson (1979) examined the extent of outward licensing by foreign-owned subsidiaries in Australia to affiliate and non-affiliate companies. In a study of research and development by Australian enterprises, the Australian Bureau of Statistics (1979b) obtained broad data on receipts from overseas for the sale of technical know-how. However, while these studies present an overall picture of the extent of outward foreign licensing by Australian companies, they provide little insight into the process of licensing. It is to this latter issue that this study has been directed.

The general objective was to analyse and assess the role of outward foreign licensing in the internationalization process of Australian companies. An important aspect of this objective was the consideration of licensing's role at the marketing level. It is hoped that, through an examination of the way in which Australian firms have utilized licensing in international business, other firms might gain useful insights into the possibilities of this relatively neglected mode of international operations—as well as some valuable lessons as to strategy and operational methods.

Outward foreign licensing has tended to be regarded as a secondary internationalization strategy by most firms within Australia and overseas. Based on evidence presented before it, an Australian government committee has recently commented that 'Too few companies in Australia seem capable of engaging in R and D with a view to recovering some of the costs through licensing later on' (Senate Standing Committee, p. 106). The findings of studies in other countries seem to confirm this pattern. In a study of US medium-sized firms, Tesar (1977, p. 1) found that 'the majority of firms do not consider licensing as a viable alternative'. Likewise from an investigation of virtually all Finnish manufacturing firms, Luostarinen (1979, p. 103) concluded that 'physical goods are, almost without exception, the first sales object to be introduced into foreign markets'.

2. METHODOLOGY

The original objective was to survey all Australian companies licensing overseas. This task is difficult as the population of companies is not known with certainty. In 1976/77, the Australian Bureau of Statistics (ABS) estimated that 124 companies were in receipt of royalties. Since then, it is known that the number of companies licensing overseas has grown but it is believed that the number falls short of 500. (This impression was gained from conversations with patent attorneys and other practitioners in the field.) From two lists, one compiled by the Australian Government's Department of Trade and Resources and the other compiled by the researchers, 502 companies were contacted. Of these, 30 firms indicated that they were not licensing. Of the remainder, 43 stated that they were licensing, giving a response rate of 9%. However, this estimate is likely to be well under the true response rate as many companies were not licensing and there was some overlap between the two lists. This could not be verified as the names on the Department of Trade and Resources' list could not be revealed to the researchers because of confidentiality reasons.

A breakdown with regard to size; number of agreements and company size; the proportion of private and public companies; and the proportion of foreign controlled companies is set out below.

Compared to the ABS Statistics the group of firms surveyed is biased towards small to medium-sized Australian owned companies. Over 70% of the companies were small to medium-sized and only 25.6% were foreign controlled (compared to 42% from the ABS Statistics). In addition, 79% of the companies held less than six agreements.

With regard to the survey results, findings for companies with one to five agreements, are more relevant for the small to medium-sized companies whereas findings for companies with greater than five agreements are more relevant to the larger companies.

Table 1. Characteristics of the group of companies surveyed

Number of agreements and company size

	Small	Medium	Large	Total
One Agreement	5 (38.0%)	7 (54.0%)	1 (8.0%)	13
2–6 Agreements	10 (47.6%)	6 (28.6%)	5 (23.9%)	21
6–20 Agreements	2 (25.0%)	1 (12.5%)	5 (62.5%)	8
>20 Agreements	0	0	1 (100%)	1
Total	17	14	12	43

Size:	Small	below 200 employees	17	39.5%
	Medium	200–1000 employees	14	32.5%
	Large	more than 1000 employees	12	28.0%

Public and private companies: public (55.8%), private (44.2%)
Foreign control (>25% foreign equity): 25.6% of the companies were foreign controlled.

The degree of representativeness, however, cannot be measured with any accuracy. It is accepted that the very small firms and inventors and the very large (particularly foreign owned companies) are not represented adequately. As the survey was investigating the process of licensing rather than attempting to accurately predict given magnitudes for the population of licensing firms as a whole, this is not seen as critical.

The survey was conducted in two phases. First, the questionnaires were sent to the two company lists. Second, respondents were followed up wherever possible with interviews. Twenty-nine companies (67.4%) were interviewed. In addition, patent attorney practices were surveyed in order that checks could be conducted on some of the information generated by companies. Of the 29 practices in existence at the time replies were received either through the mail and/or interview from representatives of seven practices. Also one licensing consultant was interviewed.

Some companies responding to the questionnaire were attempting to license overseas for the first time. Five were interviewed. While their responses have not been included in the tabulations, their experience provided useful insight into how companies initially entered licensing arrangements.

3. THE ROLE OF LICENSING IN THE INTERNATIONALIZATION PROCESS OF THE FIRM

3.1. The adoption process

3.1.1. The licensing choice

Other studies have shown that outward foreign licensing is frequently adopted as a secondary or residual international strategy. Where foreign markets are too small or risky, or the firm has limited resources or experience to develop foreign markets by exporting or foreign investment, licensing may well appear as a feasible and simpler alternative. In a US study, Budack and Susbauer (1977, p. 17) noted that the common view of licensing at the outset is that it is relatively easy to implement. In many cases too, the licensing option is virtually forced on the firm if it is not prepared to risk the foreign investment step, because the imposition of various types of import restrictions constrain the ability to service a foreign market.

In the survey, firms were requested to indicate the most important factors involved in the decision to license overseas. Difficulties associated with exporting to a foreign market, combined with an unpreparedness to undertake foreign investment, were considered to be the most important by the respondents. Table 2 shows the most important factors (in order) mentioned by the proportion of firms noting them. In the main, licensing was not adopted because of a positive view of its value as a strategy for developing foreign markets.

A typical example of the operation of the export difficulties factor was the case of a firm with 120 employees which had signed six foreign licensing agreements. The general manager, and instigator of the licensing programme, pointed out that the company had a preference for exporting but the attempt to export had not been successful. He stated that the combination of actions by foreign governments (import restrictions) and the cost of

Table 2. Licensing decision factors

Factors in decision to license	Proportion of firms mentioning each factor
High costs of shipping goods	53.5%
Tariff and non-tariff barriers	41.9%
High production costs in Australia	25.6%
Difficulties in selling goods overseas (e.g. poor distribution)	23.3%
High risk associated with foreign investment	18.6%
Lack of finance	11.6%

Number of respondents = 43.

shipping bulky items made licensing the only feasible path for earning foreign income, given that foreign investment had never been seriously entertained.

The emphasis on barriers to exports created by government intervention is to some extent a result of the geographical orientation of Australian international expansion activity—at least in the earlier stages. Of the 18 firms which mentioned these barriers as a factor in causing an interest in licensing, 15 (or 83%) had licensed to New Zealand, suggesting that New Zealand's traditional barriers to exports of manufactures have resulted in firms looking to licensing.

The 'residual' market approach to the use of licensing was stressed in a small number of cases. It was the assessment that a given foreign market lacked sufficient size and potential which led these firms to opt for licensing, indicating an inherent judgment that licensing was inappropriate as a basis for servicing primary markets. In addition, two firms used licensing as a strategy to sell 'residual' (non-mainstream) technology. Patentable technology was developed as a result of researching solutions to operating problems within the firm. In one case, the invention was a new instrument for sampling, in the other, a pollution control device. The first company was a manufacturer of a relatively bulky material used by producers of final consumer goods while the other was a mining company. In both cases the technology developed was only subsidiary to the main income earning activities. In the first case, licensing allowed the company to earn 'some additional income' from the invention while the mining company seemed to have almost gone into the attempt to sell technology, despite its 'nuisance value', as an outlet for its younger research personnel who were particularly keen to see this area of the company's operations develop.

For those companies licensing overseas subsidiaries, licensing tended to be used as an additional means of extracting income and, in general, maintaining control.

3.1.2. *International involvement preceding licensing*

In explaining the adoption of licensing as an internationalization strategy, an important background factor is the preceding level of foreign involvement. Responses to a survey question on the type of international activity preceding each foreign licensing agreement are shown in Table 3. In general, licensing to particular foreign markets was preceded by either no involvement or exporting. In only a small number of cases was there a direct association with foreign investment reported by respondent firms. The mainly small to

Table 3. Type of international involvement preceding licensing

| | Foreign licensing agreements | | | | | | | |
| | Total | | 1–5 | | 6–20 | | > 20 | |
	No.	%	No.	%	No.	%	No.	%
No involvement	119	56.9	38	48.1	61	77.2	20	39.2
Exporting beforehand	38	18.2	31	39.2	7	8.9	0	—
Foreign investment beforehand	12	5.7	4	5.1	5	6.3	3	5.9
Licensing and foreign investment in package	29	13.9	1	1.3	0	—	28	54.9
Other	11	5.3	5	6.3	6	7.6	0	—
Total	209	100	79	100	79	100	51	100

Number of respondents = 42.

medium-sized firms in the sample appeared to enter licensing as a separate international-ization strategy rather than as an element of a foreign investment strategy. This is undoubtedly related to them being at an earlier stage of international development.

In all but eight cases, however, licensing was not the first form of international involvement by the firm. It was generally preceded by, if not exporting to the particular foreign market, at least by exporting to other foreign markets.

Preceding international selling experience was found to make a contribution to the initial licensing step in various ways:

(a) At a general level the development of skills, understanding and knowledge about selling in international markets could be applied to some extent in the exercise of selling technology. Not all international knowledge and skills can be readily transferred to activities which are licensing specific, but some were—for example, experience in finding and selecting suitable overseas agents provided a useful background in approaching the task of finding, selecting and negotiating with suitable licensees.

(b) The large proportion of cases where exporting was directly replaced by licensing in a given foreign market necessarily means that firms developed varying degrees of market-specific knowledge and skills. Such knowledge obviously provides a basis on which to make the decision about choice of licensee. The market experience may throw up a potential licensee so that much of the search process can be short-circuited, and perhaps the selection and assessment phases.

In addition, the basis of the licensing arrangement may have been effectively created by the exporting activity in the market concerned. As an example, in the survey one firm was very successful in exporting to the Thai market but was eventually blocked out by various import restrictions.

However, because its name had become so well established in the market, it was able to license some know-how and, in the main, its trade mark to a local manufacturer. In this case the very basis for the licensing deal was established by the preceding export activity. A large number of other cases fell into a similar category in that exports established and proved a foreign market which was then threatened by various external developments (for example, import restrictions). As a result, not only did the Australian firm become interested in licensing but the end-product of the licensing exercise had been proven to potential licensees, who sometimes made the first approach to the Australian firm.

(c) The channel which was previously used for the exporting activity or for carrying on production was sometimes transferred to a licensee basis, in which case most of the pre-agreement activities were no longer necessary. The exporter to Thailand noted in (b) above is a case in point. Its Swiss export agent in Thailand became its licensee, undertaking manufacture locally. It was interesting to note the Australian firm's perception of this licensing deal as a 'riskless, troublefree income source—although still inferior to the preferred exporting mode'. In such cases then, licensing can be relatively simple and with little cost involved. It is clear however that most firms are not in a position to make such simple transfers between modes of representation in a given foreign country.

Rather than using licensing as a means of channel transfer, a small number of firms had used licensing in order to achieve some channel expansion—that is, they already had a majority-owned subsidiary or joint-venture partner within the foreign market and the formal relationship was extended by one or more licensing agreements covering various forms of technology transfer (including marketing). In all but one of these examples the purpose was to provide another means of extracting income from a New Zealand subsidiary. The odd case involved an attempt to provide a broader basis of control and income generation with respect to a joint venture partner in Malaysia where the Malaysian government had restricted the Australian firm's equity level to 40%. Control over the activities of the joint venture operation was written into the licensing agreement such that the Australian company was able to determine any important strategic decisions of the Malaysian operation.

(d) Preceding international selling operations also frequently led to organizational and resource allocation changes within the firm, as well as creating a degree of international orientation which further assisted the ultimate move into international licensing activity.

It is clear then that preceding international selling activity, in whatever form, provides an important foundation for the move into licensing and explains why some firms are able to accomplish the move with relative ease. Nevertheless, there are other forms of international involvement which can contribute to the ability and likelihood of adoption of licensing.

An important form of foreign licensing experience for Australian firms arises from the activity of licensing from foreign sources. The derivative nature of Australian technology is reflected in the reliance on technology obtained via licensing into Australia. In an earlier study, Stubbs (1968, p. 92) found that 'about four-fifths of companies in the study had signed (inward) licence agreements'. A 1976–7 survey by the Australian Bureau of Statistics (1979) revealed that licensing payments overseas were almost ten times greater than receipts while the number of firms making payments overseas far exceeded those earning receipts. The experience gained in such aspects as negotiation, drawing up of agreements, etc., can be readily applied to outward licensing activities. Certainly, given the greater prevalence of inward licensing by Australian companies, foreign licensing skills are likely to be frequently developed through this avenue. The effect of licensing into the country also seems to be useful in developing an awareness of the possibilities of using the licensing mode. While there were only four firms in the survey that specifically mentioned the contribution of inward licensing to the later outward licensing step, their experience confirms that this was not only important in producing an awareness of licensing but also provided a frame of reference for outward licensing agreements ultimately devised. Clearly the international technology purchasing exercise can feasibly open up foreign market possibilities like more outward-looking international selling modes and has more direct application to the mechanics of licensing.

Other forms of international purchasing can likewise expose licensing possibilities, although obviously not producing the same awareness of the licensing mode. There were two cases in the survey of Australian firms importing first from their eventual licensees.

Overall then, the type of international involvement which precedes the move into international licensing emerges as a key influence on the nature of the adoption process. There are a number of ways in which preceding international experience can make a contribution to removing some of the barriers associated with outward foreign licensing as a new form of international operations. International experience in its various forms has a positive effect on licensing through the development of relevant skills and knowledge, which enhance the process of risk and uncertainty reduction in the new venture. Without such experience, it can be a long road from invention to international commercial exploitation via licensing. When an inventor enters the international sphere for the first time, unless he uses an intermediary, there is not only the need to acquire licensing-specific skills but also international marketing skills.

3.1.3. Industrial property protection as a barrier to licensing

For the smaller firm or individual inventor, even the patenting stage, as a prelude to licensing, can pose a major hurdle. Particularly for the individual inventor, the establishment of ownership rights to industrial property is a crucial exercise as he tends to be less reliant on know-how. As a result, he is more exposed to any breach of his industrial property rights and more concerned about any actual or latent challenge to them. Any defence ties up the operational capacity of the inventor (and small firm), stretches his liquidity and constrains his ability and preparedness to proceed to international patenting and ultimately licensing. There were only a few firms in the sample which could be classed as inventors only (3 licensing, 1 attempting). Three small firms were also interviewed whose approach to patenting and licensing seemed to reflect similar problems to those faced by individual inventors. Two of the individual inventors and one of the small firms had faced patent litigation problems within Australia. In these cases it is clear that the threat to their industrial property rights tended to divert attention and funds away from the prospects of international patenting and licensing. Thus, the ability to exploit technology via licensing in other countries is affected by an inventor's or company's path through the patenting process.

Any concern about the viability of industrial property protection in foreign countries, whether directly related to problems experienced within Australia or not, acts as an important constraint on the activity of marketing technology internationally. Threat of patent breach and involvement in some form of patent litigation is one aspect of this concern, which is heightened in foreign countries where the problems of policing industrial property are usually seen to be greater. This concern is further accentuated where no form of protection of industrial property has been taken out in a given foreign country. For all inventors, individuals or companies, early in the life of the Australian patent decisions must be made about the international extent of patent protection to be southt. Judgments must be made in advance about the likely extent of exploitation, and the cost of carrying a large international portfolio of patents is usually prohibitive for most inventors and small firms.

Thus, it is frequently the case that inventors and small firms find themselves with inadequate foreign industrial property protection and a heightened concern about the possibility of breach of industrial property rights by foreign companies. Two instances from our sample illustrate the constraining effect these influences may have on the foreign marketing of technology. In the first case, the company had faced patent litigation within Australia and, as a result, had neglected to seek patent protection within the United States until after the expiry time for such applications. In lieu of the patent, it had registered its trade mark because of interest in US market possibilities. After undertaking some advertising in trade journals there, 25 inquiries had been received from potential US licensees, but after a year no response to these had been made. The company was not prepared to send a brochure explaining its product for fear of the concept being copied.

The second firm had registered its designs in the UK and Denmark and had undertaken a small level of exporting via a Danish agent. The company had also been visited by South Korea's chief licensing officer who was prepared to arrange a licensing deal by taking drawings of designs back to South Korea and finding appropriate licensees to undertake production. The owner of the firm had responded as follows: 'Send a potential (Korean) licensee to me and we can then discuss the prospects of a licensing agreement. I shall not send my drawings outside the country so that they can be copied.' A joint-venture proposal by the Malaysian authorities had also been turned down.

In both these examples, there were clear proposals for the sale of technology via licensing arrangements but the approach to them was constrained by a lack of official industrial property protection and a concern about how the technology could nevertheless be protected in the foreign country. However, without full access to the technology it is difficult for a foreign company to be convinced about the value of a licensing relationship. Disclosure or secrecy agreements do not appear to have filled this void.

While the problems involved in the establishment of industrial property rights are sometimes perceived to be sufficiently large to prevent foreign licensing, there are nevertheless many inventors who carry through the exercise to completion. The commitment of the inventor to his invention and belief in its ultimate commercial success is a powerful motivation towards exploitation. This drive seemed to produce two types of responses amongst inventors in the survey:

(a) There was a continued effort to sell the invention despite a host of problems which might have provoked withdrawal. A number of inventors contacted had faced difficulties such as patent litigation and had incurred expenses to the point where their basic liquidity was in jeopardy, yet they continued on to complete the task of achieving commercial success for their invention.

(b) In other cases, the inventors continued onwards into a world marketing exercise without any real knowledge of the potential problems, convinced of the invention's worth and that it would therefore sell. An understanding of the real demands of licensing came afterwards. In one example, the inventor attended a conference of manufacturers of his product in the US and was offered a licensing arrangement on the spot by one manufacturer. Only then did the real assessment of licensing take place. The offer was turned down, the inventor returned to Australia, advertised in a US trade magazine and, after a number of offers, spent some time negotiating a more acceptable agreement with the original interested party.

Thus, the background of a company or inventor is important in explaining the likelihood and form of initial outward foreign licensing involvement, and in this respect the patenting process particularly, and protection of industrial property generally, can be a crucial phase leading up to the licensing step. However, the experience of the inventors and smaller firms mentioned could not be generalized to other firms in the sample. Larger firms, although recognizing the importance of patents did not appear to display the same level of 'concern' about the protection issue. Perhaps this is because the patent is embedded in a far stronger overall framework including know-how, etc. In general, they appeared to be less reliant on the patent per se and were therefore less exposed to patent breach. It was interesting to note the examples of larger firms having a high degree of confidence in the inability of other firms to copy their essential know-how, or more importantly, confidence in the unpreparedness of other firms to incur the cost involved in attempting to reproduce the concept in a viable manufacturing operation.

3.2. The impact of licensing in the longer run

In the following section the impact of the adopted licensing strategy on the development of a firm's international operations over time is examined. The impact of licensing in the longer run is determined in part by the role to which it is initially assigned and the circumstances surrounding adoption, frequently as a residual or second-line strategy. There is clearly a danger of firms merely looking to short-run returns rather than viewing licensing as a long-run investment in international development. Where licensing is only adopted as a secondary strategy there is a danger that this will lead to insufficient development and exploitation of the foreign markets involved. Licensing tends to be a more passive form of international operations, so that it is easy to slip into an arrangement whereby the market is totally left to the licensee to develop. For example, one respondent company had commented: 'It (the licensing deal) is a good arrangement. There is no work for us to do. The income just keeps on flowing in.' In this case, the firm was undertaking no information gathering or any other activity in the licensed foreign market. The market had been left completely to the licensee. The licensor was almost totally passive in the arrangement.

There are a variety of areas of co-operation with the licensee which will be necessary in order that the technology is effectively transferred and utilized by the licensee. If there is a passive involvement by the licensor, beyond the basic demands of negotiating and policing the licence, then it is likely that the firm will become a dependent partner. As a by-product, it will only have a limited degree of control over the success of the licensing venture.

In fact, the concern that licensing produces a loss of control over a firm's technological knowledge and its foreign exploitation is enough to discourage many firms from entering into any licensing arrangements at all, except with affiliated companies. Budack and Susbauer (1977, p. 21) concluded that: 'The loss of control has, for many firms, been the fundamental reason for not entering licensing agreements.' However, the more passive the involvement in the licensing arrangement, the greater the loss of control.

This problem is accentuated for the smaller firm which has limited capacity to develop marketing activities on a broad scale. It may have gone into licensing arrangements with limited exporting experience or other international background and been stretched to the limit of its resources in the patenting, licensee search and selection, and negotiation phases leading up to licensing. The small firm particularly tends to be more susceptible to dependency on the licensee and often the only form of control tends to be that which it is able to build into the licensing agreement. This represents a partial solution, but the firm still relies on other parties for international development, while it tends to remain in a relatively passive position.

It is interesting to note that, in responses to the survey question regarding 'drawbacks of licensing', information flow and control problems emerged as paramount. These drawbacks are of course interrelated as lack of information tends to be a contributory factor to the feeling of loss of control.

Of course, not all firms used licensing as the main means of developing a particular foreign market. In a small number of cases it acted in a supportive role to a joint venture operation. For example, one company entered into a licensing arrangement when it was forced to accept only a 30% equity in the UK joint venture operation rather than the preferred 50% level. The licensing agreement was a means of ensuring an adequate return on the technology transferred as well as controlling the utilization of the technology. Another company used two licensing agreements, one covering management assistance, the other technical assistance, in order to effect control of a 40%-owned joint venture in Malaysia as well as extract income. In other words, in the joint venture situation licensing becomes an important part of the armoury of control, rather than being a reason for loss of it as in normal licensing exercises.

In the longer run, however, the concern about lack of control in licensing may act as one of the factors causing a company to move to another mode of representation in a given foreign market. No examples were encountered in our survey where foreign market channel transfer could be said to have been induced by the control problem, but many of the companies had effected various measures, some via the licensing agreement itself, to ensure a degree of effective control. Some of the approaches were positive in nature (for example, via training schemes, frequent visits and early transfer of new technology) to ensure that the licensee operated as efficiently as possible and thereby generated acceptable returns to the licensor.

3.2.1. Licensing and knowledge development

The secondary, and passive, role to which licensing is commonly assigned is, in one sense, not surprising given some of its more obvious drawbacks as an internationalization strategy when compared to exporting and direct investment. It has, for example, been argued that 'the alternative of licensing a foreign producer can match the profitability of direct investment only in certain cases' (Caves, 1972, p. 272). The 'deficiencies' of licensing are chiefly related to the limited involvement in the foreign market that it usually implies. There tends to be reduced international marketing activity when compared to exporting or foreign investment. This restricts, or removes, the growth of experience in and knowledge about foreign markets, which form such key elements in the ability to extend foreign commitments. Johanson and Vahlne (1977, p. 23) have developed and partially confirmed a model of the internationalization process of the firm 'that focuses on the development of the individual firm, and particularly on its gradual acquisition, integration and use of knowledge about foreign markets and operations, and on its successively increasing commitment to foreign markets. The basic assumptions of the model are that lack of such knowledge is an important obstacle to the development of international operations and that the necessary knowledge can be acquired mainly through operations abroad'. If we accept the validity of this model, it does lead to the conclusion that, because licensing is usually a less involving form of international operations, it will tend to be less effective in advancing internationalization.

Information flows relating to foreign markets tend to be reduced in licensing relative to other international marketing strategies (Vernon, 1972, p. 216). Once the foreign licensing agreement has been signed and the technology effectively transferred (which may include training) there is less pressure on the licensor to maintain any further involvement in the foreign market.

3.2.2. Licensing as an interaction process

Notwithstanding the fact that licensing tended to be adopted as a secondary strategy, it was clear that most interviewees had, with experience, come to recognize the importance of licensing as an interactive operation. This was expressed in terms of the need to develop an effective 'working relationship' with the licensee. The emphasis on developing a 'licensing relationship' appeared to arise from a concern to ensure that licensing succeeded and the business developed as well as providing a means to achieve a degree of control over the nature and technological quality of the licensee's operations. Many firms commented that a 'hit-and-run' attitude to licensing ensured that there would be little future in the licensing business. It was not enough merely to transfer the technology under the terms of the agreement and leave it at that. It was stressed that the success of the licensor depended on the success of the licensee and that it was therefore in the interests of the Australian company to provide the best possible service to the licensee. This included frequent up-dating of the technology available. By such means, the licensee was made more dependent on the licensor, while the continuing royalty payments appeared as less of a millstone and there was less incentive to break the terms of the licensing agreement. A frequent comment in interviews was that a satisfactory two-way relationship could never be guaranteed by a legal document.

Thus, in time, the elements of a more positive approach to licensing seemed to emerge, with a more longitudinal view of its role and an emphasis on the effectiveness of interaction with the licensee. A general assessment of the experience of companies in the survey would be that failure to recognize the interactive nature of licensing put the long-run viability of the licensing strategy at risk.

The return benefits of effective interaction with the licensee can be considerable. For example, in response to a question about the long-run benefits of licensing, the three most commonly expressed items were (in order): return flow of technology and other information from the licensee; contribution to foreign market knowledge and skills; and exports of equipment to the licensee. In one case, the Australian company had participated in a joint venture in a third country with its licensee, while in another the Australian licensor had begun importing machinery from its US licensee in order to widen its local product range. There were also benefits in the expansion of consultancy services to the host country for a small number of firms. Such positive effects emphasize the potential role of licensing as a means of penetrating a foreign market and opening up wider market possibilities beyond licensing itself. A study of Finnish companies found that exports of related equipment to independent licensees (in aggregate) were more than double the value of licensing income (Oravainen, 1979, p. 99).

3.2.3. Licensing as a stepping stone strategy

From a longitudinal perspective, licensing is a phase in internationalization which may well create other marketing possibilities. In the long-run, it can become a springboard or bridge to these other openings, operating positively as a means of risk and uncertainty reduction. In some cases, the licensing arrangement opens up the possibility of takeover or a joint-venture relationship at a later stage. As such, foreign licensing can be viewed as a feasible experimentation phase by which a more direct involvement with, or takeover of, an existing manufacturer can be tested. Particularly in the early stages of internationalization, when a firm is often restricted by limited resources in its expansion activity, licensing can operate as an indirect means of securing a manufacturing base in a foreign market until it is better equipped to undertake direct investment. However, for such an approach to be effective, licensing has to be planned and adopted within a framework of the future potential for an altered marketing mode in the foreign market. In other words, if licensing is to operate as a stepping stone in the internationalization process, it should be seen not as an end point but as potentially a creative phase for developing alternative international possibilities.

The survey revealed few cases where licensing was utilized positively as a stepping stone strategy to other international marketing modes. The general impression was that the strategic role of licensing in the firm's internationalization process had not been clearly planned. Licensing tended to be adopted without consideration of its ultimate role. Although small in number, responses to the question regarding termination of licensing agreements tend to indicate that rather than being the subject of a planned disengagement from licensing to more effectively service a foreign market, termination tended to have been forced by outside circumstances and was generally not replaced by other modes of representation.

Even in cases where manufacturing companies have embarked on a licensing-only strategy for internationalization, there will be a tendency in the long-run to shift to other forms of international operations. Over time, the expanding licensing company will have developed international skills and is likely to have exposed new opportunities which are not exploitable by licensing alone.

Table 4. Reasons for termination of licensing agreements

Reason given	Number of firms
Licensee unwilling to renew agreement	2
Problems with licensee (e.g. licensee ceased operations, unsatisfactory performance)	6
Change in foreign market conditions	2
Product did not sell	1
Total	11

Table 5. Replacement activity where licensing agreement terminated

Replacement activity	Number of firms
Company has ceased to operate in host country	7
Another licensee adopted	1
Licensing replaced with exporting	3
Total	11

In this sense, it is not the limitations of licensing per se that lead to an interest in an alternative approach, but rather that opportunities emerge *because* of the licensing activity. The success of licensing opens up and supports the move into hitherto uncharted territory. In the long run, an excess capacity for international operations beyond licensing is created within the firm at the same time as the uncertainty of new ventures is reduced. In individual foreign markets, market-specific skills and knowledge can often be best exploited by advancing to a more involved form of operations than licensing. By this means, a return is obtained on these other skills as well as on the original technological advantage.

A case in point is the Australian firm, Rocla Industries, which has extensively internationalized through the sale of technology embodied in licensing arrangements and in machinery. The initial stimulus to overseas operations came as a result of Rocla's patented invention, the roller suspension concrete pipe-making machine. This was developed in the 1940s and quickly sparked overseas interest. Rather than invest directly overseas, which would have required scarce capital and involved some risk, Rocla decided to market the patent via a licensing system. Capital was needed for Australian use. From 1948 onwards, Rocla began to sell the licence together with concrete pipe-making machinery. Since that time, it has steadily expanded the number of licensing agreements with foreign producers to the point of having now achieved near-global coverage. As a result, despite the market contact and knowledge 'deficiencies' normally associated with licensing, over such a long period Rocla developed considerable international knowledge, expertise and contacts and established its international reputation in the field. It was in a better position to perceive and act upon opportunities outside the normal licensing techniques. As the company has noted:

> Licensee arrangements can lead to investment opportunities in joint ventures, either for special contracts or normal production. In Northern Ireland, a licence agreement led to a joint venture operation for a major pipeline contract and then, eventually, to Rocla's own investment in Britain (Department of Overseas Trade, 1974, p. 363).

3.3. Overview

The mainly small to medium-sized companies in this investigation tended to utilize licensing because of various constraints on the use of other international marketing techniques, rather than because of a positive preference for licensing as such. Despite its adoption in a secondary or residual manner, though, many firms were still able successfully to expand their international operations via licensing. A key factor in the success of licensing appeared to be the development of effective interaction with the licensee in a long-run relationship. Effective interaction not only contributed to the commercial viability of the licensee but also produced return benefits for the licensor of technological and market information as well as exports of equipment and components and co-operation in other ventures in some cases. Few firms however, were able to develop the positive potential of licensing as a stepping stone strategy to other, more involving, forms of international market commitment. Perhaps this requires an altered strategic assessment of the potential for expanded international activities flowing from a more effective utilization of the licensing phase.

4. MARKETING ISSUES

4.1. The relative roles of patents, know-how and other forms of industrial property

There are various forms of technical and commercial technology (industrial or intellectual property in the broad sense) which may be the object of licensing overseas. Both in Australia and overseas, there appears to be a growing realization of the important roles which different elements in the licensing package can play in strengthening the process of marketing technology overseas. By tying the various elements together into a cohesive package, the position of the licensor is strengthened.

Patents and technical know-how are the most common objects of licensing and the most important basis of income generated. The Australian Bureau of Statistics (1979a) only made a separation between patent licence fees and royalties, and other technical know-how. Out of the total of $7.5 million received by the manufacturing sector, $4.3 million (57.3%) was for patents and $3.2 million (42.7%) for know-how.

There is some evidence, however, that once foreign-owned companies and cases of licensing to overseas affiliates are removed from consideration, the proportionate importance of patents is reduced. In a recent investigation of *all* Finnish firms engaged in outward licensing, it was found that out of the total of agreements with independent licensees, only 48.0% included patents as one form of industrial property transferred, whereas 96.1% included technical know-how. Other proportions were trade marks 36.4%, designs 5.2%, management know-how 11.7%, and marketing know-how 24.7% (Oravainen, 1979, p. 35). It is interesting to note the emerging separate importance of commercial, rather than technical, technology as an object of licensing. This area has probably been ignored or underrated in past considerations of licensing.

In this survey, companies were requested to provide a proportional breakdown of their licensing receipts between the main objects of licensing-patents, know-how, and other (trade marks, copyright, etc.). The results are shown in Table 6.

The clear message in responses to this question, taken overall, was that sale of know-how represented the principal element in licensing agreements signed. Only three out of the total of 34 respondent firms (8.8%) had not sold any know-how as part of their licensing agreements, whereas the corresponding figure for patents was 20 out of 34 companies (58.8%) and 28 out of 34 (82.4%) for the 'other' category. At the other end of the scale for 55.9% of respondent companies the know-how component constituted 80% or more of the licensing arrangement whereas the corresponding figure for patents was

Table 6. Licensing receipts by object of licensing

	Object of Licensing					
	Patents		Know-how		Other	
Percentage of Licensing Receipts	No. of Firms	%	No. of Firms	%	No. of Firms	%
0	20	58.8	3	8.8	28	82.4
1–19	3	8.8	1	2.9	0	0
20–49	3	8.8	4	11.8	3	8.8
50–79	4	11.8	7	20.6	2	5.9
80–100	4	11.8	19	55.9	1	2.9
Total	34	100	34	100	34	100

11.8% and the 'other' category 3.0%. The overall breakdown was: patents 20.1%, know-how 69.8% and other 9.9%.

This pattern was further confirmed in responses to the question concerning overseas patenting, as shown in Table 7.

It is perhaps somewhat surprising that patents emerged as being of relatively minor overall importance in the responses. The breakdown does of course mask a great deal of variation on a company-to-company basis. While it might have been expected that smaller firms would have shown far greater reliance on patents—as is inevitably the case for individual inventors—the responses show otherwise. When the results shown in Table 7 are related to company size, and individual inventors removed, they reveal that about half of the small and medium-sized firms had not attempted to file for overseas patents whereas only one of the large firms had not done so. Although the supply of patentable technology is clearly a factor in the ability to patent overseas, the above results seemed to be a strong reflection of attitudes towards patenting held within respondent companies.

Larger firms seem to have recognized more clearly the marketing value of patents in the process of selling technology overseas, whereas many small to medium-sized firms have not only had a poor view of the value of patents but have been unprepared to commit finance to the investment in international patents. Nevertheless, it appears that the role of patents in the licensing process is currently subject to an important change, especially for small to medium-sized firms, the result of which is likely to be a greater emphasis than is indicated in the current results. This judgment is based on the interview process.

There were two cases where high technology companies had begun to pay greater attention to patenting after attaining some international experience. One company commented that while it originally did not take out patents it had learnt from that

Table 7. Has your company attempted to file for patents overseas?

	Number of agreements				
	1	2–5	6–20	>20	Total
No. of firms 'Yes'	7	10	11	1	29 (67.4%)
No. of firms 'No'	5	9	—	—	14 (32.6%)

'mistake' and now 'patented everything'. The other company noted that it had a limited understanding of patents in the 1960s leaving it with only know-how to license. It began to patent during the 1970s but had 'learnt that it was not as strong as it should be in the area and intended to become more competent'. The company was facing a court action in the US over breach of patent by an inventor who had taken out a patent on an idea which had already been developed, but not patented, by the Australian company.

A number of patent attorneys who were involved in outward foreign licensing activity on behalf of client companies were interviewed. One of these commented that there was a growing concern amongst companies that know-how is too easily lost through the movement of employees. As a result he said that companies were becoming more reluctant to buy straight know-how. He was in fact advising clients not to rely on know-how itself, but rather to use it as part of an overall package.

Thus, while there were many cases encountered of a negative or passive attitude towards the role and usefulness of patents, it was possible to discern a change in attitude within a number of firms towards a more positive approach. There appeared to be two sets of forces producing this development—technological 'push' and the 'pull' of international marketing. As a result of the involvement by firms in R&D activity, new technological know-how was being developed, some of it in patentable form, and so there was a natural defensive response of attempting to protect the ownership of the resultant industrial property. On the other side though, involvement in international marketing exercises, particularly via licensing, had produced, in many cases, a new recognition of the value of patents. Beyond the concern for protection of industrial property in foreign markets, patents have come to be viewed as an important element in strengthening the marketability of the licensing package to foreign licensees, of strengthening the hand of the licensor in the negotiation process and in ensuring compliance to the terms of agreement in the operative phase.

In general it would seem that, as Australian companies become more involved in international licensing, the value of patents and other forms of industrial property will become more apparent.

4.1.1. The know-how component

The passive approach towards patents by some companies partly reflects the importance placed on non-patented know-how. The way in which the interrelationship between patents and know-how influences judgments about patents was aptly illustrated by the experience of one manufacturer in the survey who was licensing two products overseas. One product was a component part which incorporated an idea that, once disclosed, could be readily copied. It required no back-up services to effect the transfer of technology. As a result, the manufacturer regarded the patents taken out overseas as being absolutely crucial to the generation of income from licensing. The other product being licensed overseas was a relatively complex machine used in hospitals. A high level of back-up services had to be provided to overseas manufacturers, in the form of supportive manufacturing know-how, so that the patent was considered to be a far less important factor in licensing.

The latter example is illustrative of the fact that effective international transfer of technology in a commercialized form via licensing normally requires far more than just the transfer of patent rights. In order that patent information be applied successfully, it commonly requires a 'software' element involving, in the main, the transfer of various forms of know-how. A training component of most licensing agreements tends to be an important medium for the transfer of manufacturing know-how. Pengilley has noted that:

> In a great number of patents, the patent does not necessarily tell anybody how the invention will work in a practical manner in actual operation. This disclosure is something different. It is 'know-how' . . . (a) United States survey undertaken by George Washington University showed that about 50 per cent of United States patents studied had to be supplemented by 'know-how' details before the patent became viable. Persons in industry with whom I have discussed this statistic give the uniform reply that they feel it overstates the position, that is they feel that far fewer inventions would be practically workable in the absence of 'know-how' details (Pengilley, 1977, p. 201).

Not only does the know-how factor complicate the technology transfer package, and therefore the negotiations surrounding commercialization via licensing agreement, but it also has important implications for the bargaining position of the licensor. To begin with, a strong know-how component strengthens the position of the licensor when selling the patent—he becomes less liable to patent breach, because the patent of itself is not enough to enable another manufacturer to go ahead with production, without considerable development cost and manufacturing experimentation. One inward licensor in the survey stressed that know-how was far more important than the patent because it could design around a patent, but it was far cheaper to purchase the licence, and thereby the manufacturing know-how, rather than attempt to replicate the development process itself. Given that much know-how tends to be developed through manufacturing experience, the individual inventor is at a significant disadvantage when compared to a manufacturing firm that is seeking to exploit an invention. The individual inventor is far more dependent on the patent—and is therefore far more exposed to patent breach. Should a large manufacturer be required to undertake considerable design and development work to make a licensed invention not only marketable but amenable to large-scale manufacturing techniques, it becomes questionable whether the invention is the same at the end of this process as the one originally offered. As a result, it is not surprising that proprietary rights are sometimes questioned. In fact, many manufacturers are not prepared to enter into patent licensing arrangements, as licensee, unless the product of the patent has already been commercialized, obviating the need for design work etc., and avoiding any potential problems regarding proprietary rights to any new technology developed. As a result, the individual inventor faces a difficult exercise when relying solely on the patent and attempting to sell technology overseas.

In contrast, a larger manufacturing company, with R&D facilities, normally has a strong know-how component to support the basic patent, as well as the ability to gain from technology swap arrangements, sell some related plant and equipment, etc. The availability of R&D facilities enhances the position of a manufacturer as a licensor because of the possibility of creating a more permanent flow of technology and back-up technological support. As Limbury (1979, p. 19) notes, 'it is usually the totality of the know-how concerning the use, manufacture and marketing of the item which is given the greatest weight by the potential licensee, particularly if the licensor is able to update it regularly'. The large manufacturer is therefore in a relatively stronger position by selling a technology 'package' rather than simply a patent. The returns will not only tend to be greater, but the patent is effectively secured within the total package.

Thus, while the patent can play an important role in strengthening the total package for licensing purposes, it appears that, not only does the know-how component perform a similar role, but it is the crucial element in most cases of effective technology transfer via licensing.

4.1.2. Other components

While patents and know-how are the major components of most licensing packages, other elements—mainly trade marks and designs—also play a part. For some industries, as noted earlier, and for certain companies they play a vital role in the ability to license overseas and obtain a degree of industrial property protection where patenting is not possible or could be readily bypassed. In fact in interviews both design and trade mark protection emerged as far more important components of industrial property protection overseas than was indicated by responses to the questionnaire. For example, one company mentioned that it was interested in expanding its overseas licensing activities beyond the one outward agreement currently held. However, it held few patents—none of these being overseas—and yet it had registered designs and product names in a number of prospective overseas markets as a basis for future licensing possibilities.

Trade marks can be a useful contributory factor in the development of a market via licensing. In this context Limbury (1979, p. 19) has noted that 'licensees usually can be required to use the licensor's trademark in relation to the licensed products or processes and this develops good-will attaching to the licensor rather than to the licensee. Should it ever be necessary to change licensees, the licensor's identity in the market, through its trademark, will already be established.' Likewise, when licensing occurs subsequent to a period of exporting, exporting having led to goodwill associated with the registered trade mark, the licensor may be able to make the trade mark an important element of the licensing package. The trade mark tends to be elevated as a component of the company's industrial property and improves the marketability of the total package. In one case a trade mark established via a successful exporting programme subsequently became the principal object of an enforced switch to licensing. However, it appeared that, for those firms in the survey licensing trade marks, trade marks were a relatively unimportant basis for generating licensing income in most instances.

While know-how emerged as the principal component of technology transfer via licensing, there is a clear trend that the elements within the licensing package are expanding, with the result that the licensing package in the future is likely to involve a more complex amalgam of elements than is presently the case. Not only will this tend to strengthen the basis of protection of the package but will enhance its marketability and widen the basis of income generation. As a by-product of the greater use of licensing in international marketing, it can be argued that a greater recognition of the useful contributory role which can be played by even the more minor components of the total package is likely to emerge. Overseas evidence suggests a further spread in the types of know-how being licensed, with an increase in emphasis on commercial 'technology'.

4.2. The timing factor

An important factor in the success of licensing is the timing of the attempt to sign up overseas licensees relative to the stage of technical and commercial development of an invention or other form of new technology. In most cases in the survey, there was relatively limited attention to this question because the timing move was determined by outside forces. Since licensing generally followed exporting, the technology was normally relatively well developed and had been effectively commercialized before the licensing step. The decision to license was promoted by a variety of commercial and strategic considerations which had little to do with a planned assessment of the most appropriate phase in the life of the technology to exploit it overseas via licensing. Similarly, a recent US investigation found that US innovations were more likely to be exploited internationally via licensing in the second five years after commercialization than in the initial five years (Mansfield et al, 1979, p. 56).

For most firms in the survey then, the timing was not strategically determined. Nevertheless, there was a fortuitous benefit in this situation, as the Australian licensors were able to approach licensees with generally proven technology—proven in both commercial and technical senses. For a licensee there is obviously a greater attraction in being able to utilize such technology because there tend to be limited risks in adoption, while the costs of further development and design work are saved. As Limbury (1979, p. 19) has noted:

> The most favourable environment in which to grant licences is where the licensor is already successfully exploiting the products in his home market. Potential licensees can thus realistically evaluate the operating conditions they are likely to encounter . . . If the licensor has already solved his manufacturing and marketing problems he would possess a body of know-how which would enable the licensee to start promptly . . . A potential licensor is often better advised to postpone attempts to market a relatively untried patent until he can simulate actual operational conditions when negotiating with potential licensees.

One relatively large and successful licensor in the survey commented that while it was always a problem of when to offer technology for sale, it erred on the side of commercializing the product first. While most respondent companies went into licensing with established technology, it is clear that not all companies are in a position to license in such an evolutionary way because of, for example, rapid technological progress. In fields of rapid introduction of new ideas, long periods of commercial and technical development may jeopardize later attempts to license internationally. In such situations, interest may be shown by potential licensees who are seeking early solutions to technological competition within their home markets. Licensing new technology is an attractive alternative to the time and cost which would be taken up in a firm's own R&D efforts (Stubbs, 1968, pp. 92–6). In industries where there is a certain fashion element to product designs, such as the furniture industry, there is considerable pressure on companies to exploit any newly developed technology as rapidly as possible. Thus, it may be necessary to advance the timing of the attempt to sell technology overseas to the phase of early commercial experimentation, despite the clear advantages in selling a well-proven product or process. McInnes (1979, p. 128) has argued that:

> Typically in the life of a patent the first five years are spent bringing the idea to an initial commercial level . . . Obviously and especially in a market as small as Australia's it is not logical to wait until the process is obsolescent before introducing it to the larger market overseas . . . For this reason I advocate taking technology overseas at the stage of pilot commercial development.

In a number of cases in the survey, companies were licensing principally to middle-income or developing countries in the Asian and African regions. The technology involved was well established, but more 'appropriate' to the developing countries and there was minimal danger of technological obsolescence. As a result, there seemed to be virtually no pressure on the companies to seek rapid exploitation of the technology. It is therefore in fields of high and/or rapidly changing technology where other technically advanced countries are the principal markets that the timing question becomes a critical issue. In these situations though, the risks involved in advancing the timing of sale of technology are reduced when the licensee is a well established overseas client, perhaps involving the broadening of an already established licensing relationship.

With regard to the commercial implications of selling technology before proving commercial success, Limbury (1979, p. 19) maintains:

> More difficult to conclude are successful licences where the licensor merely has a pilot plant or prototype to offer for demonstration purposes to licensees. Lack of actual commercial success is usually reflected in less satisfactory royalty terms since the licensee requires recognition of the risks and delays in pioneering.

The timing problem for individual inventors with no manufacturing base is even more acute. Inventors have difficulties not only in demonstrating commercial feasibility but also in proving technological operation under manufacturing conditions. Such difficulties tend to be accentuated when the technology concerns an industrial process or a large item of capital equipment where scaling up is important. One inventor in the sample attempted to license his building systems technology to a Middle-Eastern market but, while interest was shown, prospective clients were not prepared to consider seriously a licensing arrangement without evidence of its use within the housing and construction industry within Australia. The inventor has since switched to a programme of active commercial exploitation within Australia. Clearly he has attempted to sell the technology overseas too early in its life given that the idea involved a major departure from existing systems and included a large machine whose operation could not be readily demonstrated overseas.

This case was in direct contrast to the experience of another inventor whose product was very small, and consumer oriented. From conception to first sample the product had only taken six months, and was licensed soon thereafter to a Hong Kong toy manufacturer for world distribution. The idea used in the product was simple and its operation could be readily demonstrated. Given that the commercial life of the product was likely to be relatively short, there was considerable pressure on the inventor to seek maximum exploitation as quickly as possible.

Thus, while it is sometimes suggested that the attempt to license overseas by inventors should proceed immediately after the provisional patent application has been lodged, the small number of case studies examined in the survey indicate that the appropriate time to begin the attempt to license overseas for individual inventors as with manufacturing companies, relates to such broader questions as the rate of change of technology, the extent of departure from existing technology and the complexity of the product.

In general though, for both individual inventors and manufacturing firms, the strongest pressure in regard to the timing of exploitation of technology via international licensing appears to lie in the direction of some technical and commercial proving beforehand, at least within the home market. The marketing exercise is likely to be significantly more difficult without such background, unless there is strong commercial pressure on a potential licensee in the foreign market in favour of the early adoption of new technology.

4.3. Selection of the licensee

Interviews with companies revealed that there was considerable variation in the criteria used to select licencees. However, a picture emerged of companies taking greater care in the selection process as they increased the number of agreements. There seemed to be a strong consensus that the selection of a good licensee was far more important than a tight legal document. The terms most commonly used were 'trust' and 'confidence'.

Many companies put considerable time and resources into assessing the market first before finding licensees. The following were seen as important:

- the depth of political stability. Frequent changes of government were not as worrisome if the basic administrative structure was stable.
- the existence of a US or British legal system. Some companies would not license unless a strong British system existed.
- the end uses of the licensor's product and any peculiar requirements which may favour or disadvantage the product. For example, provision for insulation is necessary in external building panels in Scandinavia.
- establish what competitive product lines exist in the country.

One company even went to the trouble of having more than one executive travel through the country making independent assessments before embarking on the selection process.

With regard to short-listing several techniques were used. Some companies would not short list potential licensees unless they were already known to the licensor. However, for most, licensors were prepared to investigate previously unknown companies. A common technique was to advertise both in host country newspapers and other trade journals. Also, exhibitions during the short-listing period proved to be useful.

Uppermost in firms' minds in selecting licensees was the problem of competition. Even though much of the licensing which had taken place was in countries to which the licensor could not export, care was taken not to license firms that were able to compete in other markets and also not to license companies which produced competitive lines. The emphasis was on complementarity. Complementarity was also seen as important where there was considerable trade in technology. In these situations, licensees sought were those keen and able to participate in technology interchange.

In the selection process a number of characteristics of potential licensees seemed to have been examined closely:

4.3.1. Size

The largest companies were frequently avoided because of a concern that the technology offered would be relatively minor or unimportant to them. It was material that the technology make an important contribution to the licensee's operation and that the licensee was prepared to push the products. Small private firms tended to be avoided because they could quite easily close down and re-open under another name still holding the technology.

4.3.2. Distribution

The ability to distribute and market the licensor's product was considered paramount. This factor is of course partly connected to the size and extent of the licensee's operation.

4.3.3. Growth

Notwithstanding the above factors, in general companies preferred to select licensees which were keen to grow.

Finally, compatibility was seen as significant. The licensee needed to have the capacity to manufacture the product. Where firms were selected which were not producing competitive products it was still important that the firm had been working with similar materials. Compatability was also strengthened if the licensee possessed quality technical staff and if necessary quality design staff. In general, there was a strong emphasis on the technical side.

Overall then, the selection of the licensee emerged as a crucial phase in the licensing process. The investment of considerable time and resources in the selection process was common and was justified by the fact that the licensee effectively becomes the long term representative of the licensor in the designated foreign market and ultimately determines the success of the licensing venture.

4.4. Negotiation

Having selected a target group of potential licensees, the next step for the licensor is the negotiation of an acceptable licensing agreement. In approaching a potential licensee, an important issue at the outset is the extent of information disclosure. This is a difficult area as the potential licensee must be aware of what is being offered before he can begin to make an assessment. Often licensors do not think out carefully what is to be offered and how it is to be protected. Negotiations can be aborted if the licensor needs to divulge confidential information but is not prepared to waive company secret status. If the licensor desires the potential licensee to sign a secrecy agreement the information must be clearly identifiable and separable from public information and information already in the potential licensee's possession. The interviews indicated that secrecy agreements were generally not used and licensors tended to take calculated risks after carefully choosing targets. With smaller companies often too much information was divulged in the early stages.

To sell the technology some licensors felt it necessary to collect intelligence on the potential market for the product embodying the technology and prepare cost estimates. Accuracy was considered to be important to ensure that the licensor was not vulnerable in negotiations.

Companies saw it as rewarding to leave the potential licensee with a list of questions which should be answered before further rounds of negotation took place. These questions were seen to serve two purposes:

(a) force more people in the recipient company to become involved in the agreement, and;

(b) provide more information to the licensor.

Companies were also careful to stress the need to take particular care over key clauses in the agreement. In assessing royalties licensors had to be able to calculate the likely savings or likely profits which would arise from adopting the technology.

Notwithstanding these calculations the most common royalty rate was 5%.[1] The royalty rate was varied by turnover, the need for warranties and servicing, and the field of activity. Pharmaceuticals, chemicals and engineering products (with low turnover) appeared to attract higher royalties.

Of course all companies desired an up-front lump sum payment. Clearly, the firm must be able to bargain from a position of strength if it hopes for a lump sum payment as well as a reasonable royalty payment.

This is highlighted by the survey data. Those firms with only one licence agreement had had no lump sum payments included in their agreements. Out of the 11 companies which indicated that they had only one agreement (10 or 91%) received royalties based on sales levels alone. The remaining agreement was based on a technology swap arrangement. As expected the proportion of agreements attracting lump sum payments tended to increase for firms holding a larger portfolio of agreements. After taking into account conjointness with other forms of payment for firms holding 2–5 agreements 30.3% of agreements included lump sum payments. The proportion rose to 38% for firms holding 6–20 agreements.

It was stressed that licensors must realize that they are negotiating with individuals rather than companies at the negotiating table. Executives tend to be wary of committing their companies to high expenditure as such a decision may rebound against them in future promotional rounds.

Throughout weight was given to the need to be 'reasonable'. Notwithstanding the recognition that minimum royalties were important and perhaps more important than performance clauses, it was accepted that minimum royalties must be practical. Insufficient allowance for a settling-in period can destroy an agreement. Furthermore, exclusivity was seen in a similar light. 'It is unreasonable to expect a licensee to buy technology without exclusivity' was a common view.

Finally, most companies attempted to draw up a tight agreement. This was done not so much to keep two hostile parties together but rather to serve as a reminder or point of reference for both parties in the event that key personnel leave and in case a dispute requiring litigation arises.

5. COSTS

A common view in economic literature is that the marginal cost of transferring technology will be very low once the set-up cost associated with developing technology has been incurred. This view is naïve in practice, albeit because of the premise upon which it is based; that transfer involves no more than the provision of blueprints already developed. Indeed, if we accept this premise, we could go further and say that where a patent is involved no transfer is necessary as the specifications are on file in the host country and for a patent to be granted the specifications must be capable of being used successfully by an independent manufacturer. But the above view is discredited in practice by the complexity of the transfer. Often a transfer will require a composite of patents, unpatented know-how (technical, managerial and marketing), designs (both registered and unregistered) and sometimes trade marks and copyrights. The assignment of rights to use a patent is more complicated too. First, the specifications in the patent may be insufficient as they have been necessarily restricted to cover very narrow claims. Second, negotiations often take place during the pre-publication period. Consequently, supplementary procedures are necessary. Third, many patents do require additional know-how for others to activate them.

Two overseas investigations add support to the above rebuttal. Teece (1977) analysed the cost of transfer of technology by US multinationals. His general conclusions were that there was a decline in the cost of transfer with each new transfer but on average his costs amounted to 19% of the total project cost associated with new technology acquired by the transferee. In the study by Oravainen (1979) which is perhaps more relevant to the Australian situation, there is a measure of all explicit and implicit costs[2] associated with establishing an agreement. Having acquired information on all Finnish firms licensing to independent licensees, he calculated that in 1977 the average total cost per agreement was 456,000 Finnish marks or approximately 100,000 Australian dollars.

5.1. Evidence from interviews

Because of the sensitivity of Australian companies to the release of cost data, it was not possible to obtain information on absolute costs. However, it became readily apparent in the interviews that the transfer process was a costly exercise. Many companies were surprised at the time, cost and difficulty of entering into licensing agreements. The opportunity costs associated with this exercise are highlighted where a small firm with an owner/manager is involved. He must make a decision as to where he devotes his time and his financial resources.

The costs and time scale associated with the initial phases of licensing appeared to be related to three main factors:

(a) The necessity to undergo a considerable amount of learning about the process of licensing. Where authority cannot be delegated as in the case of smaller firms this is a major problem.

(b) The location and assessment of suitable licensees. This cost is often increased as licensors became more aware of the importance of 'getting things right at the outset'. It was observed with some of the more successful licensors that considerable time was taken assessing the licensee, his market and the general economic environment, and;

(c) the negotation was often very costly in time and airfares as the licensor needed to negotiate in the host country rather than his own country.

Some of the smaller firms had attempted to circumvent these costs by using agents. To date it is difficult to assess how successful and cost effective this alternative has been. The use of outside assistance from government was certainly looked upon favourably. However, licensors could go little further than use these services for general information and some contacts.

5.2. Survey results

Licensors were asked to indicate the relative importance of particular costs. This required them to apportion total costs, costs associated with establishing an agreement and costs associated with maintaining agreements. The results are set out in Table 8.

Table 8(a) indicates that establishment costs were seen as the most important. However, the breakdown demonstrates that if the absolute costs are significant for the company then protection of industrial property and maintenance cannot be ignored. The high level associated with protection is perhaps a consequence of the desire on the part of many companies to patent wherever they saw potential for foreign sales. Of the 29 companies which filed for patents overseas, 16 (55.2%) had done so in countries where they adjudged a potential for licensing, export or foreign investment. As a result, some of the industrial property costs may in fact be connected with exporting and foreign investment. The relative importance of maintenance is also interesting. This indicated that many agreements are not 'one off' but require servicing, a natural outcome of the licensor's desire to build a licensing relationship.

Table 8(b) shows that well over half the expenses are involved in discovering, and striking an agreement with, the licensee. The relatively low figure for adaptation and testing may be partly explained by the fact that a high proportion of licences were struck after the firm had been exporting to the market. In addition much of the adaption could have been implemented by personnel training by the licensor.

Finally, in Table 8(c) there is a breakdown of the maintenance costs. Here we can see the outcome of the licensing relationship emerging quite strongly. A number of firms stressed that a large part of this figure is attributable to frequent visits to the licensee.

The relatively low figure for on-going market research is also interesting. Perhaps it indicates that even though much is being spent on building a licensing relationship relatively little is being spent on attempting to forge the next step in the internationalization process. Clearly then, the costs of transferring technology via licensing are significant, and greater than many firms embarking on a licensing strategy realize. The establishment costs of licensing are particulary significant, but if a licensing agreement is to be effectively maintained, substantial continuing costs must also be incurred. Over the longer run, the general pattern is for the cost of each new licensing agreement to decline.

Table 8. The relative costs of licensing overseas

(a)	*Breakdown of total costs of licensing overseas*	%
	Protection of industrial property	24.8
	Establishment of a licensing agreement	46.6
	Maintenance of licensing agreement	29.0
(b)	*Breakdown of establishment costs*	
	Search for suitable licensees	22.8
	Communication between involved parties	44.7
	Adaption and testing of equipment for licensee	9.9
	Training personnel for the licensee	19.9
	Other (additional marketing activity and legal expenses)	2.5
(c)	*Breakdown of maintenance costs*	
	Audit of the licensee	9.7
	On going market research in the market of the licensee	7.2
	Backup services for the licensee	65.0
	Defence of industrial property rights in the licensee's territory	11.0
	Other	7.1

For this to occur though, some economies need to be effected in each establishment phase. In this respect the beneficial effects of learning-by-doing in licensing have been reported for one Australian company:

> Rocla gained most of its know-how about licensing in overseas countries the hard way. Since it began in 1948, the company has found there are pitfalls as well as benefits. The license agreement now incorporates clauses to overcome the problems experienced during the life of its early arrangements (Department of Overseas Trade, 1974, p. 363).

6. CONCLUSION

In this study of outward foreign licensing by Australian companies the role of licensing in the internationalization process of individual firms was examined, along with important aspects of the associated marketing exercise. The emphasis has been on the use of licensing as an international business strategy other than as part of the transfer flows of a foreign affiliate network.

In general it was found that licensing tended to be utilized as a second-line or residual international marketing mode because external pressures constrained or prevented the use of exporting to particular foreign markets. As a result, there was limited assessment and planning of the longer term role of licensing. Nevertheless, many firms had recognized the need to work closely with their licensees over time in order to ensure that the licensing arrangement worked successfully and that it generated satisfactory returns. In some cases the development of an effective working relationship with the licensee had led to spin-off benefits in terms of technical interchange and co-operation beyond the confines of the licensing arrangement.

However, few firms appeared to have a clear perception of the positive potential of licensing as an international penetration strategy—either in the form of complementary operations built around licensing or as a bridge to alternative, deeper forms of market involvement.

The study does show that licensing has a positive role to play in extending and deepening the international operations of individual firms. For licensing to fulfil this role though, it must be employed with far more strategic purpose, involving a longer term perspective of a company's foreign market involvement. In addition, to secure any long-term benefits from licensing, considerable care needs to be taken in the timing of technology transfer; the choice of foreign market; the selection of licensee; the negotiation process; and assembly of the contents of the licensing package to be offered.

NOTES

1 The royalty was usually based on the licensee's invoice value for the products associated with the techniques less: (a) Sales tax; (b) Agent's commission; (c) Cash discounts; (d) Packaging, freight and delivery charges; (e) Site installation costs.

2 The Oravainen study involved probably the most comprehensive effort yet to assess the implicit costs associated with licensing. An import component of costs which is generally ignored is managerial time. The Finnish licensing executives provided details of their own and subordinates' activities concerning licensing, and the time spent in each. The time spent was valued at the appropriate salary level. Not only did these 'time costs' constitute a major component of the total licensing costs, but they caused most early licensing agreements of the Finnish firms to be unprofitable.

REFERENCES

Australian Bureau of Statistics (1979a) *Foreign Control in Research and Experimental Development: Private Enterprises, 1976–77.* Canberra.

Australian Bureau of Statistics (1979b) *Research and Experimental Development: Private Enterprises, 1976–77.* Canberra.

Budak, P. R., Susbauer, J. C. (1977) International Expansion Through Licensing: Guidelines for the Small Firm. *Journal of Small Business Management* **15**(1): 17–21.

Caves, R. E. (1972) International Corporations: The Industrial Economics of Foreign Investment. In J. H. Dunning (ed) *International Investment*, Penguin: Harmondsworth.

Department of Overseas Trade (1974) Rocla Builds Business Through Licensing. *Overseas Trading* July 26, 1974: 363–364.

Johanson, J., Vahlne, J. E. (1977) The Internationalization Process of the Firm—Model of Knowledge Development and Increasing Foreign Market Commitments. *Journal of International Business Studies* **8**(1): 23–32.

Limbury, A. (1979) Manufacturing Licence Deals Can Produce Export Profits. *Overseas Trading* January 19, 1979: 19.

Luostarinen, R. (1979) *The Internationalizatin of the Firm*, Acta Academiae Oeconomicae Helsingiensis, Helsinki School of Economics: Helsinki.

McInnes, A. D. (1979) Now Is the Time To Market Technology. *Overseas Trading* March 2, 1979: 128.

Mansfield, E., Romeo, A., Wagner, S. (1979) Foreign Trade and US Research and Development. *Review of Economics and Statistics* **61**(1): 49–57.

Oravainen, N. (1979) *Suomalaisten Yritysten Kansainvaliset Lisenssi—Ja Know-How—Sopimukset* (International Licensing and Know-How Agreements of Finnish Companies). Helsinki School of Economics, FIBO Publications, No. 13: Helsinki.

Parry, T. G., Watson, J. F. (1979) Technology Flows and Foreign Investment in the Australian Manufacturing Sector. *Australian Economic Papers* **18**(6): 103–118.

Pengilley, W. (1977) Patents and Trade Practices—Competition Policies in Conflict. *Australian Business Law Review* **5**(3): 172–203.

Senate Standing Committee (1979) *Industrial Research and Development in Australia.* Australian Government Publishing Service: Canberra.

Stubbs, P. (1968) *Innovation and Research: A Study in Australian Industry.* Cheshire: Melbourne.

Teece, D. J. (1977) Technology Transfer by Multinational Firms. *Economic Journal* **87**(346): 242–261.

Tesar, G. (1977) Corporate Internationalization Strategy Through Licensing Arrangements in Industrial Marketing. Paper presented at the annual meeting of the Academy of Marketing Science, Akron, Ohio, May 4–6, 1977.

Vernon, R. (1972) *The Economic Environment of International Business.* Prentice-Hall: Englewood Cliffs.

This reading is based on a report for the Industrial Property Advisory Committee and the Licensing Executives Society of Australia, December 1981.

7

Foreign Direct Investment by Small- and Medium-sized Enterprises: The Theoretical Background

Peter J. Buckley

1. DEFINITIONAL PROBLEMS

It is apparent that definitions of 'small firm' vary according to author and context. Definitions are not right or wrong, just more or less useful. Table 1 shows the definitions employed by the Wilson Committee and the UK 1981 Companies Act. On these definitions, the companies of our British study (worldwide turnover less than £10 millions) are relatively large (Buckley et al, 1988). However, when we examine the criteria used for instance in the Bolton Report based on 'economic' criteria, then we are justified in terming our firms 'smaller'. The Bolton Report took as its criteria: (1) Market share, the characteristic of a small firm's share of the market is that it is not large enough to enable it to influence the prices or national quantities of goods sold to any significant extent, (2) Independence, which means that the owner has control of the business himself—this rules out small subsidiaries of large firms, (3) Personalized management, which implies that the owner actively participates in all aspects of the management of the business and in all major decision making processes with little devolution or delegation of authority. On these grounds the 43 firms analysed in the study by Buckley et al (1988) qualify for the epithet 'smaller'. Further, on the world scale they are in the tail of the size distribution of international firms. The criterion of £10 million turnover was chosen so as to exclude large multinationals but to leave a population such that a viable sample could be chosen.

Comparable definitions for other countries relate to the size of the economy. A study of US 'midsized companies' defines midsized companies as those with sales between $25 million and $1 billion (Cavanagh and Clifford, 1983). An alternative US definition of a medium-sized company is 15–50 million US dollars in sales (Fierheller, 1980). A study of strategic planning in small and medium-sized companies in the Netherlands took lower limits of 50–75 employees, 3–10 million DF sales and 2–8 million DF in assets and higher limits of 300–500 employees, 25–100 million DF sales and 20–120 million DF assets (van Hoorn, 1979).

Reprinted by permission of Kluwer Academic Publishers from *Small Business Economics*, Vol 1, pp 89–100
Copyright © 1989 Kluwer Academic Publishers

Table 1. Definitions of small firms

A. Wilson Committee 1978 (cmnd. 7503)

Manufacturing	200 employees or less
Retailing	Turnover 185 000 p.a. or less
Wholesale trades	Turnover 730 000 p.a. or less
Construction	25 employees or less
Mining and quarrying	25 employees or less
Motor trades	Turnover 365 000 p.a. or less
Misc. services	Turnover 185 000 p.a. or less
Road transport	5 vehicles or less
Catering	All excluding multiples and brewery managed public houses

B. 1981 Companies Act

1. Medium-sized
A company may be classified as medium sized if, for the financial year and the one immediately preceding it, two out of the following three conditions apply:
    (i)   turnover did not exceed 5.75 m
    (ii) balance sheet total did not exceed 2.8 m
    (iii) average weekly number of employees did not exceed 250

2. Small
A company may be classified as small, if for the financial year and the one immediately preceding it, two of the following three conditions apply:
    (i)   turnover did not exceed 1.4 m
    (ii) balance sheet total did not exceed 0.7 m
    (iii) average weekly number of employed did not exceed 50

Balance sheet total means the total of all its assets without deduction of any liabilities.

2. THE ANALYSIS OF FOREIGN DIRECT INVESTMENT BY SMALL FIRMS

There exists a variety of approaches to the analysis of small firm foreign direct investment. The economics of the firm's growth points to internal and external constraints on the growth of the firm. Questions about the size of firm may indeed be misplaced. Both the underutilized resources approach (Penrose, 1959) and the internationalization approach (Buckley and Casson, 1976; 1985) suggest that the size of firm is merely a point of time view of a dynamic process of growth and that it is the growth process which is critical. The export literature has seen the foreign expansion of firms as part of a generalized view of deepening international commitment, with foreign direct investment as a final stage in an evolutionary process beginning with the 'pre export phase'. A specific hypothesis on foreign investment behaviour in the early post war period, the 'Gambler's Earnings Hypothesis' may be relevant to the explanation of the foreign operations of smaller firms. The corporate decision making approach exemplified by Yair Aharoni's *The Foreign Investment Decision Process* (1966) also represents a contribution to our understanding of decision making in first time foreign investors. Finally, the international business approach has been to attempt to define successful foreign operation and to relate this outcome to the subdecisions going into the investment decision. The following sections investigate these approaches in more detail.

2.1. The economics of the firm's growth

The economic theory of the multinational enterprise, drawing on industrial economics, international economics, the theory of finance and the economics of location has integrated and expanded concepts relevant to the growth of the firm (Buckley and Casson, 1976; 1985). Many of these concepts are relevant to the international expansion of smaller firms. (For a review of these concepts see Casson, 1983; and Buckley, 1983a,b.)

The role of management is central in this process. The function of management is to adjust to change. The faster the rate of change, the higher the demand for management. Foreign direct investment is (or should be) a management intensive activity because of the risks involved in the move and because of the necessity to collect and, crucially, to channel information in order to support effective decisions. Smaller firms are constrained by a shortage of management time and consequently frequently take short cuts in decision making and information gathering which can be disastrous. However, the exercise of entrepreneurial ability is often difficult to rationalize from an observer's viewpoint. Individual managers endowed with foresight, flair, imagination (or luck) may be able to cut through the planning process and achieve success.

The availability of managerial skills and their successful absorption may be important constraints on the growth of the firm (Penrose, 1959). Further constraints arise from technological and contractual factors. The optimum scale of a production plant is a constraint on operations in an individual location, not on the size of firm because optimum scale plants can be replicated at different locations (Scherer et al, 1975). The true constraints are co-ordination (via management) and contractual. The minimization of transactions costs are a major explanation of firm size. The difficulties of diversification and expansion out of a given sector and product are well known (Teece, 1983), as are barriers to entry to new areas of growth (Bain, 1956). Smaller firms are vulnerable to product, market and technological changes because they are not diversified and are often one product, one market companies. Thus, although the state of technology may not be a constraint on firm size, changes in technology may curtail or reverse the growth of individual firms.

Organizational issues are also important in the growth of the firm. A balance must be achieved between hierarchical control and co-operation which suits the unique situation of the firm (Casson, 1983). This problem is highlighted, for example, by the difficult choice of chief executive of the newly created foreign subsidiary. This is bound up with the issues of exercising adequate control at a distance. Our findings (Buckley et al, 1988) were that a British chief executive was chosen where hierarchical control was envisaged and a local national where a co-operative mode of operation was sought. Such a simplistic device did not, in many cases, succeed, but it illustrates a response to the organizational/ management style problem which becomes more acute in international operations.

The availability of finance is often adduced to be a constraint on the expansion of small firms. Where external finance is not available, funds for expansion are limited to the profits generated by past investment. Beyond this, small firms must win the confidence of the market for funds. This confidence can be won by technological achievement, attempts at proof of future success, recruiting individuals who have the confidence of the market or astute political lobbying. In most cases financial constraints are secondary to managerial constraints. However the lack of funds for future investment in new products and processes (and for recruitment of managerial talent) is a constraint at particular points of time. As such, in a dynamic environment, they can be fatal by preventing the reduction of the vulnerability which besets smaller firms. A further corollary of lack of funds is that attempts to minimize outlays, e.g. on the acquisition of information, on salaries for key individuals and on product adaptation can be disastrous.

2.2. The evolutionary approach: internationalization

The export literature has seen exporting as an innovative strategy and as a first step in internationalizing, possibly a step which ends in failure. Thus exporting can be seen as launching a process of deepening international commitment, possibly leading to direct investment (for a full review of the literature, see Buckley, 1982).

This evolutionary approach is, to a degree, embodied in Figure 1. All but 7 of the 43 firms in the sample used by Buckley et al (1988) had exported prior to making their first direct investment in a particular country. This deepening investment, and the success which goes with having a number of intermediate states (exports, agency, sales subsidiary) before a production subsidiary is capable of two explanations. The first is that each stage allows a learning process to take place. The second explanation is that the unsuccessful firm can drop out at any one of the intermediate states and thus never appears as a direct investor. In other words, looking back in time from a position where a direct investment is established, 'failures' are weeded out (Buckley et al, 1988.)

The internationalization approach has identified crucial interactions between internal and external pressures in the firm's development and, in particular, has highlighted the crucial role of management activity and awareness. All forms of international activity are

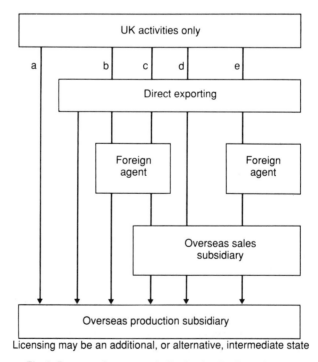

Licensing may be an additional, or alternative, intermediate state

Fig. 1. Routes to Investment in Production Facilities Overseas.

management intensive, foreign investment particularly so. Information gathering, a crucial part of the feedback process, is particularly time intensive. The 1978 study shows the heavy costs of information gathering for a small firm with severe constraints on management time (Buckley et al, 1988).

Information also plays a crucial role in reducing risk. One way of minimizing the risks arising from foreignness is to invest in a country as similar as possible to the home country. This suggests an expansion strategy based on 'psychic distance', investing in psychically 'nearby' countries first. The results of our study show that, often, psychic distance and physical distance are inversely correlated. It is unwise, however, to underestimate psychic distance between two ostensibly 'close' countries, as the 1978 study by Buckley et al (1988) and those of British investment in Australia show (Buckley and Mathew, 1979, 1980; Mathew, 1979).

The switch from exporting to direct investment is a crucial decision. Models of the switch, based on the different costs involved in these methods of market servicing, have been put forward by Vernon (1966) and Hirsh (1976). The more complex model of Buckley and Casson (1981) specifies the optimal timing of the switch by reference to the costs of servicing the market, demand conditions in the market and host market growth. This decision emerges as highly complex and in a highly uncertain world, its correct execution demands a great deal of management judgment.

Alternative modes of technology transfer can be incorporated into this model by considering licensing as an alternative intermediate stage. This should not imply that licensing is merely a step towards a direct investment in all cases—it can be a viable, permanent and optimal choice under certain circumstances (Buckley and Davies, 1981).

2.3. The 'gambler's earnings' hypothesis

The 'gambler's earnings' hypothesis was put forward in the mid-1950s to explain an empirical phenomenon associated with foreign direct investment. This phenomenon was the large ploughback of profits in foreign owned subsidiaries (notably in General Motors' Holden subsidiary in Australia). Consequently multinational firms were likened to gamblers who, beginning the game with a small stake (the initial investment, usually small) continually ploughed back their 'winnings' (profits) into the game until a real 'killing' was made. In foreign investment this meant that when a dividend repayment was eventually made to the parent firm, it was large in relation to the initial investment (Barlow and Wender, 1955; Penrose, 1956). Such behaviour poses adjustment problems for the host country because a large repayment can disrupt its balance of payments stability.

Underlying this behaviour are three features of interest. First, the subsidiary is assumed to be very largely independent of the parent. This may be because of distance (both physical and psychic), because of the need for local judgment or because of the lack of firm-wide policy co-ordination. Second, the differences in setting up a foreign rather than a domestic subsidiary are relevant. The rate of return on a foreign subsidiary needs to be higher in order to compensate for the greater risks. Moreover, foreign investment is often in the nature of an exploratory strategy in order to see if further foreign investment is desirable. Therefore, the risk averse firm is likely, initially at least to underinvest and to begin with a small stake. The small initial investment thus economizes on the costs of investigation and organization. Third, the process has a dynamic of its own. When the firm has a (small) successful foreign subsidiary, uncertainty is lower and the costs of search for further profit approximate to zero. The argument thus is that rather than scanning the world for further, possibly more profitable, opportunities, the firm will re-invest in its safe bet—the existing subsidiary. Thus, the investor will keep reinvesting long after this is justified by relative rates of return from other (unconsidered) alternatives. In other words, foreign investors are hypothesized to exhibit a bias in the allocation of investment funds toward existing, profitable subsidiaries. The 'gambler's earnings' hypothesis is no longer a valid explanation of the behaviour of large, diversified multinational firms used to monitoring worldwide opportunities, managerially integrated and often highly centralized. However, the hypothesis may hold for small firms where the costs of information and co-ordination are high. For first-time foreign investors in particular, the costs of decision making may make such behaviour optimal. However, in the longer run, 'gambler's earnings' behaviour results in missed opportuntities, declining overall rates of return and lost gains from internationalization. It may be a phase in the development of an international strategy before full international co-ordination is justified, but for the successful firm it must not be more than this.

2.4. The corporate decision making approach

The corporate decision making approach sees foreign direct investment (by small firms) as a managerial process. It is exemplified by Yair Aharoni's *The Foreign Investment Decision Process* (1966). In this approach, competition is insufficiently perfect to prevent there existing an area in which managers can exercise discretion and pursue their objective function. Consequently, the objectives of managers, which may involve the search for an easy life, or concern for the share price, or managerial rewards, can be sought. Also included in the approach are the costs of information, the limited decision horizons of managers, conflicts within the firm and uncertainty of outcomes.

Aharoni's study based on a survey of US investors and non-investors in Israel suggests a five stage process as typical of the foreign investment decision. It is a basic finding of Aharoni's work that a strong 'initiating force' (Stage I) is necessary to propel an inert non-investor along the path towards a foreign direct investment. Such pressure may come from within the firm, an executive with an interest in such an investment perhaps, or from the environment, e.g. an outside proposal from a powerful source such as a client, distributor or government agency. Aharoni suggests that the existence of a profitable opportunity is not a sufficient stimulus, and the venture must have extra appeal. Given a sufficiently strong initiating force, Stage II is the investigation process. This is the beginning of the firm's search process. It is a biased search, however, carried out in a sequential way with built-in check points. If at one of these checks, a negative answer is found, the rest of the work is abandoned. Thus, the order of search is of crucial importance. The inexperienced foreign investor needs to know many factors in addition to those involved in its dramatic investment decisions. The phases of the search are: (1) general indicators, to establish the degree of risk, (2) on the spot indicators, and (3) presentation of a report. Before Stage III 'the decision to invest' is reached, a process of building commitments in the firm takes place. The very fact of investigation is sufficient to create a commitment amongst the investigators, whence such a commitment diffuses throughout the decision makers. In Stage IV 'reviews and negotiations' a bargaining situation occurs where powerful groups within the firm impose their wishes and attempts to reduce uncertainty (and outlay) are made.

The first few stages of Aharoni's model then represent a description of short-run decision making under uncertainty. The fifth stage 'changes through repetition' adds a longer run element. In this stage, the firm changes organizationally so as to bring its foreign operation(s) within central control via, Aharoni suggests, an international division. The attitude to risk and uncertainty of foreign ventures alters radically, for the firm now finds them intrinsically little more risky than domestic ventures and the firm thus progresses to full international status.

2.5. The international business approach: defining 'success'

In discussing the foreign investment behaviour of smaller firms it is difficult to avoid normative statements. The observer is tempted to discuss 'what ought to be done' rather than the decisions which have been made. It was to avoid this difficulty that the methodology of the Bradford study was designed (Buckley et al, 1988). Briefly, the methodology is as follows. First, an attempt is made to define success. This is done by a 'success index' made up of measures of profitability, growth, managerial perception of success, synergy and an appraisal of the investment as a step towards full internationalization. Second, each investment is then rated on a five point scale or 'success index'. Third, each subdecision is then evaluated on the basis of the outcome in terms of average success of those investments making that subdecision. On this basis, a best practice set of decisions can be defined. Fourth, the findings of the success index are tested against external factors which may have influenced the outcome. For instance, longevity of investment may positively influence the success rating. Indeed Lupo et al (1978) showed that profitability of US multinationals in 1966 was strongly related to the ages of the subsidiary after controlling for the industry and country where the subsidiary was located. To eliminate such possibilities, the success rating is tested on these external factors which are shown not to be decisive. In view of this, the success index outcome is deemed to depend on managerial decision making. A variant of this model is also used in the companion volume (Buckley et al, 1983) to evaluate the direct investments of smaller European firms into the UK.

A similar approach is used by Sikander Khan (1978) to evaluate export ventures. In classifying firms' export ventures, he uses (1) objective criteria; profit and sales penetration, (2) semi-objective criteria; the degree to which expectations are met compared to the actual outcome with respect to costs, export volume and profitability, (3) subjective criteria; the firms' assessment of the degree of success and failure concerning individual export markets. No attempt was made to combine or aggregate these criteria and Khan notes (p. 220) that the objective and subjective evaluations were not significantly different.

3. SPECIAL ISSUES RAISED BY SMALL FIRM FOREIGN INVESTORS

A crucial issue arising from the above discussion is the extent to which small firms are at all different in their foreign investment behaviour. There are several key areas in which small firms are different and these raise a set of important conceptual and strategic issues.

In comparison with larger firms, two critical shortages may affect smaller firms: capital and management time (Buckley, 1979). The lack of pull in the capital market may lead to less than optimal arrangements. Decisions taken in order to minimize capital outlay sometimes have negative consequences. One example is entering into joint venture arrangements where they bring in finance but subsequently prove to be a serious liability. In raising capital, the small firm faces a 'Catch 22': how to raise finance without disclosing its competitive advantage secrets. Capital rationing can thus adversely affect small firms who therefore rely greatly on internally generated finance.

The shortage of skilled management in smaller firms is often a more serious liability. Small firms do not often have specialist executives to manage their international operations, nor do they possess a hierarchy of managers through which complex decisions can be sifted. Decision making is much more likely to be personalized involving *ad hoc*, short term reckoning based on individual perceptions and prejudice. Shortage of management time leads to firm taking short cuts without proper evaluation of alternatives. Linked to management shortage are the problems of information costs, which (like any fixed costs) bear heavily on small firms. Attempts to avoid these costs, for instance by making no attempt to appraise a potential joint venture partner, can be disastrous. The horizons of small firms are limited by managerial capacity and there is little 'global scanning' for opportunities. Therefore, when an opportunity appears, it is often taken without proper evaluation. Given this problem, why does the firm not recruit management from outside the firm? An important point here is the crucial phase of growth from a family firm to a wider management controlled organization (Casson, 1982). One issue is the desire to retain (family) control; the other is the difficulty in obtaining specialist knowledge of how to evaluate outsiders. Lack of these crucial skills constrains recruitment and makes endemic the burden on management. Consequently, small firms with inexperienced managers have an inevitable degree of naïvety. They are politically naïve because they lack the public relations skills, lobbying power and sheer economic muscle of larger firms. In the international sphere they lack knowledge of the local environment, the legal, social and political aspects of operating abroad.

Small firms face a high degree of risk in going international. It is likely that the proportion of resources committed to a single foreign direct investment will be greater in a small firm than a large one. Failure is more costly. It is arguable that owner-managers are greater risk takers than other types of decision makers.

The financial strategy of small firms also requires explanation. It is clear that the 'Gambler's Earnings Hypothesis' shows up an important empirical phenomenon. An explanation is given by analogy with ploughing and harvesting. A period of ploughing may be set by the firm (say 5 or 7 years). In this time it is given a great deal of leeway. After that, it either generates a stream of income for the next project (the next ploughing) or it is sold off to obtain a return. The short horizon arises because of restricted capital and management time. Thus a target rate of return and payback period are discovered by trial and error.

It is important to distinguish two types of relationship between firm size and market size. In the first case we can envisage a small firm attempting to grow in a 'big-firm' industry, i.e. an industry where optimal scale is large in relation to market size. Secondly, there are many industries with few economies of scale where many small firms exist. Industries requiring a wide range of specialist intermediate inputs, in particular, present a situation of a small firm in equilibrium with a small market. In such a situation, foreign direct investment can enable a small firm to service optimally a growing market (Buckley and Casson, 1981). This role of small firms to fill a market niche is a major advantage and has been noted for Third World multinationals who are seen as versatile users of flexible equipment (Wells, 1983). There is an argument that disinternalization brought about by the need to decentralize in large companies and by the need for specialized services such as consultancies and oil industry services, makes this role loom larger on the world scale. However, in the first case, it is difficult for a small firm to grow in competition with large firms. In such situations, the vulnerability of small firms and the danger of becoming overstretched often lead to bankruptcy or selling out.

3.1. Synthesis

Several key points emerge from the theoretical literature. First is the importance of the relationship between firm and market. This is reflected in the crucial balance between firms size and market size. The growth of the firm by internalization of markets is a key to understanding the velocity and direction of the growth of small- and medium-sized firms. The importance of market niches is also of great potential in explaining the industrial distribution and pattern of the foreign activities of SMEs.

Second, the importance of constraints on the international activities of SMEs emerges from the literature. Both internal and external constraints can be seen to influence growth patterns. Internal constraints are shortages of capital and management and informational constraints. The acquisition of greater resources is impeded by the necessity to retain (family) control and institutional difficulties of borrowing and raising finance (capitalizing knowledge). External constraints arise from the market, from the dangers of takeover and from institutional restraints, both governmental and non-governmental.

Third, the role of uncertainty looms large in the decision making of SMEs. Partly, this can be offset by information acquisition, but this is costly and interacts with management shortages. Taking short cuts and inadequate evaluation of alternatives often result.

Fourth, the alternative forms of technology transfer must be evaluated. Licensing and other 'new forms' (Buckley, 1983b; also Chapter 3 in Buckley and Casson, 1985; Buckley and Davies, 1981; Oman, 1984) of industrial co-operation must be considered as alternatives to foreign direct investment. It is notable that technology transfer by SMEs via licensing was also significant (White, 1983, pp. 272–273; and White and Campos, 1986, where of 32 cases of technology transfer to Argentina and Brazil, 14 were arms length technology agreements and 8 were minority foreign joint ventures, p. 82). Indeed, it has recently been hypothesized that smaller firms are likely to become important users of 'new forms of international co-operation' such as licensing, joint ventures, turnkey operations and production sharing (Oman, 1984). Whilst such operations economize on capital outlay, they tend to be management-intensive and this may choke off the ability of small firms to enter into the more complex forms of such arrangements (Buckley, 1983). Licensing and joint ventures remain viable options, although the 1978 study (Buckley et al, 1988) shows that the tolerance of small firms to joint venture arrangements can be low and that such arrangements can adversely affect success.

Fifth, the vulnerability of SMEs to technological, political, institutional and market changes must be stressed. Against this the flexibility of SMEs is often an important competitive advantage.

Sixth, the motives for foreign investment follow several patterns. (1) SMEs may be 'pulled' into foreign markets by larger firms, by government, e.g. tariff imposition, or other powerful influences. (2) They may be 'pushed' abroad by domestic conditions, e.g. a declining home market or avoidance of (foreign exchange) restrictions. (3) They may follow the classic motives of foreign direct investment—raw material or input control, market oriented or cost oriented. These forms of investment require very different types of analysis. Previous studies have shown that there are differences in predominant motives related to the nationality of SMEs. Ozawa (1985) found that many Japanese SMEs were investing in LDCs as offshore production platforms in order to export back to Japan whilst most Western European SMEs invest abroad in order to secure market access (Onida et al, 1985, for Italy; Buckley et al, 1988, for UK; Berger and Uhlman, 1984, for Germany; and Bertin, 1986, for France). See White and Campos (1986) for further elucidation. (4) SMEs are susceptible to 'spurious' investment based on inadequate evaluations of alternatives, over zealous actions in following up an approach from an external body or misinformation. (5) SMEs may invest abroad as a result of entrepreneurial foresight, which may or may not be rewarded.

Seventh, we should note that the large multinationals often have highly sector-specific expansion routes. This leaves market niches or 'interstices' for SMEs to exploit. It is in these 'small firm industries', not characterized by economies of scale where we should look for successful SMEs (see White and Campos, 1986).

Eighth, the international structure of industries should be examined. As well as industries populated by small firms, we can often observe a 'fringe' of small firms in 'large firm industries'. This pattern should be investigated. Is it an historical legacy or a reaction to efficiency and optimum locational criteria?

The growth of the industry, too, is relevant. A cycle can be envisaged where in the early stages lots of small firms vie for position. As the industry matures, economies of scale become prevalent and dominance of the few ensues in an oligopolistic structure. Over time fragmentation takes place as new entry erodes the existing competitor's dominance. The role of SMEs over the life cycle of the industry needs to be examined.

Ninth, the location strategy of SMEs and multinationals is of great importance in determining the pattern of activity by both groups of foreign investors. Specifically, several forces are at work. (1) There are increasing returns to scale in many activities and this will affect location strategy and bias these activities towards large firm dominance. (2) The performance of many non-routine activities, such as research and development and marketing by modern firms, means that such activities will exercise a locational 'pull' on production. The inputs to these activities and the scale economies in their performance may dictate centralization within the firm. (3) Many (multinational) firms operate in imperfect markets and cannot be considered as price takers. Consequently, large firms can often force down input or factor prices and will concentrate their activities in countries or regions intensive in these inputs. Such distortions will have important effects on the opportunities for SMEs to compete with or supply such monopolistic multinationals. (4) Avoidance of government intervention at home or in the host country will affect location. Biases towards low interference countries and to the use of transfer pricing will distort location of both SMEs and multinationals away from what would be, in the absence of government interference, least cost location. (5) Communications costs within the firm dictate the centralization of high communication intensive activities and the decentralization of routine, low communication cost activities. These influences on location must be evaluated for SMEs as there is a differential impact on the activities of integrated multinationals and more loosely organized SMEs.

4. THE NATURE OF FOREIGN DIRECT INVESTMENT BY SMALL AND MEDIUM-SIZED ENTERPRISES

There are a number of suggestions in the literature as to the important factors in the existence of SMEs as direct investors. The range of industries and nature of production have been characterized in a number of studies.

Foreign investment by SMEs covers a wide range of industries. White (1983) characterizes the operations as 'highly specialized', covering one or two product lines, with short production runs, often serving the 'contractual markets' given by other industries (p. 274). Typical industries include metal working, capital goods production, textiles and clothing, food, furniture, ceramic products and non-metallic products. These industries are well represented in the sample of UK outward investors which have been studied in detail (Buckley et al, 1988).

UK smaller outward investors are largely engaged in the production of intermediate and component products and services for other firms. Thirty-six of the 43 investors studied made producer goods or services; only four were entirely engaged in consumer good production and four firms made both producer and consumer goods. A large proportion was engaged in the engineering and metal goods sectors (SIC orders VI, VII, VIII, IX, XI, XII)—fully 31 out of 43 (Buckley et al, 1988, Table 2.2, p. 9).

Medium sized firms investing in the UK were also concentrated in these sectors (SIC VI, VII, VIII, IX, XI, XII) which accounted for 21 out of 35 production subsidiaries. Textiles also was well represented with 5 production subsidiaries. Again producer goods were dominant—27 production subsidiaries made only producer goods; 2 made both, and only 6 were consumer goods specialists (Buckley et al, 1983).

Smaller Japanese foreign investors cover a variety of labour intensive light manufacturing such as light metal articles, furniture, bags, footwear, apparel, toys, plastic products, etc. It is expected that the 1980s will see many more smaller firm foreign investors in electrical machinery, non-electrical machinery and transport equipment as smaller suppliers and subcontractors follow large enterprises abroad (UNCTAD, 1984).

Foreign direct investors from less developed countries (many of them SMEs) were largely small scale manufacturers, with high adaptability to local conditions (including input availability) and flexible users of capital equipment. Local procurement, small scale manufacturing, special products and access to markets were picked out as competitive advantages of 'Third World multinationals' (Wells, 1984). The existence of cross-national ethnic ties (e.g. overseas Chinese, expatriate Indian communities) should not be ignored.

These findings provide empirical support for the conjectures above supporting the hypothesis that balanced growth in 'small firm industries' is conducive to success.

4.1. The scale of UK SME foreign investment

In the case of United Kingdom foreign investors, according to the latest survey conducted for 1981, an estimated 1500 enterprises had 9100 foreign affiliates. Two thirds of these foreign investors (i.e. 1000 firms) with net foreign assets less than £2 million accounted for 0.8% of the total net book value of UK foreign direct investment at the end of 1981 (British Business, 2 March 1984) (see Figure 2). This is in sharp contrast to the 34 enterprises with net assets over £200 million and 1550 overseas affiliates which account for 55% of the total stock of British foreign investment.

When foreign investment in the UK is examined, it is found that about 3000 foreign countries had UK affiliates, three quarters (2150) of these had UK affiliates with a book value of less than £2 million, accounting in total for 2.4% of inward direct foreign investment in the UK (excluding oil, banking and insurance) (see Figure 3). In contrast, 21 foreign countries had assets valued at over £150 million in the UK, and account for one third of the total (British Business, 2 March 1984). Inward investment was less concentrated than outward: the 100 largest inward investors account for 60% of total direct investment; the 100 largest outward investors account for 80% (again excluding oil, banking and insurance).

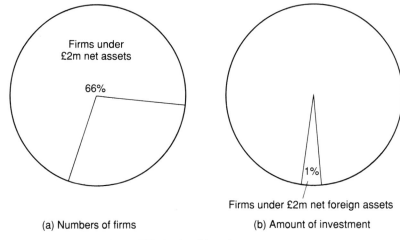

(a) Numbers of firms   (b) Amount of investment

Fig. 2. UK Foreign Direct Investment.

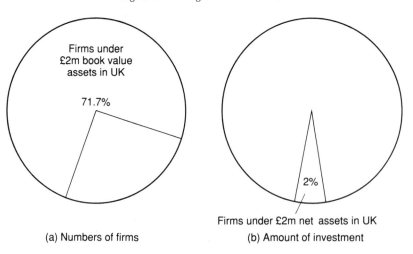

(a) Numbers of firms   (b) Amount of investment

Fig. 3. Inward Investment into UK.

4.2. The direction of UK foreign investment by SMEs

The study by Buckley et al (1988) examined first time foreign direct investors. None of these investments was in a middle income or developing country. However, the 52 firms (43 with foreign production subsidiaries and 9 with foreign sales subsidiaries) made a total of 39 further foreign investments—33 production and 6 sales subsidiaries. Six production subsidiaries and two sales subsidiaries were in middle income and developing countries as Table 2 shows. This study also shows two marked shifts in overall UK foreign direct investment—one away from the old Empire and Commonwealth towards the countries of the European Communities dating from the late 1960s to late 1970s succeeded by a wave of investment to the USA. It appears, from very partial evidence that SMEs followed these general trends.

Table 2. Later foreign production and sales subsidiaries of the 52 UK smaller firms*

Location	Foreign production subsidiaries	Foreign sales subsidiaries
Developed countries		
South Africa	5	1
Australia	4	—
Netherlands	4	—
France	3	1
USA	3	—
Canada	2	2
New Zealand	2	—
Ireland	2	—
Belgium	1	—
Norway	1	—
	27	4
Middle income and developing countries		
Mexico	1	1
India	1	—
Nigeria	1	—
Malta	1	—
Spain	1	—
Portugal	1	—
Bahamas	—	1
	6	2
Totals	33	6

*43 with foreign production subsidiaries, 9 with foreign sales subsidiaries.
Source: Derived from the research reported by Buckley, Newbould and Thurwell (1988).

5. CONCLUSION

The problems facing SMEs in foreign direct investment are most acute for first time investors. Risks are perceived to be great and the firm has no international experience on which to draw. Many firms in the 1978 study had unsuccessful first foreign ventures but went on to undertake later successful foreign investments. Learning from mistakes is a vital part of business progress. However, the dice are stacked by the type of industry and environment faced by the firm. SMEs have a natural constituency in industries characterized by insignificant economies of scale and specialized demand. In such industries there is no 'critical minimum scale' at which a firm can be expected to succeed in foreign direct investment. Attempts to move into areas of great potential demand where economies of scale are prevalent are fraught with danger and emphasize the vulnerability rather than the sensitivity of small firms.

The author would like to thank Mark Casson, Hafiz Mirza, Nick Wilson and Roger Brooksbank for constructive comments on an earlier draft.

University of Bradford Management Centre

REFERENCES

Aharoni, Y., 1966, *The Foreign Investment Decision Process*, (Boston, Mass: Graduate School of Business Administration, Harvard University).

Bain, J. S., 1956, *Barriers to New Competition*, (Cambridge, Mass: Harvard University Press).

Barlow, E. R. and Wender, I. T., 1955, *Foreign Investment and Taxation*, Englewood Cliffs, NJ: Prentice-Hall).

Berger, M. and Uhlman, L. 1984, *Auslandsinvestitionen kleiner und mittlerer Unternehmen*, IFO Schnelldienst 30/84 (Munich: IFO Institute).

Bertin, G. Y. (1986). Le Transfert de Technologie aux Pays en Developpement par les Petites et Moyennes Enterprises Françaises, Paris: Mimeo.

Buckley, P. J. (1979). 'Foreign Investment Success for Smaller Firms', *Multinational Business* 3, 12–19.

Buckley, P. J. (1982). 'The Role of Exporting in the Market Servicing Policies of Multinational Manufacturing Enterprises: Theoretical and Empirical Perspectives', in M. R. Czinkota and G. Tesar (eds.), *Export Management: An International Context* (New York: Praeger).

Buckley, P. J. (1983a). 'A Critical View of Theories of the Multinational Enterprise', *Aussenwirtschaft* **36**, 70–87. Revised version in Buckley and Casson (1985) *op. cit.*

Buckley, P. J., (1983b). 'New Theories of International Business: Some Unresolved Issues', in Mark Casson (ed.) *The Growth of International Business*, (London: George Allen & Unwin).

Buckley, P. J., Berkova, K. and Newbould, G. D. (1983). *Direct Investment in the UK by Smaller European Firms* (London: Macmillan and New York: Crane Russak).

Buckley, P. J. and Casson, M. (1976). *The Future of the Multinational Enterprise* (London: Macmillan and New York: Holmes-Meier).

Buckley, P. J. and Casson, M. (1981). 'The Optimal Timing of a Foreign Direct Investment', *Economic Journal* **91**, 75–87.

Buckley, P. J. and Casson, M. (1985). *The Economic Theory of the Multinational Enterprise: Selected Papers* (London: Macmillan).

Buckley, P. J. and Davies, H. (1981). 'Foreign Licensing in Overseas Operations: Theory and Evidence from the UK', in A. G. Hawkins and A. J. Prasad (eds.), *Research in International Business and Finance*, Vol. 2 (New York: JAI Press).

Buckley, P. J. and Mathew, A. M. (1979). 'The Motivation for Recent First Time Direct Investment in Australia by UK Firms', *Management International Review* **19**(1), 57–69.

Buckley, P. J. and Mathew, A. M. (1980). 'Dimensions of the Market Entry Behaviour of Recent UK First Time Direct Investors in Australia', *Management International Review* **20**(2), 35–51.

Buckley, P. J., Newbould, G. D., and Thurwell, J. (1988). *Foreign Direct Investment by Smaller UK Firms*, Macmillan, London. Previously published as Newbould, G. D., Buckley, P. J., and

Thurwell, J., 1978, *Going International—The Experience of Smaller Companies Overseas* (London: Associated Business Press; New York: Halsted Press).

Casson, M. (1982). *The Entrepreneur: An Economic Theory* (Oxford: Martin Robertson).

Casson, M. (1983). 'Introduction: The Conceptual Framework', in M. Casson (ed.), *The Growth of International Business* (London: George Allen & Unwin).

Cavanagh, D. K. and Clifford, R. E. (1983). *The Winning Performance of the Midsized Growth Companies* (New York: McKinsey & Co Inc).

Fierheller, G. A. (1980). Jan/Feb, 'Planning in the Medium Sized Company', *Managerial Planning*, pp. 258–270.

Hirsch, S. (1976). 'An International Trade and Investment Theory of the Firm', *Oxford Economic Papers* **28**, 258–70.

Khan, S. M. (1978). *A Study of Success and Failure in Exporting* (Stockholm: Akademilitteratur).

Lupo, L. A., Gilbert, A., and Liliestedt, M. (1978). 'The Relationship between Age and Rate of Return of Foreign Manufacturing Affiliates of US Manufacturing Parent Companies', *Survey of Current Business* **58**, 60–6.

Mathew, A. M. (1979). 'Recent Direct Investment in Australia by First Time UK Investors', Unpublished PhD thesis, University of Bradford Management Centre.

Oman, C. (1984). *New Forms of International Investment in Developing Countries* (Paris: OECD).

Onida, F., Balcet, G. et al. (1985). *Technology Transfer to Developing Countries by Italian Small- and Medium-Sized Enterprises* (Geneva: UNCTAD).

Ozawa, T. (1985). *International Transfer of Technology by Japan's Small and Medium Enterprises in Developing Countries* (Geneva: UNCTAD).

Penrose, E. T. (1956). 'Foreign Investment and the Growth of the Firm', *Economic Journal* **66**, 230–5.

Penrose, E. T. (1959). *The Theory of the Growth of the Firm* (Oxford: Basil Blackwell).

Savary, J. (1984). *French Multinationals* (London: Frances Pinter/IRM).

Scherer, F. M. et al. (1975). *The Economics of Multi-Plant Operation—An International Comparisons Study* (Cambridge, Mass: Harvard University Press).

Teece, D. J. (1983). 'Technological and Organisational Factors in the Theory of the Multinational Enterprise', in M. Casson (ed.), *The Growth of International Business* (London: George Allen & Unwin).

UNCTAD, (1984). International transfer of technology to developing countries by small and medium sized enterprises (Geneva: Report by UNCTAD Secretariat TD/B/C 6/119).

Van Hoorn, T. P. (1979). 'Strategic Planning to Small and Medium-Sized Companies', *Long Range Planning* **12** (April), 84–91.

Vernon, R. (1966). 'International Investment and International Trade in the Product Cycle', *Quarterly Journal of Economics* **80**, 190–207.

Wells, L. T. (1983). *Third World Multinationals: The Rise of Foreign Investment from Developing Countries* (Cambridge, Mass: MIT Press).

White, E. (1983). 'The Role of Third World Multinationals and Small and Medium Sized Companies in the Industrialization Strategies of Developing Countries', in *Industrial Development Strategies and Policies for Developing Countries* (Vienna: United Nations Industrial Development Organisation).

White, E. and Campos, J. (1986). *Alternative Technology Sources for Developing Countries: The Role of Small and Medium Sized Enterprises from Industrialized Countries* (Buenos Aires: Cederi Estudios).

8

Are Entry Strategies for Foreign Markets Changing? The Case of Swedish Investment in Japan

Gunnar Hedlund and Adne Kverneland

1. INTRODUCTION

A basic conclusion or assumption in many studies of foreign market entry strategies has been that lack of knowledge and experience is critical to the development of international operations, and that such knowledge is acquired mainly through actual operations abroad (Behrman, 1969; Johanson and Wiedersheim-Paul, 1975; Johanson and Vahlne, 1977; Newbould, Buckley and Thurwell, 1978; Davidson, 1980). The internationalization of the firm in these studies has been regarded as a process where the firm gradually increases its international involvement. Johanson and Vahlne, for example, confirmed what had been reported before: 'Sales subsidiaries are preceded in virtually all cases by selling via agent; similarly, local production is generally preceded by sales subsidiaries.' Newbould, Buckley and Thurwell also found that companies which followed this pattern of development were more satisfied with their performance. There has been a general acceptance of this framework, and we have not noticed any study questioning the concept of gradually increasing involvement on a foreign market. (At least not for greenfield establishments. Acquisitions change the picture somewhat.)

In our view, the concept needs to be critically scrutinized on two accounts. First, the empirical support is weak due to methodological limitations of previous studies. Second, some of the assumptions lending theoretical support to the theory can be questioned, particularly in the light of changes in the international business environment and in companies' ability to manage international operations.

The purposes of this paper are to describe Swedish companies' entry and growth strategies in Japan, to establish to what extent the pattern is consistent with the 'gradual learning' theory, to assess whether gradual entry is associated with high performance or not, and to discuss the effects of some possible determinants of company strategies in this respect. In particular, the influence of a corporation's degree of international experience is discussed.

2. PREVIOUS STUDIES OF ENTRY STRATEGIES ON FOREIGN MARKETS

It has been generally agreed that the pattern and pace of the firm's internationalization process are consequences of a series of incremental decisions. Caves, in his study from 1971, argues that a company exports to test the market and later engages in production 'for better adaption of the product to the local market or the superior quality or lower cost of auxiliary service that can be provided'. Some studies regard the increasing involvement and commitment as a consequence of the competitive situation in the home or host market (Vernon, 1966; Gruber, Meta and Vernon, 1967; and Knickerbocker, 1973). Gruber, Meta and Vernon further stress the importance of the size of the market, the technological level of the company, and the ability to organize and maintain a large and complex organization. They argue that, when a company has established a sales subsidiary, the additional costs of engaging in production will be small due to the market knowledge the company has acquired.

Many contributions to the study of foreign direct investment focus on the importance of dissimilarities between national markets as one explanation for the timing of foreign market entry and for the observed, or hypothesized, slow and step-wise entry strategy. Beckerman, in a study from a 1956, argued that trade patterns in Europe indicated that economic and geographic distance between countries strongly influenced the direction of international trade. Burenstam-Linder's (1961) and Vernon's (1966) observations that similarities in market conditions influence the direction of foreign direct investment flows rest in part on similar assumptions.

Several other studies dealing with the forces behind the internationalization of the firm implicitly make similar assumptions. (See for example Hymer, 1960; Kindleberger, 1969; Servan-Schreiber, 1969; Caves, 1971; and Dunning, 1979.) They stress that a foreign company must possess an advantage of some kind to compensate for local competitors' superior ability to deal with local conditions. Studies dealing with multinational companies' organizational development have argued for a more decentralized structure as the company's foreign operations grow, in order to better deal with different environments, thus assuming inter-country differences to be critical.

The concept of 'psychic distance' has been the focus of some Swedish studies. Psychic distance is defined as differences in language, level of education, business practice, industrial development and culture. (See Wiedersheim-Paul, F. (1972).) Johanson and Wiedersheim-Paul (1975), in a study of four Swedish multinational companies, looked at the relations between the pattern of establishment and psychic distance. Johanson and Vahlne (1977), in a study of knowledge development and increasing foreign market commitments, developed an internationalization model based on the assumption 'that lack of knowledge due to differences between countries with regard to, for example, language and culture, is an important obstacle to decision-making connected with the development of international operations'.

Thus, in most previous studies of entry strategies, lack of knowledge and resources are either explicitly or implicitly regarded as the most important obstacles to internationalization. The temporal order of successive establishments in new countries is related to the psychic or economic distance between the home and the host country. The pattern and pace are thus consequences of a process of incremental adjustments to changing conditions of the firm and its environment. The decision-process is influenced both by knowledge about international operations in general and specific market knowledge.

The present stage of internationalization is thus regarded as one important factor explaining the course of future internationalization. Perceived opportunities and risks are affected by the stage of internationalization, and in their turn influence decisions and current activities (Johanson and Vahlne). Additional commitments will be made in small steps unless the market conditions are stable and homogeneous, or the firm has much experience from other markets with similar conditions. Johanson and Wiedersheim-Paul expect jumps in the establishment chain (export sales–agent–sales company–manufacturing subsidiary) in firms with extensive experience from other foreign markets. They also argue that the size of the market is important in determining the choice between various establishment forms, and further that the different stages are dependent on the organizational structure of the firm. Johanson and Vahlne stress that market growth will speed up the step-wise increase in scale of operation.

There is a large and growing normative literature concerning choice of foreign market entry strategies. Root (1982) provides a list of factors influencing the entry mode decision. He also subscribes to a 'stage model' of evolution of the strategy. Companies with large international experience are claimed to have greater freedom in the choice of entry mode.

3. CHALLENGES TO GRADUAL COMMITMENT THEORIES

As mentioned above, there are expectations that stability of market conditions, market size, market growth, a company's market experience, international experience in transferring technology and product lines, the present stage of internationalization, a company's resources, and the organizational structure all influence the pace and pattern of internationalization. Several further factors are mentioned by Root (1982). We shall make no attempt to discuss all such factors. Instead, we will focus on a few aspects which modify the conclusions, or assumptions, concerning the effectiveness of a gradual entry strategy.

3.1. International experience

Vernon (1979) discusses multinational enterprises' spread of the geographical network and shows how it has been extended for US firms.

Table 1. Networks of foreign manufacturing subsidiaries of 315 multinational companies in 1950 and 1970

Number of enterprises with networks included	180 US-based MNCs		135 MNCs based in UK and Europe	
	1950	1975	1950	1970
Fewer than 6 countries	138	9	116	31
6 to 20 countries	43	128	16	75
More than 20 countries	0	44	3	29

Source: Harvard Multinational Enterprise Project. From Vernon (1979).

The development also reflects another change. The disposition to move first into the traditional area declined.

> For product lines introduced abroad by the 180 firms before 1946, the probability that a Canadian location would come earlier than an Asian location was 79 per cent, but for product lines that were introduced abroad after 1960, the probability that Canada would take precedence over Asia had dropped to only 54 per cent. (Vernon, 1979, page 258.)

This development is also reflected in the fact that the time between the introduction of any new product in the US and its first production in a foreign location has been rapidly shrinking.

The development concerning the growth of international experience has been similar for Swedish companies. In 1965, 82 Swedish companies had manufacturing subsidiaries abroad, increasing to 118 in 1978 (Swedenborg, 1979).

Of the 82 companies in 1965, 47 companies were still represented in 1978. These companies had 52% of their sales outside Sweden in 1965. This share had increased to 70% in 1978. They also account for a large portion of the growth in the number of foreign subsidiaries. Foreign production's share of total sales for all companies with some foreign production increased from 25% to 39% in the same period. Furthermore, in 1978, 76% of the companies' foreign sales was through foreign subsidiaries.

As hypothesized in Johanson and Wiedersheim-Paul (1975), greater international experience should lead to jumps in the establishment chain. The magnitude of the change in this respect leads us to question the relevance of the 'slow learning approach' for a large and increasing number of firms.

3.2. Organizational structure

As reported in several studies, there has been a general change in organizational form as the multinational companies have extended their foreign networks. (See for example Stopford and Wells, 1972; Franko, 1976; Wicks, 1980.) The 1960s and 1970s saw a trend towards more decentralized organizational structures, which supposedly were more suitable to deal with local conditions in foreign markets and thus decreased the uncertainty related to foreign environments. Egelhoff (1982) found that the more decentralized structures were common in companies with large foreign operations, high level of foreign manufacturing, and a large number of foreign subsidiaries.

Of particular interest is perhaps the emergence of globally divisionalized structures. Such structures enable headquarters to integrate the foreign operations more fully into the overall strategy of the corporation. In fact, global divisions may see wholly owned

Table 2. Comparison of Swedish companies with manufacturing subsidiaries

	1965	1978	Increase
Swedish companies with manufacturing subsidiaries	82	118	43.9%
Manufacturing subsidiaries	468	699	49.4%
Total	832	1864	124%

Source: Swedenborg (1979).

subsidiaries under parent company control as less of a risk than selling through agents or joint ventures. The mother–daughter structure (see Franko, 1976) meant that head-quarters top management has very little time to devote to each subsidiary, which may have contributed to a rather slow, step-wise expansion strategy. The move away from this structure would—everything else being equal—speed it up. (For a discussion of the Swedish case, see Hedlund and Aman, 1983.) We will not, however, analyse this aspect empirically since we do not have data on the evolution of organizational structures for Swedish firms established in Japan.

3.3. Oligopolistic market structures

Oligopolistic reaction to competitors' location decisions (see Knickerbocker, 1973) entails the possibility that companies feel forced to move more rapidly into new markets than caution would dictate. There has been a steady move in the direction of global oligopolies in many areas with significant foreign direct investment. Therefore, one would expect an increased preference for more direct and faster establishment strategies.

3.4. Changes in the environment of international business

During the 1960s and 1970s, economic growth in the industrialized countries in Europe and the industrialization of Asia have narrowed differences in per capita income. Vernon (1979) argues that this has weakened a critical assumption of the product cycle hypothesis; namely, 'that the entrepreneurs of large enterprises confronted markedly different conditions in their respective home markets'. The differences in market conditions and factor costs in Europe, USA and Japan have been declining, and the companies from these countries are facing conditions that are much more similar than they have been in the past. Several studies confirm that there have been striking convergences also on other points. A US study shows that there has been an equalization in, among other things, education level, R&D spendings, and capital intensity in production in the industrialized world. (US Department of Labor, 1980.) A study by Fisher (1977) of technology transfer from foreign subsidiaries acquired in the United States, found that the direction of technology flow was overwhelmingly into the United States. This is not surprising, foreign companies invest abroad to exploit some specific advantages. It confirms, however, what several other studies have found; namely, that non-US companies to an increasing extent have their advantages in areas earlier dominated by US companies. Vernon (1979) argues: 'although the gap between most of the developing countries and the advanced industrialized countries palpably remains, the difference among the advanced industrialized countries are reduced to trivial dimensions'.

These changes reduce the knowledge deficiencies prohibiting rapid entry in large steps into foreign markets. More dramatically, but slightly beyond the scope of the present paper, they imply a new kind of multinational corporation without any genuine 'home country'. Perlmutter's (1965) concept of 'geocentric companies' constituted an early recognition of this tendency. Theories of foreign direct investment are still primarily based on the exploitation of company-specific advantages derived from a home country base. The new developments mean that the theory needs to be modified.

3.5. Methodological limitations of earlier studies

Johanson and Vahlne (1977) investigated four Swedish firms. Therefore, the generality of their conclusions can be questioned. Although their unit of analysis is the foreign establishment rather than the parent company, idiosyncrasies pertaining to the strategies of the four firms may well have influenced the results.

Newbould, Buckley and Thurwell interviewed 43 firms. Their study was explicitly limited to small (below £10 million in annual sales) companies from the UK and their first foreign manufacturing subsidiary. Thus, the relevance for larger firms with greater international experience is limited. Contrary to the results of the Swedish studies, Newbould et al found that 36 out of 43 firms established their first manufacturing subsidiary without first having formed a sales company in the country (Newbould et al, p. 46). This in its turn throws a strange light on their findings concerning the correlation between a long establishment chain and positive performance. Although the authors make no claim of transferability of their results to other situations, their work is sometimes misinterpreted to lend support to more far-reaching conclusions.

Moreover, the small size of the sample and the possible influence of other variables on both performance and entry strategy (for example, country of location of the subsidiary) make causal interpretation problematic even for the sample itself. A particularly difficult methodological problem is that companies are compared as they have gone through alternative 'learning routes', and firms which have left the chain in stages prior to establishing a manufacturing subsidiary are not investigated. In this way, one introduces a bias in the estimation of performance in favour of firms following a long route. It is normal that you find more successes relating to setting up a foreign manufacturing subsidiary among firms who have successfully mastered related forms of international business, than among firms which go directly for a more ambitious form of entry. However, this does not necessarily mean that *all* firms which try the 'slow road' will make it. The study population should ideally be identified at the typically early entry stages rather than at the late ones. Newbould et al chose the latter method since it conformed better to the specific purposes of their study. However, this means that the results concerning the relationship between speed of entry and performance have to be interpreted very carefully.

3.6. Expected changes in the pace and pattern of internationalization

As we have seen, there have been significant changes affecting the assumptions put forward in previous studies of the internationalization process. The industrialized countries have developed more similar market conditions, multinational companies have extended their international networks, and thus gained significant experience from dealing with different market conditions. The companies have also developed organizational structures better capable of dealing with environmental differences. We would therefore expect to find an increasing tendency for these companies to shorten their time of penetration, make more substantial investments and thus increase their commitment in larger steps. This tendency should be particularly evident on large and rapidly growing national markets.

4. EMPIRICAL STUDY OF SWEDISH ESTABLISHMENTS IN JAPAN

Our hypotheses of changes in market entry and growth strategies will be applied to Swedish companies' establishments in Japan. As a part of a larger research project, all Swedish direct investments in Japan have been investigated during 1981 and 1982. A questionnaire was sent out to all Japanese subsidiaries of Swedish firms in late 1981. Most subsidiaries were interviewed, in Japan, in late 1982.

At the beginning of 1982, 51 Swedish companies had made direct investment in 70 subsidiaries in Japan (25% or more Swedish capital). Total sales from these subsidiaries were Y172.610 billion (1981) (US$ 785 million), and total employment was 4545 (1981). For the purposes of this paper, the analysis focuses on 18 companies, together controlling or participating in 32 subsidiaries or joint ventures in Japan. We have excluded companies established in service industries, companies with only a branch office, trading companies, and companies with their headquarters in Japan even if they have Swedish owners. All Swedish companies with manufacturing in Japan are included in the sample. The 18 companies accounted for 62% of total sales from all Swedish affiliates in Japan in 1981.

The companies were interviewed in Japan during 1982. Ten of the companies were also interviewed at their headquarters in Sweden.

Out of 18 companies, 15 were engaged in manufacturing in Japan. In some of the companies the value added in Japan was a small part of the turnover, and some companies had all their manufacturing subcontracted to local Japanese companies.

The majority of the firms belong to mechanical and electric engineering industries (14 out of 18). Companies in pharmaceuticals, pulp and paper, and metallurgy are also represented in the sample. The size of the parent company varies from MSEK 25.781 to MSEK 261 (US$ 3.305 million to 34 million) in annual turnover in 1982. Their Japanese operations range from Y42.500 million to Y840 million in annual turnover (US$ 193 million–3.8 million) in 1981.

The limited size of the sample (and the population!) obviously restricts the possibilities to generalize from the findings and to infer causal relationships. However, since all data refer to investment in Japan, the difficulty of controlling for variation in host country characteristics is avoided. Restricting ourselves to Swedish firms allows comparison with the results of Johanson and Vahlne (1977).

The choice of Japan as a testing ground for our hypotheses has both advantages and disadvantages. The most interesting advantage comes from the fact that the Japanese market has been heavily protected through various measures restricting capital inflow during the period after the second world war. The restrictions were gradually lifted between 1967 and 1973. The market has been legally open for foreign companies since May 1973. This means that we have a kind of controlled experiment situation. Before the end of the 1960s, there was no or very little choice open to foreign investors concerning their entry strategies. Selling through an agent was the dominant and, for most firms, only practical form. After 1973, there was suddenly an opportunity to choose. Therefore, we can analyse the behaviour of firms during a relatively short and recent period of time without having to assess to what extent differences in strategies between firms are due to the historical date of implementation. Thus, we have variation between companies in their degree of international experience and a 'virgin market', in the sense of containing very few subsidiaries, for legal reasons. For most industrialized countries, one would find that the experienced firms had already established subsidiaries a long time ago. Disentangling the influence of historical circumstance, general international experience and specific market experience on the choice of entry mode and speed would be very difficult indeed. Therefore, the experience in Japan is in a way uniquely appropriate in shedding light on our hypotheses of recent changes in company strategies.

We see two main disadvantages with the method. First, we cannot assess the influence of decreasing differences between countries, since we measure at only one point in time. Furthermore, Japan is probably still relatively distant in a psychological sense, and certainly so in a geographic sense. (In a way, this adds significance to any findings about more direct establishment patterns, since psychic distance is supposed to lead to incremental, slow entry strategies.)

Second, the Japanese case can be argued to be 'special'. Although the same can be said for any study restricted to one country or region, we do believe that there are two aspects which make interpretation of our results difficult. The first has to do with the probable existence of country-specific advantages of manufacturing in Japan. Particularly if use is made of the system of small-scale subsuppliers, production costs in Japan are very competitive. Therefore, there is an added incentive to move more quickly to local production.

The second aspect concerns the market structure in Japan. Although much research remains to be done here, it is likely that entry strategies for foreign as well as for indigenous Japanese firms is affected by long-term relationships between suppliers and customers. As already indicated, subcontracting is much used in manufacturing, and the relationships between component supplier and (industrial) buyer is somewhere between arm's-length and dependency.

The same situation seems to apply between sellers of industrial goods and their customers, whether they be middlemen or 'final' customers. These characterisitics of the Japanese economy influence entry strategies, but the direction of the effect is not entirely clear. On the one hand, one would expect foreign firms to try to adapt, for example by trying to get access to the system of low-cost subcontractors. On the other hand, the entry-restricting inertia in strong long-term relationships should hinder too rapid and direct entry. A lot of time should be needed to learn about the market, and learning by small, incremental steps would seem to be a reasonable strategy. (For a discussion of the effects of the market structure on entry strategy, see Hägg and Johanson, 1982; Hammarkvist et al, 1982.)

Japan constitutes a very large market, which has been growing more rapidly than in most industrialized countries. It is politically stable and has a stable and not overvalued currency. In many industries, Japanese firms are world-scale competitors to Western corporations. For all these reasons, one would expect that foreign firms would use the opportunity provided by the liberalization of the early 1970s. However, although the stock of foreign direct investment increased by 300% between 1973 and 1980, it grew by 400% in the United States. Foreign companies' share of total sales in Japan has been stable around 2% during the 1970s. Why this is so is a problem outside the scope of this paper, but it does illustrate the difficulties of penetrating the Japanese market. This is an advantage for the purposes of our analysis, since ineffective strategies are likely to be more rapidly exposed as such.

5. RESULTS

5.1. The first market contact

Exports through a local agent are a common way of opening up a new market. A substantial part of trade to and from Japan is organized through the large Japanese trading houses. This very well-developed system of trading-houses, and the fact that several Swedish trading-houses already before World War II were well established in Japan, made exports through an agent a natural first form of market contact. The Japanese restrictions on capital imports and foreign direct investments, and generally tight control over the development of industry introduced in the 1940s and the beginning of the 1950s, made export, licensing and—for a few foreign companies with unique technology needed in the reconstruction of the Japanese economy—joint ventures with a local partner the only possible market penetration strategies from the 1940s up to around 1973.

Of the 18 Swedish companies, 17 introduced their products on the Japanese market before 1973. All companies did so through an agent. Of the 17 firms, 11 used Swedish trading-houses.

Seven of the companies also licensed one or several of their product lines in the period between the first market contact and their direct investment.

The Japanese market restrictions made it difficult for any new trend in growth strategy to manifest itself in the way the Swedish companies first made contact with the market. This is the main reason for none of the companies to directly establish themselves through foreign direct investment. Any new trend in establishment and growth strategy has to be tested on company behaviour after the restrictions were lifted in 1973.

5.2. Establishment through direct investment

Fourteen of the companies established their subsidiaries in 1973 or later (see Appendices 1 and 2).

A high number of companies have adopted the 'short route' strategy (agent–manufacturing). Eight, or 44%, of the companies were engaged in manufacturing from the first year of foreign direct investment. 53% of the companies with some manufacturing in Japan preferred the 'direct route' strategy. This is a substantially higher share than the one reported in the study by Johanson and Vahlne (1977).

Furthermore, of the 12 companies with manufacturing, established in 1972 or later, eight preferred the 'short route' strategy.

Table 3. Swedish companies' first market contact in Japan (number of firms)

Market contact	−1950	1950–72	1973–81	Total
Swedish agent	8	3		11
Japanese agent	1	5	1	7
Total	9	8	1	18

Table 4. Swedish companies' establishments and growth strategies

Growth strategy	Number of companies	Average number of years with FDI in Japan, 1981
Agent—sales subsidiary	3	8
Agent—sales subsidiary, manufacturing	7	19*
Agent—manufacturing	8	7

*One company established a sales subsidiary already in 1932, one in 1953 and one in 1962.

Table 5. A comparison of establishment and growth strategy (% of firms using various routes)

Strategy	Sales subsidiary		Manufacturing subsidiary	
	n ↓ s	a ↓ s	a ↓ p	s ↓ p
Japan (18 firms)	0	56	53	47
Johanson and Vahlne (1977) (all countries for 4 firms)	9	78	24	76

n = no activity
s = sales subsidiary
a = agent
p = production

The Swedish companies have preferred a more 'short route' strategy in Japan. The Johanson and Vahlne study looked at four Swedish companies' strategies in various markets. We have concentrated on one market, and so investigated a much larger sample. We believe, as also argued by Johanson and Vahlne, that psychic distance and market conditions have substantial explanatory power. The average psychic distance between the countries and Sweden in the Johanson and Vahlne study is lower than between Sweden and Japan. The explanation for the difference in result has thus to be found in the changes in the environment and within the companies which have taken place in the time period covered by the two studies. (Assuming that the samples are comparable in other respects.) The Johanson and Vahlne study looked at market growth strategies from the first stage of internationalization of the companies up to around 1970. Our study looks at market growth strategies in the 1970s. Although our method cannot rigorously isolate the effects of such changes over time from effects of differing samples of firms and host countries, the results do lend some support to our hypotheses about changing patterns of entry and growth strategies.

5.3. Factors influencing the market growth strategy

5.3.1. Knowledge of the Japanese market

We will in this part examine to what extent the companies adopting different strategies also differ in terms of market knowledge at the time of the establishment.

Table 6 shows that the companies going directly from agent to manufacturing to a much higher degree have used Swedish agents. They have also been represented substantially longer on the market. Many companies have also been engaged in licensing to Japan, and two of the companies had branch offices in Japan prior to the establishment of a Japanese subsidiary. (Appendix 3 gives a more detailed description of all companies engaged in production.) Thus, although there are companies going more directly into the market than a classical establishment chain would indicate, they seem to prepare their moves by other mechanisms of learning than setting up a sales subsidiary. The use of Swedish rather than Japanese agents complicates the picture, however. One could argue that the latter would be more consistent with a (modified) learning theory of market entry.

Table 6. The establishment and growth strategy and the manufacturing companies' 'market knowledge' activities (number of companies)

	Nationality of agent		Market knowledge activities		
Strategy	Japanese	Swedish	Licensing prior to FDI	Branch office prior to FDI	Average year of agent relation
a→s→p	4	3	2	0	15
a→p	1	7	5	2	41

a = agent, s = sales subsidiary, p = production

Table 7 shows that the companies adopting a 'short route' strategy use joint ventures and subcontracting to a greater extent. Six out of eight companies are joint ventures, and six out of eight companies have subcontracted most of their production to local Japanese companies. For the companies following the traditional establishment chain, the situation is different. Most of the companies are wholly owned and they have preferred to internalize the production. One interpretation of this difference would support a modified version of the theory of gradual involvement. By co-operating with local partners, the firms which move into the market rapidly compensate for the losses of prior knowledge, which a slower strategy would have generated. However, one should remember that also

Table 7. The establishment and growth strategy and the manufacturing companies' use of joint ventures and subcontracting (number of companies)

	Ownership		Manufacturing	
Strategy	Wholly owned	Joint venture	Mainly internal production	Mainly sub-contracting
a→s→p	5	2	5	2
a→p	2	6	2	6

a = agent, s = sales subsidiary, p = production

Japanese companies use subcontracting to a great extent. Therefore, the observed pattern can be interpreted as an adaptation to the Japanese way of organizing manufacturing, rather than as a risk reduction and learning strategy.

5.3.2. International experience

We will in this section look more closely at the companies' international experiences at the time of the first foreign direct investment in Japan.

The companies that preferred to establish production directly at the time of establishment in Japan had more experience from foreign operations in the form of subsidiaries. All eight companies preferring a 'direct route' strategy had a production subsidiary in more than five countries, compared to only one out of seven of the companies preferring to establish a sales subsidiary prior to production (see Table 8).

Table 8. Growth strategy and international experience at the time of the first direct investment in Japan (Number of companies)

Strategy	a ↓ p	a ↓ s ↓ p
Number of countries with subsidiary:		
5	0	0
6–15	2	4
16–25	2	1
25	4	2
whereof production subsidiary:		
5	0	6
6–15	5	0
16–25	3	1
25	0	0

a = agent, s = sales subsidiary, p = production

The difference is especially large when it comes to production subsidiaries. The result is the same if we exclude the three companies established prior to the regulations concerning foreign investment in Japan (see Table 9). Multinational companies with extensive international experience thus seem to increase their commitments on the market in large steps.

Table 9. Average number of countries with subsidiary at the time of establishment in Japan, for companies following different strategies

Strategy	Average number of countries with subsidiary	Average number of countries with prod. subsidiary	Average number of countries with prod. subsidiary for companies established 1972 or later
a→p	25	13	13
a→s→p	15	4	5

a = agent, s = sales subsidiary, p = production

It is, however, difficult to determine the relative importance of specific market knowledge and general international experience. The companies which preferred to establish production directly have, as we have seen, been more involved in both kinds of activities.

Degree of market knowledge activities*	International experience*	
	High	Low
High	Short route 5 Long route 0	Short route 2 Long route 0
Low	Short route 0 Long route 2	Short route 1 Long route 5

*We have divided the sample in the high/low categories to obtain approximately the same number of companies in each category. High in international experience is companies established in more than 18 foreign countries, and high in market knowledge activities are companies with 6 to 9 points according to the grading in Appendix 3.

All companies with many market knowledge activities have preferred the 'short route' strategy. (Going directly from agent sales to local production.) Two of the companies with high international experience and low degree of market knowledge had preferred to follow the traditional establishment design (see Table 9). Thus, both variables seem to be important.

5.3.3. Size

Still another problem is the influence of the companies' resources on the growth strategy.

Companies preferring the 'short route' strategy are larger on average. However, even the average for the other companies is quite high, or US$ 236 million.

Another test could be to try to determine the relative importance of firm size and international experience. However, these factors are highly interrelated. All the large companies in the sample have extensive and long international experience.

5.3.4. Other factors influencing the choice of strategy

Other factors than the ones mentioned could be expected to influence a company's establishment and penetration strategy to some extent. The need for service, product

Table 10. Total sales, sales in Japan in 1982, and total sales at the time of establishment in Japan for companies established in Japan 1972 or later (Total sales at the time of establishment adjusted to 1981 prices by Swedish export price indexes)

Growth strategy	Average turnover in Japan 1982 (mill. JPY)	Average total turnover (mill. SEK)	Average total turnover at the time of establishment in Japan (1981 prices, mill. SEK)
a→s→p	5,800	5,100	1,800
a→p	4,300	10,800	4,800

adaptation, and the company's technical level are often mentioned. We did not find any significant differences between the two sets of companies in this respect.

Another factor of interest is the companies' sales in Japan at the time of direct investment in Japan. There is reason to expect that larger sales would give a better economical base for production in Japan. Unfortunately, full information on this has not been available. There are, however, indications that this factor has been less important. The companies that established a production subsidiary directly had on average a lower turnover in Japan in 1982 than companies going over a sales company. Furthermore, the sales development for companies with sales subsidiaries has been negative during the last years (1979–1982), while most companies with production have had a substantial increase in sales.

5.4. Establishment and growth strategy and performance

Newbould et al (1978) concluded that companies following the establishment chain performed better than companies preferring a more aggressive growth strategy.

Performance is, as is well known, difficult to relate to action in some limited sense. The effect on the company as a whole as well as on the subsidiary's profitability and future potential should be taken into account. In lack of better information, we have used the following three factors: (1) the subsidiary's profitability in 1981; (2) sales growth between 1977 and 1982; (3) the opinion of the subsidiary general manager about the performance during the last five years. Appendix 4 gives the scores for each of the three dimensions. A composite subjective index has been constructed by us on the basis of this information and the in-depth interviews.

We have used the following classification:

1 = Very bad performance
2 = Bad performance
3 = Average performance
4 = Good performance
5 = Very good performance

The difficulties of attributing causes to the differences in performance makes us hesitate in drawing any firm conclusions on the basis of our data. However, we do feel that they cast doubt on a generalized hypothesis about the desirability of a strategy of gradual commitment on a foreign market. Our doubts are reinforced by the results of the study by Lundgren and Hedlund (1983) of Swedish investment in South-East Asia. The incidence of 'short route' strategies, as well as the association of these with good performance, is much higher than one would expect given the gradual commitment hypothesis. Since the

Table 11. Establishment and growth strategy and performance

Strategy	Performance					Average
	1	2	3	4	5	
a→s→p	2	2	1	2	0	2.86
a→p	0	1	5	1	1	3.25

eight markets investigated in the beforementioned study are very different from Japan, reservations emanating from the uniqueness of Japan lose in significance.

6. SUMMARY AND DISCUSSION

The experiences of Swedish firms in Japan suggest that establishment and growth strategies on foreign markets are changing towards more direct and rapid entry modes than those implied by theories of gradual and slow internationalization processes. Around half of the companies investigated went directly from a sales agent to manufacturing in Japan, rather than taking the route over a sales subsidiary. The companies' degree of general international experience is associated with the degree of directness of approach. Also knowledge about the Japanese market—in the form of long relations with local agents, licensing in Japan, and relations with joint venture partners—is related to the establishment strategy. The relative influence of size of the parent company and degree of international experience is difficult to separate since the variables were very closely related in our sample.

No clear association between establishment strategy and company performance could be established. Although the methodological difficulties involved in interpreting the data are staggering—in ours as well as other studies—the results show doubt on the hypothesis of better performance by following a slower and more gradual establishment chain in approaching a foreign market.

The results suggest that theories of the firm's internationalization process need to be developed in order to take account of changing environmental conditions—such as diminishing differences between the industrialized countries—and changes in corporations' ability to handle the complexities of international business. Also, the benefits of fast learning and entering a market early in the competitive game need to be weighed against the advantages of lower risks associated with more cautious strategies.

For managers of international companies, the results imply that firms should seriously consider whether they cannot move more quickly and directly towards more ambitious forms of representation on a foreign market than the common wisdom of gradual entry would dictate. For Japan specifically, involvement in local production is desirable for many firms.

Appendix 1 Swedish companies which have followed the traditional establishment chain, agent/ licensing–sales company and eventually production in Japan

| | | Form of establishment | | | | |
Company	Agent (A)/ −1950	1950–72	1973–82	Sales company (year)	Manufacturing (year)	Ownership policy
1		A (1960)		1973	—	WO[a]
2		A (1965)		1974	—	JV[b]
3			A (1974)	1976	—	WO
4	A			1932	1974	WO
5	A			1953	1979	WO
6		A (1957)		1962	1971	WO

Appendix 1—*contd*

Form of establishment

Company	Agent (A)/ −1950	1950–72	1973–82	Sales company (year)	Manufacturing (year)	Ownership policy
7		A (1968)		1973	1981	WO
8	A			1975	1978	JV
9		A (1971)		1976	1979	JV
10	A			1979	1981	WO

[a] WO = wholly owned subsidiary
[b] JV = joint venture

Appendix 2. Swedish companies which have gone directly from agent to manufacturing affiliate in Japan

Form of establishment

Company	Agent A/ −1950	195(...)−73	1973–82	Manufacturing (year)	Ownership policy
11	A			1972	JV[a]
12	A			1974	JV
13	A			1974	WO[b]
14		A (1954)		1974	JV
15	A			1975	WO
16				1975	JV
17	A			1979	JV
18	A			1981	JV

[a] WO = wholly owned subsidiary
[b] JV = joint venture

Appendix 4. The manufacturing companies' performance in Japan[a]

Profits 1981 (% of sales)	Increase in sales 1979–82	Subsidiary managers' opinion ( )	Our rating
6.0	67	As expected	3
0.7	39	Not quite as good as expected	2
6.0	4	As expected	3
6.6	5	Much better than expected	4
Negative	47	Not quite as good as expected	2
Very high	23	Much better than expected	5
0	135	As expected	3
Very high	—	Better than expected	4
0.6	− 33	Not quite as good as expected	1
Very high	10	As expected	5
1.3	− 12	Not as good as expected	1
5.0	79	As expected	3
0	76	As expected	3
Very high	97	Much better than expected	5
Negative	—	Not as good as expected	2

[a] For reasons of confidentiality, we have chosen not to relate the data in this table to company establishment strategies

Appendix 3. Ownership policy, market knowledge, and use of joint venture and subcontracting in manufacturing

| Company | Ownership policy | | Manufacturing policy | Market knowledge | | | | Grading[b] |
	Wholly owned	Joint venture	Mainly subcontracting	Swedish agent	Licensing prior to FDI	Branch office prior to FDI	Years of agent relation[a]	
4	x		x	x			22	4
5	x			x			4	2
6	x				x		6	1
7	x		x				6	2
8		x			x		46	4
9		x					6	2
10	x			x			10	2
11		x	x	x	x		20	7
12		x	x	x	x		30	8
13	x			x	x	x	100	7
14		x	x	x			21	6
15	x		x	x	x		30	9
16		x					21	3
17		x	x	x			59	7
18		x	x	x			48	7

[a] For three of the companies in the 'agent-manufacturing' group the years of agent relations are approximate
[b] 3 points for Branch office, 2 points for joint venture, subcontracting and Swedish agent, and 1 point for licensing and agent relations longer than average (29 years)

REFERENCES

Beckerman, W. (1956) Distances and the Pattern of Intra-European Trade. *The Review of Economics and Statistics*, **38(1)**.

Behrman, J. (1969) *Some Patterns in the Rise of the Multinational Enterprise*. Chapel Hill: London.

Burnenstam-Linder, S. (1961) *Essays on Trade and Transportation*. Wiley: New York.

Caves, R. E. (1971) International Corporations: The Industrial Economics of Foreign Investment. *Economica* **38(149)**.

Davidson, W. H. (1980) *Experience Effects in International Investment*. UMI Research Press.

Dunning, J. H. (1979) Explaining Changing Patterns of International Production: In Defence of the Eclectic Theory. *Oxford Bulletin of Economics and Statistics* **41**.

Egelhoff, W. G. (1982) Strategy and Structure in Multinational Corporations: An Information-Processing Approach. *Administrative Science Quarterly* **27**.

Fisher, H. W. (1977) *Technology Transfer as a Motivation for United States Direct Investment by European Firms*. Final report to National Science Foundation, Battelle Columbus Laboratories: Columbus.

Franko, L. G. *Multinationals: The International Activity of Continental European Enterprises*. Harper & Row: New York.

Gruber, W., Mehta, D., Vernon, R. (1967) The R&D Factor in International Investment of United States Industries. *Journal of Political Economy* **75(1)**.

Hammarkvist, K-O., Håkansson, H., Mattsson, L.-G. (1982) Markets as Networks—An Approach to the Analysis of Specific Marketing Situations. Paper presented at the 1982 Annual Meeting of the European Academy for Advanced Research in Marketing, Antwerp.

Hedlund, G., Aman, P. (1983) *Managing Relationships with Foreign Subsidiaries—Organization and Control in Swedish MNCs*. En Mekanpublikation: Sweden.

Hymer, S. (1960) *The International Operations of National Firms: A Study of Direct Investment*. Doctoral dissertation, MIT: Boston, MA.

Hägg, I., Johanson, J. (1982) *Företag i nätverk—ny syn på konkurrenskraft*. SNS: Stockholm.

Johanson, J., Vahlne, J.-E. (1977) The Internationalization Process of the Firm—A Model of Knowledge Development and Increasing Foreign Market Commitment, *Journal of International Business Studies* 23–32.

Johanson, J., Wiedersheim-Paul, Finn. (1975) The Internationalization of the Firm—Four Swedish Cases, *Journal of Management Studies*, **12,** 3.

Kindleberger, C. P. (1969) *American Business Abroad*. New Haven, CT, Yale University Press.

Knickerbocker, F. T. (1973) *Oligopolistic Reaction and Multinational Enterprise*. Harvard Business School: Boston.

Lundgren S., Hedlund, G. (1983) *Svenska företag i Sydostasien*. Stockholm School of Economics, Institute of International Business.

Newbould, G. D., Buckley, P. I., Thurwell, J. (1978) *Going International—The Experience of Smaller Companies Overseas*. Associated Business Press: London.

Perlmutter, H. V. (1965) L'Enterprise Internationale—Trois Conceptions, *Revue Economique et Sociale* **23**.

Root, F. R. (1987) *Foreign Market Entry Strategies*. Amacom: New York.

Servan-Schreiber, J. J. (1968) *The American Challenge*. Hamish Hamilton: London.

Stopford, J. M., Wells, L. T. (1972) *Managing the Multinational Enterprise*. Basic Books Inc.: New York.

Swedenborg, B. (1979) *The Multinational Operations of Swedish Firms. An Analysis of Determinants and Effects*. Industriens Utredningsinstitut: Stockholm.

US Department of Labor—Office of Foreign Economic Research (1980) *Report on US Competitiveness*.

Vernon, R. (1966) International Investment and International Trade in the Product Cycle, *Quarterly Journal of Economics*, **80**, 190–207.

Vernon, R. (1979) The Product Cycle Hypothesis in a New International Environment, *Oxford Bulletin of Economics and Statistics* **41**.

Wicks, M. E. (1980) *A Comparative Analysis of the Foreign Investment Evaluation Practices of US based Multinational Companies*. McKinsey & Co: New York.

Wiedersheim-Paul, Finn. (1979) *Uncertainties and Economic Distance—Studies in International Business*. Almqvist & Wiksell: Uppsala.

9

Direct Foreign Investment in Japan as a Means of Market Entry: the Case of European Firms

Peter J. Buckley, Hafiz Mirza and John R. Sparkes

Previous versions of this paper have been given at the Royal Institute of International Affairs (Chatham House), Meiji Gakuin University, Tokyo, the Nissan Institute for Japanese Studies, Oxford, and the Centre for the Study of Contemporary Japan, University of Essex. We are grateful for comments from participants at each of these seminars. The first phase of this study was financed by the Japan Foundation. The current phase is financed by the Great Britain Sasakawa Foundation. Additional help has been received from the University of Bradford Research Committee and the Japan Foundation Endowment Committee. The authors are grateful for this financial support.

The research reported here is to be published in Peter J. Buckley, Hafiz Mirza and John R. Sparkes (1988) *Success in Japan: How European Companies Compete in the Japanese Market*, Oxford, Basil Blackwell.

Direct foreign investment in a market is the most risky form of entry because it carries the highest capital risk. However, it has long been recognized that direct foreign investment is the best way to defend a market share. The alternatives, exporting and licensing, do not allow on-the-spot, controlled reactions to competitors' moves, nor do they allow the firm to gauge precisely the market's needs as an investment presence does (Buckley and Casson, 1985). In the current context of globalization of markets, more and more firms are feeling the strategic necessity for a triangular presence in the world's leading economic centres: USA, Europe and Japan (Ohmae, 1985; Buckley et al, 1984).

Despite these compelling long-term reasons for a strategic investment presence in Japan, European companies have been reluctant to secure an investment base in the market. Section 1 of this paper examines the amount and nature of direct investment in Japan, Section 2 examines the objectives and strategies of entry, based on a sample of European firms with a Japanese manufacturing presence, Section 3 analyses the success of these ventures and the Conclusion gives predictions for the future of direct market entry into Japan.

Reprinted from *Journal of Marketing Management*, Vol 2, No 3, pp 241–258

1. FOREIGN DIRECT INVESTMENT IN JAPAN

Foreign direct investment in Japan has been slow to evolve and still has not reached a level which would be expected for an economy of Japan's size. This has been partly because of regulation of inward investment and partly because of the reluctance of foreign multinationals, even the largest ones, to tackle the undoubted difficulties of establishing a presence in the Japanese market (although the perception of some of these difficulties is greater than the reality).

Table 1 shows the evolution of regulations governing foreign investment in Japan. Effective liberalization began only in the early 1970s, although many US companies had established a presence during the Occupation and even earlier. This piecemeal removal of

Table 1. Measures taken by Japan to liberalize direct foreign investment

	Establishment of new business		Acquisition of existing firms Limits on foreign ownership	
	(A) Number of sectors liberalized up to 100% foreign ownership	(B) Number of sectors liberalized up to 50% foreign ownership	Individual (%)	Total (%)
July 1967 First round of liberalization	17	33	7	20
March 1969 Second round of liberalization	44	160	7	20
September 1970 Third round of liberalization	77	447	7	25
April 1971 Liberalization of automotive industry	77	453	7	25
August 1971 Fourth round of liberalization	228	All except 7 sectors	10	25
May 1973 100% liberalization in principle	All except 5 sectors		100% where the investment has been duly approved by the firm concerned 10 Others	25
June 1975 Liberalization of retail businesses	All except 4 sectors (agriculture, forestry and fisheries, mining, petroleum and leather manufacturing)			
December 1980 Enforcement of amended foreign exchange control law	All investment was liberalized in principle with the former approval system replaced by a report system			

Source: JETRO (1983) *How Can Foreign Affiliates Succeed in Japan?* Tokyo

the regulations was carried out in parallel with the revival and growth of the Japanese economy, so much so that one European executive, interviewed in the firm's Japanese affiliate described investing in Japan as 'rather like being invited to the cinema when all the best seats have been taken!' The situation now is of free entry, except for areas, at the government's discretion, which are felt to harm national security, public order or welfare, or where investment might 'adversely affect the national economy'.

This history of regulation and bureaucratic interference gave Japan a 'closed door' image to potential investors. This, combined with ignorance of Japan, potential language problems and other 'cultural differences', together with fears of the arcane distribution system, led foreign multinationals, particularly European ones, to shun Japan. However, the threat posed by Japanese multinationals in world markets, the difficulties of penetrating the Japanese market in any other way and the realization that a market of nearly 120 million potential consumers cannot be ignored, has led to an awakening of interest in an investment strategy. Figure 1 is McKinsey's summary of the relative difficulties of penetrating the Japanese market (McKinsey and Co., 1983). An investment joint venture in Japan faces constraints of laws and regulations, communication problems and costs in developing personnel, but it may well avoid cultural constraints. As we see below, the joint venture route is the preferred means of initial direct investment entry into Japan.

The extent of foreign direct investment in Japan is shown in Table 2. Direct investment up to 1984 amounted to approximately $4.5 billions although this is based on approvals or notifications. This is a tiny figure by world standards. Table 3, based on actual investments, gives Japan $3.7 billions of investment. This compares to $143.3 billions in the USA, $53.5 billions in the UK, and even Italy has five times as much inward investment, at $15.5 billions. Although investment in Japan grew by 54% between 1979

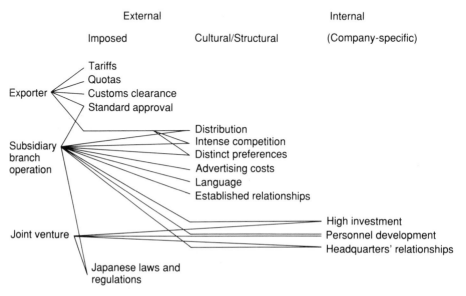

Source: McKinsey & Company, 1983, p. 18.

Figure 1. Constraints Faced by Foreigners in Japan.

Table 2. Foreign direct investment in Japan by source country up to 1984

Source country	Total accumulated investment ($ millions)	(%)
USA	2,655	59.3
Canada	111	2.5
(North America)	(2,766)	(61.8)
Switzerland	310	6.9
UK	260	5.8
Germany	227	5.1
Netherlands	120	2.7
France	116	2.6
Sweden	80	1.8
Denmark	11	0.2
Belgium	5	0.1
Others	50	1.1
(Europe)	(1,180)	(26.3)
Hong Kong	215	4.8
Panama	32	0.7
Taiwan	26	0.6
Others	260	5.8
Total	4,479[1]	100.0

[1] Figures based on approvals or notifications
Source: JETRO

Table 3. Foreign direct investment in major industrialized countries, 1979–1984

Country	Stock of inward FDI ($bn) 1979	1984	Percentage Increase 1979–84
USA	52.6	143.3	172
Canada	45.1	49.3	9
UK	36.2	53.5	48
Germany	30.9	35.5	15
France	17.5	29.0	66
Italy	10.5	15.5	48
Japan	2.4	3.7	54

Source: Based on United Nations Centre on Transnational Corporations, Salient Features and Trends in Foreign Direct Investment, UN, New York, 1983; and IMF, Balance of Payments Yearbook, 1985, Part 2, Washington, 1986

and 1984, this only parallels the rates of UK and Italy. It is well behind the growth rate in France and the USA. So, even though investment is minuscule, it is not rapidly growing, even from this small base.

The European contribution to direct investment in Japan is small. Table 2 shows that Europe in total accounts for only 26.3% of total accumulated investment in Japan. This contrasts markedly with the USA's share of 59.3%. The leading investors from Europe are Switzerland, UK and Germany, accounting together for 17.8% of total investment in Japan.

Table 4 shows that, up to September 1985, 1,032 investors from the European Communities (EC) had made 1,112 investments in Japan, accounting for Y 165 billion. German companies made 392 of these investments, British companies 280 and French companies 203. However, Dutch and British companies tended to have larger than average home capital invested per venture.

Very few of the European ventures in Japan are engaged in manufacturing. The EC delegation in Japan estimated that only 35% of all EC ventures in Japan were engaged in manufacturing and extraction. The survey reported in Ohmori (1986) discovered only 176 factories owned by foreign-affiliated companies; of these only 62 (35.2%) were European owned (Table 5).

The industrial classification of these factories is shown in Table 6. The chemicals industry was the most frequently represented, followed by the electrical industry, general machinery and pharmaceuticals.

Table 4. Size and value of EC investments in Japan up to September, 1985

	Number of EC investors	Percentage of total number of EC investors	Number of ventures made in Japan	Percentage of total number of ventures	Number of ventures incorporated in Japan	Amount of capital paid-up by EC investors (¥m)	Average EC capital invested per venture (¥m)
Belgium	14	1.3	17	1.5	11	1,964	179
Denmark	57	5.5	56	5.0	41	3,329	81
W. Germany	360	34.9	392	35.3	335	40,260	120
Greece	4	0.4	5	0.4	2	64	32
France	187	18.1	203	18.3	152	20,140	132
Ireland	5	0.5	6	0.5	6	45	8
Italy	60	5.8	64	5.8	47	4,462	95
Luxembourg	6	0.6	6	0.5	5	179	36
Netherlands	75	7.3	83	7.5	77	34,802	452
UK	264	25.6	280	25.2	223	59,695	268
Total	1,032	100.0	1,112	100.0	899	164,940	183

Source: EC delegation, Tokyo, September 1985

Table 5. Factories owned by foreign-affiliated companies

By country	(%)
USA	107 (60.8)
W. Germany	18 (10.2)
Switzerland	12 (6.8)
France	11 (6.3)
Britain	8 (4.5)
Sweden	7 (4.0)
Canada	5 (2.8)
Netherlands	4 (2.3)
Denmark	2 (1.1)
Australia	1 (0.6)
Hong Kong	1 (0.6)
Total	176 (100)

Source: Tatsuya Ohmari, 'Foreign-affiliated companies in Japan', *Journal of Japanese Trade and Industry*, Vol. 5, No. 6, 1986

Table 6. Factories owned by foreign-affiliated countries

By industry	(%)
Chemical	47 (26.7)
Electronics, electrical	36 (20.5)
General machinery	22 (12.5)
Pharmaceuticals	18 (10.2)
Nonferrous metal, metal	11 (6.3)
Glass, ceramics	6 (3.4)
Foodstuffs	5 (2.8)
Paper, pulp	4 (2.3)
Auto parts	4 (2.3)
Transportation equipment	3 (1.7)
Precision instruments	3 (1.7)
Oil, oil products	2 (1.1)
Textiles, clothing	2 (1.1)
Other manufactured products	11 (6.3)
Others	2 (1.1)
Total	176 (100)

Source: Tatsuya Ohmari, 'Foreign-affiliated companies in Japan', *Journal of Japanese Trade and Industry*, Vol. 5, No. 6, 1986

Overall, therefore, foreign direct investment has not been a favoured means of market penetration in Japan. This is particularly true for European companies and for direct investment in manufacturing. This route has not been chosen because of government restrictions in the past and because of perception of its difficulty by potential investors.

The next section examines the objectives and strategies leading to market entry by investment in manufacturing, based on structured interviews with executives of parent companies in Europe and affiliated companies in Japan.

2. OBJECTIVES AND STRATEGIES LEADING TO ENTRY

The sample of 24 European firms in our study, all with a manufacturing presence in Japan, is shown by nationality of parent in Table 7. They divide into the industrial sectors shown in Table 8. The ownership arrangements entered into by our sample of firms are shown in Table 9.

The European parent firms in the sample were asked to give the major factor which led them to establish an affiliate(s) in Japan. The most frequently cited reason was the size and growth of the Japanese market, a factor usually coupled with the difficulties foreign companies face of penetrating the Japanese market in any other way, for example, by exporting.

The difficulties for foreign companies of penetrating the Japanese market require investors to adopt a long-term view of their objectives in Japan. Most of the companies interviewed had not expected short-term profits. The initial aim, in some cases regardless of the profitability of the venture, was to seek a presence in the market and establish customer loyalty. For the new entrant, establishing a market presence is a prime objective,

Table 7. The sample of firms by nationality of parent

	Parent	Affiliates
Belgium	2	4
Denmark	4	5
France	3	15
German Federal Republic	4	17
Italy	2	5
Netherlands	3	9
Sweden	1	4
Switzerland	3	4
United Kingdom	2	2
Total	24	65

Table 8. The sample of firms by broad industrial sector

Industrial sector	No. of parent companies
Ceramics	1
Chemicals, including pharmaceuticals, cosmetics, etc.	12
Machinery: electrical, general, precision and transport	9
Metal products	2
Total	24

Table 9. Ownership arrangements in the sample

Arrangement	Number of affiliates
European participation (100%)	16
Majority European participation	7
50:50 European–Japanese participation	28
Minority European participation	6
Not known	8
Total	65

and the time taken in achieving this frequently renders profitable operation a long-term aim.

A further element in this motivation was the fact that the firms wished to 'exchange threat' with Japanese-owned competitors in Europe. A presence in Japan enables firms in highly concentrated oligopolistic industries to meet competition directly.

The second most frequently cited factor leading to establishment of a Japanese affiliate was the parent company's global strategy. Several of the larger firms referred to their 'triangular concept' of the world market, which necessitates having a manufacturing presence in the three major power bases of the world economy—Europe, Japan and the USA. It was widely acknowledged that Japan is a major market for strategically important products. In consequence it was felt necessary to be active in the market by establishing a production facility there.

In a highly competitive market, feedback is important for product development. Feedback was variously interpreted to mean the exchange of technical views on product development, the acquisition of knowledge about Japanese production processes, as well as feedback from end-users. Such feedback was considered beneficial for the group as a whole and not just for the company's Japanese involvement.

Japanese market size and growth and the company's global strategy were the most frequently cited reasons for setting up an affiliate in Japan. Another mentioned as a primary factor was 'control of the business'. Establishing a market presence begs the question of how best to achieve that—whether through a joint venture, a wholly-owned subsidiary, or through agents and distributors.

All of the companies interviewed had made a direct investment in their own operation in Japan, either on a joint venture basis or wholly owned. But many had also used agents prior to establishing a facility of their own, and some still made use of agents. The objective of increasing sales was generally considered to be best achieved by expansion of an affiliate's own manufacturing capability. Only then, it was felt, could companies hope, long term, to control the selling and distribution of their own products.

Japan is, by consensus, not a market for quick returns. Entrenchment and acceptance as a Japanese company, were widely thought to be critical to successful operation in Japan. The most favoured route for the great majority of parents *and* affiliates interviewed was clearly the joint venture. This was considered to offer greater flexibility for the new entrant than the more 'commercial' alternatives, for example, with agencies.

For some companies, of course, the objective for their Japanese operations will be highly specific. One company in our survey, for example, saw as its basic reason for being in Japan the dilution of research costs. The company concerned was in a field where Japanese technology and technical expertise were in the van of development, and in consequence technical co-operation was of benefit to the group's activities worldwide.

Other companies that had succeeded in building up a market share by exports and licensing had subsequently established joint-venture arrangements to protect their market share.

It was widely acknowledged that the Japanese customer demands and expects very high quality and service. To succeed in Japan, European companies must offer products generally of a higher standard than the Japanese equivalent. Not all of the executives interviewed might agree with the observation that 'a low-price strategy in Japan is wrong' but that view was echoed in the aim of many of the companies to create market consciousness for high price/high quality products.

If Japan is, as suggested, a strategically important market, and the most effective competitive strategy in relation to the market is to invest in Japan, why is the joint venture still the preferred route? Prior to 1973 government restrictions on direct foreign investment were an obvious reason for the joint-venture option as a means of entry. But it has continued to be the most usual form of entry and for only one of the companies in our sample using this route was its joint-venture partner considered an encumbrance.

The reasons why a joint-venture entry strategy is often preferred are many and various. Among the reasons typically advanced are the following. A green-field development is too expensive in time and money whereas a joint venture satisfies a foreign company's desire for local knowledge and expertise. In particular, a local partner of appropriate size and experience can appoint and support local management—a notoriously difficult thing for a foreign company to do in its own right. Even then problems of allegiance arise, the stronger association with the Japanese joint venture partner than with the venture itself usually giving the partner great influence in the management of the affiliate.

Some foreign investors find it necessary to involve a joint-venture partner to overcome distribution problems. This is of course possible without a joint-venture arrangement. But a company using a distribution agency without itself becoming a fully-integrated Japanese entity with manufacturing facilities in Japan faces the distinct possibility that the company and the agency have different goals and profit objectives. This makes it unlikely that the company will achieve anything like its full potential. A joint venture, even with a distributor, is most likely to reconcile any such conflict.

In the absence of a manufacturing base, a joint venture has also been the basis for the development of licensing programmes to capitalize on existing brand awareness while utilizing the strength of the partner to finance such a programme. A joint venture is the shortest route towards establishing a Japanese identity and a market presence. It offers the prospect of close contact between the customer and the manufacturer and can facilitate the need to respond quickly to customer demand.

Joint ventures are not without problems, but the advantages seem to outweigh the disadvantages. Where the joint venture arrangement has been effective is in situations where conflicting interests between the joint venture company and the Japanese partner have resulted in competition in other market segments—occasionally to the extent that a company can be bidding against itself!

We have encountered no joint venture arrangement where there was not some area of conflict between the partners, although the will to seek resolution makes conflict too strong a word in the great majority of cases. But the more muted description often applied, such as 'matters for discussion' masks one of the most apparent frustrations of a joint venture which is the painstaking and often laborious way in which decisions are reached. Consensus, with all its ramifications in terms of Japanese-style management, is a time-consuming process.

3. OUTCOME AND ACHIEVEMENTS: THE LESSONS OF EXPERIENCE

Commentators on international investment in Japan are apt to stress the relatively high profitability of foreign manufacturing subsidiaries, particularly when compared to domestic concerns (Figure 2). However, having allowed for different measures of profitability, it is important to recognize that the comparison is an unfair one, since highly competitive, internationally-orientated companies are being juxtaposed with an average of *all* companies operating in Japan. When like is compared with like, the result is not so flattering.

The range and composition of European investment in Japan is similarly biased. Table 8 shows that most companies in our sample are engaged in a small range of industries: speciality chemicals, pharmaceuticals, and industrial machinery. In general this implies technological and niche advantages and, in particular, means that most companies are orientated towards *industrial* customers (Table 10). However it does not follow that objectives are easy to achieve and there is considerable scope in terms of the most effective form of market entry (see below).

The complexity of entry into the Japanese market does not allow the assessment of success based on a single measure. Most executives interviewed argued that their companies were successful in terms of the objectives set (Table 11) though many discussed specific problems and failures in frank terms. Of particular value to potential European investors in Japan was their evaluation of the major factors underlying success and failure (Figure 3), though, needless to say, specific factors vary from industry to industry.

There was considerable variation in more objective measures of success. Market share, for example, varied from 1–2% of the Japanese market for some more diversified entrants, to up to 75% for particular specialized companies and products. The latter type

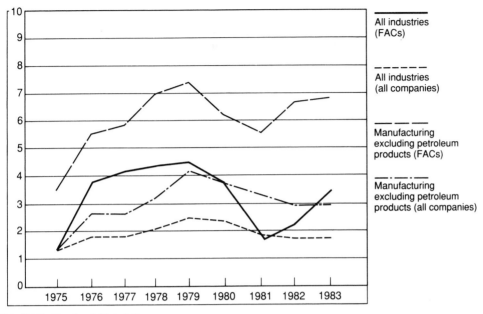

Note: FAC = Foreign Affilated Company.
Source: The 18th Survey of Foreign Affiliates in Japan, MITI. Cites in Tatsuya Ohmari, "Foreign affilitated companies in Japan", *Journal of Japanese Trade and Industry*, Vol. 5, No. 6, 1986.

Figure 2. Profit Ratios for all Japanese Companies and Foreign Affiliated Companies.

Table 10. The target market of European investors in Japan

	Number
Industrial customers only	10
A range of customers[1]	9
Not known	5
Total	24

[1] Of which 2 or 3 companies are almost entirely consumer-market orientated

Table 11. The perception of success of the affiliate at the European head office

	Number of firms
Very successful	11
Successful	6
'Satisfied, but more could be achieved'	6
Unsuccessful	1
Total	24

of company tended to sell to a small number of industrial customers and was relatively profitable. Companies with small market shares or lower rates of profit were either in more competitive markets (i.e. normally competing with efficient Japanese firms with local knowledge) or/and involved in consumer products—and hence faced with customer

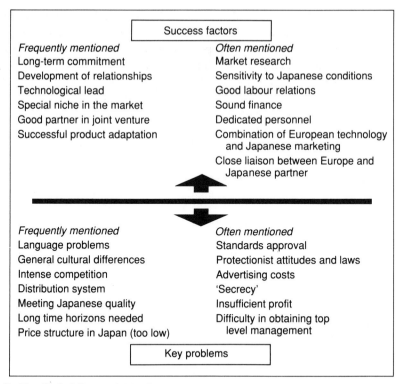

Source: Peter Buckley, Hafiz Mirza and John Sparkes, "Key to successful investment by foreign companies", *Investors Chronicle*, September 19, 1986. (Part of a survey on Japan).

Figure 3. Key Factors in Success and Failure in Japan.

resistance to foreign products and complex distribution systems. One executive gave the example of a specific market:

> 65 per cent of this market is virtually closed to foreigners because of the links between smaller outlets and existing suppliers. There are about 5,000 bigger stores but they represent only 35 per cent of the market. Therefore if we are to achieve a market share of 5 per cent in this sector we need to capture 15 per cent of the large store sales—a huge problem which requires considerable marketing effort, including advertising.

Yet even this executive stressed that 'presence effects' (enhanced knowledge of the local market, capacity to produce customer-specific goods, acceptance as a 'Japanese' company) meant that manufacturing direct investment was vital, and underlined his company's commitment to long-term goals rather than short-term profits or similar objectives.

Though the companies in the sample had been chosen because of their manufacturing investments in Japan, the modes of penetration of the market were very varied indeed. Some European companies employed virtually the entire gamut of forms: manufacturing and sales subsidiaries, wholly-owned subsidiaries, joint ventures, joint research and a variety of 'co-operative' agreements with Japanese partners; and the use of a variety of agents and distributors, including Sogo Shosha (general trading companies). This diversity of forms produces valuable advice on entry methods. Virtually all firms were still involved in exporting to Japan and saw this as the appropriate vehicle for a variety of products (e.g. low-volume, highly technical goods where the necessary resource inputs were already well-developed in Europe). Even so, a sales subsidiary was deemed appropriate, especially when it could adapt products to local market requirements (e.g. tests on pharmaceuticals). Most companies abjured licensing, except under extreme circumstances, but a few were very licensing-orientated. These were late high-tech entrants into a Japanese market dominated by indigenous concerns. Under these oligopolistic conditions cross-licensing was prevalent, but a manufacturing presence could be maintained in some products when the European company had a lead—it could also be viewed as an insurance.

Though joint ventures remain the dominant ownership arrangement (Table 9), many well-established firms are gradually redefining their role and new affiliates are frequently wholly owned, now that legislation allows this option. However, most new entrants in our sample were still inclined towards joint ventures because of their lack of knowledge in the highly intricate Japanese market. Earlier European investors still urged this as the least risky way for a company to ease itself into Japan. Entry by acquisition was extremely rare, because this strategy is regarded as a hostile act in Japan, and most new ventures were either green-field or, more usually, established on the partner's site.

Executives were also able to comment on a number of other issues affecting the net benefits or costs of a manufacturing subsidiary. For example, executives asked to compare Japanese productivity performance generally conceded that it was on par with, or exceeded, European levels (Table 12). However, productivity is perhaps not the best word and one manager's response is enlightening:

> It is difficult to compare productivity because notions of efficiency differ between Japan and Europe. The Japanese apparently waste a lot of time: their meetings take longer and personal relations are established as late as 10.30 p.m. in bars. However this is necessary because relationships are of paramount importance—and outside of office hours junior personnel are allowed to criticise managers without hindrance. This builds trust and increases output. The power of a Japanese team working well together is superior to a similar Western group. However I must repeat that we are talking about two different things.

Table 12. Relative productivity performance

	European parent
Japanese productivity is:	
Higher than European productivity	8
The same as European productivity	5
Lower than European productivity	4
Don't know	7
Total	24

Table 13. Does your presence in the Japanese market stimulate the home company to make better and more competitive products?

	Number of companies
Yes	13
Not yet, but expected to	4
No	5
Not known	2
Total	24

A number of European companies have tried to encourage some of these practices at the head office (and other subsidiaries). A particular example of worker-participation apparently bearing fruit on transfer is the institution of quality control circles.

A related question was whether a manufacturing presence in Japan encouraged the production of better products. In general the answer was in the affirmative (Table 13) and in many cases technology developed in Japan had been transferred to Europe. One executive explained this phenomenon thus:

> Operating in the Japanese market has meant that we have had to pay great attention to matters such as packaging, image, technology, quality standards, purity requirements, precision and reliability. Although there are similar feedbacks from elsewhere the Japanese market is particularly sophisticated both at an industrial and consumer level. We have adapted many products based on our Japanese experience and our sales and exports have benefited considerably.

Two potentially negative consequences of establishing a subsidiary in Japan were especially stressed by a number of companies. First, given the shortage of European managers experienced with Japan and (perhaps more importantly) the need to establish local relationships and links in accordance with Japanese business customs, most managers in these affiliates are ethnically Japanese. This can create rifts between the European parent company and the Japanese affiliate because of differing management philosophies and practices. A number of Japanese executives felt they were under pressure to 'do it the European way'. The issue is complex, but one German firm summed up the problem thus: 'the goal in Germany is profit, in Japan it is harmony'. Second, though most firms were happy to comply with local personnel policies, a number of European investors were unhappy with specific practices, particularly where there was little chance of change given the philosophy of the Japanese partner company. Various executives voiced their misgivings about certain Japanese personnel practices, including seniority-based promotion, 'life-time' employment and certain wage and fringe benefits. The greatest fear was (tongue in cheek), 'What if the Europeans find out?!'

4. CONCLUSION

Investment in Japan as a means of market entry is an under-used method as far as European firms are concerned. Most of our sample of manufacturing affiliates in Japan consider their Japanese affiliate to be successful, although it must be recognized that Japan is not a location in which high returns can be expected quickly. The joint venture route is the most popular method which European firms use to establish manufacturing facilities in Japan. Joint ventures allow lower cost and lower risk entry although the dangers of loss of control are evident. Abegglen and Stalk (1985) feel that the era of joint ventures in Japan is coming to an end with US foreign investment moving more towards acquisitions in Japan. This does not appear to be the case for entry by European firms—in our sample only European firms already established in Japan have carried out acquisitions (which generally have to be by consent in Japan). In their projections, most European companies feel that joint ventures will continue to be important.

The strategic arguments for a presence in Japan are compelling for global companies: the costs and drawbacks must be balanced against the dangers of not being there. For

Table 14. The percentage of the global sales of the European firms represented by Japan

	Number of companies
Up to and including 1%	3
2–4%	6
5–10%	11
11–15%	2
Over 15%	1
Don't know	1
Total	24

medium and small companies, caution is warranted, but our research shows that a successful investment presence in Japan is not crucially dependent on large size.

A useful final measure of success in Japan is the proportion of global sales of the company represented by the Japanese market (Table 14). A useful rule of thumb suggested to us by one of the European executives interviewed is: 'If the Japanese market represents 5% of worldwide sales, then the company is doing very well indeed'. On this measure 15 of the 24 firms in our sample are doing well as Table 14 shows. For companies hoping to achieve these levels of market penetration in Japan, a presence is essential.

REFERENCES

Abegglen, J. and C. Stalk, G. (1985). *Kaisha: The Japanese Corporation*, New York, Basic Books.

Buckley, P. J. and Casson, M. (1985). *The Economic Theory of the Multinational Enterprise*, London, Macmillan.

Buckley, P J., Mirza, H. and Sparkes, J. R. (1964). *European Affiliates in Japan*, Report for the Japan Foundation, Tokyo, December.

Buckley, P. J., Mirza, H. and Sparkes, J. R. (1988). *Success in Japan: How European Firms Compete in the Japanese Market*, Oxford, Basil Blackwell.

Buckley, P. J., Mirza, H. and Sparkes, R. (1986). 'Key to successful investment by foreign companies', *Investors Chronicle*, September 19. (Part of Special Survey on Japan.)

EC Delegation, Tokyo (1985). *EC Investment in Japan*, September.

International Monetary Fund (various), *Balance of Payments Yearbook*, Washington DC, IMF.

JETRO (1983). *How Can Foreign Affiliates Succeed in Japan?*, Tokyo.

McKinsey & Company Inc. (1983). *Japan Business: Obstacles and Opportunities*, New York, John Wiley.

Ohmae, Kenichi (1985). *Triad Power: The Coming Shape of Global Competition*, New York, Free Press.

Ohmori, Tatsuya (1986). 'Foreign affiliated companies in Japan', *Journal of Japanese Trade and Industry*, Vol. 5, No. 6.

United Nations Centre on Transnational Corporations (1983). *Salient Features and Trends in Foreign Direct Investment*, New York, UNCTC.

10

Joint Ventures and Global Strategies

Kathryn Rudie Harrigan

Kathryn Rudie Harrigan is an Associate Professor at the Graduate School of Business, Columbia University.

This research was supported by the Strategy Research Center, Columbia University. It is a condensation of materials from *Strategies for Joint Ventures* (1985). It has benefited from suggestions by William H. Newman, Director of the Strategy Research Center, as well as suggestions by Donald C. Hambrick, Robert Drazin, James Fredrickson, Leonard Sayles, E. Kirby Warren, and Boris Yavitz.

As business risks soar and competition grows more fierce, firms will embrace joint ventures with increasing frequency. This should not be surprising. Joint ventures have long been used by entrepreneurial firms to expand into new markets, particularly within newly industrializing nations. But what of the use of joint ventures within mature economies? What of the firms whose markets are being invaded by global competitors? Little attention has been devoted to other uses of joint ventures, and this is a serious shortcoming. Joint ventures represent a significant change in industry structures and in competitive behaviour. They can be a more versatile competitive tool than earlier studies have indicated.[1] They could help domestic firms to enter the global milieu or find a new way of competing. This article sketches firms' uses of 'operating joint ventures' in light of the pressures created by international competition. It presents a framework for predicting how parent firms might configure joint ventures to achieve these competitive purposes.

OPERATING JOINT VENTURES DEFINED

This definition suggests a defensive approach. 'Operating joint ventures' are partnerships by which two or more firms create an entity, a 'child,' to carry out a productive economic activity. Each partner takes an active role in decision-making, if not also in the child's operations. Operating joint ventures do not include passive financial investments made by parties who are not involved in the new entity's strategic business decisions. Nor do they include interfirm arrangements that do not create a separate entity.

Operating joint ventures could include manufacturing arrangements, such as the titanium steel mill of Allegheny International, Sumitomo Metal, and their partners. They could include distribution arrangements, like that of Coca-Cola Bottling and Seagram, or research and development arrangements, like those formed by a consortium of electronics firms. Each party to the operating joint venture makes a substantial contribution in the form of capital and technology, marketing experience, personnel or physical assets. But most importantly, partners contribute access to distribution networks. If neither partner controls market access, it will be more difficult for the joint venture to succeed, particularly within industries where other firms have longer track records. This will be so because of the nature of global competition and the greater difficulties encountered in hurdling entry barriers when an industry's structure is well-established. Similarly, when a nation's economy is mature, distribution infrastructures will be better established, and more costly to duplicate.

GLOBAL STRATEGIES DEFINED

'Global strategies' are those which recognize that competition can no longer be confined to a single nation's boundaries. Industries become global for many reasons, and firms need an approach appropriate to meet new challenges when this change occurs.[2] When this occurs, firms must re-examine their assumptions concerning how competitive advantage can be gained by integrating the operations of diverse geographic locations. Perhaps firms may use joint ventures to co-ordinate their activities within a global system. This is a novel suggestion. Although firms will often think of production scale economies, technological innovation, and new sourcing arrangements as a means of meeting the global challenge, fewer firms may recognize the advantages of joint ventures. Yet operating joint ventures offer a means of leveraging firms' advantages to succeed within global industries. As is explained below, competitive advantages could be gained through operating joint ventures.

A JOINT VENTURE FRAMEWORK

What determines the viability and durability of joint ventures? How should firms design and run them? This section presents a framework that predicts, from the parent firm's perspective, how the joint venture bargain might be struck. The framework is dynamic, as Figure 1 indicates, and it involves external forces as well as the considerations detailed below.

In Figure 1, competitive forces combine with the interests of two or more parent firms to make a joint venture feasible. (Figure 2 details these forces.) The combination of strategic needs and parent firm resources determine the configuration of the child. The configuration—the control mechanisms, vertical integration relationships and other points of the bargaining agreement—may change over time, due to many stimuli, as depicted in Figure 2.

The ultimate success (or failure) and disposition of the resources committed to the joint venture are also determined by these stimuli. A brief explanation of the framework follows. The forces giving parent firms more (or less) bargaining power to forge particular joint venture configurations are discussed more fully below.

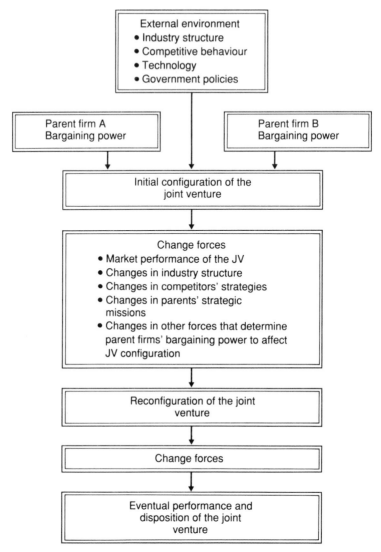

Figure 1. A Dynamic Model of Joint Venture Activity.

Parent firm considerations

In Figure 2, Parent Firms A and B desire certain (1) benefits from their joint venture. These are their reasons for co-operating with other firms. They recognize that co-operation in joint ventures entails (2) costs, which some firms may consider too significant to accept. In such cases, their negotiations to form joint ventures will be fruitless or will take other forms, instead. If a joint venture can be negotiated, each potential partner has resources and skills which could serve as (3) inputs to the joint venture. Paradoxically, the greater firms' resources, the greater their (4) bargaining power. But the greater their (5) need to co-operate, the less their bargaining power will be in negotiating the configuration of the joint venture. The magnitude of the opportunity costs or other disadvantages firms

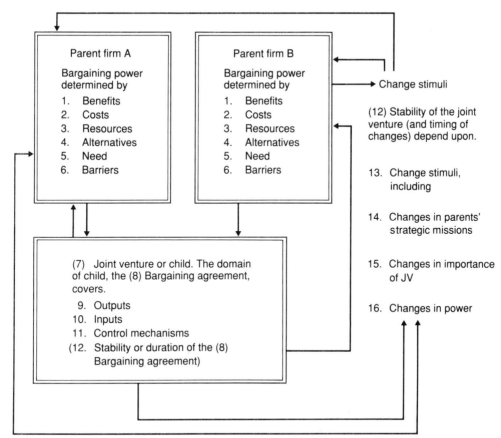

I thank Donald C. Hambrick for suggesting this diagram.

Figure 2. A Dynamic Model of Joint Venture Activity.

perceive in co-operating will determine the height of their (6) barriers to co-operation. It is necessary to overcome these barriers if a joint venture is to be formed. Later, if asymmetries develop between joint venture partners, exit barriers must be overcome to change the terms of the bargaining agreement, which is discussed below. Thus there are barriers in forming and in re-configuring joint ventures.

Child firm considerations

In Figure 1, the (7) child, or joint venture (JV), is the result of the bilateral bargaining power of its parents. Its form, inputs, outputs, and control mechanisms are defined by a (8) bargaining agreement. This agreement, which defines the child's domain of activities, specifies its (9) outputs, and it may specify its customers, as well. The purpose of the joint venture's existence is usually defined by these outputs. The bargaining agreement specifies the (10) inputs necessary for the joint venture to attain its objectives. These resources may be provided for by its parents through a variety of vertical integration arrangements, or they may be obtained from outsiders. The child cannot be viable, however, if its parents do not provide for an economic source of (or means of attaining) these inputs. The bargaining agreement also specifies the (11) control mechanisms its parents will use to ensure that the benefits they desired were received. These control mechanisms should also provide for the (12) stability of the joint venture.

Change stimuli

Both the formation and the stability of a joint venture agreement depend upon the nature of the bargaining agreement that can be struck between parents and the impact of (13) change stimuli upon the perceived attractiveness of the joint venture agreement. Joint ventures are formed within dynamic environments. Environmental conditions may change. Parent firms may change, and the child itself will evolve over time.[3]

A joint venture's (17) performance within its markets will affect its attractiveness to its parents. An industry's structure can change due to past competitive behaviours, and with it, change the potential for future profitability. Competitive conditions may change within the child's industry due to technological, political or other uncontrollable changes. The child's abilities to command resources or satisfy its customers may deteriorate or improve, depending upon its past performance. Another part of the child's performance is determined by the suitability of its strategy for serving its customers, and by its effectiveness in implementing its chosen strategy (past performance will be, in part, the source of the child's current market power). Since this strategy must accommodate the dynamics of at least three entities, the joint venture's relationship with one or both of its parents may change due to changes in their strategies.

These or other (13) stimuli may force the joint venture's parents to renegotiate the terms of the bargaining agreement. The timing of changes in the bargaining agreement will depend upon the forces motivating a particular parent to co-operate or modify the terms of co-operation (and whether they can overcome (6) the barriers which constitute impediments to their strategic flexibility). The re-configuration and ultimate disposition of the child will depend upon its parents' (14) strategic missions, (15) the strategic importance they attach to the child, and the alternatives parents possess to attain the same benefits which their joint venture may have provided in other ways. Possessing alternatives gives parents a new source of bargaining power that may be strong enough for them to change their bargain and hurdle inertia barriers. The sources of these barriers are sketched in the discussion of parent firm bargaining power which follows.

DETERMINANTS OF PARENT FIRM BARGAINING POWER

Firms will co-operate in forming joint ventures only if the needs of each partner are great enough and if they can add resources which are complementary to the other's attributes. The resources firms possess will give them the basis for bargaining power when entering joint ventures, but if their needs for co-operation are great enough this potential power will be mitigated.[4] The balance between these opposing forces will be realized in the form the joint venture takes. It will be apparent in the control mechanisms partners use to control their interests in the JV, in the vertical relationships they maintain with the JV, and with its stability. The stability of joint ventures will be affected by a variety of forces.

This section discusses the net impact of parent firms' resources upon the ultimate bargaining agreement that determines the child's configuration, alternatives for attaining the benefits joint ventures promise, needs to co-operate and barriers to forming (and dissolving) joint ventures.

Successful joint ventures serve their purpose without disrupting their parents' strategic well-being. The key to successful joint ventures will be a meeting of minds.[5] Effective joint ventures depend upon trust, but they are often forged as a compromise between two or more parent firms who would rather own the child wholly.[6] Like a marriage, they tolerate their wayward partners to attain some advantage that satisfies their needs. The key to forging mutually satisfactory joint ventures will be realistically assessing firms' strengths (and weaknesses) in the proposed venture. It is also necessary to assess potential partners' commitments to the venture's success and their willingness to contribute resources (or provide a market for outputs) in a manner that accommodates their partners' needs.[7] Joint ventures may be transitory organizations firms embrace to attain an advantage faster, but the most stable joint ventures will be those where the child can stand on its own economically.

Benefits of joint ventures

Parent firms embrace joint ventures because they are ways to implement changes in their strategic postures or to defend current strategic postures against forces too strong for one firm to withstand.[8] They allow each partner to concentrate their resources in those areas where they possess the greatest relative competence, while diversifying into attractive but unfamiliar business arenas. Joint ventures should not be seen as a way to hide weaknesses. Rather, if they are used prudently, joint ventures are a way of creating strengths.

Managers have often disparaged joint ventures in the past, believing them to be too complex, too ambiguous or too inflexible.[8] But as the challenges of global competition increase, as projects grow larger and more risky, and as technologies become too expensive for one firm to afford, managers must learn how to use joint ventures, even in their firms' home markets. They have been an important structural trait within emerging national economies; joint ventures will become an important way to cope with uncertainties in established national economies, as well.

Often firms cannot afford to acquire the resources and competences they need.[10] Frequently, the knowledge and assets they seek cannot be purchased.[11] As an intermediate option (between acquisition or internal development and dependence upon outsiders) joint ventures represent a special, highly flexible means of enhancing innovation or achieving other strategic goals which managers should not overlook as their industries become global.[12] Joint ventures offer firms a window on promising new technologies, such as genetic engineering, videotext and synfuels.[13] They can be a means of utilizing a new manufacturing process (such as continuous casting in the steel industry), a by-product (as in many chemical processes), or a new capability (such as transmitting services over existing communications lines). Joint ventures offer salvation for firms within older global industries (such as automotive, farm equipment and petrochemicals), as well. Given the political realities of offsets and co-production requirements in order to conduct international trade, joint ventures among partners of different nationalities are becoming imperative.[14] Joint economies, co-production, common procurement and other aspects of joint ventures are being used to ward off competitors which are making inroads into firms' key markets.[15]

In brief, joint ventures offer many internal, competitive and strategic benefits. They provide firms with resources for which there are no equally efficient and available substitutes.[16] Some projects would never be undertaken without this means of spreading costs and risks.[17] Some firms could not retain their positions, given the rapid pace of change in global competition, without joint ventures.[18] Timing will be an important part of competitive strategy in this situation because firms which move first can gain access to better partners. If the ventures are 'exclusive' (explained below), firms could gain a competitive advantage which late entrants could not capture as easily. Joint ventures could be a means of pre-empting suppliers (or customers) from integrating to become competitors, and they could blunt the abilities of ongoing firms to retaliate as firms expand their domains.[19] By binding potential rivals to them through joint ventures, firms can make them allies.[20]

The benefits firms perceive from using joint ventures will differ according to whether they are 'insiders' or 'outsiders' with regard to the activities in question. Firms which are new to the market or activity ('outsiders') may see joint ventures as an insurance policy against domestic trade barriers or as a way to diversify.[21] Firms which are already in the market or engaged in the activity ('insiders') may see joint ventures as a way to curb potentially tough competitors or gain technological assistance. They must find some benefit in opening their markets to outsiders, else they would not consider joint ventures. Moreover, they must retain control over the enduring competitive advantage their market access gives them. Insiders should not trade away too much of this advantage for fleeting technological benefits.

Costs of joint ventures

Joint ventures are not without risks. Some industrialized nations, like the United States, have strict antitrust laws that prohibit those joint activities which function like monopolies.[22] When firms plan joint ventures within such environments, it will be particularly important to show a pro-competitive design and an antitrust-sensitive explanation of the need for the joint venture.[23] This justification must include a convincing portrayal of the inability of *either* parent to go it alone.[24] Parents may differ in their time horizons, the synergies they see with the joint venture, and other operating details. The objectives of host governments are not always the same as those of joint venture partners.[25] Decisions regarding whether to license knowledge or form joint ventures cannot follow the traditional patterns of technology transfer if host governments (or local partners) exert substantial bargaining power.[26] If partners possess such power, they could disrupt the schedule by which firms had intended to transfer the sources of their competitive advantage within global systems.[27]

Joint ventures can result in deadlocks if partners have not created equitable mechanisms for resolving day-to-day deadlocks in decision-making.[28] If deadlocks are not overcome, firms will suffer from foregone opportunities, loss of control over invested capital, technical resources, and proprietary information.[29] If the reasons for forming the joint venture were poorly conceived, if partners were not chosen carefully, or if the agreements and systems used to manage the venture were inadequate, firms may be worse off than they were before entering the joint venture.[30]

Firms' needs to co-operate

Firms' strategic missions determine their need to co-operate with others. If a business is close to firms' technological cores, they will often be less willing to enter joint ventures in those businesses, particularly if they distrust potential partners' motives. The technological core of many firms is the essence of their corporate strategies and business purpose. Their unwillingness to bare their technological cores to partners who could not protect this knowledge adequately from technological bleed-through makes them want majority control, if not full ownership.[31] It also makes them hover over every decision the child might make. Paradoxically, autonomous joint ventures have been more prolific innovators than JVs which were not allowed to operate in their own rights.[32] Yet parent firms are often reluctant to grant JVs the freedom to develop into viable entities.

Resources

By contrast, some firms use joint ventures pre-emptively to protect turf that is of great value to them. They form joint ventures with aggressive outsiders in businesses which are important to them in order to co-opt outsiders.[33] Their secret seems to be their awareness that they control crucial resources. Access to technology and market are the key bargaining chips in negotiations leading to joint-venture creations, reconfigurations and terminations. Firms' preferences concerning how many joint ventures to form (and with whom) depends on which resources they control. Market access permits firms to absorb aggressive outsiders. This approach seems to work best, for example, where domestic firms understand the importance of their control over market access and can prevent their joint-venture partners from gaining this resource. To do so, they configure the joint venture to prevent it from ever becoming a competitor. They may form parallel, in-house entities that duplicate the joint venture's activities and learn from its mistakes. Or they may form a spider's web of joint-venture relationships on the basis of their market power.

Alternatives

The balance of power ultimately agreed upon between firms will not necessarily be symmetrical because some partners will accept a lesser degree of control in order to achieve other objectives. Recognition of others' strategic needs and resource strengths can suggest how much latitude domestic firms will have in forming ventures that play off competing firms against each other.

'Spider's Web' joint ventures link many firms to one pivotal partner.[34] Depending upon the need to be satisfied and the sensitivity of information and resources to be exchanged, a domestic firm could forge a variety of patterns for co-operation that keep outsiders at bay while strengthening its own position. This approach is appropriate early in an industry's development when it is unclear which firm's technological standards will be adopted. It is the opposite of an approach whereby firms pick a future industry champion early and bet all resources on it through an 'exclusive' joint venture.

Where firms possess bargaining power over outsiders, spider's web joint ventures are more likely to result, unless the resources in question are so sensitive that neither firm wants to share information with others. Less powerful firms can only accept the terms dictated to them, so their ability to form multiple alliances is by mutual consent of its ongoing joint-venture partners.

Barriers

Joint ventures should be used to fortify parent firms' weaknesses in the face of global competition. Recognition of this and other weaknesses does not come easily to complacent firms.[35] Their unwillingness to see that their industries have become global creates barriers to firms' uses of joint ventures or other adaptive strategies.

The principal barriers to forming joint ventures are strategic in nature. Uncertainties regarding their abilities to manage operating joint ventures also erect barriers to joint-venture formation. Briefly, the strategic costs (detailed above) are valued more highly than the benefits firms believe they can attain. The high entry barriers that would normally deter a single firm from penetrating a new market or learning about a new technology are reasons to band together in forming joint ventures in the face of global competition.

Externally-imposed barriers to joint ventures include political restrictions on ownership, patent restrictions, competitor retaliation or other conditions. These may be easier to overcome than firms' own attitudinal barriers. For example, the comparative costs of off-shore manufacturing would inevitably drive domestic firms to relocate unless governments permitted them to join forces with efficient world-scale firms. Furthermore, joint ventures allow firms whose technologies have grown obsolete to replenish themselves.

USING JOINT VENTURES

Successful joint ventures require the correct choice of partners and symmetrical parent outlooks, but since most parents have diverse strategic outlooks and their strategies evolve dissimilarly, the inevitable tensions which develop must be managed. It is unreasonable to expect that joint ventures can preserve the relationships that existed when they were first created. Sometimes a change in managers is sufficient to change how a parent firm values its child. Joint ventures may be terminated, or they may be turned into a new opportunity to co-operate. The key to successful use of these tensions for competitive advantage lies in remembering the parent firm's sources of bargaining power.

It is useful to recall the inherent fragility of joint ventures when choosing partners to bring into one's home markets.[36] Today's partners could become tomorrow's competitors. Joint ventures are often reconfigured when partners have gained knowledge of markets which they previously did not understand. Thus it is important for domestic firms to avoid losing their competitive advantages to their partners. Providing for joint-venture disposition is also important, lest firms encounter difficulties in recovering the value of their investments in their child. One would expect that a market existed for the resources they had committed, but the ability to exit can be ensured better if firms manage for this contingency. Given firms' fundamental aversions to joint ventures, they would be expected to press to renegotiate their agreement into a fully-owned acquisition which they can control more fully. The flaw in this attitude is its assumption that the joint venture was sub-optimizing in its decisions while it was jointly-owned. If, instead, the child were given the freedom to make the best economic decisions, its profitability potential will not change after its ownership changes, unless its new owner imposes a *strategy* change on the child. The joint venture that is integrated well into its parents' global networks can be divested with greater ease should one of its parents' orientations change. Then 'fade-out' provisions can be exercised in a manner that permits firms to part amicably.[37]

CONCLUSION

Joint ventures are assuming greater importance in global strategies because product lives are shorter, cost advantages are becoming more pronounced and greater numbers of firms who formerly operated only in domestic markets are becoming international competitors. These changes have ominous ramifications for non-global firms, for they are likely to be offered partnership in joint ventures by firms who covet their strengths (transitory though they may be). A timely analysis of how joint ventures fit the interests of such firms could help them to forge configurations which leave them better off.

In the past, joint ventures have often been read as a signal of lesser corporate commitment to the project in question (unless firms purposely signalled high commitment to the markets in question in other ways). Firms have been particularly loathe to use joint ventures where local governments did not require them as a condition of entry for domain-expanding multinationals. In environments of scarce resources, rapid rates of technological change and massive capital requirements, however, joint ventures may be the best way for some underdog firms to attain better positions in global industries which they consider to be important. Joint ventures may be used as pre-emptive manoeuvres to ensure that access to distribution channels, suppliers and technology in promising industries are not foreclosed to them because they ventured too late. They are also a way of ensuring that potential entrants do not team up with more dangerous opponents. As long as firms recognize the dangers and limitations of joint ventures and manage these shortcomings, there will be a chance for joint ventures to play a useful role in global strategies.

NOTES

1. Berg, Sanford V. and Friedman, Philip, 'Corporate Courtship and Successful Joint Ventures,' *California Management Review*, Vol. 22, No. 2, Spring 1980, pp. 85–91.

2. Porter, Michael E., *Competitive Strategy: Techniques for Analyzing Industries and Competitors*, (New York: Free Press, 1980) and Hout, Thomas; Porter, Michael E. and Rudden, Eileen, 'How Global Companies Win Out', *Harvard Business Review*, Vol. 60, No. 5, Sept.–Oct. 1982, pp. 98–108.

3. Edström, Anders, 'The Stability of Joint Ventures,' (working paper, University of Gothenburg, 1975b).

4. Fowaker, Lawrence E. and Siegel, Sidney, *Bargaining Behavior,* (New York: Mc-Graw-Hill, 1963).

5. Riker, W. H., *The Theory of Political Coalitions,* (New Haven: Yale University Press, 1962).

6. Schermerhorn, John R., Jr., 'Determinants of Interorganizational Cooperation,' *The Academy of Management Journal*, Vol. 18, December 1975, pp. 846–956 and 'Openness to Interorganizational Cooperation: A Study of Hospital Administrators,' *Academy of Management Journal*, Vol. 19, June 1976, pp. 225–236.

7. Schelling, Thomas C., *The Strategy of Conflict*, (Cambridge: Harvard U. Press, 1960) and Telser, L. G., *Competition, Collusion and Game Theory,* (New York: Addine-Atherton, 1972).

8. Edstrom, Anders, 'Acquisition and Joint Venture Behavior of Swedish Manufacturing Firms,' (working paper, University of Gothenburg, 1975a) and Pfeffer, Jeffrey, and G. R. Salancik, *The External Control of Organizations: A Resource Dependence Perspective*, (New York: Harper & Row, 1978).

9. Killing, J. Peter, 'How to Make a Global Joint Venture Work,' *Harvard Business Review*, Vol. 61, No. 3, May–June 1982, pp. 120–127, and Wright, Richard W., 'Canadian Joint Ventures in Japan,' *Business Quarterly*, Autumn 1977, pp. 42–53.

10. Pfeffer, Jeffrey, 'Merger as a Response to Organizational Interdependence,' *Administrative Science Quarterly*, Vol. 17, 1972, pp. 382–394, and Pfeffer, Jeffrey and P. Nowak, 'Joint Ventures and Interorganizational Interdependence,' *Administrative Science Quarterly*, Vol. 21, No. 3, September 1976, pp. 398–418.

11. Williamson, Oliver, *Markets and Hierarchies: Analysis and Antitrust Implications*, (New York: Free Press, 1975).

12. Gullander, Stefan, 'Joint Ventures and Corporate Strategy,' *Columbia Journal of World Business*, Vol. XI, No. 1, September 1976, pp. 104–114.

13. Drucker, Peter, *Management: Tasks, Responsibilities, Promises*, (New York: Harper & Row, 1974), Hlavacek, James D. and Victor A. Thompson, 'The Joint Venture Approach to Technology Utilization,' *ILEE Transactions on Engineering Management*, Vol. EM-23, No. 1, February 1976, pp. 35–41, and Berg, Sanford V. and Philip Friedman, 'Corporate Courtship and Successful Joint Ventures,' *California Management Review*, Vol. 11, No. 2, Spring 1980.

14. Vernon, Raymond, *Storm Over the Multinationals*, (Cambridge, MA: Harvard University Press, 1977).

15. Harrigan, Kathryn Rudie, *Strategies for Declining Business* (Lexington, MA: D. C. Heath & Company, 1980), Harrigan, Kathryn Rudie, 'Deterrents to Divestiture,' *Academy of Management Journal*, Vol. 24, No. 2, June 1981, pp. 306–323, and Orski, C. Kenneth, 'The World Automotive Industry at a Crossroads: Cooperative Alliances,' *Vital Speeches*, Vol. 47, No. 3, November 15, 1980, pp. 89–93.

16. Bachman, Jules, 'Joint Ventures in the Light of Recent Antitrust Developments: Joint Ventures in the Chemical Industry,' *Antitrust Bulletin*, Vol. 10, Jan.–April 1965, pp. 7–23, and Brodley, Joseph F., 'Joint Ventures and the Justice Department's Antitrust Guide for International Operations,' *Antitrust Bulletin*, Vol. 24, Summer 1979, pp. 337–356.

17. Ballon, Robert J., ed., *Joint Ventures and Japan*, (Tokyo: Sophia University, 1967), and Franko, Lawrence G., *Joint Venture Survival in Multinational Corporations*, (New York: Praeger Publishers), 1971.

18. Bivens, Karen Kraus and Enid Baird Lovell, *Joint Ventures with Foreign Partners*, (New York, National Industrial Conference Board, 1966).

19. MacMillan, Ian C., 'Preemptive Strategies,' *The Journal of Business Strategy*, Vol. 4, No. 2, Fall 1983, pp. 16–26, and Harrigan, Kathryn Rudie, *Strategies for Vertical Integration*, (Lexington, MA: D. C. Heath & Company, 1983).

20. Harrigan, Kathryn Rudie, 'Strategies for Domestic Joint Ventures,' (book-length manuscript, forthcoming, 1985).

21 Meehan, James W., 'Joint Venture Entry in Perspective,' *Antitrust Bulletin*, Vol. 15, Winter 1970, pp. 693–711, and Daniels, John D., *Recent Foreign Direct Manufacturing Investment in the United States: An Interview Study of the Decision Process*, (New York: Praeger Publishers, 1971).

22. Mead, W. J., 'The Competitive Significance of Joint Ventures,' *Antitrust Bulletin*, Vol. 12, Fall 1967, pp. 819–849, Davidow, Joel, 'International Joint Ventures and the US Antitrust Laws,' *Akron Law Review*, 10, Spring 1977, and Rowe, Frederick M., 'Antitrust Aspects of European Acquisitions and Joint Ventures in the United States,' *Law and Policy in International Business*, Vol. 12, No. 2, 1980, pp. 335–368.

23. Marquis, Harold L., 'Compatibility of Industrial Joint Research Ventures and Antitrust Policy,' *Temple Law Quarterly*, Vol. 38, No. 1, Fall 1964, pp. 1–37.

24. Treeck, Joachim, 'Joint Ventures and Antitrust Law in the United States, Germany and the European Economic Community,' *Journal of International Law and Politics*, Vol. 3, No. 1, Spring 1970, pp. 18–55, Brodley, Joseph F., 'Joint Ventures and the Justice Department's Antitrust Guide for International Operations,' *Antitrust Bulletin*, Vol. 24, Summer 1979, pp. 337–356, and Ewing, K. P. Jr., 'Joint Research, Antitrust and Innovation,' *Research Management*, Vol. 24, No. 2, March 1981, pp. 25–29.

25. Vernon, Raymond, *Sovereignty at Bay: The Multinational Spread of US Enterprise*, (New York: Basic Books, 1971), Wright, Richard W. and Colin S. Russel, Joint Ventures in Developing Countries: Realities and Responses,' *Columbia Journal of World Business*, Vol. X, No. 2, Summer 1975, pp. 74–80; and Gregory, Gene, 'Japan's New Multinationalism: The Canon Giessen Experience,' *Columbia Journal of World Business*, Vol. XI, No. 1, Spring 1976, pp. 122–126.

26. Vernon, Raymond, 'International Investment and International Trade in the Product Cycle,' *Quarterly Journal of Economics*, Vol. 53, No. 2, May 1966, pp. 191–207, Gabriel, Peter P., *The International Transfer of Corporate Skills*, Boston: Harvard Business School, Division of Research, 1967, and Harrigan, Kathryn Rudie, 'Innovations by Overseas Subsidiaries,' *Journal of Business Strategy*, Vol. 5, Summer 1984 B, pp. 47–55.

27. Franko, Lawrence G., *The European Multinationals*, (London: Harper & Row, 1976), Vernon, Raymond and Louis T. Wells, Jr., *Manager in the International Economy*, (Englewood Cliffs, NJ: Prentice-Hall, Inc., 1976), and Young, G. Richard, and Standish Bradford, Jr., 'Joint Ventures in Europe—Determinants of Entry,' *International Studies of Management and Organizations*, Vol. 1–2, No. 6, 1976, pp. 85–111.

28. March, J. G. and H. S. Simon, *Organizations*, (New York: Wiley, 1958).

29. Friedman, W., and G. Kalmanoff, *Joint International Business Ventures*, (New York: Columbia University Press, 1961), Picard, Jacques, 'How European Companies Control Marketing Decisions Abroad,' *Columbia Journal of World Business*, Vol. XII, No. 2, Summer 1977, pp. 113–121.

30. Tractenberg, Paul, 'Joint Ventures on the Domestic Front: A Study in Uncertainty,' *The Antitrust Bulletin*, Nov.–Dec. 1963, pp. 797–841. Ray, Edward John, 'Foreign Direct Investment in Manufacturing,' *Journal of Political Economy*, Vol. 85, No. 2, April 1977, pp. 283–297, and Davies, Howard, 'Technology Transfer Through Commercial Transactions,' *Journal of Industrial Economics*, Vol. XXVI, No. 2, December 1977, pp. 161–175.

31. Killing, J. Peter, 'Technology Acquisition: License Agreement or Joint Venture,' *Columbia Journal of World Business*, Vol. 15, No. 3, Fall 1980, pp. 38–46.

32. Franko, Lawrence G., *Joint Venture Survival in Multinational Corporations*, (New York: Praeger Publishers, 1971).

33. March, J. G., 'The Business Firm as a Political Coalition,' *Journal of Politics*, Vol. 24, 1962, pp. 662–678.

34. Gullander, Stefan O., 'An Exploratory Study of Inter-Firm Cooperation of Swedish Firms,' (doctoral dissertation, Columbia University, 1975).

35. Harrigan, Kathryn Rudie, *Strategies for Declining Business*, (Lexington, MA: D. C. Heath & Company, 1980), and Harrigan, Kathryn Rudie, *Strategies for Vertical Integration*, (Lexington, MA: D.C. Heath & Company, 1983).

36. Franko, Lawrence G., *Joint Venture Survival in Multinational Corporations*, (New York: Praeger Publishers, 1971); Gullander, Stefan O., 'An Exploratory Study of Inter-Firm Cooperation of Swedish Firms,' (doctoral dissertation, Columbia University, 1975); Gullander, Stefan, 'Joint Ventures and Corporate Strategy,' *Columbia Journal of World Business*, Vol. XI, No. 1, September 1976, pp. 104–114; and Young, G. Richard, and Standish Bradford, Jr., 'Joint Ventures in Europe—Determinants of Entry,' *International Studies of Management and Organizations*, Vol. 1–2, No. 6, 1976, pp. 85–111.

37. Meeker, Guy B., 'Fade Out Joint Venture: Can It Work for Latin America?' *Inter-American Economic Affairs*, Vol. 24, 1971, pp. 25–42.

REFERENCES

Bachman, J., 'Joint Ventures in the Light of Recent Antitrust Developments: Joint Ventures in the Chemical Industry,' *Antitrust Bulletin*, Vol. 10, Jan.–April 1965, pp. 7–23.

Ballon, R. J., ed., *Joint Ventures and Japan*, (Tokyo: Sophia University, 1967).

Berg, S. V., Duncan, J., Jr., and Friedman, P., *Joint Strategies and Corporate Innovation*, (Cambridge, MA: Oelgeschlager, Gunn & Hain, Publishers Inc., 1982).

Berg, S. V. and Friedman, P., 'Corporate Courtship and Successful Joint Ventures,' *California Management Review*, Vol. 22, No. 2, Spring 1980, pp. 85–91.

Bivens, K. K. and Lovell, E. B., *Joint Ventures with Foreign Partners*, (New York, National Industrial Conference Board, 1966).

Bourgeois, L. J. III and Singh, J., 'Organizational Slack and Political Behavior Within Top Management Terms,' (working paper, Stanford University, December 1982, presented at 1983 National Academy of Management Meetings, Dallas).

Brodley, J. F., 'Joint Ventures and the Justice Department's Antitrust Guide for International Operations,' *Antitrust Bulletin*, Vol. 24, Summer 1979, pp. 337–356.

Cyert, R. M. and March, J. G. *A Behavioral Theory of the Firm*, (Englewood Cliffs, NJ: Prentice-Hall, 1963).

Daniels, J. D., *Recent Foreign Direct Manufacturing Investment in the United States: An Interview Study of the Decision Process*, (New York: Praeger Publishers, 1971).

Davidow, J., 'International Joint Ventures and the U.S. Antitrust Laws,' *Akron Law Review*, 10, Spring 1977.

Davies, H., 'Technology Transfer Through Commercial Transactions,' *Journal of Industrial Economics*, Vol. XXVI, No. 2, December 1977, pp. 161–175.

Drucker, P., *Management: Tasks, Responsibilities, Promises*, (New York: Harper & Row, 1974).

Duncan, W. J., 'Organizations as Political Coalitions: A Behavioral View of the Goal Formulation Process,' *Journal of Behavioral Economics*, Vol. 5, No. 1, 1976, pp. 25–44.

Edström, A., 'Acquisition and Joint Venture Behavior of Swedish Manufacturing Firms,' (working paper, University of Gothenburg, 1975a).

Edström, A., 'The Stability of Joint Ventures,' (working paper, University of Gothenburg, 1975b).

Ewing, K. P. Jr., 'Joint Research, Antitrust and Innovation,' *Research Management*, Vol. 24, No. 2, March 1981, pp. 25–29.

Filley, A. C., House, R. J. and Kerr, S., *Managerial Process and Organizational Behavior*, (Glenview, IL: Scott Foresman, 1976).

Fouraker, L. E. and Siegel, S. *Bargaining Behavior*, (NY: McGraw-Hill, 1963)

Franko, L. G., *The European Multinationals*, (London: Harper & Row, 1976).

Franko, L. G., *Joint Venture Survival in Multinational Corporations*, (New York: Praeger Publishers, 1971).

Friedman W., and Kalmanoff, G., *Joint International Business Ventures*, (New York: Columbia University Press, 1961).

Gabriel, P. P., *The International Transfer of Corporate Skills*, (Boston: Harvard Business School, Division of Research, 1967).

Gregory, G., 'Japan's New Multinationalism: The Canon Giessen Experience,' *Columbia Journal of World Business*, Vol. XI, No. 1, Spring 1976, pp. 122–126.

Gullander, S. O., 'An Exploratory Study of Inter-Firm Cooperation of Swedish Firms,' (doctoral dissertation, Columbia University, 1975).

Gullander, S., 'Joint Ventures and Corporate Strategy,' *Columbia Journal of World Business*, Vol. XI, No. 1, September 1976, pp. 104–114.

Hambrick, D. C. and Mason, P. A., 'Upper Echelons: The Organization as a Reflection of Its Top Managers,' (working paper, Columbia University, 1982).

Harrigan, K. R., 'Deterrents to Divestiture,' *Academy of Management Journal*, Vol. 24, No. 2, June 1981, pp. 306–323.

Harrigan, K. R., 'Innovations by Overseas Subsidiaries,' *Journal of Business Strategy*, Vol. 5, Summer 1984, pp. 47–55.

Harrigan, K. R., *Strategies for Declining Business*, (Lexington, MA: D. C. Heath & Company, 1980).

Harrigan, K. R., 'Strategies for Domestic Joint Ventures,' (book-length manuscript, forthcoming, December 1984).

Harrigan, K. R., *Strategies for Vertical Integration*, (Lexington, MA: D. C. Heath & Company, 1983).

Hlavacek, J. D. and Thompson, V. A., "The Joint Venture Approach to Technology Utilization,' *ILEE Transactions on Engineering Management*, Vol. EM-23, No. 1, February 1976, pp. 35–41.

Killing, J. P., 'How to Make a Global Joint Venture Work,' *Harvard Business Review*, Vol. 61, No. 3, May–June 1982, pp. 120–127.

Killing, J. P., 'Technology Acquisition: License Agreement or Joint Venture,' *Columbia Journal of World Business*, Vol. 15, No. 3, Fall 1980, pp. 38–46.

MacMillan, Ian C., 'Preemptive Strategies,' *The Journal of Business Strategy*, Vol. 4, No. 2, Fall 1983, pp. 16–26.

March, J. G., 'The Business Firm as a Political Coalition,' *Journal of Politics*, Vol. 24, 1962, pp. 662–678.

March, J. G. and Simon, H. S., *Organizations*, (New York: Wiley, 1958).

Marquis, H. L., 'Compatibility of Industrial Joint Research Ventures and Antitrust Policy,' *Temple Law Quarterly*, Vol. 38, No. 1, Fall 1963, pp. 1–37.

Mead, W. J., 'The Competitive Significance of Joint Ventures,' *Antitrust Bulletin*, Vol. 12, Fall 1967, pp. 819–849.

Meehan, J. W., 'Joint Venture Entry in Perspective,' *Antitrust Bulletin*, Vol. 15, Winter 1970, pp. 693–711.

Meeker, G. B., 'Fade Out Joint Venture: Can It Work for Latin America?' *Inter-American Economic Affairs*, Vol. 24, 1971, pp. 25–42.

Orski, C. K., 'The World Automotive Industry at a Crossroads: Cooperative Alliances,' *Vital Speeches*, Vol. 47, No. 3, November 15, 1980, pp. 89–93.

Pfeffer, J., 'Merger as a Response to Organizational Interdependence.' *Administrative Science Quarterly*, Vol. 17, 1972, pp. 382–394.

Pfeffer, J. and Nowak, P., 'Joint Ventures and Interorganizational Interdependence,' *Administrative Science Quarterly*, Vol. 21, No. 3, September 1976, pp. 398–418.

Pfeffer, J. and Salancik, G. R., *The External Control of Organizations: A Resource Dependence Perspective*, (New York: Harper & Row, 1978).

Picard, J., 'How European Companies Control Marketing Decisions Abroad,' *Columbia Journal of World Business*, Vol. XII, No. 2, Summer 1977, pp. 113–121.

Porter, M. E., *Competitive Strategy: Techniques for Analyzing Industries and Competitors*, (New York: Free Press, 1980).

Ray, E. J., 'Foreign Direct Investment in Manufacturing,' *Journal of Political Economy*, Vol. 85, No. 2, April 1977, pp. 283–297.

Riker, W. H., *The Theory of Political Coalitions*, (New Haven, CT: Yale University Press, 1962).

Rowe, F. M., 'Antitrust Aspects of European Acquisitions and Joint Ventures in the United States,' *Law and Policy in International Business*, Vol. 12, No. 2, 1980, pp. 335–368.

Schelling, T. C., *The Strategy of Conflict*, (Cambridge, MA: Harvard University Press, 1960).

Schermerhorn, J. R. Jr., 'Determinants of Interorganizational Cooperation,' *The Academy of Management Journal*, Vol. 18, December 1975, pp. 846–956.

Schermerhorn, J. R. Jr., 'Openness to Interorganizational Cooperation: A Study of Hospital Administrators,' *Academy of Management Journal*, Vol. 19, June 1976, pp. 225–236.

Shubik, M., *Strategy and Market Structure*, (New York: Wiley, 1959).

Telser, L. G., *Competition, Collusion, and Game Theory*, (New York: Aldine-Atherton, 1972).

Tractenberg, P., 'Joint Ventures on the Domestic Front: A Study in Uncertainty,' *The Antitrust Bulletin*, Nov.–Dec. 1963, pp. 797–841.

Treeck, J., 'Joint Research Ventures and Antitrust Law in the United States, Germany and the European Economic Community,' *Journal of International Law and Politics*, Vol. 3, No. 1, Spring 1970, pp. 18–255.

Vernon, R., 'International Investment and International Trade in the Product Cycle,' *Quarterly Journal of Economics*, Vol. 53, No. 2, May 1966, pp. 191–207.

Vernon, R., *Sovereignty at Bay: The Multinatinal Spread of U.S. Enterprise*, (New York: Basic Books, 1971).

Vernon, R., *Storm Over the Multinationals*, (Cambridge, MA: Harvard University Press, 1977).

Vernon, R. and Wells, L. T. Jr., *Manager in the International Economy*, (Englewood Cliffs, NJ: Prentice-Hall, Inc., 1976).

Von Neumann, J. and Morgenstern, O. *Theory of Games and Economics Behavior*, (Princeton, NJ: Princeton University Press, 1944).

Williamson, O., *Markets and Hierarchies: Analysis and Antitrust Implications*, (New York: Fress Press, 1975).

Wright, R. W., 'Canadian Joint Ventures in Japan,' *Business Quarterly*, Autumn 1977, pp. 42–53.

Wright, R. W. and Russel, C. S., 'Joint Ventures in Developing Countries: Realities and Responses,' *Columbia Journal of World Business*, Vol. X, No. 2, Summer 1975, pp. 74–80.

Young, G. R. and Bradford S. Jr., 'Joint Ventures in Europe—Determinants of Entry,' *International Studies of Management and Organizations*, Vol. 1–2, No. 6, 1976, pp. 85–111.

Part III

The Internationalization Process

CONTENTS

11

Internationalization: Evolution of a Concept

Lawrence S. Welch and Reijo Luostarinen

Over the last two decades there has been growing interest in the international operations of business companies. Academic activity in the area has both stimulated and been stimulated by the many strands of concern—for example, the business firms themselves, with a concern to make such operations more effective and efficient in a more competitive global environment; governments, with a concern to ensure that the overall process has a positive effect on the national interest; and trade unions, with a concern about the impact on working conditions, wages and their own power.

At the outset much academic interest and analysis focused on the multinational corporation. Studies such as Servan Schreiber's (1) *American Challenge* alerted governments and others to the already extensive international operations of these companies. Much of the academic research in the early stages was involved with documenting and explaining the spread of multinational corporations, and assessing their impact, with an emphasis on their foreign investment activities. This was reflected in a spate of studies of foreign investment in various recipient countries (2) (3) (4).

However, much of the early research took the multinational, or at least foreign investment, as a starting point in the analysis, leaving many questions unanswered regarding the development process which preceded this stage, and undoubtedly affected the later steps. Horst (5), for example, after finding that firm size was a significant factor in the firm's decision to invest abroad concluded that: 'The principal deficiency in this line of analysis, I believe, is the absence of dynamic considerations. Nowhere is there a description of how a firm came to acquire its current attributes . . . But if we are even to unravel the complexity of the foreign investment decision process, a systematic study of the dynamic behaviour of firms must be undertaken.' In essence a more longitudinal view, a process perspective, was called for.

Already, though, a shift in this direction had begun with Aharoni's (6) study of the various steps involved in the foreign investment decision process. As well, Wilkins (7) (8) had begun to delineate some of the dynamic factors contributing to the historical evolution of American multinational corporations.

This developing longitudinal approach was taken a stage further with a number of studies of the international operations of Nordic-based companies, studies which considered the expansion activity as an internationalization process (9) (10) (11). Specifically, their research was important in advancing our knowledge of the process not only because of its identification of patterns of internationalization, and a method for examining them, but also because of the attempt to outline the key dynamic factors which formed the basis of forward progress. In the Nordic case the overall pattern was one of gradual, sequential development of international operations.

At the same time as this overall longitudinal research was developing in the 1970s, an interest was growing in the analysis of specific steps which contribute to the ongoing process. Inevitably the shift to a more longitudinal approach led to an interest in the earlier steps which formed a foundation for later moves. For example, considerable analysis of early exporting activity has been undertaken in a number of countries (12) (13) (14) (15) (16). While each new step of the development of international operations can be considered unique, each nevertheless provides insight into the broader longitudinal forces at work.

In general therefore research into the process of internationalization has tended to be carried on at the level of specific decisions to increase involvement as well as overall patterns and dynamic causative factors. Nevertheless, although considerable progress has and is being made in unravelling the nature and cause of internationalization—much remains to be accomplished. The various contributions represent an incomplete patchwork. As Buckley (17) has noted: 'The development from naïve entrant to established multinational has been inadequately modelled . . . and its implications for theory are as yet unassimilated.'

THE MEANING OF 'INTERNATIONALIZATION'?

At the very outset it is difficult to discuss a 'theory of internationalization' because even the term itself has not been clearly defined. Although widely used, the term 'internationalization' needs clarification. It tends to be used roughly to describe the outward movement in an individual firm's or larger grouping's international operations (18) (19) (20). As a starting point this common usage could be broadened further to give the following definition: 'the process of increasing involvement in international operations.' An important reason for adopting a broader concept of internationalization is that both sides of the process, i.e. both inward and outward, have become more closely linked in the dynamics of international trade.

The growth of countertrade in its many forms, from pure barter to buy-back arrangements and offset policies, is indicative of the way in which outward growth has become tied in with inward growth (21) (22). In effect, countertrade has meant that, for many companies, success in outward activities is partly dependent on inward performance. This, in combination with supportive government action in some cases, has led to a number of large companies setting up trading arms to facilitate the process (23) (24). The inward-outward interlink is further illustrated in the growth of international subcontracting which has played an important role in the international viability of many companies through the ability to tie in cheap component/raw materials imports from international suppliers—from clothing manufacture through to sophisticated systems selling (25) (26) (27). From a general perspective therefore, it seems to be inappropriate to restrict the concept of increasing international involvement merely to the outward side, given the growing inward-outward interconnection.

Having put forward a working definition of 'internationalization' it should be stressed that once a company has embarked on the process, there is no inevitability about its continuance. In fact the evidence indicates that reverse of 'de-internationalization' can occur at any stage, as the example of Chrysler and other disinvestments in the late-1970s illustrate, but is particularly likely in the early stages of export development (28) (29).

So far the concept of 'internationalization' has been couched in relatively broad terms deliberately, to cover a multitude of possibilities. However, to apply the concept, considerable elaboration is required. For example, on what basis can we assess the degree of internationalization of one firm versus another? What does the concept mean as an outcome? Perhaps the simplest objective basis for assessing the degree of internationalization is some measure of foreign sales relative to total sales. The proportion of total sales exported has often been used as an indication of export performance despite its drawbacks (30). Such a measure can also be extended out to the national economy as exports/gross domestic product. Although this measure is attractive because of its simplicity and measurability it provides very little information about the nature of and capacity to conduct international operations. Given the diversity of international operations, types of markets, degree of organizational commitment and types of international offering, there is obviously a need for a broader framework for assessing the extent of 'increased international involvement'—i.e. on a number of different dimensions. An example of such a framework is presented in Figure 1. In general internationalization can be expected to be associated with, and perhaps dependent upon, developments along each of the dimensions shown:

Operation method (how)

Evidence indicates that as companies increase their level of international involvement there is a tendency for them to change the method/s by which they serve foreign markets (31) (32) (33). The Nordic studies indicate that this change occurs in the direction of increasing commitment, a typical pattern being from no exporting, to exporting via an agent, to a sales subsidiary and finally to a production subsidiary. One of the reasons for the considerable attention on the operational method as a means of assessing a pattern of internationalization is that it does represent a clearly overt manifestation of the overall process.

As well as increasing commitment though, the pattern appears to be one of greater operational diversity as internationalization proceeds (34). This appears to be related not only to the greater experience, skills, and knowledge of foreign markets and marketing which develops within the firm, but also to the exposure of a wider range of opportunities and threats. Sometimes the sheer success of one method of operation, for example exporting, causes the erection of import barriers by a foreign government thereby necessitating a shift to some other form such as licensing or foreign investment if a market presence is to be maintained. An Australian study found that outward foreign licensing was mainly adopted because of various constraints on the use of other, more preferred methods of operation in foreign markets (34). The recent strong move by Japanese firms into foreign investment has been partly stimulated by the various forms of protection imposed in key markets (35) (36). In a similar manner, the exploitation of market opportunities in the socialist countries, because of the emphasis of their governments on

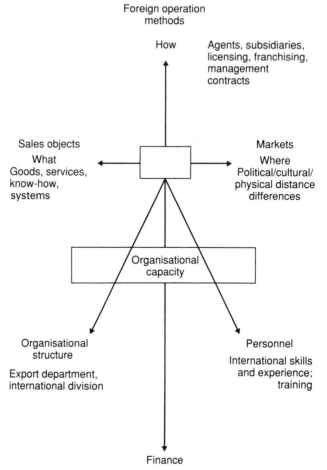

Figure 1. Dimensions of Internationalization.

counter-trade, is likely to force some shift towards operational diversity. Clearly, the degree of market diversity has an impact on the degree of operational diversity.

Thus, on the method of operation dimension we would expect internationalization to be reflected in both increasing depth and diversity of operational methods. At a global level, this is evident not just in the growth of foreign investment but also in the rise of countertrade in its various guises, of the technology trade, of franchising, of management contracts and so on. It is difficult, if not impossible, to go far in the internationalization process simply by using one preferred operational method. One can perhaps argue that the future international success of companies will partly depend on their ability to master and successfully apply a range of methods of foreign operation.

Sales objects (what)

As a company increases its involvement in international operations there is also a tendency for its offering to foreign markets to deepen and diversify (37). This may occur at two levels:

- Expansion within an existing, or into a new, product line (38).
- Change in the whole product concept to include 'software' components such as services, technology, know-how, or some combination. Over time the blending of hardware and software components is often developed into more packaged forms, representing project or systems solutions (39).

Target markets (where)

As with sales objects and operation forms, it is difficult to develop internationally merely by concentrating on a limited number of countries. Expanded operations and offerings increasingly link with a wider range of foreign markets—typically more distant over time in political, cultural, economic and physical terms. There is a basic tendency for companies, particularly in the early stages of internationalization, to approach markets which appear simpler, more familiar and less costly to penetrate—and these are most commonly those which are closest in physical and cultural terms (40) (41). It is not uncommon for Australian firms to view operations in New Zealand as merely an extension of domestic activities, as also for Finnish firms moving into Sweden. A company's shift of activities to more 'distant' locations can therefore be seen as one indication of greater maturation in its internationalization process.

Organizational capacity

The internationalization process of a company is perhaps most overtly demonstrated by the preceding three dimensions: the further advanced a firm is along them the more 'internationalized' it may be regarded as being. For example, a Finnish company with a high export/total sales ratio of say 80% but which is selling only one product, via an agent, to one country, Sweden would be regarded, according to the above framework, as still being only in the earliest stages of international development.

Nevertheless, although providing a broader-based assessment of internationalization, the first three dimensions concentrate on the components of actual foreign market activity. Such an approach leaves aside the variety of internal company changes which are consequent upon, and therefore reflect, the degree of internationalization but also form the foundation for additional steps forward in the overall process (42). In the resources area finance and personnel are obviously important, but so also is the organization structure developed for handling foreign activities. In Figure 1, three of these areas—finance, personnel and organization structure—are noted because of their importance, but they are by no means exclusively so.

Personnel

The success of internationalization in any company depends heavily on the type of people both initiating and carrying through the various steps in the process, and on overall personnel policies. Lorange (43) has recently argued that 'the human resource function is particularly critical to successful implementation of (such) co-operative ventures (joint ventures, licensing agreements, project co-operation . . .)'. In the initial exporting phase the background of the decision-maker, in such areas as work and foreign experience, education and language training, has been shown to be potentially important in the preparedness to commit a firm to the exporting activity (44) (45). At a general level though, internationalization both feeds upon and contributes to the development of international knowledge, skills and experience of the people involved (46). While learning-by-doing appears to be a key part of the whole process, it is also possible to obtain some assistance through effective training and recruitment policies. Tung (47), for example, concluded from a study of a number of US, European and Japanese companies that 'the more rigorous the selection and training procedures used, the less the incidences of poor performance or failure to work effectively in a foreign country'. Clearly, unless the people involved, through whatever means, become more international in their capacities and outlook, the ability to carry through any international strategy is bound to be severely constrained. International personnel development therefore remains as a prime indication of the internal extent to which a company has effectively become internationalized, although it is perhaps more difficult to measure than the preceding three dimensions.

Organizational structure

As the administrative and organizational demands generally of carrying out international operations grow and diversify, the organizational structure for handling such demands ultimately needs to respond. A variety of formal and informal organizational arrangements have been used by companies in different countries to cope with the increasing amount and complexity of continuing internationalization (48) (49) (50). The changes, and their sophistication, as the company seeks to improve the organizational mechanism and focus of international operations, provide a further signpost of the state of internationalization. Organizational changes are often a clear statement of commitment to the objectives of international involvement. In an Australian study the shift from experimental to committed exporting was often marked by the establishment of an export section or division in some form (51).

Finance

The growth of international operations inevitably also places increasing demands on the availability of funds to support the various activities. The nature and extent of the company's financing activities for international operations provide a further indicator of the degree of internationalization. We might expect that the range of finance sources (both local and international) and the sophistication of financing techniques would develop with international growth. However, the relationship is by no means clear-cut—depending on such aspects as the type of product/service, operation methods and payment method, as well as the extent of government support (52).

Framework overview

By examining the above six dimensions it is possible to derive a substantial overview of the state of internationalization of a given company, which could then form the basis of comparison to others. It is not the intention at this stage to consider scales of measurement along the different dimensions, although work has already taken place in this area—as for example in Luostarinen's (53) composite of business distance (including cultural, economic and physical distance). At a general level though it is possible to foresee the development of more precise composite measures along the various dimensions, providing a better basis for relative assessment of the internationalization progress of different companies. For example, the hypothetical patterns for two companies are presented in Figure 2. Comparing the two patterns it is clear that company 1 has gone further than company 2 in its foreign market activities, yet its internal development to support these is less developed than company 2. Perhaps this is a sign of potential problems for company 1.

PATTERNS OF INTERNATIONALIZATION

From the discussion so far it is clear that there is a wide range of potential paths any firm might take in internationalization. Nevertheless, are there any consistent patterns observable from the research? In answering this question a major contribution has been made by Nordic researchers (54) (55) (56). Their work points generally to a process of evolutionary, sequential build-up of foreign commitments over time. Johanson and Wiedersheim-Paul studied the establishment chains of four large Swedish multinationals from the beginning of their operations. Typically the growth of foreign establishments

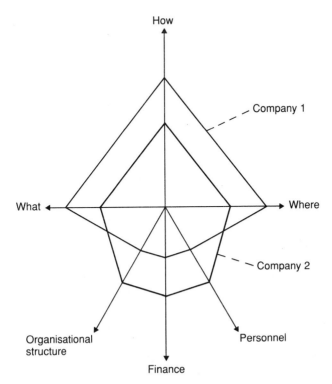

Figure 2. Hypothetical Company Comparison.

was distinguished by a series of small, cumulative steps over time: the setting-up of a sales subsidiary was preceded by an agency operation in about three-quarters of cases.

This general pattern of evolutionary development was perhaps most strongly confirmed in Finnish research. In a study of around three-quarters of the population of Finnish industrial companies with foreign operations of any type Luostarinen found that, in 1976, 65% of the companies had only non-investment marketing operations abroad, 33% had production operations abroad which had been preceded by non-investment marketing operations, whereas in only 2% of the total had production operations abroad begun without preceding operations. This result has apparently continued, although being less pronounced, according to a more recent examination of the shift to foreign direct manufacturing investment during the period 1980–82 by Finnish companies (57). In only 13% of cases did the shift occur without preceding alternative operations in the country concerned.

Luostarinen's research revealed a process of evolutionary development not only in terms of the depth of operational mode, but also in terms of the diversity of modes used, as well as in product offerings and the range of markets penetrated. For example, product offerings were divided into four categories: goods, services, systems and know-how. The offering to foreign markets consistently began in the simplest form—i.e. goods (for 99% of companies)—while sales of services systems and know-how came later, and approximately in that order (58). The gradual development towards systems or package selling has also been noted in the growth of Swedish multinational corporations where skills and knowledge (software) were added to the hardware sale until a more complete problem-solving package was on offer (59). This trend has broader implications as a growing software/service component clearly places greater stress on effective communication skills and understanding of user needs and the user's environment, which is a more demanding exercise once cultural and other distance barriers have to be surmounted, thereby reinforcing the impact of such distance variables on internationalization.

Research in other countries, although differing in sample size, period of study and subject of analysis, nevertheless has revealed a degree of consistency with the results of Nordic research. In examining Japanese foreign investment in South-East Asia, Yoshihara (60) found that 'the pattern of investment seems to substantiate the evolutionary theory of foreign investment'. This echoes a similar conclusion drawn from a longitudinal study of American direct investment abroad (61). Small sample studies of first time UK smaller firm direct investors and of Continental European direct investors in the UK have confirmed the pattern of intermediate steps being used as build-up to foreign investment (62) (63). While 15.4% of cases involved a direct move to foreign investment, 'over half of these firms were prevented from exporting by the nature of their product—transport cost barriers or a high 'service' element effectively ruled out exporting as a means of servicing the foreign markets' (64).

The pattern is not completely consistent though as an Australian study of 228 outward direct investment cases revealed that in 39% of these cases there was no pre-existing host country presence (65). To some extent this can be explained by the high proportion (43.8%) of service companies involved in the investment activity, given that it is often more difficult to operate with intermediate steps to the foreign investment stage in the services sector. However, service companies were only slightly under-represented (40.7%) amongst those affiliates with a pre-existing presence (66). Of particular note though is the fact that 65.5% of the investments were undertaken during the period 1970–79. This is perhaps suggestive of a change in the rate at which firms have been accomplishing internationalization in more recent times, through leapfrogging of intermediate steps to the foreign investment stage in some countries. Further support for this development has been forthcoming in the more direct move to foreign investment by Swedish companies into the Japanese market from the early 1970s (67). Perhaps a more general indication of the desire by companies to short-circuit the process of gradually building-up activities in foreign markets over time has been the switch in foreign investment towards acquisition and away from greenfield ventures (68) (69) (70). Acquisition is not only a path to more rapid establishment in a given foreign market, which has become a more important consideration in the light of stronger global competition, but it is also potentially a means of obtaining faster access to a developed international network. For example, when the Australian company Wormald International purchased Mather and Platt in the UK it obtained as well a network of subsidiaries in Europe, Japan, Brazil, South Africa and New Zealand. The managing director commented that to have built such a network from scratch would have taken 20–30 years (71) (72).

Of course, it should be expected that observed patterns of internationalization will vary from country to country, and over time, because of environmental differences at the outset, as well as the inevitable changes in the environment. A combination of the more competitive international environment of the 1980s and the general demonstration effects of other companies' increased international efforts from different national environments has probably contributed to a less cautious approach to internationalization, at least in the latter stages.

It should also be stressed that the concept of a sequential, cumulative process of internationalization does not necessarily mean some smooth, immutable path of development. The actual paths taken are often irregular. Commitments are frequently lumpy over time with plateaux while previous moves are absorbed and consolidated. Particular steps are affected by the emergence of opportunities and/or threats which do not usually arrive in a continuous or controlled manner. The outcome tends to be derived from a mixture of deliberate and emergent strategies (73).

In fact, some of the argument which appears to be developing about the evolutionary or stages model of internationalization (74) seems to have occurred because of a lack of specification of what this process actually means for an individual company: does it mean evolution or a stepwise process for each individual foreign market or rather development of involvement in an overall sense? So far concentration has been on the former situation where the number and type of steps up to, for example, foreign investments are considered. A reduction in, or absence of, intervening steps in a foreign market is taken as some indication that the evolutionary or stages model is not functioning (75). Such a result is of course more likely in particular markets where unique circumstances might apply, perhaps in the form of government policy. More importantly though it is probably more appropriate to analyse the process of international involvement at the company level, looking across total foreign market activities. As skills, experience and knowledge in the use of a more advanced form of operations are developed in some foreign markets we might expect that this will eventually allow a company to leapfrog some intermediate steps in others (76). This proposition is illustrated in Figure 3. Taken on its own, company X's move directly to foreign investment in Foreign Market No. 6 might be regarded as a shift away from the sequentialist pattern revealed in other markets. However, when taken in the overall context of the steps taken in other markets it is certainly far removed from a

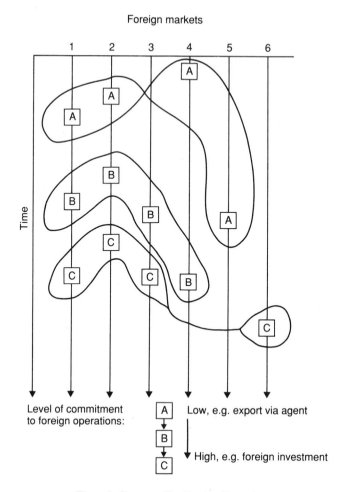

Figure 3. Company X—Foreign Operations.

leap into the unknown. Thus, leapfrogging moves in given markets should be examined as part of the overall operational pattern of the company before any definite conclusions can be drawn about a 'shift' from the evolutionary pattern.

Likewise the concept of what is evolutionary could be related back to the type of preceding experience of international operations that key individuals in the company might have had. For example an Australian company with four years of operating and marketing experience in a small Australian city (Toowoomba) considered its first 'export' move as an attempt to penetrate a large Australian city 130 kilometres away (Brisbane). By contrast a Sydney company was exporting within three months of beginning operations and to 52 countries in three years. The differences in behaviour were strongly related to the owner-managers of each company. In the Toowoomba example the individual had very limited personal or company experience beyond the local area, whereas in the second case the manager was a migrant with over 20 years of international experience in the industry concerned which had exposed an unexploited market niche. His perception of the market place was international in character from the outset. In this context, the international moves of the Sydney company were less startling than at first sight. One person's (or company's) evolution often appears as a revolution to others (77) (78).

Overall then, the research has revealed a reasonable degree of consistency, at least up to the mid-1970s, that the pattern of internationalization for most firms has been marked by a sequential, stepwise process of development. More recently, limited evidence has been emerging of a departure from the gradualist path as some firms seek to by-pass the steps to deeper commitment, resulting in a speeding up of the whole process. Just how widespread the change is can only be determined from further research, but pattern variation should be expected in response to the many environmental changes, both nationally and globally, which have occurred in the 1970s and 1980s.

WHY INTERNATIONALIZATION?

While we can expect continued debate on the nature of the shifting pattern of internationalization, an important question remains to be settled: why internationalization? What is it that drives the process, leading a firm from little or no involvement to, in some cases, widespread multinational investments? Obviously, if we are to understand the process then we have to explain why a company undertakes each particular step in an overt pattern. As Starbuck (79) has noted, growth is not spontaneous, it is the result of decisions. As such, the separate analysis of these distinct steps contributes to our understanding of why and how the internationalization process is initiated and maintained. For example, the recent research on the export involvement decision has considerably elucidated how and why a company's internationalization begins, and what sort of base is established for subsequent forward moves, if any (80) (81) (82). However, each of the decision points inevitably has a variety of unique causative elements as well as bearing the impact of any general on-going influential factors, as noted in Figure 4. In developing any overall explanation of internationalization it is important to examine those continuing influences which play such a key role in maintaining forward momentum—in building the company to the point where it is more receptive to the possibilities of increased involvement, and better prepared to respond to them. These dynamic factors also help to explain why there is some degree of consistency of internationalization

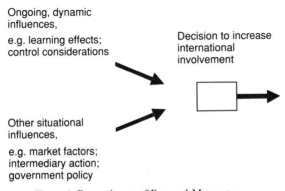

Figure 4. Determinants of Forward Momentum.

patterns across countries because of their general effect. At the same time they represent reasons why so many companies feel constrained to a more gradual, sequential path of development, as revealed in the research noted earlier.

Overall pattern explanatory factors—resources availability

The ability to undertake any form of international operations is clearly limited by the means accessible to the firm to carry it out. For smaller firms, given their limitations in many areas, this is an obvious reason why less demanding directions of international development can be undertaken first, with major commitments only occurring well into the longer run. By the same token, this means that we should expect larger firms, based in large domestic markets, to reveal more advanced involvement far earlier, and generally to move through the overall process at a faster rate. While there is some argument about the research results which consider the impact of size, there does not appear to be any clear relationship between size of firm and export performance (83) (84). Instead of size, Czinkota and Johnston (85) concluded that 'what really does seem to make for export success is the attitude of management'. Some of the constraints which face companies of whatever size, when considering international expansion, particularly financial ones, are sometimes more apparent than real. Outside financial sources and creative funding of takeovers, have been used by some companies to permit faster expansion than directly accessible means would imply (86). While resource availability may limit expansion at any given point in time, the constraint is not static, so that any action or developments which widen availability provide the basis for increased foreign operations over time.

Knowledge development

Clearly, there is something more to the resources question than just physical or financial capacity. A critical factor in the ability to carry out chosen international activities is the possession of appropriate knowledge: this includes knowledge about foreign markets, about techniques of foreign operation, about ways of doing business, about key people in buyer organizations, and so on. Such information and understanding is not easily, cheaply or rapidly acquired. Much of it is not readily acquired 'off-the-shelf' as it is developed through the actual experience of foreign operations (87). The learning-by-doing process explains much in the evolutionary patterns of internationalization revealed in research (88).

Communication networks

Personal contact and social interaction play an important part in the development of international markets—especially where more complex industrial products are concerned (89). Networks between buyers and sellers which form the basis of effective communication must be established. Network establishment can be a demanding and time consuming process where the gap between buyer and seller is large due to an initial lack of knowledge of each other and is accentuated by physical and cultural distance barriers. There is considerable inertia amongst buyers who feel more secure with suppliers from familiar sources and locations. While this constrains the development of operations at the outset, the initial gaps are not necessarily static: they are susceptible to reduction over time. With wider experience, greater contact at all levels and more diverse cultural exposure on both sides, there is a potential for deeper and more long-standing relationships to evolve, forming the basis for deeper commitments (90).

Risk and uncertainty

As foreign buyers are loath to establish networks with unknown foreign suppliers at the outset so too the foreign suppliers, because of initial lack of knowledge and experience, tend to feel uncertainty about taking on additional or new foreign operations, especially in unfamiliar locations. Inevitably there is a response of seeking ways to reduce the uncertainty exposure. It is not surprising therefore to find the pattern noted earlier that companies are attracted to foreign operations first in more familiar (culturally) and closer locations and that only small steps in operational commitments are undertaken initially thereby limiting exposure. This also allows experimentation without high risk and the time required to gather relevant knowledge and experience, before any deeper commitment is contemplated.

In general therefore the need to develop relevant knowledge and skills and communication networks, as well as to reduce risk and uncertainty exposure, interact and play a key role at given points in constraining international moves. Over time, however, the inevitable changes in these areas consequent upon foreign activities also change the capacity of the company to contemplate and carry through more involving commitments (91).

Control

Given the limited foreign market knowledge and experience of many companies during the early stages of internationalizaton it is not surprising that they will often look to outside foreign intermediaries to assist in market penetration. With more experience, however, if a company's knowledge about a given market increases through active involvement, there is a tendency for it to scrutinize the activities of its foreign intermediary more closely, especially when sales potential has been proven by preceding operations. The concern about control is reflected in a variety of efforts to more closely direct the operations of the intermediary on its behalf. Sometimes this will result in 'positive' steps such as training or the provision of promotional materials. In other cases a more 'negative' approach will be adopted, leading to more stringent checks and guidelines. Under these changing circumstances, with the power positions being subtly reversed and the principal feeling less dependent on its foreign intermediary, it is not uncommon for dissatisfaction about perceived under-performance to grow. Ultimately, perhaps sparked by other developments, the principal may feel that the effective way of dealing with the 'problem' is for it to take over the running of the foreign operation itself, in some altered form. Inevitably this will mean increasing its commitment in the given foreign market. Thus, the control factor, interacting with knowledge development and risk perception, tends to be a growing influence over time which pushes a company towards increasing involvement in foreign operations. In general, increasing market control means increasing involvement and thereby greater cost and risk (92).

Commitment

As international operations are developed there is necessarily a commitment of resources, and by people, to the process. This commitment is particularly strong when key management staff are involved in developing the international strategy (93). It creates a need for fulfilment and provides strong forward momentum whereby justification is sought in further operations and deeper involvement along the same line (94). The commitment factor therefore represents a further dynamic driving force in the overall internationalization process.

The above factors taken together help to explain the continued forward momentum of the internationalization process of individual companies and also why the evolutionary pattern has been found in so many studies in different countries (95). In essence, these factors, apart from any general market size and potential considerations, help us to understand why for example a given environmental change—such as protectionist action by a foreign government or a change in foreign investment rules—is unlikely to cause a shift to foreign investment by a company with limited foreign experience but is more likely to do so at a later stage after the development of market knowledge, contacts, a sales organization, etc., as illustrated in Figure 5.

CONCLUSION

Taken overall the concept of internationalization has yet to be clearly developed as a research object. Nevertheless, considerable progress has been made in establishing its conceptual and empirical foundations, while the emerging debate about the 'stages thesis' or 'gradual internationalization' can be considered a healthy step in clarifying the subject.

Given the focus of the concept, a development process through time, much research remains to be conducted that is responsive to its longitudinal character. Inevitably this is a

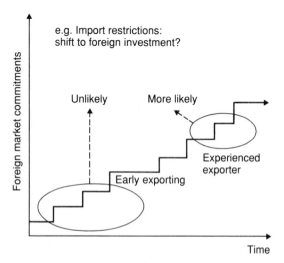

Figure 5. Response to Environmental Change.

difficult activity (96): take for example the attempt to trace the impact of individuals and the evolution of communication patterns in the past. It can be expected however that research will continue along the dual lines of analysis of particular decisions or steps in the overall process and those elements which tie together total progress.

REFERENCES

1. Servan-Schreiber, J. J., *Le Defi American*. Editions de Noel, Paris, 1967.
2. Brash, D. T., *American Investment in Australian Industry*, Harvard University Press, Cambridge, Mass., 1966.
3. Safarian, A. E., *Foreign Ownership of Canadian Industry*, McGraw-Hill, Toronto, 1966.
4. Dunning, J. H., *American Investment in British Manufacturing*, Allen and Unwin, London, 1958.
5. Horst, T., 'Firm and Industry Determinants of the Decision to Invest Abroad', *Review of Economics and Statistics*. Vol. 54. 1972, pp. 264–5.
6. Aharoni, Y., *The Foreign Investment Decision Process*, Harvard University Press, Boston, Mass., 1966.
7. Wilkins, M., *The Emergence of Multinational Enterprise*, Harvard University Press, Cambridge, Mass., 1970.
8. Wilkins, M., *The Maturing of Multinational Enterprise*, Harvard University Press, Cambridge, Mass., 1974.
9. Johanson, J. and Wiedersheim-Paul, F., 'The Internationalization of the Firm—Four Swedish Cases', *Journal of Management Studies*, Vol. 12, No. 3, October, 1975.
10. Johanson, J. and Vahlne, J.-E., 'The Internationalization Process of the Firm', *Journal of International Business Studies*, Vol. 8, Spring/Summer, 1977.
11. Luostarinen, R., *The Internationalization of the Firm*, Acta Academic Oeconomica Helsingiensis, Helsinki, 1979.
12. Bilkey, W. J. and Tesar, G., 'The Export Behavior of Smaller Wisconsin Manufacturing Firms', *Journal of International Business Studies*, Vol. 8, Spring/Summer, 1977.
13. Welch, L. S. and Wiedersheim-Paul, F., 'Initial Exports—A Marketing Failure?' *Journal of Management Studies*, Vol. 17, October, 1980b.
14. Joynt, P., 'An Empirical Study of Norwegian Export Behavior', *Skriftserie*, No. 1. 1981.
15. Piercy, N., 'Company Internationalisation: Active and Reactive Exporting', *European Journal of Marketing*, Vol. 15, No. 3, 1981.
16. Denis, J.-E., and Depelteau, D., 'Market Knowledge. Diversification and Export Expansion', *Journal of International Business Studies*. Vol. 16, Fall, 1985.
17. Buckley, P. J., 'New Theories of International Business', in M. Casson (ed.), *The Growth of International Business*, Allen and Unwin, London, 1983, p. 48.
18. Johanson, J. and Wiedersheim-Paul, F., op. cit.
19. Piercy, N., op. cit.
20. Turnbull, P., 'Internationalisation of the Firm—A Stages Process or Not?', paper presented at the conference on Export Expansion and Market Entry Modes, Dalhousie University, Halifax, October 15/16, 1985.
21. Koury, S. J., 'Countertrade: Forms, Motives, Pitfalls, and Negotiation Requisites', *Journal of Business Research*, Vol. 12, No. 2, June 1984.
22. Huszagh, S. M. and Huszagh, F. W., 'International Barter and Countertrade', *International Marketing Review*, Vol. 3, No. 2, Summer, 1986.
23. Dizard, J. W., 'The Explosion of International Barter', *Fortune*, Vol. 107, No. 3, February 7, 1983.
24. Cohen, S. S. and Zysman, J., 'Countertrade, Offsets, Barter, and Buybacks', *California Management Review*, Vol. 28, No. 2, Winter 1986.
25. Carstairs, R. and Welch, L. S., 'Australian Offshore Investment in Asia', *Management International Review*, Vol. 20, No. 4, 1980.
26. Hornell, E. and Vahlne, J.-E., 'The Changing Structure of Swedish Multinational Companies'. Working Paper 1982/12. Centre for International Business Studies, University of Uppsala.
27. *Business Week*, 'The Hollow Corporation', March 3, 1986.
28. Boddewynn, J. J., 'Foreign Divestment: Magnitude and Factors', *Journal of International Business Studies*, Vol. 10, Spring/Summer, 1979.
29. Welch, L. S. and Wiedersheim-Paul, P., op. cit., 1980b.
30. Cavusgil, S. T. and Godiwalla, Y. M., 'Decision-Making for International Marketing: A Comparative Review', *Management Decision*, Vol. 20, No. 4, 1982.
31. Johanson, J. and Wiedersheim-Paul, F., op. cit.
32. Luostarinen, R., op. cit.
33. Luostarinen, R. op. cit., pp. 105–124.

34. Carstairs, R. T. and Welch, L. S., 'Licensing and the Internationalization of Smaller Companies: Some Australian Evidence', *Management International Review*, Vol. 22, No. 3, 1982, p. 35.

35. Roscoe, B., 'Getting round protectionism by the direct route', *Far Eastern Economic Review*, June 13, 1985, pp. 82–3.

36. Emmott, B., 'Japan: A Survey', *Economist*, December 7, 1985, pp. 26–30.

37. Luostarinen, R., op. cit., pp. 95–105.

38. Price Waterhouse Associates, *Successful Exporting*, Australian Government Publishing Service, Canberra, 1982, pp. 30–34.

39. Hornell, E. and Vahlne, J.-E., op. cit., p. 8.

40. Vahlne, J.-E. and Wiedersheim-Paul, F., 'Psychic Distance—An Inhibiting Factor in International Trade', Working Paper, 1977/2. Centre for International Business Studies, University of Uppsala, Sweden.

41. Luostarinen, R., op. cit., pp. 124–172.

42. Cavusgil, S. T. and Godiwalla, Y. M., op. cit.

43. Lorange, P., 'Human Resource Management in Multinational Cooperative Ventures', *Human Resource Management*, Vol. 25, No. 1, Spring, 1986, p. 133.

44. Reid, S. D., 'The Decision-Maker and Export Entry and Expansion', *Journal of International Business Studies*, Vol. 12, Fall, 1981.

45. Welch, L. S., 'Managerial Decision-Making: The Case of Export Involvement', *Scandinavian Journal of Materials Administration*, Vol. 9, No. 2, 1983.

46. Johanson, J. and Vahlne, J.-E., op. cit.

47. Tung, R. L., 'Selection and Training of U.S., European, and Japanese Multinationals', *California Management Review*, Vol. 25, No. 1, Fall 1982, p. 70.

48. Stopford, J. M. and Wells, L. T., *Managing the Multinational Enterprise*, Basic Books, New York, 1972.

49. Bartlett, C. A., 'Multinational Structural Change: Evolution Versus Reorganization', in L. Otterbeck (ed.), *The Management of Headquarters—Subsidiary Relationships in Multinational Corporations*, Gower, Aldershot, 1981.

50. Hedlund, G., 'Organization In-Between', *Journal of International Business Studies*, Vol. 15, Fall, 1984.

51. Welch, L. S. and Wiedersheim-Paul. F., op. cit., 1980b.

52. Price Waterhouse Associates, op. cit., pp. 56–62.

53. Luostarinen, R., op. cit., p. 151.

54. Johanson, J. and Wiedersheim-Paul. F., op. cit.

55. Luostarinen, R., op. cit.

56. Juul, M. and Walters, P., 'The Internationalization of Norwegian Firms: A Study of the U.K. Experience', *Management International Review*, Vol. 27, No. 1, 1987.

57. Larimo, J., 'The Foreign Direct Manufacturing Investment Behaviour of Finnish Companies', paper presented at the 11th European International Business Association Conference, Glasgow, December 15–17, 1985.

58. Luostarinen, R., op. cit., pp. 95–105.

59. Hornell, E. and Vahlne, J.-E., op. cit., p. 8.

60. Yoshihara, K., 'Determinants of Japanese Investment in South-East Asia', *International Social Science Journal*, Vol. 30, No. 2, 1978, p. 372.

61. Wilkins, M., 1974, op. cit., p. 414.

62. Buckley, P. J., Newbould, G. D. and Thurwell, J., 'Going International—The Foreign Direct Investment Behaviour of Smaller U.K. Firms' in L. G. Mattsson and F. Wiedersheim-Paul (eds), *Recent Research on the Internationalization of Business*, Acta Universitatis Upsaliensis, Uppsala, 1979.

63. Buckley, P. J., Newbould, G. D. and Berkova, Z., 'Direct Investment in the U.K. by Smaller Continental European Firms', Working Paper, University of Bradford, 1981.

64. Buckley, P. J., 'The Role of Exporting in the Market Servicing Policies of Multinational Manufacturing Enterprises', in M. Czinkota and G. Tesar (eds), *Export Management*, Praeger, New York, 1982, pp. 178–9.

65. Bureau of Industry Economics, *Australian Direct Investment Abroad*, Australian Government Publishing Service, Canberra, 1984, p. 115.

66. Bureau of Industry Economics, op. cit., p. 128.

67. Hedlund, G. and Kverneland, A., 'Are Establishments and Growth Strategies For Foreign Markets Changing?', paper presented at the 9th European International Business Association Conference, Oslo, December 18–20, 1983.

68. Hornell, E. and Vahlne, J.-E., op. cit.

69. Larimo, J., op. cit.

70. OECD, 'International Direct Investment: A Change in Pattern', *OECD Observer*, No. 112, September, 1981.

71. Korporaal, G., *Yankee Dollars: Australian Investment in America*, Allen and Unwin, 1986, ch. 12.

72. Department of Trade, 'Fire Protection firm sparks new sales in China, U.S.S.R.', *Overseas Trading*, Vol. 31, No. 10, 25 May, 1979, p. 345.

73. Mintzberg, H. and McHugh, A., 'Strategy Formation in an Adhocracy', *Administrative Science Quarterly*, Vol. 30, June, 1985.

74. Turnbull, P., op. cit.

75. Hedlund, G. and Kverneland, A., op. cit.

76. Buckley, P. J., op. cit.

77. Welch, L. S. and Wiedersheim-Paul, F., 'Domestic Expansion: Internationalization At Home', *Essays in International Business*, No. 2, December 1980a.

78. Layton, R. (ed.), 'Magna Alloys and Research Pty. Ltd.', *Australian Marketing Projects*, Halstead Press, Sydney, 1969.

79. Starbuck, W. H., 'Organizational Growth and Development', in W. H. Starbuck (ed.), *Organizational Growth and Development*, Penguin, Harmondsworth, 1971.

80. Welch, L. S. and Wiedersheim-Paul, F., op. cit., 1980b.

81. Cavusgil, S. T., 'Organizational Characteristics Associated With Export Activity', *Journal of Management Studies*, Vol. 21, No. 1, Jan. 1984.

82. Yaprak, A., 'An Empirical Study of the Differences Between Small Exporting and Non-Exporting US Firms', *International Marketing Review*, Vol. 2, No. 2, Summer, 1985.

83. Czinkota, M. R. and Johnston, W. J., 'Exporting: Does Sales Volume Make a Difference', *Journal of International Business Studies*, Vol. 14, Spring/Summer, 1983.

84. Cavusgil, S. T., op. cit.

85. Czinkota, M. R. and Johnston, W. J., op. cit., p. 153.

86. *Euromoney*, 'Elders IXL', Supplement, August, 1985.

87. Johanson, J. and Vahlne, J.-E., op. cit.

88. Carlson, S., *How Foreign Is Foreign Trade*, Acta Universitatis Upsaliensis, Uppsala, 1975.

89. Hakansson, H. (ed.), *International Marketing and Purchasing of Industrial Goods*, John Wiley, Winchester, 1982.

90. Ford, D., 'The Development of Buyer-Seller Relationships in Industrial Markets', *European Journal of Marketing*, Vol. 14, 5/6, 1980.

91. Johanson, J. and Vahlne, J.-E., op. cit.

92. Luostarinen, R., op. cit., p. 117.

93. Aharoni, Y., op. cit.

94. Johanson, J. and Vahlne, J.-E., op. cit.

95. Cavusgil, S. T. and Godiwalla, Y. M., op. cit.

12

A Challenge to the Stages Theory of the Internationalization Process

Peter W. Turnbull

Theories of internationalization, in particular 'stages' based models, are usually offered to explain the export structures that firms adopt, and to provide normative or prescriptive approaches for assisting export decision making. This chapter empirically questions the validity and premises of the internationalization thesis using data gathered from the Industrial Marketing and Purchasing (IMP) Group's research project on the international marketing of industrial products in Western Europe.

The sample consists of British companies operating in three industry sectors: large marine diesel engines, motor vehicle components, and telecommunications equipment. These industries show considerable variation in their dependence on foreign markets and in their penetration of Western Europe.

The results presented refute current explanations of firm foreign involvement and cast considerable doubt on the usefulness of such approaches for understanding the process through which foreign market expansion takes place. In addition, some specific comments are offered concerning the conceptual and methodological problems associated with operationalizing and investigating firm foreign market expansion and export involvement.

The analysis is divided into five sections: (1) a survey of the internationalization literature, (2) a critical discussion of the internationalization thesis, (3) a description of the research methodology, (4) an overview of the research results, and (5) implications and conclusions from the research findings.

THE INTERNATIONALIZATION CONCEPT

The 'stages theory of internationalization' argues that firms proceed in a consistent stepwise fashion along some organizational continuum as they develop their international activities. This core assumption that is explicit in the 'stages approach' is also found in

The author recognizes the funding support of the British Economic and Social Research Council, which made this research possible. The help of Doreen Li Wan Po, Sheena Ellwood, and Gillian Blackwell in data collection and analysis is also gratefully acknowledged.

many explanations of how firms internationalize. For example, Tookey (1969) sees three steps in terms of 'exporting', 'international marketing', and 'international business'. These steps are differentiated by the objectives they aim to achieve. In the exporting stage, firms emphasize selling surplus products or obsolete inventory to foreign markets; in the second stage of international marketing, firms make consistent efforts to maximize profitable sales and meet needs in world markets. In the final stage, international business, firms are principally concerned with managing global operations.

While other writers conceptualize internationalization differently, they still view it as an orderly and progressive sequence. Wind, Douglas, and Perlmutter (1973), for example, consider it as a process in which specific attitudes or 'orientations' are associated with successive stages in the evolution of international operations. They identify four attitude types—ethnocentrism, polycentrism, regiocentrism, and geocentrism, that are reflected in the goals, philosophies, and exporting stages of international companies—and specific exporting strategies. The ethnocentric business (which is primarily 'oriented' to the home country) views overseas operations as secondary to domestic ones, and mainly as a way of disposing of surplus domestic production. This type of orientation and export emphasis gradually changes until a final stage of foreign involvement is reached. In this final 'geocentric' (world orientation) phase, the entire world is seen as a potential market, and policies are developed on an international basis.

Other interpretations of internationalization as a sequential and orderly process of organizational development exist. The most well-developed is that presented in the work of the Uppsala School (Johanson and Vahlne 1977; Johanson and Wiedersheim-Paul 1975) and of Bilkey and Tesar (1977). The Uppsala School considers internationalization as having four stages, whereas Bilkey and Tesar propose six. These writers, however, differentiate the internationalization stages in terms of 'levels of export involvement' in contrast to the attitude criterion used by Wind, Douglas, and Perlumutter (1973).

Bilkey and Tesar (1977) primarily consider internationalization from the perspective of increased export dependence in a growing number of markets, while Johanson and Vahlne (1977) focus on the organizational forms that are associated with such dependence. The stress on export organizational forms that are associated with growing export involvement is a distinct feature of the Uppsala School's proposition on internationalization.

Johanson and Vahlne (1977) emphasize the link between resource commitment, the approach used to acquire market information, export dependency, and export organization. For example, sales subsidiaries are considered to give firms more 'controlled' channels through which they can direct the type and amount of information flowing from and to the market. In this stage, it is argued, firms have direct experience of 'resource influencing factors' and these experiences will govern entry into establishing direct production facilities, the final stage of foreign involvement. Bilkey's (1978) conclusion that exporting occurs in development stages is also shared by Cunningham and Homse (1982), who proposed that internationalization

is a continuous process of choice between policies which differ maybe only marginally from the status quo. It is perhaps best conceptualized in terms of the learning curve theory. Certain stimuli induce a firm to move to a higher export stage, the experience (or learning) that is gained then alters the firm's perceptions, expectations and indeed managerial capacity and competence; and new stimuli then induce the firm to move to the next higher export stage, and so on.

CRITICAL ISSUES IN INTERNATIONALIZATION

It is surprising just how 'popular' and widely accepted the stages approach to inter-nationalization has become since, as Reid (1984) points out, it largely rests upon only two significant empirical studies: the original research into the export behaviour of four Swedish companies (Johanson and Wiedersheim-Paul, 1975) and the research into Australian firms reported by Wiedersheim-Paul, Olson, and Welch (1978). The degree to which this theory has been accepted is evidenced by almost universal references to it in international marketing texts (for example, see Kirpalani, 1985).

The popularity of the concept is inconsistent with empirical and theoretical evidence that contradicts its propositions. For example, Young and Hood (1976) in their survey of US multinationals in Scotland show that firms can have significant sales in a market prior to establishing manufacturing subsidiaries. Other writers, such as Turnbull and Valla (1986) and Buckley, Newbould, and Thurwell (1979), also show that firms do not necessarily follow any consistent organizational approach as they enter foreign markets or expand exports. Even large companies with substantial international experience and commitment use a variety of export marketing organizations, which can change from market to market (Li Wan Po, 1982).

A further and perhaps more important challenge to the stages theory has been consistently propounded by Reid (1983a, b; 1984), who questions the fundamental theoretical validity of the approach. The theory's underlying assumption that companies develop more formal structures for handling export markets as their dependence on these markets increase is extensively criticized. Reid's writings view foreign expansion as contingency based and offer an export transactional cost approach to explain the process. The writer notes that this interpretation of firm behaviour is consistent with other writers, notably Penrose (1959) who proposes that firms strategically and situationally adapt to market circumstances.

The above view on internationalization is best summed up as follows:

> Since exporting results from a choice among competing expansion strategies that are guided by the nature of the market opportunity, firm resources, and managerial philosophy, it represents a selective and dynamic adaptation to the changing character of the foreign market. . . . Market factors and requirements are therefore closely intertwined with deciding whether to go international and what form this expansion should take (Reid, 1983a, 137–138).

Apart from the empirical and conceptual challenges the stages theory has received, there are additional interpretive and methodological problems that should be considered. The first problem is a definitional one. An examination of international companies, particularly large or multiproduct ones, reveals extremely complex and dynamic organizational forms, with product divisions, regional divisions, or other administrative groupings. Depending on which discrete organizational unit is observed within a complex company, one can find different degrees and types of internationalization. The second problem is the lack of clear distinctions between internationalization stages and confusion in their measurement.

Internationalization is sometimes indicated by such criteria as export value or number of markets served (Cavusgil, 1977) or by type of international organizational form (Johanson and Wiedersheim-Paul, 1975). The two measures are often combined in the sense that it is assumed that each export organizational form is automatically a consequence of the stage of internationalization achieved. Thus, in Johanson and Wiedersheim-Paul's research, exporting through agents is considered as a primary stage of internationalization. We do not accept this neat association and our previous IMP work (Turnbull and Valla, 1986) has shown that companies with substantial international experience and commitment can still use this type of export marketing organization.

A third conceptual difficulty arises when we try to define a company's degree of internationalization. In large multiproduct/multidivisional firms, one commonly finds variance in extent of export dependence, number of export markets served, and export structure across and among business units. For example, in one of our sampled firms, a *division* had export sales of less than 2% of its total sales, whereas the *company* export sales amounted to nearly 50% of total turnover. Evidence of this sort questions whether internationalization as a concept can be meaningfully applied across all organizations irrespective of their varying structures.

The issue of which organizational forms are being examined is of course paramount. Proper classification of organizations is necessary for both descriptive and analytical purposes. Many different classifications can be found in the literature. Ansoff (1982) uses a very simple classification of direct export, international and multinational; Rothchild (1983) proposes a classification of domestic, quasi-domestic, and multinational; Johanson and Wiedersheim-Paul (1975) suggest four types of exporting: direct, indirect (using agents), local sales (sales office or subsidiary), and local manufacturing; while Bilkey and Tesar (1977) offer a more complex six-stage typology.

None of the above classifications offers organizations with pure export properties or characteristics that are practically consistent. They in fact do provide scope for potential confusion. This is most likely when we compare the classifications of export *activity* or *orientation* that underlie Rothchild's and Bilkey and Tesar's frameworks with other classifications of export marketing *organizational forms*. While the two may be closely linked they are not necessarily interchangeable.

The organizational form adopted—which can be seen as an output of the process on the one hand, and a facilitator of the process on the other hand—need not follow such sequential change. Thus there may be limited correspondence between a company's stage in export development and the organization structure it employs.

THE RESEARCH METHODOLOGY

The empirical results presented in this section are drawn exclusively from British data gathered by the UK research team over a five-year period. This research team is part of the Industrial Marketing and Purchasing project conducting programmatic investigations in the export development pattern of companies marketing industrial products. The IMP project research focus and methodology are extensively described elsewhere (Turnbull and Cunningham, 1981; Hakansson, 1982). It is necessary, however, to enumerate briefly the study's objective and its relevant methodological points.

The IMP studies are primarily aimed at providing empirical and theoretical knowledge of buyer-seller relationships in industrial firms operating across international markets. This particular research uses convenience samples of industrial companies located in the

United Kingdom who have European export markets. No public data are available that provide a listed population of such firms. The research is mainly exploratory in nature and is based on data secured from in-depth personal interviews with senior executives in the general and marketing management functions. The respondents were identified and selected by a sequential process involving interviews at various levels in the sampled companies.

Preliminary analysis of the IMP data revealed two interesting findings that lead to the more detailed analysis reported here. First, the most common forms of export marketing organization used by the British companies are direct sales representation from the United Kingdom and the agency system, even among companies that are highly export-oriented. Second, no major differences are apparent in the structures used regardless of the firm's dependence on exports.

In light of these findings and in order to obtain a clearer understanding of the organizational structures, further data analyses were conducted. The industry variable is considered to be of major significance and 24 companies from three industries—marine diesel engine, motor vehicle components, and telecommunication equipment—were selected to allow interindustry comparison.

Each industry sector is significantly different in terms of export orientation. The marine diesel engine industry (MDE) has a high level of export performance (over 60% of value of turnover). The motor vehicle components industry (MVC) is much less export oriented with exports accounting for 10–12% of turnover, while the telecommunications equipment industry (TE) currently exports less than 2% of turnover. The MVC and TE industries also have considerably higher unit manufacturing volume than the MDE industry sector.

It should be noted that only four MDE companies were included because of that industry's concentrated nature. In contrast, twelve motor vehicle component and eight telecommunications companies are in the sample. The basis for the research analysis is 72 organization structures in France, Germany, and Sweden. A case study approach for examining the companies was adopted since it better facilitates the exploratory focus on organizational processes and issues in international expansion. This chapter presents only a preliminary first-stage analysis of the data. Further statistical analyses are currently being conducted.

RESEARCH RESULTS

The results for a total of 24 UK-based companies operating in France, Germany, and Sweden are presented in Table 1. Overall, 72 export structures are identified by company type, country, and such firm characteristics as size and gross and export sales turnover, multiplying each figure by a constant factor in order to preserve data confidentiality.

It is important to note that Table 1 shows only the direct export organizational form or unit for each country. In almost every case technical support service, including direct contact with customers, was provided from either a UK base or other manufacturing or product development unit in some other country. In no cases did the country-based marketing unit, whether it be a full sales subsidiary or not, act completely autonomously in terms of customer service and marketing operations.

Table 1. Key characteristics of the sample companies and their exporting operations

Company[a]	Size[b]	International Orientation[c]	France Sales ($000)	France Organization[d]	West Germany Sales ($000)	West Germany Organization[d]	Sweden Sales ($000)	Sweden Organization[d]
D1	Small	High	65	A+SR	65	A+SR	45	A+SR
D2	Medium	Very high	500	A+SR	450	A+SR	59	A+SR
D3	Small	High	420	A+SR	580	A+SR	65	A+SR
D4	Medium	High	234	A	58	A	52	A+SR
C1	Medium	High	650	SO+SR	780	SO+SR	1,560	SO+SR
C2	Small	Low	208	SO+SR	95	SO+SR	830	SO+SR
C3	Small	Low	100	SO+SR	400	SO+SR	195	SO+SR
C4	Large	Low	0	SR	12	MS+SO+SR	8,000	SO+SR
C5	Small	Medium	520	SO+SR	0	SO+SR	1,300	SO+SR
C6	Small	Medium	260	SO+SR	0	SR	280	SO+SR
C7	Medium	High	2,210	A+SR	2,600	SO+SR	3,770	SO+SR
C8	Small	Low	0	NIL	0	SO	0	NIL
C9	Small	Low	40	SO+SR	400	SO+SR	60	SR
C10	Small	Medium	650	SO+SR	400	SO+SR	400	A+SR
C11	Small	Medium	780	SO+SR	1,690	SO+SR	1,400	SO+SR
C12	Medium	Low	520	SO+SR	N/A	SO+SR	N/A	A+SR
T1	Small	Low	48	D	58	D	0	D
T2	Very large	Very high	110	SS	800	SS	45	SS
T3	Very large	High	80	SS	0	SS	0	SS
T4	Small	Very high	68	D	110	D	25	A
T5	Medium	Medium	0	SR	180	SO	250	SO
T6	Very large	Very high	1,400	D	2,200	SO	280	D
T7	Large	Low	750	D	2,800	MS+D	550	SS
T8	Very large	Low	620	SS+D+SR	100	SS	0	SS

[a] Companies are coded by type of industry:
D = marine diesel engine manufacturers
C = motor vehicles component manufacturers
T = telecommunications equipment manufacturers

[b] Size is broadly defined in annual sales turnover terms as follows:
Small   Less than $65 million
Medium $65 million–129 million
Large $130 million–649 million
Very large $650 million or more

[c] International orientation in terms of contribution to sales turnover from foreign market sales:
Low   Less than 25%
Medium   25–49%
High   50–74%
Very high   75% or more

[d] Key to organizational abbreviations
MS = Manufacturing subsidiary
SS = Sales subsidiary
SO = Sales office
SR = Direct sales representation
A = Agent
D = Distributor

Source: Compiled by the author

Before examining the data in aggregated form by comparing industries, size of companies, and so on, we provide a brief description of each industry and the 'typical' export organizational patterns that may exist (Table 2).

The UK marine diesel engine industry

The marine diesel engine industry is concentrated and only four manufacturers were included in the sample, giving a total of 12 export structures across the three countries. Table 1 details the various structures in use and Table 2 summarizes the frequency of occurrence of each structure. All four firms rely to a great degree on agents in European markets, but in most cases direct selling through company-employed representatives is also used. It is interesting to note that no company has established a sales subsidiary or sales office in any of the countries. Where representatives were based in the export market they were working without the support of an official sales office in the country.

There appears to be no significant relationship between the total company sales turnover in any country market and the sales organization used (see Table 1). This evidence shows that for these firms a sequential development of overseas markets has not occurred. Despite their dependence on export markets (exporting over 50% of turnover), these companies all rely extensively on direct selling and agents. There is a marked difference, however, in the tasks performed by the agents and those performed by representatives.

The main activities of the agents, as identified by respondents, are to:

1. Fill the market intelligence function. Agents act mainly as listening posts and are 'the companies' eyes and ears' and are responsible for the identification of opportunities.

2. Produce supplier's contracts with the authorities and customers and facilitate interaction with customers. Agents were, in general, appointed on the basis of their political and industrial contacts or their reputation in customer industries.

Table 2. Frequency of export organization structure by industry

Export organization structure	Marine diesel engines	Motor vehicle components	Telecommu- nications equipment	Total
No organization	0	2	0	2
Distributors (D) only	0	0	9	9
Agents (A) only	2	0	1	3
Direct sales representation (SR) only	0	3	1	4
D/A + SR	10	3	0	13
Sales office (SO) only	0	1	2	3
SO + SR	0	26	0	26
Sales Subsidiary (SS)	0	0	9	9
SS + D + SR	0	0	1	1
Manufacturing subsidiary (MS) + D/A	0	0	1	1
MS + SO + SR	0	1	0	1
Total	12	36	24	72

Source: Compiled by the author

3. Provide after-sales and maintenance functions. Agents, generally, carry spares and stocks and act as service agents.

The division of tasks between agents and supplier representatives allows engine manufacturers to carry out their marketing activities economically. The market intelligence function and initial contacts are the prime responsibility of the agent, while the negotiation process is dealt with by company salesmen. Both market and product knowledge, the two vital ingredients for an effective marketing programme for engine manufacturers are ensured at minimum costs to suppliers.

The fluctuating nature of demand together with a highly fragmented market suggest that agency systems are the most appropriate structure for marketing large diesel engines. No costs are incurred in terms of structure in times of low demand and no resources are tied to a specific market, while a constant eye is nevertheless kept on developments within individual markets. Through the agency system any pickup in demand can be brought quickly to the suppliers' attention as agents are usually in close touch with customers through the sale of other products. This provides a high level of flexibility within the company's marketing organization since selling effort can be adjusted to the state of demand.

In summary, then, no evidence is found of a sequential process of internationalization in the four companies studied. Market characteristics are the primary factors associated with the organizational structures that these firms use for exporting. In those instances where companies have been selling to overseas markets for many years, they still had not progressed beyond the stages of agency relationships and direct selling.

The UK vehicle component industry

Since the UK vehicle component industry is more diverse and fragmented than the diesel engine industry, a larger sample of companies (12) covering a wider range of size by turnover and a total of 36 organization structures were identified and examined. Again using Tables 1 and 2, it is clear that by far the most 'popular' organization form was local representation in the market, through sales offices, backed up by direct selling support from the UK company (26 cases). Direct sales support was also provided in 3 cases where markets were serviced by agents. Even where a manufacturing subsidiary (1 case) existed, it was supported in the local market by a sales office and by direct sales representatives from the UK parent company.

While in general companies favoured the country-based sales office together with head-office sales support, different combinations of structures across the markets and between companies were common. Again, these firms provide little apparent evidence of a stages form of international development.

The telecommunications industry

The telecommunications industry, which is now a part of the rather loosely described information technology industry, faces rapid and dramatic change. Technological convergence of telecommunications, computing, and office systems, together with changing political and economic factors, have led to a major reorientation, particularly among the telecommunications companies, away from a domestic to an international outlook. (For a detailed discussion see Turnbull and Hug, 1984 and Turnbull and Ellwood, 1984.) Western Europe and the United States are seen as prime targets for international development by these companies throughout the world. Consequently, the market entry and development strategies and the structure of the international organizational forms adopted by these expansionist companies are of particular relevance to understanding the internationalization process.

Table 1 shows the extent of industry diversity in terms of international orientation. In two cases (T7 and T8), large and very large companies go together with very low degrees of international orientation, indicating little apparent relationship between size and degree of internationalization. It should be noted here that a number of the sales and manufacturing subsidiaries had been established as joint ventures between the original equipment manufacturer, the supplier, and a local company. These joint ventures varied significantly in terms of their responsibilities but have been established in response to trade or non-tariff barriers in respective country markets.

Our sampled firms tend to adopt the same organizational structures across the various country markets. This structural uniformity applies regardless of existing sales volume in the country concerned. Thus a company such as T3, which has substantial existing export business in Germany and has an established sales subsidiary there, also adopts a similar structure for entering the Swedish and French markets. We believe that the source for this type of consistency can be traced to the organizational philosophy and strategy of companies. This export behaviour is again at variance with a sequential or stepwise development of the organization structure.

Evidence is also provided in Tables 1 and 2 of some companies adopting a mixed approach involving two or more forms of marketing organization in individual countries. Thus company T8 has a wholly owned sales subsidiary in the French market, yet also employs agents and distributors, and these are supplemented by sales and service support direct from the head office in the United Kingdom. Again, this finding brings into question the stages theories of internationalization in terms of organizational development.

Having briefly examined the findings by industry it is useful to bring the data of the three industry samples together to examine if other variables are significant influences on a company's marketing overseas organization.

Company size and export organization

It has already been noted that within each industry little evidence was found to suggest that either the value of sales in an overseas market or company size (as measured by total sales) affects the form of organizational structures. Table 3 shows frequency of occurrence of each structure by size of company across all three industries. For the small and medium-size groupings there is no clear pattern of relationship, but a sales office supported by direct selling was most frequently found. Although there are only six large companies in the sample, no apparent relationship and indeed no one structure is repeated in any two countries.

It is particularly interesting to note the apparent disparity among very large companies. In nine of the twelve cases, companies have established sales subsidiaries. In all cases these

Table 3. Frequency of export organization structure by company size

Export organization structure	Company size*				
	Small	Medium	Large	Very large	Total
No organization	2	0	0	0	2
Distributors (D) only	5	0	1	3	9
Agents (A) only	1	2	0	0	3
Direct sales representation (SR) only	2	1	1	0	4
D/A + SR	7	6	0	0	13
Sales office (SO) only	1	2	0	0	3
SO + SR	18	7	1	0	26
Sales subsidiary (SS) only	0	0	1	8	9
SS + D	0	0	0	1	1
Manufacturing subsidiary (MS) + A	0	0	1	0	1
MS + SO	0	0	1	0	1
Total	36	18	6	12	72

* Small = less than $65 million annual sales
  Medium = $65–129 million
  Large = $130–649 million
  Very large = $650 million or more
Source: Compiled by the author

are TE companies and often the sales subsidiaries have been set up in countries where there were little or no existing sales (see T1, T2, T3, and T8). In contrast, company T6, with quite high sales in France and Germany, uses a distributor system for its export sales. A case study approach is necessary to understand this anomaly.

International orientation and export organization

Table 4 compares the frequency of occurrence of the various organization structures with the degree of international orientation (as measured by the proportion of sales turnover accounted for by exports). It is clear from the table that there is little or no relationship between the two variables. It is surprising to note the relatively frequent use of distributors and agents by highly internationalized companies, while in 14 of 30 instances companies with low international development have established sales offices in Western Europe. What is perhaps more remarkable is the setting up of sales subsidiaries and manufacturing subsidiaries by companies with little international sales volume. As previously noted, this strategy has been one adopted by telecommunications companies, for the strategic reason of gaining access and market presence in the markets concerned.

Another commonly used measure of international orientation is the number of foreign markets served by the company. Although not shown here, this research shows a strong association between this measure and the percentage of sales accounted for by exports. This finding is consistent with other evidence showing that British companies tend to expand their international sales volume through market spreading, rather than concentrating on a selected and limited number of markets (Doyle, Saunders, and Wong 1985; Betro Trust, 1979).

Table 4. Frequency of export organization structure by international orientation

Export organization structure	International orientation*				
	Low	Medium	High	Very high	Total
No organization	2	0	0	0	2
Distributor (D) only	4	0	0	5	9
Agent (A) only	0	0	2	1	3
Direct sales representation (SR) only	2	2	0	0	4
D/A + SR	1	1	8	3	13
Sales office (SO) only	1	2	0	0	3
SO + SR	14	7	5	0	26
Sales subsidiary (SS) only	3	0	3	3	9
SS + D/A + SR	1	0	0	0	1
Manufacturing subsidiary (MS) + D + SR	1	0	0	0	1
MS + SO + SR	1	0	0	0	1
Total	30	12	18	12	72

* Low = less than 25% of sales turnover is from foreign markets
  Medium = 25–49%
  High = 50–74%
  Very high = 75% or more
Source: Compiled by the author

Country and export organization

Analysis of Table 5 shows that there is little or no evidence that the country variable is a significant determinant of structure. The sales office and sales representation type of organization is overwhelmingly the most 'popular' in all three countries. It should be noted, however, that sales or manufacturing subsidiaries are more prevalent in the French

Table 5. Frequency of export organization structure by country

Export organization structure	France	Germany	Sweden	Total
No organization	1	0	1	2
Distributor (D) only	4	3	2	9
Agent (A) only	1	1	1	3
Direct sales representation (SR) only	2	1	1	4
D/A + SR	4	3	6	13
Sales office (SO) only	0	2	1	3
SO + SR	9	9	8	26
Sales subsidiary (SS) only	2	3	4	9
SS + D/A + SR	1	0	0	1
Manufacturing subsidiary (MS) + DR	0	1	0	1
MS + SO + SR	0	1	0	1
Total	24	24	24	72

Source: Compiled by the author

and German markets. We might tentatively conclude that this is related more to the size of these markets, they being significantly larger than the Swedish market for all three product groups, than to other characteristics of the countries.

IMPLICATIONS AND CONCLUSIONS

This analysis indicates that a stages theory of internationalization inaccurately portrays the international expansion of British companies in Europe for the three industries studied. It does not support the proposition that the pattern of export organizational development follows an evolutionary path. Companies in the industries studied use a combination of organizational approaches in single markets, and not the dichotomous structures implied by the stages theory. Even where these firms have established more 'advanced' structures, such as sales or manufacturing subsidiaries, a strong and active involvement of the company-based sales representatives exists. Further, in a number of cases, companies reported a 'reversal' of stages whereby a sales office, for example, had been closed in favour of direct export selling from the United Kingdom or the use of distributors and agents.

Our research suggests that a company's 'stage' of internationalization is largely determined by the operating environment, industry structure, and its own marketing strategy. Thus, diesel engine manufacturers mainly used agents because of the fragmented nature of the market, the irregular pattern of demand, and the degree of competition. Vehicle component manufacturers, facing more concentrated markets, used sales offices and changed their organizational structures as exports became strategically important. Sales offices were established in European countries by many companies prior to any sales to that market. In the telecommunications industry, which is at an even earlier stage of export market development, firms used distributors, sales offices, and subsidiaries, as well as direct selling to quickly establish a presence in Western Europe. It appears that some experimentation is taking place.

Consequently, we find supportive evidence of Chandler's (1962) claim that 'structure follows strategy'. The nature of export strategies pursued by domestically oriented British companies may be different from those of more internationally oriented Swedish companies, on which the Uppsala stages theory was based. British companies' export trade, until recently, could be associated more with selling rather than marketing. Similarly, as changes in the wider operating environment occur, so do the nature of company strategies. Hence, what may have been successful strategies in the 1960s, when the stages theory was initially conceived, may no longer be appropriate for the changed and extremely competitive environment we find today.

Thus we agree with Reid's (1983b, 62) view that 'we have shown that there will exist significant inter- and intra-firm variations in the way exports are handled and these variations have their genesis in firm and market specific factors'.

In conclusion it can be said that the stages theory has merit in its use as a framework for classification purposes rather than for an understanding of the internationalization process itself. This is not surprising, since an understanding of how companies internationalize can be achieved only through a knowledge of the environment within which they operate. It is this environment that determines the nature of their strategies. We therefore suggest that patterns of organizational development in particular markets can be best studied at the industry level and that generalized models of organizational development should be discarded.

A final comment relates to the organizational structure classifications commonly used in the field and discussed earlier. We have found these classifications inadequate for categorizing the real pattern of structures that exist. While any classification system must be limited to some degree, it is important that its use reflects the complexity and breadth of reality being examined. It was necessary for this research to use six basic organizational descriptions and various combinations of these where relevant. It is important that marketers working in the field of international organizations agree on common and consistent classifications for advancement of export theory and practice.

REFERENCES

Ansoff, H. I. (1982). 'Strategic Dimensions of Internationalization.' European Institute for Advanced Studies in Management, Brussels, *mimeo*, October.

Betro Trust (1979). 'Languages and Export Performance.' A Study Prepared for the Royal Society of Arts (London), September.

Bilkey, W. J. (1978). 'An Attempted Integration of the Literature on the Export Behavior of Firms.' *Journal of International Business Studies* 9 (Spring/Summer): 33–46.

Bilkey, W. J. and G. Tesar (1977). 'The Export Behavior of Smaller Wisconsin Manufacturing Firms.' *Journal of International Business Studies* 8 (Spring/Summer): 93–98.

Buckley, P. J., G. D. Newbould, and J. Thurwell (1979). 'Going International—The Foreign Direct Investment Behaviour of Smaller UK Firms.' In Recent Research on the Internationalization of Business—*Proceedings* of the Annual Meeting of the European International Business Association, Uppsala, Sweden, December, 72–87.

Cavusgil, S. T. (1977). 'A Proposed Conceptualization of International Marketing Activities and Some Observations.' *Studies in Development* 16 (Summer): 28–42.

Chandler, A. D. (1962). *Strategy and Structure*. Cambridge, Mass: MIT Press.

Cunningham, M. T. and E. Homse (1982). 'An Interaction Approach to Marketing Strategy.' In *International Marketing and Purchasing of Industrial Goods: An Interaction Approach,* edited by H. Hakansson. Chichester: John Wiley, 328–345.

Doyle, P., J. Saunders, and V. Wong (1985). 'A Comparative Investigation of Japanese Marketing Strategies in the British Market.' *Proceedings* of the Annual Conference of the European Academy, Bielefeld, West Germany, April, 73–84.

Hakansson, H. (1982). *International Marketing and Purchasing of Industrial Goods: An Interaction Approach*. Chichester: John Wiley.

Johanson, J. and J. Vahlne (1977). 'The Internationalization Process of the Firm—A Model of Knowledge Development and Increasing Foreign Market Commitment.' *Journal of International Business Studies* 8 (Spring/Summer): 23–32.

Johanson, J. and F. Wiedersheim-Paul (1975). 'The Internationalization Process of the Firm: Four Swedish Case Studies.' *Journal of Management Studies*, October: 305–322.

Kirpalani, V. H. (1985). *International Marketing*. New York: Random House.

Li Wan Po, D. (1982). 'Organizational Issues in International Industrial Marketing.' Unpublished MSc. thesis, University of Manchester Institute of Science and Technology.

Penrose, E. (1959). *The Theory of the Growth of the Firm*. London: Basil Blackwell.

Reid, S. (1983a). 'Export Research in a Crisis.' In *Export Promotion: The Public and Private Sector Interaction,* edited by M. Czinkota. New York: Praeger, 129–153.

Reid, S. (1983b). 'Firm Internationalization. Transaction Costs and Strategic Choice.' *International Marketing Review* 2 (Winter): 45–56.

Reid, S. (1984). 'Market Expansion and Firm Internationalization.' In *International Marketing Management,* edited by E. Kaynak. New York: Praeger, 197–206.

Rothchild, D. (1983). 'Surprise and the Competitive Advantage.' *Journal of Business Strategy* **4(3):** 10–18.

Tookey, D. (1969). 'International Business and Political Geography.' *British Journal of Marketing* **3(3):** 18–29.

Turnbull, P. W. and M. T. Cunningham (1981). *International Marketing and Purchasing*. London: Macmillan.

Turnbull, P. W. and S. Ellwood (1984). 'Internationalization in the Information Technology Industry.' In *Proceedings* of the International Research Seminar on Industrial Marketing, Stockholm School of Economics, August.

Turnbull, P. W. and F. Hug (1984). 'The Telecommunications Industry and its Markets.' University of Manchester, Institute of Science and Technology, Occasional Paper No. 8404, July.

Turnbull, P. W. and J-P. Valla (1986). *Strategies for International Industrial Marketing*. London: Croom Helm.

Wiedersheim-Paul, F., H. C. Olson, and L. Welch (1978). 'Pre-Export Activity: The First Step in Internationalization.' *Journal of International Business Studies* 9 (Spring/Summer): 93–98.

Wind, Y., S. P. Douglas, and H. V. Perlmutter (1973). 'Guidelines for Developing International Marketing Strategies.' *Journal of Marketing* 37 (April): 14–23.

Young, S. and N. Hood (1976). 'Perspectives on the European Marketing Strategy of US Multinationals.' *European Journal of Marketing* **4(5):** 240–256.

13

Organizing the Multinational Firm: Can the Americans Learn from the Europeans?

John M. Stopford

The continued rapid growth of foreign direct investment has been accompanied by an increasing awareness among businessmen of the vital role that the organization structure can play in the successful conduct of their international operations. This awareness has stemmed in part from the fact that there has been a succession of well-publicized structural changes among firms already heavily committed on a global scale. The organizational practices of these leaders in the international business area can set precedents that others follow eagerly and sometimes blindly in the effort of promoting their own version of the fashionable image of 'multinationality'. For many firms foreign ventures are a relatively new form of activity. As they grapple with the problems of developing organizations, skills and control systems appropriate to their new and unfamiliar environments managers tend to find that the structures previously built up on the domestic front are not entirely appropriate abroad, so they look outside their own firms for guidance from their most internationally experienced competitors.

Any given strategy of growth demands an ordering of priorities among the various management tasks if the strategy is to be effectively implemented. These priorities tend to become established by the form of the management structure that is developed in the firm. Unless the characteristics of the structure match the needs of the strategy inefficiencies are likely to occur.[1] Hence decisions made to change the strategy of growth are likely to be accompanied by changes in the structure. Each of the possible strategies of achieving the international growth and development of a firm leads to a particular structure. The form of the structure is closely associated with the firm's style of management, so that different firms may develop different strategies to implement similar structures.

Management style is greatly influenced by the attitudes and assumptions of the senior executives in the firm. These attitudes and assumptions vary enormously among individuals, but there are certain common denominators among United States executives that differentiate them from their European colleagues. These differences reflect the divergent cultural and social philosophies on either side of the Atlantic. The management style and

This reading is taken from Brooks, M. Z., Remmers, H. (eds) (1972) *The Multinational Company in Europe* Longmans: London.

organization structure that is appropriate for implementing one strategy in the United States may not, therefore, be appropriate for the implementation of a similar strategy in a European firm.

The growth of international operations as an integral and increasingly important component of a firm's total business has made the export of one managerial style from one country to a large number of foreign countries increasingly difficult. The foreign activities are more and more being managed by foreign nationals who do not share the attitudes and assumptions of the senior executives in the parent company. Adaptations of the organization structures to allow these differences in style to be managed effectively and to reduce the possible conflicts are beginning to appear. These adaptations are occurring on a two-way basis across the Atlantic as Americans learn about the distinctive skills of the Europeans and vice versa.

The purpose of this chapter is to describe and contrast some of the American and European practices in managing foreign operations and to speculate about the changes that are beginning to appear. Naturally the descriptions contain a high degree of generalization about factors that are subject to widely differing interpretation and to the criticism that no generalizations in this complex field are possible. The analysis therefore should be considered as an attempt to map the gross dimensions of change in international organizational practice and not as an attempt to define the full spectrum of management practices in different cultures.

THE AMERICAN EXPERIENCE

The development of organization structures for administering the foreign activities of United States manufacturing firms has followed three distinct stages, with a fourth stage possibly in the process of emerging. The first three stages are similar to the phases of development that have been identified for the domestic activities of American manufacturing enterprises.[2] First, there is the initial expansion and accumulation of manufacturing resources abroad; second, the foreign activities are centralized under the responsibility of a single executive; and third, further expansion into new products and new markets abroad is accompanied by the development of new organizational arrangements to ensure the continued effective administration on a global scale of the resources of the firm. A discussion of the fourth emerging stage is delayed until the end of this section.

The evidence on which these generalizations are based is described in detail elsewhere.[3] The sample used for this study comprised 170 United States manufacturing firms that were in the 1964 or the 1965 *Fortune 500* classifications and that had manufacturing subsidiaries in six or more foreign countries at the end of 1963, and where the parent company owned 25% or more of each subsidiary. These firms represent over three-quarters of all American-controlled manufacturing activity abroad. By using interviews, annual reports, and secondary sources,[4] histories of each firm were developed to describe the organizational and strategic changes involved in the process of expansion outside the United States.

The initial foreign expansion of firms has been well described by others.[5] The early penetration of foreign markets through exports generally precedes the investment in manufacturing facilities within the export markets. The initial manufacturing investments typically do not have a great deal of management input from the corporate headquarters, since there are few, if any, executives in the firm with experience in managing foreign business. The fledgling operations may have only a dividend reporting responsibility to the corporate controller, or they may have a reporting relationship with the president of the firm if he happens to have a personal interest in the international scene. Control procedures are largely non-existent, and the men running the foreign subsidiaries are left virtually on their own.

The uncertainties that surround the initial foreign investments are so great that many firms regard them as portfolio gambles, not subject to the usual investment criteria for domestic expenditures. So long as they continue to be treated in this way the lack of direct management may continue. However few United States firms are prepared to gamble large sums of money for very long without introducing a control mechanism. The first stage of foreign expansion, therefore, is likely soon to give way to the second stage when controls and organization are introduced.

The typical organizational response to the perceived need for control is to place all the foreign subsidiaries in a single division, normally called the international division. The single executive who has the profit responsibility for this division is charged with the additional responsibility of developing the appropriate control system. The early timing of this organization change in the growth of a firm's international commitments is indicated by the fact that fifty-seven of the 106 firms for which data were available established an international division when they had four or fewer foreign subsidiaries. A few firms even missed out the first stage of unco-ordinated expansion altogether and charged one man with full responsibility for spearheading the move abroad. Such men were normally recruited after they had acquired international experience in other firms.

The international division is at the same organization level as the domestic divisions, but does not have their autonomy. It is dependent on the co-operation and assistance of the product divisions and is therefore in a position that can readily generate conflicts and organizational stresses. The product division managers, who are evaluated on their own domestic profit performance, tend not to provide the services that are in the interests of the firm as a whole, leaving the international manager to fend for himself. While the international division accounts for only a small proportion of the business, the costs of these natural responses are usually outweighed by the benefits that accrue from having a centre of international expertise to provide the foreign subsidiaries with the necessary inputs that would not otherwise be available.

If the foreign markets are growing faster than domestic markets, which has often been the case during the last twenty years, the international division starts to account for an increasing share of the firm's operations. Problems of capital allocation and transfer pricing become relatively more important. Consistent and rational resolution of these problems requires better communication across the domestic–international fault in the organization. Top management has responded to this need for better communication by giving domestic product and functional managers international experience by means of short-term assignments abroad. Such action, however, has proved in many firms to be only a limited palliative for the more fundamental need to establish practices and procedures capable of bringing a global perspective to the management responsibilities of the firm.

Reorganization by replacing the international division with new structure has been a second and important response. By the end of 1968, fifty-four of the firms studied had introduced alternative structures. In twenty-four other firms, where growth abroad had been primarily through merger with other firms whose foreign activities were in different industries, the problems of the international division had been bypassed altogether.

Three alternative structures have been used to replace the international division. Firms choose one of these structures in accordance with their strategies of growth abroad.

In cases where the principal international growth vehicle has been the transferring of diversified product lines sequentially from the United States to the foreign subsidiaries, the international division has been divided into its product components regardless of location. These components are attached directly to the erstwhile domestic product divisions. This change contains many of the potential conflict areas within a single division, and in addition reduces the problems associated with containing product diversity within a single division. Such problems are similar to those experienced by firms that attempted to diversify byproduct in the United States whilst maintaining a centralized structure of functional departments.[6] Most of the thirty firms adopting worldwide product divisions were heavily engaged in research and development activities. They were transferring abroad relatively new products for which the technology is still developing, requiring close control and rapid communication among the manufacturing units and the laboratories. The new structure facilitates such communication.

A second strategy of growth abroad is to expand a limited product line into an increasing number of foreign markets. Products for which manufacturing in a large number of markets is justified tend to be mature and technologically stable;[7] marketing being the crucial management ingredient. Since marketing requires a detailed knowledge of local conditions, directives from the head office to the subsidiaries are often inappropriate. The communication requirements in implementing this strategy are, therefore, less than they are for the previous one. The typical structural adjustment to the successful implementation of this strategy is the formation of regional divisions partitioning the world. Product diversity, if it is present in the firm, is largely confined to the United States division and managed by its separate subdivisions. Firms generally make this structural change when the foreign activities are a very large and important part of the overall firm. In fifteen firms choosing this combination of strategy and structure, the international component of each accounted for at least 30% of the total activity, and in some cases more than 50%.

A third possibility is a combination of product and area diversification. One mature product line is extended by manufacturing in many foreign countries, and at the same time newer products are introduced in a limited number of foreign markets. For example, several international food companies that have diversified into chemicals in the United States have chosen to manufacture some chemicals abroad. The typical organizational response to this strategy is to separate the product lines by retaining the international division for the food lines and establishing a chemical division with worldwide responsibilities. Twenty-six firms had chosen this 'mixed' structure by 1968. They adapted the organization to the needs of the subsidiaries on a product basis with little or no attempt to integrate the diversified product lines on an area basis.

These three structures are used to replace the international division and all have various characteristics in common. They all require more than a single international general manager. Indeed the shortage of such men may often delay the reorganization until well after the need to cope with the organizational stresses has been clearly recognized. The organization has to be divided into clearly separated units for which responsibility is assigned on the basis of establishing product differences or area differences as the variable of prime importance. Such organizational choices provide a clear focus for identifying where the conflicts and stresses are to be managed and how performance is to be measured. Each operating division has the minimum possible overlap in responsibility with other groups. Divisional autonomy, however, is often provided at the cost of duplication of effort. For example, a firm with worldwide product divisions can have many subsidiaries in one foreign country, each subsidiary having its own facilities for functions such as law, government and industrial relations that might be shared among all of them. Other costs of these choices have been described in some detail elsewhere and need not be elaborated here.[8] In general, though, firms attempt to develop a form of structure that minimizes these costs.

A significant feature of the development of the firms studied is the consistent direction of organizational change. Only a few instances were observed where firms abandoned their international divisions and later reformed them. These few firms had all had severe problems of profitability abroad; a situation where recentralization of management attention is a natural response under conditions of severe 'threat'. The implication of this consistency in the direction of chance is that the eighty-two firms that retained an international division in 1968 may be expected to adopt one of the other structures in the future when their foreign operations reach the levels of foreign diversity by product or area that characterize the operations of the firms in stage three.

The three stages in international development correspond closely to the organizational practices that are central to the conduct of these firms' domestic activities. They are based on a number of management principles that are exported with little or no modification. These principles appear in turn to be closely related to the American culture and philosophy of personal behaviour in a managerial context. If comparisons are to be made with European organization practices these principles and cultural attributes need to be explored, since the procedures by which a given strategy is implemented in an organization are inevitably influenced by behavioural characteristics of the men concerned.

One author[9] summarized a number of these underlying American management characteristics and discussed reasons for the differences between them and the characteristics of management in other cultures. This agrees with much of the work of others[10] and provides a convenient framework for analysis. The American manager is seen as a man who believes strongly in his ability to determine to a large degree the future fruits of his own labours, who is committed to forward planning both personally and for his firm and who values facts more highly than intuitive judgments. His primary commitment is to the success and growth of the enterprise. He expects promotion on the basis of ability rather than social status, and shares the belief that frequent changes from one assignment to another are stimulating for the individual and productive in terms of training for future increased responsibilities. He considers interfirm mobility to be consistent with his attitude that executives perform a 'professional' service. These management concepts allow United States enterprises to develop into networks of co-ordinated action and to assume a vitality of their own divorced from the individuals who manage the various intersections of the network. Consistency of behaviour in all parts of the network is vital.

> Enthusiasm for decentralisation rests on assumptions that men down the line share similar *mores* regarding self-determination, hard work, morality of commitments, and the significance of time. If such *mores* prevail then supervision can be general and consultative, instead of close and disciplinarian. The nature of control can become constructive feedback rather than suspicious verification.[10]

If the *mores* are changed, the shape of the resulting network must necessarily be changed. Transferring the American style of management to other cultures cannot, therefore, be accomplished without major and painful modifications.

These characteristics and *mores* of the United States are usually expressed in familiar operating practices that may be summarized as:

- Unity of command.
- Clear definitions of responsibility, especially between line and staff functions.
- Clear definitions of reporting relationships.
- The setting of detailed budget targets.
- Evaluation of performance by profit performance against budget.
- Rapid promotion patterns.
- The development of large staff groups to process information.

The first three stages of the international expansion are managed largely according to these principles. Firms that have not adapted their basic procedures to the needs of the foreign environment have paid some penalties. For example, American personnel and labour relations policies are a common and expensive source of friction in the foreign subsidiaries. Furthermore in spite of the extreme difficulties of forecasting accurately even twelve months ahead in countries subject to rapid political, social, or economic change, detailed budgets are prepared and executive effort directed towards achieving the set goals. Often in such environments the critical function is not so much the setting of targets but the speed with which the appropriate responses to changed market circumstances are made. An elaborate reporting system may act to delay a rapid re-direction of effort.

Offsetting this penalty is the advantage that, under conditions of rapid executive turnover in the international activities, an elaborate reporting system allows newcomers to become effective in a short time by providing a rule-book of behaviour. Perhaps it was the function of the system rather than inexperience internationally that prompted Max Gloor of Nestlé to observe:

Many American companies seem (here as in other things) to have a tendency to establish and follow gospels, either those of centralised or decentralised management or management by exception or so forth. Being mostly newcomers to international management I guess they have to be more dogmatic and start with certain policies, learn from mistakes and re-adapt them. They have had no time to follow a pragmatic approach.[11]

Such rigidities in the organization may not be a serious problem when the foreign environments are favourable to American firms, as was generally the case during the 1950s and early 1960s. With an enormous initial advantage over local competition in terms of technology, products and money, the highest degrees of managerial effectiveness were not required in order to generate rates of growth and profitability far in excess of those recorded by the domestic side of the firm. Decentralized operations, often administered by second rate managers[12] working with procedures designed in the head office, were adequate.

In the last few years the international competitive situation has become much less favourable to United States firms. These are now competing fiercely among themselves for the same foreign markets, and competition from local firms has increased. An indication of the degree of this competition is the rapid decline in the profitability of all United States direct investments in Europe from 14% in 1960 to 8% in 1968.[13]

Abandoning the international division and introducing a global perspective to the management task is only one part of the response to these changed conditions. Other responses are common. In more and more firms foreign assignments are now becoming accepted as prerequisites for promotion to the highest executive levels and first-class men are taking over the foreign subsidiaries. These changes in top management attitude have stimulated a far greater effort to streamline the control of the international commitments. Duplication of staff groups that could previously be rationalized by the performance of the subsidiaries is now being carefully examined to find cheaper and better ways of performing the same functions. New procedures are being tried out, often at the prompting of foreign nationals who have risen far on the executive ladder.

In a few firms these new efforts have resulted in further major reorganizations, heralding the emergence of a fourth stage in international development. They responded to the international organizational dilemma that has been expressed as: 'How to provide for functional and geographic specialization, and for corporate guidance and coordination on a company-wide basis, without blurring lines of accountability and authority, and without impairing the freedom of action and the drive of the executives in charge of the major operating divisions.'[14] These firms were all highly diversified by product abroad and the foreign operations accounted for a very large proportion of total business, usually more than 40%. None of the alternative structures previously described had proved to be a satisfactory solution to the dilemma; each provided clarity of responsibility and authority on one of the dimensions, product or area, at the expense of co-ordination and clear responsibility on the other equally important dimension.

The reorganization has taken the form of abandoning the principle of unity of command and establishing a grid structure, in which worldwide product divisions and area divisions are profit centres of equal status and share spheres of responsibility. Functional departments perform a worldwide staff function. This three-dimensional structure reflects the three-dimensional nature of the dilemma. One large chemical firm has even introduced a fourth dimension, that of time, in the attempt to resolve the conflicts of overlapping responsibility. In this firm, the product divisions take prime responsibility for all investment projects with a time horizon of more than eighteen months, and the area divisions have prime responsibility for all operations with a time horizon of less than eighteen months.

The final forms that these grid structures will eventually adopt cannot be predicted yet with any degree of certainty, as they are still in a formative and turbulent stage. New ways of budgeting and controlling, and perhaps even new ways of thinking about the problems, need to be worked out and proven by experience. Furthermore, managers will have to adjust their assumptions about what constitutes the 'American' way of doing business. Yet the fact that these very large firms consider the expense and disruption of further reorganization to be worth while suggests that others will soon follow suit as they also become highly diversified by area and by product around the world.

One possible alternative to the problems of establishing this multidimensional structure is to choose not to attempt to achieve a full reconciliation of the dilemma. Some firms may value the benefits of executive autonomy more highly than those of full co-ordination and accept the possible consequences of imbalance among the three dimensions of the enterprise; others may start to divest those parts of the enterprise that are not readily susceptible to integrative treatment. There are, as yet, few examples of this latter course. The Olin (a large international chemical, plastics, metals and paper enterprise) divesti-ture of its worldwide pharmaceutical business is one of the rare examples. The current difficulties of the American conglomerates may, however, help to reinforce the attractiveness of this alternative.

THE EUROPEAN EXPERIENCE

European manufacturing firms have long been actively engaged in foreign operations. Indeed if the proportion of the total assets held abroad is an indication of international commitment, many European firms are far more international than their American competitors. Yet organization developments that have accompanied their expansion abroad have not followed the American pattern. This is perhaps not surprising, because the management practices and styles used abroad almost of necessity reflect domestic practices; European practices differ in many important respects from American. A brief description of some aspects of European management in its home environment is needed before the international extensions of those practices may usefully be examined.

The wide differences in cultural and social assumptions between the various nations in Europe make single generalizations about aspects of European management behaviour necessarily controversial. Quite possibly no general truths exist. The discussion that follows is intended to provide no more than an identification of aspects that appear to be different on either side of the Atlantic. No attempt to delineate them precisely is made. To make such an attempt would be foolhardy, as some of the available evidence appears to be contradictory.[15] Besides European business practice is in a state of such rapid change that judgments based on data collected even five years ago are suspect in terms of their current and future validity. For example, the changes in attitude in Britain's British Leyland Motor Corporation have been described as follows:

> Until four or five years ago we were a highly authoritarian company. The hallmark of the company style was action; thinking was something you did in your spare time. And as all the important decisions were made by the men at the top there really did not seem to be much point in setting up a management development programme. . . . Over the next five to ten years a steady improvement in the quality of management is going to be of crucial importance in a business which in the past has given the emphasis to engineering excellence. Clearly management training must be given a high priority and we have a great deal of leeway to make up.[16]

The European executive in the middle-1960s was perceived by one writer[17] to have certain distinctive traits. He was more concerned with the past than with the future; he valued wisdom more highly than vitality and preferred values to facts; he preferred experience to training in management; he tended to spend his career within a single company and did not accept that the American concept of job rotation had great value; he disliked egalitarianism among his colleagues; and he preferred thrift and secrecy in his organizational practices. To these traits others may be added. The European manager did not accept the American gospel that all men are created with equal managerial aptitude; social status and, increasingly, education were important prerequisites for promotion to some jobs. There was an acceptance of impersonal regimentation at lower levels of management, and what has been described as 'a fear of the face-to-face situation'.[18] An easy interchange of ideas and plans among men at different levels in the hierarchy was difficult to establish. Furthermore, many Europeans were reluctant to accept business success as their prime goal in life, preferring to retain other cultural ideals of the individual in society.

This perception of the European manager is essentially a caricature. Caricatures are useful nevertheless for highlighting important influences of characteristics that can become obscured in more detailed and comprehensive portraits. Each of the traits above has a bearing on the organization structures and procedures that are of interest here.

Until recently cartels and a seller's market were pronounced characteristics of the European scene. In such circumstances a historical perspective among managers is hardly surprising as there was little need for investment in expensive forward-planning procedures. Planning where it existed tended to be intuitive, short term in focus and largely production-oriented.[19] The established markets yielded high profit margins and were capable of continued growth; firms could be successful without having to use a complex array of control techniques. In the absence of pressures for planning and control, targets and budgets, the European manager could perform perfectly adequately without the necessity of giving his prime loyalty to the firm.

The most prevalent European organization structure, the centralized assembly of functional departments, reflects these factors. Such a structure has many bureaucratic features that are congruent with the attitudes of many of the managers. The interdependence of the departments means that it is virtually impossible to assign autonomous responsibility to one man and to measure this performance by results. Promotion tends to be slow and to be contained within a single functional activity.[20] As a result, the senior management group in many firms is dominated by men who have spent many years working together and who have built up close personal relationships. In the absence of a factual basis for evaluating their colleagues, top management uses subjective criteria of evaluation. It has been observed that, even if the functional structure gives way to an arrangement of product divisions, the basic tendency to rely on personal judgments and to put faith in values rather than facts persists.[21] Promotion to the highest levels in the firm can readily be justified on a class or educational basis if the subjective values of senior men are preferred to an objective assessment of a man's performance.

The men at the top of these structures are often relatively free to behave in the tradition of the merchant trader. They make alliances for business purposes, but their stock in trade is a capacity to outbargain and out-manoeuvre other businesses.[22] Their freedom stems in part from a sophisticated application of the principle of divide and rule. Their subordinates are experienced in only one part of the general management task, and they cannot do much more than carry out orders.

Once decisions have been made at the top, the functional departments can be enormously efficient in undertaking the necessary actions. Close co-ordination is possible by means of established hierarchical procedures. Such close co-ordination is essential in the management of vertically integrated chains of production. Many firms with functional structures have as a result relied on vertical integration as their principal means of growth.

The cohesiveness of the functional structure makes it an inefficient vehicle for the management of diverse activities. The structure has only a single general manager, the president or managing director. It tends therefore to behave in the manner of a single problem solver; problems are dealt with one at a time in some order of priority. When the activities of the firm become diversified, the number of problems requiring decision exceeds the available decision-making capacity. Serious delays and inefficiencies are created as the queue of problems awaiting decision lengthens.

Firms typically respond to this situation by breaking the structure into separate divisions or subsidiaries. Many firms have established a holding company arrangement; the subsidiaries have almost complete autonomy and share with one another only ties of ownership to a common parent firm. Some firms have established divisions in the American fashion, and control the activities of the division through the financial function and procedures for allocating resources on a company-wide basis. This latter group of firms has been a small minority among diversified European firms, but may be expanding.

Integration of the different functions or product divisions is commonly achieved in European firms by means of group or 'collegial' management at the top. These firms have not placed any store on the notion of unity of command. In Germany, the 'Vorstand', and in Holland the 'Directie', are examples of collegial management. In the United Kingdom, it is becoming increasingly common in large firms for members of the Board of Directors to wear 'two hats'; one 'hat' is responsibility for a functional department, the other is responsibility for a product line, group of subsidiaries, or an area of operations.

Decisions in these groups are reached by consensus rather than by personal decision. The individual, however, has considerable negative decision-making powers through the use of the veto. Such a management system tends to slow down decision-making, to favour compromise solutions, and to diffuse responsibility.[23] Yet it can work extremely effectively. Why? The answer appears to lie in well-established personal relationships between the managers so that they can operate on the basis of mutual respect and trust.

The reader should note that 'collegial' management in European firms is fundamentally different from the use of executive committees of senior officers in American firms. In American executive committees, many of the committee members are divisional managers, each held personally responsible for the economic performance of his division. These men have, of necessity, to defend their own interests. The most successful of them have enormous power. Their 'track records' of superior past performance allow them to predetermine to a considerable extent the outcome of the deliberations of the committee. In other words, they have an authority based on achievement that can reduce the function of the committee to that of a rubber stamp. In contrast, the members of a 'collegial' group do not have to defend so vigorously their personal performance. There is the possibility of a much greater exchange of opinion before a collective decision is reached; the committee can act as a decision-maker with far fewer constraints than in the American case.

From a base of centralized, functional structures, many European firms have established large and successful foreign operations. Before the Second World War the bulk of European foreign investment was portfolio.[24] Direct investment, even where 100% of the equity was owned, was not concerned so much with management control as with profitable enterpreneurial ventures. Men were sent abroad and expected to run the business independently, maintaining little more than a dividend relationship with the head office. Until recently it was common for European firms to manage numerous foreign subsidiaries in this way. Unco-ordinated arrays of more than fifteen foreign manufacturing ventures were not uncommon in the United Kingdom. Joint ventures abroad were far more prevalent among these firms than was true for the Americans who required greater degrees of control.

The absence of direct control mirrored the pattern of the holding company arrangements for diversified activities in the domestic market; there was no organizational pressure to establish a management system equivalent to the international division. The managers of these foreign subsidiaries were exposed to the general management task far earlier than they would have been had they stayed within the domestic company. With no one at an equivalent level in the parent organization performing an equivalent function, the managers of the foreign subsidiaries were seldom overmuch constrained by directives from the head office. Although they were often subjected to a constant stream of directives, they could ignore many of them. Many had considerable latitude in pursuing their own product policies, a characteristic that is seldom found in American companies. Training, however, was virtually non-existent; men had to learn from their own mistakes how to run a business.

Recently there have been major changes in the domestic and foreign structures of many European firms. Increasing competition, greater product diversity, the development of foreign manufacturing bases serving more than a single national market, a greater awareness of American methods, and many similar factors have acted to make Europeans start introducing controls, planning, and general management centres at many levels in the firm. They have been adapting the American techniques to suit their style of doing business.

The tradition of working in management groups and the acceptance of multiple responsibilities have allowed firms to introduce new management techniques without building up elaborate staff groups for co-ordinating purposes. For example, one highly successful and large United Kingdom firm has diversified into six major industry groups and has three-quarters of its turnover outside the United Kingdom. Yet this firm has less than thirty executives, line and staff, in its head office. The long-established working relationship among management groups helps to reduce the need for staff groups, because relevant information can be exchanged rapidly on a personal basis.

The effect of these domestic changes on the international organization has been pronounced. The increasing awareness of the need for planning, especially on a global scale, has acted to integrate the foreign subsidiaries into the emerging domestic corporate structures. Managers of the foreign subsidiaries are being bombarded with more and more orders, which they can no longer afford to ignore.

The common denominator among these changes is that the links established between domestic and foreign activities do not conform to a consistent pattern in any one firm. They are tailored to the needs of each subsidiary without a single priority among area, product, or function being assigned equally to all subsidiaries.

Naturally the form of the domestic organization affects the shape of these foreign linkages. For example, where there is dual responsibility between functions and areas in the head office, the subsidiary manager may report direct to several executives. The frequency of his reports is determined by the extent of the operating problems and changes he encounters. The budgets and targets for the subsidiary are established by consensus between the subsidiary manager, the area executive, and the functional executives. The manager of an African subsidiary of a British oil company commented recently that he never knew to whom he was directly responsible. This diffusion of responsibility, he added, did not matter; the system worked efficiently to provide him with all the support he needed for expanding his business profitably.

Flexibility and strong personal working relationships among the executives are critical features of the new structures. They are particularly important in the international sphere where the appropriate responses to events may not be determined easily or rapidly by formal, objective analysis. On this aspect of international management one executive commented: 'There have been moments in our company's life, and they may come again, when the cohesion of the group depended on such [personal] links more than on anything else.'[25]

A further example of how personal relationships can affect the workings of the formal organization is provided by the case of a German electrical goods firm. Superficially, the structure resembles the American international division alongside domestic product divisions. The divisions, however, share an equal status with the functional departments and there are elements of dual responsibility and authority. One observer commented:

> Rationalising production within the EEC or worldwide is simply not a major problem. The company does not as yet see any need to tie the foreign operations to the domestic product divisions. And the equality of the functional and product divisions, with the lack of clear responsibility lines, causes no particular strains among a management that has worked together for many years.[26]

Although such systems of shared responsibility are probably restricted as yet to the largest of the European-based multinational enterprises, the manner in which they are being developed provides a pointer for the future. The multiplicity of informal links of different kinds allows a firm freedom to expand the many directions simultaneously. Furthermore, the systems appear to be able to tolerate a wide spectrum of different kinds of management procedure. They are based on skills in international management that were acquired many years ago, and do not have to depend on efforts to communicate newly acquired knowledge throughout the organization. As a result, they have been able to concentrate relatively more attention on developing less formal structures. There is much less need to institute the type of standardization in management practice that characterizes most United States-based multinational firms; the adaptations of domestic practice to the needs of complex multinational operations are in some ways less for the Europeans than for the Americans.

To be sure, there are many difficulties in making the adaptations. As European firms expand further abroad and continue to diversify their product lines, the present organization practices may not continue to prove equally effective. Increasing size and complexity place a heavy burden on informal and personal methods of achieving communication and co-ordination. The growing body of ambitious young men who do not share a common set of attitudes with their superiors may also help to spur further changes. The establishment of more clearcut allocations of responsibility seems likely to occur.

It is interesting to note that these changes have been occurring during a period when European multinational firms have been growing fast. Although no cause and effect relationships can be established, one can speculate that the ways in which Europeans have traditionally managed their businesses will be an important source of strength for them in managing multinational operations.

CONCLUSIONS

Many American-based multinational enterprises are beginning to find that the difficulties of managing complex, multiproduct operations in many countries pose new managerial challenges. For a few firms, these challenges have induced responses that are beginning to break down their adherence to traditional ways of organizing and managing a business. By working out ways of sharing responsibilities among managers, by learning how to manage multiple reporting relationships, by modifying standards of measurement to include some of the intangible factors that affect performance, and by increasing their dependence on informal relationships, these firms are moving in a direction in which they are becoming, at least superficially, more akin to their European-based multinational competitors.

At the same time there is evidence that European-based enterprises are themselves changing. They are beginning to adopt many of the American methods of management. Among European firms, those that have expanded widely abroad appear to have moved furthest in the direction of resembling American firms.

Do these directions of change mean that there is a convergence of management practice among United States and European multinational enterprises? At best, the answer to this question appears to be a qualified speculation that, for a handful of the multinational giants, some convergence is likely. Those that have undertaken the strategy of diversifying widely both by product and by area face common problems in their world markets. These common problems will probably induce some common responses, regardless of the national origin of the firm.

Nevertheless, there are many constraints on the extent of any such convergence. National origin will be most likely to continue to affect behaviour no matter how widely the managers are experienced in international business. Besides, the changes observed in the organization of the diversified giants are experiments; it is by no means certain that they will succeed. Faced with difficulties in implementing new solutions to their problems, some firms may pull back and attempt to use the old methods in management.

Differences in strategic choice will add further constraints on any general movement towards convergence. There is no intrinsic reason why firms facing the same changes in their markets should all choose the same strategies; European enterprises have a perspective that differs from American ones simply because of the location of their headquarters. Very few firms will become so totally multinational in outlook that the location of the headquarters becomes of no consequence in their decision-making.

Although the constraints are formidable, the pressures for some convergence are strong. No United States multinational enterprise that attempts to co-ordinate the activities of multiproduct subsidiaries scattered around the world can escape altogether the dilemma of how to establish the appropriate blend of policies that allow adequate local autonomy and at the same time provide for adequate control. As they search for ways to resolve the dilemma, these firms would be well advised to take a long, hard look at how European-based firms have approached these problems in the past.

To be sure, the European approaches have not been wholly adequate or successful. The lack of complete success, however, does not mean that such approaches are worthless. On the contrary, they are capable of adaptation on some selective basis to American needs. By learning from European experience and practice, United States multinational enterprises may find ways of dealing with their problems more quickly than might otherwise be the case. Solutions, however incomplete, that are generated in this fashion might also hold a greater promise of success than those generated solely from an internal process of trial and error.

NOTES

1. Chandler 1962 provides a comprehensive discussion of this necessary correspondence between strategy and structure.

2. See Chandler 1962, p. 479.

3. See Stopford and Wells 1972.

4. Such as Lovell 1966.

5. See, for example, Kolde 1968, chapter 15; Aharoni 1966 gives an excellent description of the initial foreign manufacturing decisions.

6. See Chandler 1962 for a graphic description of such problems.

7. See Vernon 1968a for an economic assessment of this relationship.

8. See Lovell 1966.

9. See Newman 1970.

10. See, for example, Haire, Ghiselli and Porter 1966; the quotation is from p. 9.

11. 'Nestlé's multinational mode', *Management Today*, October 1968.

12. See McCreary 1964.

13. US Department of Commerce, *Survey of Current Business* (Washington, DC: Government Printing Office, October 1969), Chart 15.

14. See Lovell 1966, p. 84.

15. Contrast, for example, Haire, Ghiselli and Porter 1966 with Harbison and Myers 1959 on the question of European attitudes to trust, authoritarianism, and participative management.

16. 'Leyland: spending £25 to make a manager', *The Sunday Times*, 22 March 1970.

17. See Nowotny 1964.

18. Crozier 1964, p. 288.

19. Haas 1967, p. 103.

20. Chandler 1962, p. 50 describes the same phenomenon occurring in American firms with similar functional structures. In the United States, however, functional structures have largely been replaced by divisional structures. For example, only 8 of the 170 firms in the US sample described earlier retained their functional structure in 1968.

21. Haas 1967, p. 135.

22. This analogy is developed in an illuminating way in Fayerweather 1960.

23. Parks 1966.

24. Normally considered to be 25 per cent or less of the equity of a firm, or preference shares, or bonds.

25. 'Nestlé's multinational mode', *Management Today*, October 1968.

26. Lombard 1969, p. 43. Data on many other similar cases are contained in *Organizing for European Operations*, New York; Business International, 1968.

REFERENCES

Aharoni, Y. (1966). *The Foreign Investment Decision Process*. Harvard Business School.

Chandler, A. D. (1962). *Strategy and Structure*. Massachusetts Institute of Technology.

Crozier, M. (1964). *The Bureaucratic Phenomenon*. Tavistock.

Fayerweather, J. (1960). *Management of International Operations: texts and cases*. New York: McGraw-Hill.

Haas, H. Van Der (1967). *The Enterprise in Transition*. Tavistock.

Haire, M., Ghiselli, E. E. and Porter, L. W. (1966). *Managerial Thinking: An International Study*. New York: Wiley.

Harbison, F. H. and Myers, C. A. (1959). *Management in the Industrial World: An International Analysis*. New York: McGraw-Hill.

Kolde, E. J. (1968). *International Business Enterprise*. Englewood Cliffs, NJ: Prentice-Hall.

Lombard, A. J. Jr. (1969). How European companies organise their international operations. *European Business* **22 (July)**, 37.

Lovell, E. B. (1961). *Organizing Foreign-Base Corporations*. National Industrial Conference Board.

McCreary, E. A. (1964). Those American managers don't impress Europe. *Fortune*, December.

Newman, W. H. (1970). Is management exportable? *Columbia Journal of World Business*. **(Jan–Feb)**, 5: 7–18.

Nowotny, O. H. (1964). American versus European management philosophy. *Harvard Business Review*, (**Jan–Feb**).

Parks, F. N. (1966). Group management, European style. *Business Horizons*, **9(3)**: 83.

Stopford, J. M. and Wells, L. T. Jr. (1972). *Managing the Multinational Enterprise*. New York: Basic Books.

Vernon, R. (1968a). *Manager in the International Economy*. Englewood Cliffs, NJ: Prentice-Hall.

14

Towards a New Approach for Studying the Internationalization Process of Firms

Jesper Strandskov

1. INTRODUCTION

Business corporations with international activities or multinational operations are continually changing, and therefore the natural mode of internationalizational behaviour is development. Movements in international conditions of marketing and production such as competition, consumer's environment (socioeconomic and cultural variables), political and institutional environments (governmental policies) represent more or less uncontrollable elements of an external business reality, which require new business strategies, methods of working, and changing capabilities of organizing the international activities. Also internal factors may promote change in that the managers and other members of an international firm may seek not just its maintenance but also its growth, in order to secure improved benefits and satisfaction to themselves.

Internationalizational behaviour of firms has received significant research attention recently. Although conceptualizations and theory development have been scarce, the internationalization process has been conceived as a gradual process, taking place in incremental stages and over a relatively long period of time. This paper has a three-fold purpose. Firstly, it aims at reviewing recent contributions to the study of the internationalization process, including the stage-of-development models within the theories of export behaviour of firms as well as the evolution process of multinational corporations. Secondly, it is intended to discuss the epistemological implications of a stage-approach concerning the problems related to the underlying assumption; the possibilities of distinguishing between various internationalization stages, and the difficulties in identifying important time-sensitive dimensions and variables describing the process. Finally, the paper suggests a new approach to studying the internationalizational behaviour of firms.

Presented at the Annual Conference of European International Business Association, Glasgow, Scotland, 15–17 December 1985.

The present paper has been worked out in connection with an ongoing research project on 'The Internationalization Process of Danish Firms', being conducted at the Institute of International Economics and Management at the Copenhagen School of Economics and Business Administration by the author of this article.

Although preliminary in progress the paper argues for the identification of the configurations of international firms in attempting to find richly described natural clusters among a broad variety of international environmental variables, firm contextual factors and managerial variables.

2. THE INTERNATIONALIZATION PROCESS OF FIRMS: BASIC ISSUES

Change processes are the starting point for the investigation of firm internationalization: How can the process of internationalization be characterized concerning changes in strategies, functions, and structures? Which factors determine this process? What are the managerial and organizational consequences of the adoption process?

Generally, among the studies on organizational development there has been considerable emphasis upon growth in particular, although growth does not represent the only strategy of the development of business firms. From this research there has been a debate as to how far one should seek to interpret the development process as a product of environmental forces or as a product of managerial behaviour on the part of those within the corporation who decide on strategies.

The debate provides a framework within which the process of development may be analysed. The approach of environmental determinism has recently been proposed within organizational theory where a natural-selection model has claimed that environmental characteristics select organizations for survival and growth, according to how good a fit there is between their activities, structures and environmental characteristics, Hannan and Freeman (1977) and Aldrich (1979). Although the model does not explain why certain organizations and not others adapt to external requirements, it draws explicit attention to the environmental determinants which may facilitate or constrain change. The second approach, however, draws attention to the actions which are taken by decision makers aimed at generating new conditions, and also to the motivations and political processes which lie behind such decisions and the strategies for managing or adapting to the environment, Pettigrew (1973).

Within the studies of internationalizational behaviour, researchers have concentrated almost exclusively on finding industry and firm determinants of international activities or multinational operations. Relationships between environmental variables and foreign activities have rarely been subject to a systematic, empirical analysis, see Cavusgil and Nevin (1981). In the 1970s research dealt with identifying technology and product variables as important structural factors contributing to the process of export expansion, in particular. Structural factors have often been regarded as critical determinants in the exporting activity of an enterprise, but the evidence to support the effect of size, product and technology orientation is conflicting.[1] Recently attention has been directed towards behavioural determinants of the process of internationalization, see Cavusgil (1982) and Reid (1983). Research in this respect has been dealing with the role of the decision makers' perception of foreign markets, expectations concerning these markets and the perception of the firm's capability of entering these markets. The available research does give tentative support to the existence of individual managerial factors influencing the export behaviour of firms.

In conclusion, there is no theoretical consensus or empirical evidence as to which forces generate the process of internalization or hold it back. The following section will present the stage-of-development models within the theories of export behaviour of firms and the multinational corporations.

3. DIRECTION AND STAGES OF FIRM INTERNATIONALIZATION: A REVIEW

The stage-of-development models within the theories of export behaviour of firms and multinational corporations represent an attempt to point out some common features and regularities in the basis for the development of firms. Before reviewing the various development models, a phase process can be described in several ways dependent on which 'periodization mode' has been chosen. In this context two methods will be pointed out: A unilinear and a cyclic descriptive form.[2]

Unilinear evolution

The most rigorous elaboration of a unilinear description of the process of development implies that all firms have to go through the same internationalization process in an *a priori* fixed sequence. This does not mean that all firms have to pass through every single stage, but that a reversed stage-of-development is excluded. The same forms, directions and patterns are expected to appear over time. Underlying this description is a natural selection process believed to be a powerful Darwinistic force which imposes order on internationalization paths and limits their variety and number. Structural functionalism is the dominant paradigm, and within the theories of export behaviour there are in particular supporters of such a description.

Cyclic evolution

A cyclic approach to firm internationalization is characterized by a stage-of-development process, which on one hand alternates between periods with efficient activities and structures that stipulate a stable evolution, and on the other hand transition periods with inefficient mechanism that demand fundamental renewals of international business strategies and organizational structures (often named periods of revolutions, Greiner, 1972). Compared with the unilinear variant the cyclic process of evolution represents a successive transformation to stages of a higher complexity and differentiation—characteristics related to the correlation between the corporation and its environment, and to the mutual relations within the corporation itself. The assumption underlying this view lies in the observation that organizations are systems with limited adaptability: in the short run it is possible to manage the business organization to environmental changes because of the necessity of only more or less simple (quantitatively) adjustments to changing conditions, but in the long run it is more difficult to manage alteration of the organization caused by environmental changes of, typically, a qualitative nature. A crisis has often been stressed as a necessary condition to provoke changes in the direction of the firm's development. The multinational stage models of Chandler, Stopford, and others, constitute a cyclic metamorphosis, see below.

The export development process

The theories of export behaviour emphasize that the internationalization of the firm is a continuous process with the firm gradually increasing its level of international involvement and commitment. The theories deal first of all with the initial steps. The evolutionary process has been seen as a time-phased function of the foreign experience gathered so that the exporting firm successively accumulates organizational learning over time. The learning cycles include processes by which the firm adjusts itself defensively to foreign markets as well as processes by which knowledge and experience are used offensively to improve the fits between the organization and its international environment. Several writers describe export development as a stimulus–response process, in which experimental learning has in particular been considered as an important determinant, see Carlson (1975), Bilkey (1978). Information activities, willingness to commit resources and the expectations of the favourability of exporting, managerial risk-taking behaviour, are all essentials in a description of the process. Which form and pattern the learning process constitutes has not, however, been spelled out in the literature.

Theories of export behaviours identify several stages along the process and although each scholar uses a different classification scheme, the theories all portray one common view, namely, that the decision to go international is a gradual process that can be subdivided. Various alternative classification criteria have been suggested such as for instance foreign market entry form, export activity, export involvement, export experience, managerial attitude, and combinations of these criteria.

Johanson and Vahlne (1977), Olson (1975) and Johanson and Wiedersheim-Paul (1977) use, in an early attempt of classification, the *market entry form* as a criterion based on extensive experience with Swedish firms. The classification of firms consists of four broad stages in which the following international activities take place: No permanent export, export via an agent, export via sales subsidiary, and production in a foreign subsidiary. Khan (1978) has suggested a similar scheme having investigated 165 Swedish export ventures, but his grouping consists of several other internationalization categories, including a criterion of *export area*. Based on the degrees of *export activity*, Pavord and Bogart (1975), divide the export development process into four broad categories: (1) No activity in the export market, (2) passive activity—never seek export sales but will respond to unsolicited orders, (3) minor activity—occasionally seek export sales, and (4) aggressive activity—continuously seek export sales and consider exporting to be a permanent activity. However, their empirical study of 138 US firms did not confirm the suggested categories.

Cavusgil (1980, 1982) operates with a criterion based on *export involvement* and distinguishes between five phases of internationalization: Pre-involvement; reactive involvement; limited experimental involvement; active involvement and committed involvement. In a more recent article, Cavusgil (1984) combines the three mentioned stages into one initial phase, named experimental involvement, characterized by the behaviour of those firms which exert little commitment to foreign market development, typically by responding passively (i.e. unsolicited foreign orders); employing domestic marketing strategies to psychologically closed markets; and allocating financial and managerial resources to the export activities with some degree of reluctance. The second stage, active involvement, occurs when the managers of the firm are willing to build up and penetrate foreign markets; to adapt the marketing-mix according to the specific needs of overseas markets; and to conduct the export activities on a regular basis rather than sporadically. The final stage, committed involvement, characterized by the situation in which the firm searches for business activities worldwide, not only through exports, but also by other means of foreign operations such as investments in sales and production subsidiaries abroad. Involvement of this kind implies that long-term objectives will prevail over short-term. The findings of the Cavusgil study give a preliminary indication of the existing differences among exporting firms in relation to varying levels of internationalization.

In investigating the hypothesis of the gradual internationalization process of more than 200 small and medium sized exporting US firms, Czinkota (1983) uses *export experience* (measured as the number of years of export) in a segmentation of the firms into stages. The results exhibit that changes in exporting attitudes, motivations, and perceived exporting problems are associated with growing length of exporting experience, although the defined categories did not statistically identify the precise pattern of the development process.

The work of Bilkey and Tesar (1977) consists of a more detailed framework by dividing the export development process into six stages based on *a mixture of classification criteria*, including length of export experience, volume of exports as a percentage of sales, countries exporting to, etc. They suggest the following stages:

Stage 1 Management is not interested in exporting; would not even fill an unsolicited export order.
Stage 2 Management would fill an unsolicited export order, but makes no effort to explore the feasibility of exporting.
Stage 3 Management actively explores the feasibility of exporting.
Stage 4 The firm exports on an experimental basis to some psychologically close countries.
Stage 5 The firm is an experienced exporter to that country and adjusts exports optimally to changing exchange rates, tariffs, etc.
Stage 6 Management explores the feasibility of exporting to additional countries that psychologically are further away.

The findings of their research regarding the export behaviour of more than 400 small and medium sized manufacturing firms from the US region, are in harmony with the particular stage sequence listed above. Later, Czinkota and Johnston (1981) and Czinkota (1982), find by using a revised and more elaborated model that a stage-approach is most effective in identifying homogeneous groups of firms different from each other rather than using differentiations based on managerial attitudes, size of firm, or product orientation.

The development process of the multinational enterprise

A considerable body of research within organization and management theory has been directed to the question of how developmental strategies might shape the way in which organizational structures are designed. This research has especially influenced the work of the multinational enterprises. The development has been examined primarily in terms of growing scale and diversification, and the effects these factors purportedly have on organizational strategies and structures. General analytical models of this type have been advanced firstly by Chandler (1962, 1977) followed by Salter (1971), Greiner (1972) and

Scott (1973) to mention a few. Each of these models conceives of stages in organizational development which describes the progression of an organization from its early, small and simple state to the mature stage of large scale, high complexity, financial security etc. Although the metamorphosis models differ in relation to the number of phases, dimensions and variables that constitute the developmental sequence, certain commonalities are evident in typifying the development over time: (1) A rising level of internal differentiation into specialized roles, functions, and divisions, (2) a growing complexity in terms of occupations and skills employed, (3) increasing use of formal management systems and procedures, and (4) an increased delegation and an emphasis on solving problems through direct, lateral communications rather than hierarchical communications. The essence of these descriptive models is the successive addition of new sources of diversity which result in a both more internal and external organizational complexity. What actually determines the drive behind the metamorphosis has only been superficially treated in the literature.

Much empirical research, primarily of a cross-sectional nature, has tested the relationship between organizational strategies and structure: Rumelt (1974); Channon (1973); Dyas and Thanheiser (1976); Pavan (1972); Whrigley (1976); and Itanic et al (1978), and from this research some general conclusions can be drawn.[3] Firstly, there has been a growing tendency in the United States and Western Europe in the 1960s and 1970s towards business corporations diversifying by moving from functional to divisional structures where either product or geographic dimensions dominate. Research shows that diversified strategies emerged first in the USA, then spread gradually to other countries. Secondly, Chandler's (1962) famous argument that structure follows strategy has been supported by a number of studies. In general several distinct phases characterize the diversification process for the majority of the companies studied, and only a few make either discrete jumps in classification or pass through the intermediate stages in a reverse fashion. Thirdly, the stages in organizational development have not implied a smooth and continuous process, but involve abrupt and discrete changes in the patterns of organizational development. Further there have been long time lags involved between strategic and structural changes, but how long the lag in structural adaptation to strategy and which factors explaining this process has not been studied in detail.

In addition, the research into the multinational enterprises has been directed towards investigating the relationship between MNC's strategies and structures. Smith and Charmoz (1975) have developed an interesting five stage-of-growth-model which describes the firm's evolution from the initial steps before going international to the organization moves to a global company.[4] The model is illustrated in Figure 1 and concentrates on headquarters' changing strategic focus related to control and co-ordination of the various foreign units. The model has not been empirically tested.

Phase I represents the first international engagement in which a high degree of risk and uncertainty is experienced which results in the firm's first contacts with the foreign markets being made through agents and by participation in joint ventures. This period is furthermore characterized by a low build up of international information systems, plans and strategies. Partly due to the foreign operations being new and unfamiliar and partly because they demand large investments in the establishing phase, the decisions are made at a very high managerial level at headquarters just as the day-to-day problems are attempted solved through direct personal contacts. After a period with increasing international activities, this decision structure becomes overloaded when either too many

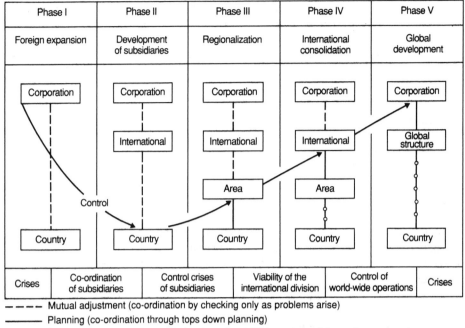

Phase I	Phase II	Phase III	Phase IV	Phase V
Foreign expansion	Development of subsidiaries	Regionalization	International consolidation	Global development

– – – – Mutual adjustment (co-ordination by checking only as problems arise)
———— Planning (co-ordination through tops down planning)
—o—o— Policy and procedure (co-ordination through establishment of policies and procedures)

Source: Smith and Charmoz (1975)

Figure 1. Evolution in Strategies and Structures of the Multinational Corporation.

decisions are made at the top, or when the quality of the decisions becomes poor and insufficient because of lack of time and foreign expertise. A typical symptom of the problem is therefore that the foreign units develop in their own way from their own interests and needs when the executive is marked by decision strains and irresolution, emphasizing the need for a co-ordinating unit located at the headquarters.

In connection with subsidiary development the transition to Phase II implies an establishment of an international department or division with the task of partly supporting the individual subsidiaries financially and partly being responsible for the co-ordination of the activities of foreign units. A division of the competence is established making the international division superior in the allocation of resources while the subsidiaries which are expected to have market expertise maintain the control of their specific market areas. In this situation the large subsidiaries are especially given much attention by the international divisions because the units' demand on resources are the largest. This structure is stable as long as the subsidiaries' interests are to no appreciable extent contrary to the superior interests of the mother company, but as a result of the decentralized structure a tendency towards increased competition for tasks and resources arises in which the international division continuously has to intervene.

Phase III is therefore characterized by changes of the structure in which the multinational company's operations are organized regionally. Regional area offices, which in decision making report to the international division, are developed in order to take part, together with the subsidiaries, in solving the day-to-day problems of marketing and production. A more formalized planning system—based on financial performance of the individual foreign units—is developed, and the tasks of the international division are now to act as a link between the top executives and the area offices. Furthermore, the international division has to cultivate the interests of the foreign operations in opposition to the product divisions concerning allocation of resources.

The transition from Phase III to Phase IV marks a period when the international commitment reaches such a level that the executives at headquarters realize that the international market expansion must give rise to a diversification. This development is reflected partly in connection with the continuous adjustment of the product programme to the individual markets' special requirements and demands and partly in relation to the emergence of new customers and market segments. The result may be a move into new areas of business where in particular global criteria for development and allocation of resources become important.

Phase IV is therefore characterized by a consolidation of the foreign operations, in which the planning and control systems are further elaborated, and at the same time top managers show an increased interest in the international activities of the corporation. However, the structure of the organization will work in a direction in which new business areas will be under-supplied as conflicts across the function areas, geographical areas and product areas continuously appear. By increasing the staff at headquarters the problems are reduced, but the cause for their existence will not be removed.

Phase V is thus marked by a further development towards a global organization structure in which the control with and co-ordination of the foreign operations either takes place in global product or area divisions. Global information and planning systems are established with a view to determining goals, resources and strategies for a portfolio of individual business areas or divisions which are more or less different regarding customers, sales functions, technology, etc.

Only a few empirical studies have been directed to analyse the relationships between the multinational corporation's selection of strategies and structures. Stopford and Wells (1972) concluded from the well-known study of the evolution of 187 American multinational enterprises (the Harvard Multinational Enterprise Project) in the 1960s that when the corporations entered foreign markets and diversified their products, they followed two definite paths of structural development. For the most diversified MNCs the common path was from stage I a functional structure to stage II a divisional structure, to stage III a product divisional structure plus international division to stage IV a global structure often based on worldwide product divisions. The other path typically followed by less diversified corporations, involved adding an international division to a functional structure before reaching stage III above. Sequences of structural development other than these two have only a few followers although among American multinationals some have moved directly from stage I to a global structure, stage IV, without ever using an international division. Cases of MNCs reversing the directions of change were only few, typically associated with failure. From the results of Stopford and Wells an international version of Chandler's thesis that 'Structure follows strategy' was further confirmed.

Only a few studies have been conducted on how American multinationals have changed their strategies and structures in the 1970s. In general the tendency has been directed towards a further shift from a traditional organizational structure with an independent international division to one suitable around worldwide or global product divisions, see for instance Curhan et al (1977), Wicks (1980) and Daniels et al (1984). The transition to global structures has been criticized in recent years by Davidson and Haspeslagh (1982). In their examination of the records of several US MNCs they concluded that the global product structure seems to retard, rather than facilitate, the transfer of resources abroad; forces companies into a defensive competitive position, and results in lower foreign sales performance. But, furthermore, this structural form on the other hand has some potential benefits, first of all in promoting cost efficiency in existing products for existing markets.

Corresponding to the American MNCs Franco (1976, 1978) has dealt with the stage of growth of European multinationals. His findings were not parallel to the results of Stopford and Wells, just like the thesis of Chandler was not confirmed in the European case.

From his research of the historical evolution of organizational structures, the most common form used by large continental corporations was the mother–daughter relations in which foreign subsidiaries report straight to corporate headquarters rather than to a division defined according to either product, market, or technology attributes. Franco emphasized that the European multinationals were built upon a 'socialized' structure of organization in which informal processes of information are prevailing because subsidiary managers have experienced a form of 'cultural affiliation' at headquarters before they were sent out. Besides the personal relations between headquarters and local management, Franco further mentioned the importance of the European multinationals' involvement in, in particular, (closed) markets with high price elasticities and limited competition. For the end of the 1960s, however, Franco points out some tendencies towards choosing an organizational form based on more global criteria. Although the studies of the historical evolution of the European multinationals in the 1970s and at the beginning of the 1980s are scarce, Swedish research confirms that European corporations have retained the mother–daughter structure for a long time, but now tend to adopt structures 'in between' a pure traditional form and a divisionalized form, defined along product or technology lines, Otterbeck (1981) and Hedlund (1984).

In summary, the literature on export behaviour and on the development of multinational enterprises points out the fact that there seem to appear only a few alternative paths of internationalization, in spite of the organizations coming from different-sized countries, facing different technological, managerial, and environmental conditions. When a number of firms repeat the same sequence of major structural changes, researchers propose that something systematic is at work and that there may be different stages of internationalization involved with each stage, having its own peculiar combination of structure, function, and process dimensions. In the following section the implications of such a stage approach will be discussed.

4. A CRITIQUE OF THE INTERNATIONAL STAGE OF GROWTH MODELS

In the following section different viewpoints of research methodology will be presented concerning the underlying basis of studying firm development generally and internationalizational behaviour in particular. Furthermore, the intention is to discuss the epistemological implications of a stage approach, including the research possibilities of investigating firm behaviour both retrospectively and prospectively. Finally, the existing research will be conducted with a view towards discussion of some considerations for the direction of future research on internationalization.

Using a stage approach represents an attempt to systematize the development process of firms in some phases which rely on *causal relationships* between different sets of variables within the firms' inner or outer environments. Identification of various stages means to put forward several causalities, which by observing the variables, are converted into hypotheses in anticipation of testing whether business realities are similar to or differ from the assumed regularities. Thus the stages of growth can be interpreted as a condensed expression of the causalities which supporters of a given classification scheme consider to be of importance. At the same time such an approach implies not only an attempt to establish certain patterns of causalities at a specific point of time, but more to construct descriptive models which point in the definite direction of changes, i.e. a time-related process also due to causal relations. According to this underlying scientific view, every stage describing the development sequence is a result of the outcome of the activities of a previous stage and furthermore a premise of a later one. This relying on the assertions of the existence of universal regularities implies *a deterministic description* of firm evolution over time.

Such a type of description has for a long time been a scientific ideal, originating from a desire to explain and to predict. Especially within the natural sciences, the conditions for explaining and predicting exist due to the objects having a material and quantitative content, typically by observing the objects in closed and controllable environments. On the other hand, business phenomena are often of a more qualitative and immaterial nature, indicating the difficulties in observing possible fixing parameters. The actors are human beings (decision makers) with a great variety of behaviour repertoire, and at the same time the environments of the business organization, are in character differentiated and complex, which all in all implies another kind of research reality. This gives a peculiar background when studying change processes of organizations. In addition several other issues can be raised.

The first and major issue turns on the possibilities of investigating firm internationalization in retrospect. This issue may not only be considered in connection with the way the research problem presents itself, but even in relation to the ongoing research process, in particular, in those instances where the researcher investigates why and how something occurred at a distinct point of time.

The problem stated is due to the fact that research into firm development is ex post analysis, i.e. the results of firm behaviour must be taken as given which determinates the exploration of the assumptions underlying. Generally, the research methodology consists of ranging the observed phenomena in accordance with a supposed model of internationalization and thus will the ranging of the causalities also appear. This means that the results of a development process are used as a way to structuralize the process in various stages by giving the descriptive elements signification. The issue raised here has not so much to do with the way in which the phenomena of firm internationalization are related, but rather, in a wider sense, concerning the research selection of those variables to be studied. This implies that it can be difficult to speak about universal development patterns when it is complicated to separate the researcher from the phenomena studied. In the natural sciences this problem is often of minor importance because the measuring instrument neutralizes the influence of the researcher, while within business sciences, on the contrary, the researcher is himself the measuring instrument. The stated problem is obviously of a general character, but especially in describing a development process of firms (the internationalization process), it must be important how the managers (the actors) on one side and the observers (the researchers) on the other interpret and evaluate the sequence of events.

A second issue deals with whether the stage-of-growth development is a uniform process, so that all firms have to go through the same sequence. The consequence of applying a unilinear description mode is—in its most extreme and strict version—that all firms have to go through each stage in a precise manner, which means that the possibilities of skipping one or several phases are excluded, just as a reversed sequence of the development path cannot occur. Such a mechanistic explanation of firm internationalization prescribes terminal or irreversible forces reducing the influences of individual and contingency factors. It seems evident that the degree of control and influence will vary from firm to firm and from situation to situation.

Lately evolutionary explanations of firm internationalization has therefore been critized. Reid (1983) states that on one hand there are no *a priori* reasons why firm international growth should occur in a systematic fashion, and on the other hand that a stage approach is suspect on both conceptual and empirical grounds, leading him to conclude that 'a general theory is highly speculative'. In a recent empirical study by Hedlund and Kverneland (1983) it is furthermore shown that

> the experiences of Swedish firms in Japan suggest the establishment and growth strategies on foreign markets are changing towards more direct and rapid entry modes than those implied by theories of gradual and slow internationalization processes.

As a result of the critique certain reservations have to be taken, because particular factors and circumstances can cause disorder in the established chain of phases. Thus, in particular, a unilinear evolution process must be rejected as a too simple mode of description.

A third issue raised is the question whether the variables of firm strategy and structure explaining the change processes represent stability and continuity as assumed within the single stages. Turning to the cyclic process of evolution, as reviewed above, this can partly be verified empirically. According to this form of description, the evolution stages bear a certain flavour of momentum—a dominant factor in organizational development; that is, reversals in the direction of change in variables are relatively rare.

The organization literature points to a very large number of potential causes for momentum and stability. Mitroff and Kilmann (1976) have shown that enduring organizational myths and ideologies are preservative for the evolution of an organization, just as Argynis and Schon (1977) in their classical work show that orientations of organizations are few and often of a reinforced nature (past behaviour is transferred into the future). Establishing political coalitions have moreover been emphasized as resistant to change, see for instance Pettigrew (1973). Other writers stress that the realities of business corporations are built upon an organizational modus operandi (Cyert and March, 1973) characterized by continuity in line with business programmes, goals and expectations.

Besides the existence of factors resisting organizational development, the findings of various studies furthermore confirm that changes (or stability) in the variables will tend to occur together, or will follow one another after a brief interval. In building taxonomies of organizations, Mintzberg (1979) shows that there are integral relationships between environmental, organizational, and strategy-making variables. Although the realities of business organizations are complex, it points out the fact that momentum is likely to coexist among a great many variables at the same time.

While the evolution stages according to the cyclic description form are characterized by stability, the transition stages (revolution periods) are often marked by dramatic changes in which there are reversals in the direction of change across a large number of variables. In some cases a transition period can be seen as a result of unsolved (previous) problems, so that the firm is increasingly unable to meet the requirements and demands of the environments. In particular, Greiner (1972) has explained the causes of revolution periods in the organizational development process.

In summary, there seems to be some empirical evidence of the existence of continuous links between sets of variables, consisting of the dimensions of strategy-making, environment, and organizational structure, which perhaps indicate that a cyclic model of evolution can be of research interest. The process of internationalization has up until now only been discussed when explaining the historical evolution. An often formulated criterion, whether a theory is satisfactory, is its usefulness in predicting. As previously stated there are many problems involved in explaining the process which casts doubts as to whether it can be reconstructed in retrospect. But there is no basis for prediction, because an analysis of the potentialities of a given firm will be inhibited by knowledge qualitative changes in the environments and within the firm itself—changes which under all circumstances take place, but the time of breakthrough, the shape, and the lapse of time of these changes are unknown at the time of analysis.

This implies that the stage models can only be applied in order to uncover the conditions and limits of the potentials of a prospective firm development (i.e. internationalization), in assuming that the models consist of systematic data on the mode of the development process for long time periods. Comparative analysis of different decision situations may potentially give occasion to draw conclusions. Although there hardly exist two identical sequences of firm development, partial similarities tend to appear, which can give rise to adopt the internationalization experience accumulated by other firms.

5. TOWARDS A NEW APPROACH TO STUDYING THE INTERNATIONALIZATION PROCESS OF FIRMS

Although it can be hard to give a general characteristic of the overwhelming amount of research within the study of the internationalization process of firms, the following picture tends to be outlined:

First, with reference to both theory and empirical methods, research orientation has been relatively unchanged within the last ten years. The majority of the studies have investigated the internationalization process by establishing (partial) relationships between small sets of variables; between first of all the role of size and growth, the technology and the managerial characteristics of the firm on the one hand and different dimensions of international activities and foreign operations on the other. A great number of studies use simple bivariate statistics such as correlation coefficients to draw conclusions about potentially complex relationships. The trend towards multivariate regression and partial correlation is encouraging, but it is not yet as widespread as it should be. When only relatively few variables have been related, resulting in an obvious and well-known problem namely, that variables which are not considered may be influenced or may account for an observed relationship. This implies that important factors can be disregarded in inhibiting or promoting potential relationships between yet other sets of variables. Furthermore, studies on firm internationalization have been based on cross-section analysis, implying that the dimension of time has been involved only indirectly. Even though adaptation of international firms takes place over time, the time dimension is never used in studies on internationalization. Of course it would be desirable to carry out longitudinal research that investigates the changes of firms over time in identifying more clearly the progression of firms through the stage-of-growth process. Such an investigation could reveal more causality between trigger factors and establish time thresholds for alterations in a firm's internationalizational behaviour. As far as it is known no investigation has analysed the development of firms using a longitudinal approach.

Concerning the hypotheses tested, they have been highly atomistic in the sense that the significance of firm size, product and technology orientations, managerial characteristics in particular has been a dominating approach. Often there have been difficulties in finding suitable approximations for the variables underlying.

Secondly, broadly speaking research in recent years has not further added to the understanding of the functioning and adaptation of the international firm. There have not been many new findings, just as a tendency to *contradictory* findings has appeared. Conflicting results have led to researchers either investigating established relations on new samples of business firms or redefining the variables used. Still the contradictions exist, so today it is difficult to conclude what role the size of firm, the product and technology orientations, the managerial characteristics etc. have for the direction and character of firm internationalization.

The above conclusion depicts a rather gloomy picture of the present research situation, and even though the picture must be viewed as being somewhat distorted, it could be relevant to ask whether a further development and/or a modification of the existing paradigm would lead to progress.

The view held by the writer of this article is that future research must seek other and new paths. Research must go in a more pluralistic direction in which the complexity of internationalization is seen in a much richer explanatory context involving several possible variables and dimensions such as strategic choice and time. At the same time research must abstain from establishing general theories which partly intend to explain the functioning of all business firms irrespective of the context in which they operate, and partly attempt to include all types of strategic decision situations in spite of the nature and importance of each situation varying from business to business and from one time to the next.

Instead a 'middle range approach' to theory development has to be established, see Pinder and Moore (1979). The aim is to distinguish between different categories or types of international corporations and contexts, each explaining only a part of the realities of the internationalization process from different assumptions and dependent variables. Inspiration can, in particular, come from organizational researchers who have in recent years shown that there exist a limited number of richly described and common organizational forms. Miller and Friesen (1977, 1980) have from their empirical research identified ten archetypes of strategy-making which characterized strategic behaviour, structure and environment along seveal variables and a time dimension. Although there are considerable methodological issues involved, the literature seems to show that there are many promising methods available, including statistical techniques as for instance hierarchical clustering, numerical taxonomy, Q-factor analysis.

In the light of the fact that organizational literature has found certain patterns of structure and strategies of various organizations, establishment of international typologies of firms will imply a split-up of a sample into different homogeneous parts according to some desired similarity criteria instead of drawing sample-wide generalizations as done in previous research. By looking simultaneously at a large number of variables that collectively define a meaningful and coherent part of a firm reality, it should be possible to identify common types of internationally oriented corporations, business situations etc. This means a search for common criteria for classifying firms as well as for basic properties of functioning the international firm or multinational enterprise. Up to now such a research orientation is at a preliminary stage.

NOTES

1. See for instance Reid (1982), Cavusgil (1984), Czinkota (1982), Abdel-Malek (1978) for the impact of size; Abdel-Malek (1974), Erland and Wiedersheim-Paul (1977), Kirpalani and Mackintosh (1980), and Suzman and Wortzel (1984) for the impact of product and technology orientation on export behaviour of firms.
2. The concepts of periodization have their background in historical research, but in the writer's opinion can be transmitted to business phenomena.
3. For excellent review articles, see Galbraith and Nathanson (1978) and Caves (1980).
4. Here quoted from Galbraith and Nathanson (1978).

REFERENCES

Abdel-Malek, T. (1974). *Managerial Export Orientation: A Canadian Study*. School of Business Administration, University of Western Ontario: London, Ontario.
Abdel-Malek, T. (1978). Export Marketing Orientation in Small Firms. *American Journal of Small Business*, **3**: 25–34.
Aldrich, H. E. (1979). *Organizations and Environments*. Prentice-Hall: Englewood Cliffs, NJ.
Argyris, C., Schon, D. (1978). *Organizational Learning: A Theory of Action Perspective*. Addison Wesley: Reading, Mass.
Bilkey, W. J. (1978). An Attempted Integration of the Literature on the Export Behavior of Firms. *Journal of International Business Studies*, **9(1)**: 33–46.
Bilkey, W. and Tesar, G. (1977). The Export Behaviour of Smaller-Sized Wisconsin Manufacturing Firms. *Journal of International Business Studies*, **8**: 93–98.
Carlson, S. (1975). *How Foreign is Foreign Trade*, Uppsala University: Uppsala.
Cavusgil, S. T. (1976). Organizational Determinants of Firms' Export Behaviour, an Empirical Analysis. Unpublished Ph.D. thesis, The University of Wisconsin: Madison, Wisconsin.
Cavusgil, S. T. (1980). On the Internationalization Process of Firms, *European Research*, **8**: 273–281.
Cavusgil, S. T. (1982). Some Observations on the Relevance of Critical Variables for Internationalization Stages. In *Export Management. An International Context*. Czinkota, M. R., Tesar, G. (eds). Praeger: New York, pp. 276–288.
Cavusgil, S. T. (1984). Differences Among Exporting Firms Based on Degree of Internationalization. *Journal of Business Research* **12**.
Cavusgil, S. T., Bilkey, W. J., Tesar, G. (1979). A Note on the Export Behavior of Firms: Exporter Profiles. *Journal of International Business Studies*, **10(2)**: 91–97.
Chandler, A. D. (1962). *Strategy and Structure*. MIT Press: Cambridge, MA.
Chandler, A. D. (1977). *The Visible Hand. The Managerial Revolution in American Business*. Harvard University Press: Boston, MA.

Channon, D. (1973). *The Strategy and Structure of British Enterprise*. Macmillan: London.

Crookel, H., Graham, I. (1979). International Marketing and Canadian Industrial Strategy. *Business Quarterly*, **44**: 28–34.

Curhan, J. P., Davidson, W. H., Rajan, S. (1977). *Tracing the Multinationals*. MIT Press: Cambridge, MA.

Czinkota, M. R. (1982) *Export Development Strategies. US Promotion Policy*. Praeger Special Studies: New York.

Czinkota, M. R. (1983). The Export Development Process: A Validation Inquiry. Staff Paper No. 4, National Center for Export-Import Studies, Georgetown University: Washington, DC.

Czinkota, M. R., Johnston, W. J. (1981). Segmenting U.S. Firms for Export Development. *Journal of Business Research*, **9**: 353–365.

Cyert, R., March, J. (1963). *A Behavioral Theory of the Firm*. Prentice-Hall: Englewood Cliffs, NJ.

Daniels, J. D., Pitts, R. A. (1984). Strategy and Structure of U.S. Multinationals: An Exploratory Study. *Academy of Management Journal*, **27**(2).

Davidson, W. H., Haspeslagh, P. (1982). Shaping a Worldwide Organization. *Harvard Business Review*, **60**: 7.

Erland, O., Wiedersheim-Paul, F. (1977). *Technological Strategies and Internationalization*. Department of Business Administration, University of Uppsala: Uppsala.

Franko, L. (1976). *The European Multinationals*. Harper & Row: London.

Franko, L. (1978). Organizational Structures and Multinational Strategies of Continental European Enterprises. In Ghertman, M., Leontiades, J. (eds), *European Research in International Business*. North-Holland: Amsterdam, pp. 111–140.

Galbraith, J. R., Nathanson, D. A. (1978). *Strategy Implementation. The Role of Structure and Process*. St. Paul, M.

Greiner, L. E. (1972). Evolution and Revolution as Organizations Grow. *Harvard Business Review*, **50**.

Hannan, M. T., Freeman, J. (1977). The Population Ecology of Organizations. *American Journal of Sociology* **82**(5): 929–964.

Hedlund, G. (1984). Organization in-between: The Evolution of the Mother-Daughter Structure of Managing Foreign Subsidiaries in Swedish MNCs. *Journal of International Business Studies*, **15**(2): 109–123.

Hedlund, G., Kverneland, A. (1984). Are Establishment and Growth Patterns for Foreign Markets Changing? The Case of Swedish Investment in Japan. Stockholm School of Economics, Institute of International Business: Stockholm.

Johanson, J., Vahlne, J. (1977). The Internationalization Process of the Firm—A Model of Knowledge Development and Increasing Foreign Commitments'. *Journal of International Business Studies*, **8**(1): 23–32.

Khan, M. S. (1978). *A Study of Success and Failure in Exports*, Dissertation, University of Stockholm: Stockholm.

Kirpalani, V. H., Mackintosh, N. B. (1980). International Marketing Effectiveness of Technology-Oriented Small Firms. *Journal of International Business Studies*, **11**(3): 81–90.

Miller, D., Friesen, P. (1977). Strategy-making in Context: Ten Empirical Archetypes. *Journal of Management Studies*, **14**: 253–280.

Miller, D. (1979). Strategy, Structure and Environment: Context Influences upon some Bivariate Associations. *Journal of Management Studies*, **16**(3): 294–316.

Miller, D., Friesen, P. (1980). Archetypes of Organizational Transition. *Administrative Science Quarterly*. **25**(2): 268–299.

Mintzberg, H. (1979). *The Structuring of Organizations*. Prentice-Hall: Englewood Cliffs, NJ.

Mitroff, I., Kilmann, R. (1976). On Organizational Stories. In Kilman et al (eds) *The Management of Organization Design*, Vol. 1, Praeger: New York, pp. 189–208.

Olson, H. C. (1975). *Studies in Export Promotion*. Almqvist & Wicksell: Uppsala.

Otterbeck, L. (1981). The Management of Joint Ventures. In *The Management of Headquarters-Subsidiary Relationships in Multinational Corporations*, Otterbeck, L. (ed). Gower Press: Aldershot.

Pavan, R. J. (1972). *The Strategy and Structure of Italian Enterprise*, Unpublished D.B.A. thesis, Harvard University.

Pavord, W. C., Bogard, R. (1975). The Dynamics of the Decision to Export. *Akron Business and Economic Review*, **6**: 6–11.

Pettigrew, A. (1973). *The Politics of Organizational Decision Making*. Praeger: London.

Reid, S. B. (1982). The Impact of Size on Export Behaviour in Small Firms. In Czinkota, R., Tesar, G. (eds) *Export Management, An International Context*. Praeger: New York.

Reid, S. B. (1983). Market Expansion and Firm Internationalization. Paper presented to 9th Annual Conference of European International Business Association, Oslo, Norway, 18–20 December.

Rumelt, R. (1974). *Strategy, Structure and Economic Performance*. Harvard Business School: Boston, MA.

Salter, M. S. (1970/71). Stages of Corporate Development. *Journal of Business Policy* **1**.

Scott, B. R. (1973). The Industrial State: Old Myths and New Realities. *Harvard Business Review* **51(1)**.

Simpson, C., Kujawa, D. (1974). The Export Decision Process: An Empirical Inquiry. *Journal of International Business Studies*, **5**: 107–117.

Smith, W., Charmoz, R. (1978). Coordinate Line Management, Working Paper, Scarle International, Chicago, Illinois, February 1975, quoted from Galbraith and Nathanson, above.

Stopford, J. M., Wells, L. T. (1972). *Managing the Multinational Enterprise*. Longmans: London.

Suzman, C. L., Wortzel, L. H. (1984). Technology Profiles and Export Marketing Strategies. *Journal of Business Research*, **12**: 183–194.

Wicks, M. E. (1980). *A Comparative Analysis of the Foreign Investment Evaluation Practices of U.S.-Based Multinational Companies*. McKinsey & Co.: New York.

Wiedersheim-Paul, F., Johanson, J. (1975). The Internationalization of the Firm—Four Swedish Case Studies. *Journal of Management Studies*, **12**: 306–313.

Wolf, B. M. (1977). Industrial Diversification and Internationalization: Some Empirical Evidence. *Journal of Industrial Economics*, **26(2)**.

Wrigley, L. (1976). Conglomerate Growth in Canada, *Mimeo*, London. Here quoted from Caves, R. E. (1980). Industrial Organization, Corporate Strategy and Structure. *Journal of Economic Literature*, **18**: 64–92.

15

Foreign Direct Investment as a Sequential Process

Bruce Kogut

The primary advantage of the multinational firm, as differentiated from a national corporation, lies in its flexibility to transfer resources across borders through a globally maximizing network. Recent models of direct foreign investment have tended to downplay these advantages of a co-ordinated multinational system; rather, they have stressed the motivational behaviour arising out of essentially national factors and market imperfections, e.g., proprietary knowledge, domestic industrial structure, and product differentiation. The neglect of the advantages of multinationality obscures, though, an important distinction between the original motivations to establish plants in foreign countries and the subsequent investment decisions. There is, in short, a fallacy of explanation of genesis in failing to distinguish between the initial investment decision and the subsequent incremental investment flows.

This paper argues that current foreign direct investment (FDI) must be understood as largely sequential flows stemming from the advantages of flexibility of a multinational system. The empirical foundation for this argument can be seen in the change over the past 30 years of the dominant channels of US FDI from new intercompany outflows to reinvested earnings. In 1970, the ratio of equity and intercompany account outflows to reinvested earnings was 1.39. By 1979, the ratio was 0.32. (The complete time series is given in Table 1.) The predominant share of FDI flows are incremental investments in already established subsidiaries. In light of these trends, previous theories of FDI which stress the oligopolistic behaviour of corporations in their home markets provide incomplete explanations for current FDI. What is required is a greater consideration of the systemic advantages inherent in a multinational network.

These trends carry implications also for the way data on FDI flows are categorized and used. Rather than collecting data according to entries and exits, information should be gathered concerning the conduit of flows as well as changes in the stock of FDI at the firm level. Data which reveals the industry and regional breakdown of both reinvested and

This reading has been published in *Multinational Corporations in the 1980s* (1983), Kindleberger, C. P. Audretsch, D. (eds.), MIT Press: Cambridge MA. Reprinted in *International Financial Management*, ed. Lessard, D. (2nd edn). Wiley: New York (1984).

Table 1. US Foreign Direct Investment (in millions of dollars)

Year	Total	Equity and intercompany account outflows	Reinvested earnings of incorporated affiliates	Ratio of equity outflows to reinvested earnings
1950	1,088	621	475	1.31
1955	1,766	823	962	0.86
1960	2,039	1,675	1,266	1.32
1965	4,994	3,468	1,542	2.25
1966	4,318	3,625	1,791	2.02
1967	4,768	3,050	1,757	1.74
1968	5,347	2,855	2,440	1.17
1969	6,186	3,130	2,830	1.11
1970	7,387	4,413	3,176	1.39
1971	7,280	4,441	3,176	1.40
1972	7,118	3,214	4,532	0.71
1973	11,435	3,195	8,158	0.39
1974	8,765	1,275	7,777	0.16
1975	13,971	6,196	8,048	0.77
1976	12,759	4,253	7,696	0.55
1977	13,039	5,612	7,286	0.77
1978	17,957	4,877	11,469	0.43
1979	24,844	5,904	18,414	0.32

Source: Survey of Current Business. US Department of Commerce (1981), **61**(2).

new FDI flows would provide a critical platform by which the systemic advantages of the multinational corporation (MNC) can be appraised.

This is not to deny that the advantages of the MNC have been studied. The broader field of research on the MNC has been sensitive to these issues. Especially in the consideration of the political complexities posed by multinational corporations, the peculiar strengths attributed to the operation of a multinational network have been discussed.[1] Such issues as transfer pricing, tax arbitrage, bargaining or negotiating powers, and cost advantages have been analysed in isolation or in group.[2] There has not been, however, a thorough integration of these issues and the theory of foreign investment in the literature, with the partial exception of Dunning (1979).

The purpose of this paper is to move toward such an integration. Section 1 reviews briefly the recent FDI literature and introduces a more generalized model in the hope of elucidating the importance of the multinationality factor in FDI flows. The cutting edges of this model is the view of the MNC as a collection of valuable options which permits the discretionary choice of altering real economic activities or financial flows from one country to the next. Section 2 discusses the valuation of systemic advantages. Finally, Section 3 discusses the importance of this expanded theory from the point of view of host and home countries and comments upon trends likely to persist into the 1980s.

1. THE MULTINATIONALITY FACTOR IN FDI

Particular aspects of the contribution of multinationality to the value of the firm and to explaining its behaviour have been examined. Kindleberger (1969) considers the conflict between the host country and a multinational firm who are maximizing conflicting objective functions. Agmon and Lessard (1977) and Lessard (1979) note the incremental value of being able to arbitrage tax regimes. Hirsch (1976) cites in a revealing analysis the effects of joint production and trade in intermediate goods in the context of subsequent investment decisions. Vernon (1979) stresses the information- and profit-scanning functions of a multinational network. Davidson (1980) demonstrates the significance of experience effects upon FDI flows.

A growing body of research concerns the combination of location and trade theory with that of internalization. Magee (1977) argues that FDI is motivated by the difficulties of appropriating rents from the trade and licensing in proprietary knowledge. Buckley and Casson (1976) argue similarly that plant location is determined by, one, locational advantages and, two, market failure in the trade of proprietary knowledge, especially that of research and development.

Dunning (1977, 1979) has more recently expanded upon these ideas in developing what he calls the 'eclectic theory' of FDI. The theory combines usefully the macroeconomics of standard trade theory with transportation theory. Thus, a country's endowment and geographical position create certain 'locational' advantages. Dunning then proceeds to consider the factors which determine entry barriers and sustainable oligopolies. These factors, e.g. patented information, brand names, technology, form what he calls 'ownership' advantages. Ignoring the possibility of licensing, the various combinations of these advantages suggest a scheme such as shown in Figure 1. In the upper right box, for example, the firm possesses a unique technology or some cost advantage. Its home domicile is, however, characterized by higher factor or transportation costs than foreign locations. As a result, it invests overseas. Thus investment occurs only when the home firm possesses a unique asset and the host country is relatively advantaged in location. Finally, the theory of internalization is introduced to explain why licensing is not a preferred mode to FDI.[3] Thus, trade and location theory is wedded to that of internalization in order to explain FDI flows as a response to market imperfections.

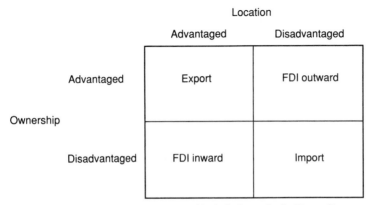

Figure 1. Trade and FDI Outcome for a Single Industry in the Home Country.

Nevertheless, the importance of a multinational network as an important contribution to the value of the firm and its economic opportunities and to the determination of the likely conduits of FDI have not been sufficiently analysed. In the view of Buckley and Casson, for example, internationalization is the by-product of the search for minimum cost production sites and the internalization of markets. The absence of uniquely international factors is starkly apparent in Hirsch's model, which is considered in more detail in the next section. While Hirsch discusses economies of scale and joint production in marketing at a single location, there is no variable that represents the revenue impact of the ownership of a globally operated system. Dunning (1981) as well does not analyse the precise systemic opportunities generated by multinationality, though he does list several types of advantages.

But does the factor of multinationality add to our understanding of the determinants of FDI? One way to answer this question is to consider whether MNCs would still have cause to exist in the absence of the commonly listed market imperfections. Let us suppose, then, that the four of the five imperfections that Buckley and Casson list in the market for technology could be eliminated. These imperfections are (1) the absence of a forwards market to hedge the risk of development, (2) the impossibility to arrange contracts that would permit discriminatory pricing, (3) the presence of monopolistic purchasers, and (4) informational impactedness. (The fifth imperfection is that of government intervention, which—along with such events as changes in exchange rates—can create unique arbitrage opportunities for the MNC.) If in some idealized state, these imperfections were altered to the requirements of perfect markets, would there still be the MNC?

The answer would be affirmative, due to three characteristics which enable the MNC to exploit uniquely international distortions in markets or production: one, the ability to arbitrage institutional restrictions; two, the informational externalities captured by the firm in the conduct of international business; three, the cost saving gained by joint production in marketing and in manufacturing. These imperfections, which are carefully considered in the studies on the political dilemmas posed by multinationals and on multinational planning and control, are curiously understated in the mainstream economic literature.

This neglect is derived largely from not considering international projects as incremental at a global level. Although conceiving international investment within a dynamic theory of the firm, the internationalization literature fails to consider the value of the *operational* flexibility and externalities of a multinational system. Rather, the stress is placed upon the *structural* elements of plant location and the elimination of transactional costs.

There is, in short, a tendency to view FDI as a decision made at a discrete point of time. This is the fallacy of genesis to which I previously alluded. The decision to transfer resources internationally is only one aspect of FDI. Given the structural outcome of this decision, the other aspect is the series of sequential decisions which determine the volume and direction of these transferred resources.

Contrary to the structural approach, consideration of the operational value of a global system places stress upon the unique ability of multinationals to reduce the costs of operating in an uncertain world.[4] This is best illustrated by considering explicitly the three factors that were claimed above to be uniquely international attributes. The first is the ability of the MNC to arbitrage institutional restrictions, e.g., tax codes, antitrust provisions, financial limitations, and even national security prohibitions on trade. In effect, the operation of an international system has provided the multinational with a string of options written on contingent outcomes. The difference between the inclusion of taxes, financial incentives, etc., as part of a theory of location and this approach is that the consideration of institutional arbitrage as an option emphasizes the unique ability of the MNC to exploit the conditions of uncertainty and of institutional environments. The MNC can, in effect, exercise an option upon the occurrence of an event, e.g., its option to choose in which country to declare its profits. Boundaries do not represent only the costs of tariffs and transport; they also represent profit opportunities which can only be exploited by a multinational corporation.

The second factor concerns the capture of externalities in information, or what we call learning cost externalities. There is an information set required of international business that is separable from that required of domestic business. Corporations spend vast resources in their recruitment of internationally skilled personnel, in political analysis, in intercultural education programmes, and in the development of monitoring and control mechanisms. They also invest in information scanning and processing in order to locate markets and customers internationally. But most critically, there are important learning curves involved in these activities as well as 'first mover advantages'. Occidental Petroleum's knowledge and status as a long-standing supplier/customer of the Soviet Union is not easily duplicated.

Joint production economies can occur in both marketing and manufacturing on a global scale. Niehans (1977) has noted that economies of scale in marketing or servicing but constant or decreasing scale economies in manufacturing can serve to explain the growth of the MNC. Similarly, joint production economies due to the creation of a multinational network reduces the physical capital or labour costs of production and marketing of incremental investments. For example, the multinational network permits the export of otherwise non-exportable goods, since the fixed costs of establishing sales offices, hiring personnel, and locating plant sites are already sunk. The incremental cost saving can permit, as Hirsch suggests, an increase in the export of intermediate products or in the market entry of new products sharing production economies. In addition, the multinational network can serve to export additional final goods or to service the export of other firms' goods in times of slack capacity; the Japanese trading companies are an example of the latter facility. Unquestionably, the formation of a multinational network poses significant barriers to entry. The implications of these barriers are analysed in greater detail in the conclusions.

2. SYSTEMIC ADVANTAGES

The implications of considering the value of international factors can be illustrated in the formulation of a capital-budgeting procedure. In an instructive article, Hirsch (1976) suggests that the decision to service a market by exports or by foreign direct investments can be modelled by four cost variables discounted at some appropriate rate: production and tax transportation costs P, research and development costs K, marketing costs M, and control costs C. Demand is assumed as given. Marketing costs are argued to be higher for exports than host-manufactured goods, while control costs rise with the internationalization of production. These assumptions are intuitively reasonable. Moreover, Hirsch argues that M and C are increasing functions of K. Implicitly, Magee argued the same in his claim that the opportunity loss of appropriability rises with information content at every stage of production. Hirsch's reasons rest in the costs of market exploration and organizational communication. Since neither argument is mutually exclusive, both can be subsumed in Hirsch's model.

Given this formulation of the model, Hirsch demonstrates convincingly that the failure of conventional trade theory is its consideration solely of the comparative costs of production. Expanding the model to include the production of several goods, Hirsch also shows that economies of joint production can change the investment decision when production for each good is maintained as an independent project. The model is also expanded to consider multistage production, whereby Hirsch shows that overseas investment production can increase the export of previously non-competitive intermediary goods.

While Hirsch discusses economies of joint production in marketing at a single location, there is no variable that represents the cost savings of the ownership of a globally operated system. As suggested earlier, these cost savings arise from considering a global network as a sunk cost and sequential investments as incremental. (There is also the factor that in a world of imperfectly diffused information, the scanning advantages of a multinational widens its set of investment opportunities.) The impact of these cost factors is to reduce the incremental values of C, K, and M and to expand the firm's investment opportunities.

We can illustrate the value of systemic advantages by considering explicitly how a capital budget formulation might account for these benefits, particularly those of the first factor. The first factor, that of arbitraging institutional and national barriers, contributes directly to the enhancement of the discounted revenue stream. Such a contribution is derived through, one, a possible reduction in the discount rate, and secondly, through the addition of a string of real but usually non-tradeable options. The advantages accrued by international diversification in financial markets and the role of MNCs in providing diversification have been commented upon by several authors, in particular by Sonlik (1974), Lessard (1976), and Agmon and Lessard (1977). In a world of no barriers to portfolio flows and of purchasing power parity, the cost of capital at the margin is the same for all investors in a taxless world, regardless of nationality. Since changes in the exchange rates and nominal interest rates would reflect equally changes in prices, discounted cash flows before taxes are the same no matter what their currency denomination.[5] When capital markets are segmented by national barriers and policies, discount rates vary between countries. These variations reflect national differences in risk bearing and in time preferences. To the extent that barriers are imperfect, discount rates tend toward a world rate plus or minus the transactional costs of subventing these barriers. Considered in this light, the equilibrium discount rates can be viewed as prices for a single commodity adjusted for transportation costs, when all countries are equally distant from one another.

The argument for the advantages of the MNC in financial markets boils down to the following set of simple statements. Multinational firms are able to invest across national borders and thereby avoid the presumably more costly barriers to portfolio flows. Because of its access to more diversified international financial markets, the MNC can, holding everything else equivalent, invest in marginal projects otherwise rejected by host firms. Since the MNC adjusts its risk according to a world portfolio and the domestic firm according to a more home-weighted portfolio (due to capital market imperfections and barriers), the risk-adjusted cost of capital is relatively lower for the MNC. Secondly, if the foreign project represents a unique asset in terms of the available portfolio investments on the world market, the home investor is willing to pay the MNC a premium for contributing an otherwise unattainable asset to his or her portfolio. In conclusion, then, in a world of imperfect international capital flows, MNCs receive a premium relative to their purely domestic home competitors—if their foreign investments are unique and non-traded assets—and invest at a lower capital cost relative to the purely domestic host country competitors.[6]

An aspect that has received less attention in the literature regarding the evaluation of a multinational network is the value of holding a string of options defined by institutional barriers. These barriers can be typified by different currencies or more exactly by changes in relative exchange rates, taxes, sovereign risk, and legal prescriptions on equity ownership, form of remittance, etc. To illustrate the importance of these options, consider an MNC operating a series of plants in several countries which serve purely domestic markets. The future cash flows are uncertain. Upon realization of its cash flows, the MNC can through transfer pricing, financial packaging, and other methods alter to a non-trivial extent the structure and level of its obligations. The contingent events are the realization of taxable earnings in each of the various countries. The nature of the option is that the MNC can choose in which geographical jurisdiction to declare these profits so as to minimize the tax burden.

Consider, for a second example, the MNC with several export markets and a few manufacturing plants. By design, the plants operate on average at less than full capacity. In country X, it must renegotiate a set of extraction or labour contracts. In response to unacceptably (however subjectively defined) bargaining positions, the MNC can shift production to other plants to service its overseas markets, given that labour constraints are not binding. (This potential has secondary effects in terms of its bargaining strength, as discussed in Section 3.) Thus given the uncertainty over the outcomes of negotiations, the MNC has the real option of mitigating the costs of factor price increases or higher taxes in the short term, and the physical adjustment costs in the long term, through maintaining excess capacity in diverse national plants. A similar case is that of a real appreciating currency. The ability to shift exports from a country whose currency is appreciating to one where other plants are located is a valuable option—assuming that pricing is denominated in the currency of the importing country and factor payments are derived out of overseas revenues.

What is important to note is that all the above-described options are valuable because the future state of the world is uncertain.[7] Moreover, the more variable the environment, the more valuable are these options. From the point of view of the MNC, the variance of its cash flows and of factor prices in the context of national restrictions presents a set of valuable options relative to the opportunity set of a purely domestic firm. Since these options are exercisable only by the MNC and cannot be traded and purchased by individual investors in any meaningful sense, the value of the firm is enhanced by the incremental value of these options.[8]

The above discussion can be illustrated through the consideration of the elements that would enter into a capital-budgeting model. The value of the firm can be described as

$$NPV = \sum_{0}^{t} \frac{(\text{cash flows} + \text{learning} + \text{joint production} + \text{options})}{(1+R)}$$

The discount rate may be lower than that available on the world market and, as is more likely, lower than that available to host country firms when capital markets are segmented. (The appropriate discount rate for each term is likely to vary according to its systematic risk, but for simplicity, we assume one rate.) The first term represents simply the discounted cash flows from a series of independent projects that are owned by globally unintegrated firms. The next three terms capture the advantages arising out of the interdependence of the cash flows of projects undertaken by an MNC. We have indicated these advantages to be learning-cost and joint-production economies, and the possession of real non-tradeable options.

How may these advantages be actually evaluated?[9] Once the initial investment is made, learning cost and joint production externalities are likely to be incorporated in the capital budget through an incremental analysis. A more complex analysis is to evaluate at the time of the initial investment the value of the option to expand into other products or into other markets. The option to arbitrage national barriers is similarly difficult to evaluate. Given the recent interest in evaluating financial options, it would appear that the analytical methods are already available to value real options numerically.[10] There are, however, serious obstacles to such an extension which are not always noted in the literature. In brief, a financial option can be valued because one assumes that there exists a shadow security whose price will follow a particular type of stochastic process. In the absence of such a shadow security, we have no reason to believe that the price of the real asset will also follow such a path since there is no means to arbitrage the real option against its shadow security. Nevertheless, the options literature provides the appropriate framework for understanding the reasoning behind the claim that the option to exercise certain rights, e.g., where to declare taxes, where to shift production, is a valuable hedge against contingent events.

The inclusion of these three elements in addition to the normal cash flows generated by project illustrates the opportunities that stem from a multinational system. As a result of these opportunities, we expect that growth in FDI is more likely to be in the form of reinvested earnings than in new entries. The consequences of this trend from the perspective of governments are discussed in the next section.

3. CURRENT TRENDS

From the firms' point of view, the flexibility to transfer resources across borders is a positive contribution to its earning stream. As discussed in an abundant literature, the viewpoints of governments are often less sanguine. Rather than consider the larger issues of government and MNC relations, we concentrate on a few specific issues, e.g., monetary stabilization, regulation, and negotiation. Through these examples, we illustrate that the well-established issues of contention between governments and the MNCs are comprehensible only within the context of the systemic flexibility of the MNCs.

How is a government likely to view these systemic advantages of MNCs when pursuing domestic monetary stabilization objectives? If an MNC speculates on currencies, its behaviour tends to give markets greater liquidity and thereby accelerates the speed of adjustment. Even if the MNC is not a speculator, it forecasts and hedges its contractual and non-contractual exposure. Whether it speculates or is able merely to shift currencies more easily from one country to the next or to write more inexpensive contractual hedges, these activities clearly tend to negate the ability of governments to pursue objectives such as the stabilization of its currency countervailing to the market trend. Thus the presence of MNCs limits further the ability of governments to pursue independent objectives in an international economy.

If governments are more constrained in their ability to pursue monetary objectives due to the existence of MNCs, are they more constrained in pursuing other objectives? Consider a government which desires to regulate a foreign-owned industry. Under closed borders, enterprises are essentially hostage to the partisan coalitions of its environment. Since exit except in the form of selling its holdings is impossible, the regulated enterprise consents to government regulation, while it may itself seek to join a political coalition.[11] For the MNC whose foreign assets are primarily in the form of proprietary knowledge, regulation is unlikely to be successful. It is especially unsuccessful in its most extreme form—that of nationalization, for as long as the ongoing value of the subsidiary is dependent on a sequential stream of innovations, nationalization results merely in the elimination of industry. The effects of less extreme interventions, e.g., an increase in taxation, invoke most likely less extreme reactions. Nevertheless, the implications are the same. To the extent that multinational corporations contribute more to the economy than that of the new policies, their partial or total withdrawal are a real loss to the host country. Moreover, if multinational corporations are truly global, then the argument applies to home countries in which governments attempt to regulate, for example, outward flows of capital.

When FDI is primarily transmitted in the form of fixed capital with known and stable technologies, the bargaining position of the MNC and host government is reversed. This situation, which is known as the obsolescent bargain, has been extensively analysed.[12] Mining is a classic example. The original investment requires a large fixed capital component. Presumably the MNC chooses to internalize this transaction in order to gain access to guaranteed supplies, to speculate on future prices when futures markets do not exist or do not trade claims on contracts many years out, or to acquire oligopolistic advantages. At the time of the investment, the host government's bargaining position is constrained by competition from the other countries. The host government can, however, capture part, if not all, of the rents ex post to the investment through a process of renegotiation. If, for example, the value of its mineral resources is higher than expected, the host government has the option of capturing part of the consequent excess returns. To the extent that this gaming behaviour is expected and that equity claims and other financial contracts are difficult to enforce, it is likely that MNCs will be reluctant to invest in mineral extraction without adequate guarantees or insurance.

What does the above analysis imply for the growth and the role of the MNC in the 1980s? There are three principal implications. First is that the entry of new firms in international markets is likely to slow, holding changes in investment opportunities constant. Evidence for this transition is suggested, as noted earlier, in the growth of reinvested earnings relative to new equity investment in total FDI flows. These figures have been given in Table 1.

The benefits of institutional arbitrage, learning curve effects, and joint production economies create, then, substantial barriers to entry. The importance of these factors is underlined in light of the present proportion of intra-firm trade which accounted roughly for 48.4% of all US imports in 1977 (Helleiner, 1979). Discussions of antitrust implications have usually stressed the feedback of FDI on competition in the home market (Bergsten et al, 1978). Perhaps a more troubling aspect is the impact of these barriers on the entry of firms from LDCs or from developed countries which were slow to create international firms. While FDI between LDCs has been increasing, such investments appear to be characterized more by the capture by small firms of investment gaps ignored by the much larger MNCs. Thus, FDI by LDCs is likely to be explained by a theory of FDI by small firms than by entry openings unique to the skills of LDC enterprises.[13]

Another implication lies in the persisting role of research and development in explaining some, though perhaps a relatively decreasing amount, of flows of proprietary capital over international borders. For those end products that are oriented towards the home market, FDI is often in the form of overseas production of intermediary products. In this case, FDI is related to research and development only insofar as the end product embodies a large value of technological expenditure. The overseas production of intermediary goods can involve minimal research and development expenditures in terms of value added. Moreover, FDI is in this form partially trade enhancing.

What should be noted is that the production of technologically sophisticated products is of less importance—though still of indubitable significance—in future FDI flows. Instead, we can imagine the development of decentralized structures that permits the delegation of product selection and research and development to subsidiaries but leaves the strategic variables of financing, production, and tax arbitrage to the home office. There is some indication that this devolution is already perceptible in the food industry (Katz, 1981).

Related to the above implications is the tendency of the MNCs to develop and expand their trading divisions. In part, this evolution is derived from the hazards of the obsolescent bargain as well as from the erosion of market advantages as the original technological edge in some products evaporates. Vernon (1977) has termed this latter trend 'senescence'. The difference between these two trends is simply that the obsolescent bargain refers to loss of property rights, senescence to loss of market shares. The underlying cause of both trends is, however, similar, i.e., the loss of some technological advantage specific to the firm which maintains its bargaining or market position. In the first case, the MNC can limit its exposure by financing extraction in the form of debt with payoffs denominated in a specified quantity of the underlying mineral or product, or by long-term contracts, or by providing managerial services and downstream marketing and relinquishing its ownership or contractual obligations. In the second case, the MNC is also induced toward eliminating its productive activities and in effect leasing the services of its global network. In both cases, the possession of a multinational network provides a stream of benefits and investment opportunities independent of the products being traded. Examples of this development are the oil industry, Japanese trading companies, and the diversification of large firms into trading third-party products, such as in the case of Thyssen.

Consequently, the MNC of the 1980s is likely to be engaged less in equity investments in primary extraction industries, but relatively more in the provision of marketing and consulting services. Trade in intermediate products is also likely to increase, because the MNC can optimize production and marketing within an already existing global system. These trends, of course, are a continuation of a pattern that has been visible for several years.

4. CONCLUSIONS

I have tried to detail the precise advantages arising from a multinational network and its implication for the identity of the agents and the type of investment flows in the future. By and large, policy implications have not been discussed. The reasons for this omission are simple. Having developed our model under the assumption of profit maximization, optimal policy recommendations which differ from a competitive profit-maximizing outcome can only be motivated if the national objective functions are specified. I have not attempted such a specification, although the dropping of the assumption of profit maximization would be an interesting exercise.

The question has been left open whether the profitability and growth of the MNC is a result of its market power or productive efficiency.[14] I have, however, implicitly suggested the importance of first-mover advantages that current MNCs possess relative to potential entrants. If we are concerned over the absence of bargaining power on behalf of many LDCs, then our analysis reinforces the recommendations for an international regulation of MNCs or the creation of countervailing institutions or enterprises to enhance the bargaining power of LDC countries. Such regional efforts as ASEAN's recent consideration of the formation of trading companies similar to those of the Japanese are illustrations of efforts to create potential countervailing enterprises. But hidden beneath such developments and recommendations is an irony often noted in the case of MNCs from developed countries. That is, though the rents from learning-curve and joint-production externalities accrue to the home MNC and hence potentially to the home countries, the creation of truly global enterprises poses challenges to the national sovereignty of governments through their maximization of global profits and through their arbitraging of institutional borders. In other words, is it reasonable to expect that an MNC originating in a developing country, which MNC maximizes its return from its global activities, should be more sensitive to the sovereignty and interests of its national government?

Consequently, the conflict of nation-states and international firms remains an issue in the 1980s. Countries face incentives not only to regulate the entry of firms, but also their exit. There has appeared the ironic evolution that LDCs have been concerned to establish strict rules of entry, whereas developed countries increasingly seek to control the exit of firms and the immediate loss of jobs and production. Whether the combined impact of these trends is to reduce the benefits of a global network remains to be seen; but, in any event, it represents the forefront of future discussions on the merits of FDI and the multinational corporation.

NOTES

I would like to thank Stephen Kobrin of New York University and Richard D. Robinson of the Massachusetts Institute of Technology for their comments on an earlier draft. I am especially grateful to Donald Lessard of the Massachusetts Institute of Technology for his comments on the first and subsequent drafts.

1. See, for example, Kindleberger (1969), Vernon (1971, 1977), or Stopford and Wells (1972).

2. Such issues as transfer pricing, tax arbitrage, bargaining or negotiating power, and regulation are discussed by Lessard (1979), Bergsten et al (1978), and Robinson (1976).

3. For a review of the internalization literature, see Rugman (1981). It should be noted that the concept of internalization is already adumbrated, like so many ideas in the literature on FDI, in Kindleberger (1969), pp. 19–22.

4. Undoubtedly, it can be claimed that the theory of internalization accounts precisely for these operational facets. (See, e.g. Buckley and Casson, 1976, p. 69.) But by placing stress upon the cost aspect of transactions, it fails to consider the profit opportunities generated by a global system.

5. This can be shown by considering whether to discount the overseas earnings by the home or foreign discount rate. If we assume purchasing power parity, changes of nominal interest rates are cancelled by identical changes of nominal exchange rates.

6. Robert Aliber (1983) has argued that FDI can be explained at the macroeconomic level, i.e., the arbitrage of international markets. Though such an approach appears weak in explaining such phenomena as cross-hauling, it has a tantalizing appeal on its attempts to link such anomalies as FDI waves to concepts as Tobin's q. There may be a macroeconomic story after all.

7. In the cases where uncertainty may appear as irrelevant, such as in tax arbitrage, governments are well equipped to develop monitoring and enforcement services. It is the uncertainty of the realized profits that keeps the costs of these services relatively high to the benefits of reducing arbitrage behaviour.

8. Some readers may be misled into inferring that the above argument suggests that total variance does matter after all to the investor. To the contrary, since these options are similar to monopoly or proprietary rents, the firms earn abnormally high rates of return but the stocks written on the firm, as long as they are traded in competitive capital markets, are priced in the expectation of a market rate of return adjusted for systematic risk.

9. See Lessard (1981) for a thorough discussion of the application of adjusted present value techniques for evaluating international projects.

10. See the path-breaking article by Black and Scholes (1973) for the evaluation of financial options. Our concern with the shadow security is directed primarily at recent extensions of the Black–Scholes model into the evaluation of real assets. MacDonald and Segal (1981) are certainly aware of these difficulties, whereas Cooper and Broglic (1981) simply assume the existence of a shadow security without substantial comment.

11. See the interesting article by Magec in this volume which discusses the impact of political coalitions on FDI flows.

12. See the writings of Vernon (1971), Stopford and Wells (1972), and Bergsten et al, (1978).

13. We have not tried here to develop such a theory of FDI by small firms. Briefly, one relevant factor would seem to be trade in custom-designed products, i.e., small producers are more sensitive to the 'voice' (in Hirschman's terminology) of smaller producers (Hirschman, 1971). Another factor is the trading by small firms of used capital equipment. Since used capital equipment is difficult to evaluate, the seller may attempt to eliminate the costs of discounting incurred through the asymmetry in information by taking an equity position. Indeed, joint ventures between LDCs are relatively common. These factors, in addition to the ones discussed above, tend to explain some characteristics of FDI between LDCs, whose markets tend after all not to be dominated by large domestic enterprises as those in developed countries. For a discussion of FDI between LDCs, see Wells (1977).

14. A number of articles in *Multinational Corporations in the 1980s* attempt to measure econometrically the relationship between the profitability of the MNC and barriers to entry. Though the factor of efficiency is not explicitly specified in these regressions, the results are nevertheless interesting in showing the significant correlation of these profits and barriers to entry.

REFERENCES

Aliber, R. (1983) in *Multinational Corporations in the 1980s*, Kindleberger, C. P., Andretsch, D. (eds). MIT Press: Cambridge, MA.

Agmon, T., and Donald L., 1977. 'Financial Factors and the International Expansion of Small-Country Firms,' in Agmon, T. and Kindleberger, C. P. (eds.), *Multinationals from Small Countries*. Cambridge, Mass.: MIT Press.

Bergsten, C. F., Horst, T., and Moran, T. (1978). *American Multinationals and American Interests*. Washington, DC.: Brookings.

Broyles, J. E. and Cooper, I. A. (1981). 'Growth Opportunities and Real Investment Decisions,' in Derkinderen, F. G. L. and Crum, R. L. (eds.), *Risk, Capital Costs, and Project Financing Decisions*. The Hague: Nijhoff.

Buckley, P. J. and Casson, M. (1976). *The Future of the Multinational Enterprise*. London: Holmes and Meier.

Davidson, W. (1980). 'The Location of Foreign Direct Investment Activity: Country Characteristics and Experience Effects.' *Journal of International Business Studies*, pp. 9–22.

Dunning, J. H., (1977). 'Trade, Location of Economic Activity and the MNE: A Search for an Eclectic Approach,' in Bertil Ohlin et al, (eds.) *The International Allocation of Economic Activity*. London: Holmes and Meier.

——, (1979). 'Explaining Changing Patterns of International Production: In Defense of the Eclectic Theory,' *Oxford Bulletin of Economics and Statistics* 41, pp. 269–96.

——, (1981). 'Explaining Outward Direct Investments of Developing Countries: In support of the Eclectic Theory of International Production,' in *Multinationals from Developing Countries*. Lexington, Mass.: Maxwell G. McLeod.

Helleiner, G. K. (1979). 'Transnational Corporations and Trade Structure: The Role of Intra-firm Trade,' in H. Giersch (ed.), *On the Economics of Intra-Industry Trade*. Tübingen: J. C. B. Mohr.

Hirsch, S., (1976). 'An International Trade and Investment Theory of the Firm,' *Oxford Economic Papers* 28, pp. 258–270.

Hirschman, A. O. (1970). *Exit, Voice, and Loyalty, Responses to Decline in Firms, Organizations, and States*. Cambridge, Mass.: Harvard University Press.

Katz, J. H. (1981). 'Does Foreign Direct Investment Theory Reflect Reality: The Case of the American Food Processors.' Unpublished paper, October: to be published as a Sloan School of Management Working Paper. Massachusetts Institute of Technology.

Kindleberger, C. P. (1969). *American Business Abroad: Six Lectures on Direct Investment*. New Haven: Yale University Press.

Lessard, D. (1976). 'World, Country, and Industry Relations in Equity Returns: Implications for Risk Reduction through International Diversification,' *Financial Analysts' Journal*. January, February, pp. 2–8.

—— (1979). 'Transfer Prices, Taxes and Financial Markets: Implications of Internal Financial Transfers Within the Multinational Firm,' in R. G. Hawkins (ed.), *Economic Issues of Multinational Firms*. New York: JAI Press.

—— (1980). 'Evaluating International Projects: An Adjusted Present Value Approach.' in Crum, R. and Derkinderen, F. (eds.), *Capital Budgeting Under Conditions of Uncertainty*. The Hague: Nijhoff.

McDonald, R. and Segal, D. (1981). 'Options and the Valuation of Risky Projects' (unpublished paper), August, presented at the Finance Research Seminar of Sloan School of Management, Massachusetts Institute of Technology.

Magee, S. P. (1977). 'Information and the Multinational Corporation: An Appropriability Theory of Direct Foreign Investment.' in J. Bhagwati (ed.) *The New Economic Order: The North–South Debate*. Cambridge, Mass.: MIT Press.

Niehans, J. (1977). 'Benefits of Multinational Firms for a Small Parent Economy: The Case of Switzerland,' in Agmon, T. and Kindleberger, C. P. (eds.) *Multinationals from Small Countries*. Cambridge, Mass.: MIT Press.

Robinson, R. D. (1976). *Natural Control of Foreign Business Entry*. New York: Praeger.

Rugman, A. M. (1980). 'Internalization as a General Theory of Foreign Direct Investment: A Re-Appraisal of the Literature.' *Weltwirtschaftliches Archiv* 116, pp. 365–79.

Solnik, B. H. (1974). 'Why Not Diversify Internationally? *Financial Analysts' Journal*. July–August, pp. 48–54.

Stopford, J. and Wells, L. (1972). *Managing the Multinational Enterprise Organization of the Firm and Ownership of the Subsidiaries*. New York: Basic Books.

Vernon, R. (1971). *Sovereignty at Bay: The Multinational Spread of US Enterprises*. New York: Basic Books.

——, (1977). *Storm over the Multinationals: The Real Issues*. Cambridge, Mass.: Harvard University Press.

—— (1979). 'The Product Cycle Hypothesis in a New International Environment,' *Oxford Bulletin of Economics and Statistics*, 41, pp. 255–267.

Wells, L. (1977). 'Firms from Developing Countries,' in Agmon, T. and Kindleberger, C. P. (eds.), *Multinationals from Small Countries*. Cambridge, Mass.: MIT Press.

Part IV

Organizing the Multinational Firm

CONTENTS

16

An Approach to Strategic Control in MNCs

C. K. Prahalad and Yves L. Doz

The extent to which the head office (HO) of a multibusiness multinational corporation (MNC) can control the strategies of its overseas subsidiaries is emerging as an issue of considerable interest to a variety of publics.[1] Top managers in MNCs, which have a significant part of their assets, sales, and profits (often more than 50%) attributable to overseas operations, would like to be assured that the strategic direction of subsidiaries is controlled from the HO. However, given that subsidiary operations are increasing in size and scope, how can the HO control effectively? Politicians—especially those from developing countries—are worried about the degree to which decisions of the subsidiaries operating on their soil are controlled by the HO of the multinational corporation. Their overriding concern is the extent to which subsidiaries can be responsive to the developmental goals of host governments.

For the researcher, this situation raises the age-old issue of centralization versus decentralization in an extremely complex setting—complexities brought about by multiple cultural environments, differences in competitive structures, pressures of host government, and the presence of joint venture partners. The key research question is: what are the dynamics of strategic control of subsidiaries by the HO in MNCs?

This article considers the problems of maintaining strategic control over subsidiaries in a multinational firm. The authors argue that the nature of strategic control by the head office over its subsidiaries shifts with time. As resources such as capital, technology, and management become vested in the subsidiaries, head offices cannot continue to rely on control over these resources as a means of influencing subsidiary strategy. The authors outline a conceptual framework that defines *organizational context*, and they argue that it can be used as an alternate means of exerting influence.

C. K. Prahalad is Associate Professor of Policy and Control at The University of Michigan, Graduate School of Business Administration. Dr Prahalad holds the B.Sc. degree from the University of Madras, the postgraduate degree from the Indian Institute of Management, Ahmedabad, and the D.B.A. degree from the Harvard Business School. His teaching, research, and consulting interests lie in the area of strategic management and control in large, complex organizations. Dr Prahalad has written articles for such publications as the *Sloan Management Review*, *Harvard Business Review*, and the *Economic and Political Weekly*. He is the coauthor of *Financial Management of Health Institutions* and *The Management of Health Care*.

Yves L. Doz is Associate Professor of Business Policy at INSEAD. Dr Doz did graduate work at the Ecole des Hautes Etudes Commerciales, and he received the Ph.D. degree from the Harvard Graduate School of Business Administration. He is the author of *Government Control and Multinational Strategic Management* and *Multinational Strategic Management: Economic and Political Imperatives*, forthcoming.

Reprinted from 'An approach to strategic control in MNCs' by C. K. Prahalad and Y. L. Doz, *Sloan Management Review*, Vol 22, No 4, 1981, pp 5–13 by permission of publisher

THE CHANGING NATURE OF STRATEGIC CONTROL EXAMINED

In this article we will present the results of our research over the last five years on the changing nature of the strategic control process between the HO and subsidiaries. (See the Appendix for a description of the research design.) Our thesis is that as subsidiaries mature and become autonomous with respect to strategic resources, such as technology, capital, management, and access to markets, the HO's ability to control the strategies of subsidiaries is significantly reduced.

The HO, faced with an inability to exert control over the subsidiaries on the basis of the subsidiaries' dependence on strategic resources, must find substitute mechanisms. Creating a sophisticated *organizational context*—a blending of organizational structure, information systems, measuremant and reward systems, and career planning and a fostering of common organizational culture—can compensate for the erosion of HO's capacity to control subsidiaries. We will illustrate why the HOs of multinational corporations must constantly be aware of the shifting importance of resource dependency and organizational context in providing a total control capability.

THE CONCEPT OF STRATEGIC CONTROL

We define strategic control as the extent of influence that a head office has over a subsidiary concerning decisions that affect subsidiary strategy. Some typical decisions that reflect the strategy of a subsidiary are: choice of technology, definition of product market, emphasis on different product lines, allocation of resources, expansion and diversification of subsidiary operations, and a willingness to participate in a global network of product flows among subsidiaries. These were the decisions we considered in the study. Further, the HO is not only interested in influencing the strategic decisions of subsidiaries but also in monitoring their progress toward fulfilling the strategic expectations.

THE HO-SUBSIDIARY MILIEU

The HO's desire to exercise strategic control over subsidiaries has been supported by two developments over the last several decades. Major companies increasingly have derived a larger share of their sales and profits from overseas subsidiaries and have sent abroad a growing share of their assets. In addition to this surge in the importance of overseas activities, several MNCs also have found that in many of their businesses, subsidiaries' markets enjoy a higher growth potential than the US market.

Impact of global competition

The changing pattern of competition during the last decade has had another critical influence on the desire of HO groups to control subsidiary strategies. Several industries—

autos, ball bearings, motorcycles, consumer electronics, chemicals, steel, tyres, heavy electrical systems, earth-moving equipment, to name a few—are increasingly dominated by a small number of worldwide competitors.[2] This implies that an MNC must develop a global strategy in addition to several national strategies to be successful. It must transcend the boundaries of national markets in determining sourcing patterns, pricing strategies, product designs, technology level, and financing. HOs are, therefore, increasingly drawn into the activities of subsidiaries by the shifting nature of competition. The HO must not only *co-ordinate* the operations of subsidiaries but also must increasingly *influence* the direction of subsidiary strategies to conform to the needs of a global strategy. The pressures resulting from the increasing importance of overseas activities and the changing character of global competition—i.e., the *economic imperatives* that pressure the MNC to rationalize global operations—tend to trigger all desires on the part of HO managers to centralize control.

Impact of host government demands

While the economic imperatives increase the tendency to centralize, host government demands (in both developing and developed countries) penalize centralization. Businesses in which an MNC is involved attract government attention and intervention for several reasons:

— They are important for national defence (e.g., jet engines);
— They represent an important infrastructure (e.g., railroads, telecommunications);
— They are key national industries that are threatened (e.g., the watch industry in Switzerland and the automobile industry in the United States);
— They are in industries in which it is difficult to gain access to key technologies (e.g., semiconductors, computers).

In some cases, effects on balance of payment and employment are key concerns of host governments. In some developing countries, all MNCs, irrespective of the nature of the business in which they are involved, attract attention (e.g., India, Mexico, Brazil). Whatever the motivations are for government intervention in subsidiary strategy, the impact of this *political imperative* encourages the subsidiary to seek greater autonomy.[3]

Joint ventures: added complexity

In addition to the political imperative, many MNCs have had to contend with joint venture partners. During the late 1960s and early 1970s, MNCs desiring greater co-ordination have found it difficult to continue to tolerate joint ventures.[4] However, joint ventures may become the only way to compete globally in several industries, such as telecommunication equipment, consumer electronics, and data processing equipment. Joint venture partners complicate the task of HO-subsidiary co-ordination.

The dynamics of HO control over subsidiary strategy are not only influenced by the conflicting demands of the economic and political imperatives of an MNC's operation but also by the changing nature of the HO-subsidiary relationship. For example:

1. As subsidiaries mature and grow in size, they can afford an adequate level of internal management talent and R&D investment.

2. As the industry matures, the technological advantage that the HO had over the subsidiary disappears.

3. Management know-how, as a distinct resource, is becoming widespread. Moreover, the management skills needed by subsidiaries operating in environments dissimilar to that of the parent—like a highly regulated environment (e.g., India, Nigeria), or a highly inflationary environment (e.g., Brazil), or a relatively low technology environment (e.g., Indonesia)—may be unavailable at the HO.

4. Subsidiaries with large volume, adequate technology, and management capability may develop their own overseas activities. Typically, this involves marketing products outside the national boundaries of the subsidiary. Staff groups in the MNC's HO may attempt to co-ordinate exports from subsidiaries to third countries, but cases where subsidiaries either ignore or contest these attempts at co-ordination are common. In some cases, subsidiaries even invest in manufacturing facilities in third countries without subjecting themselves to the co-ordination of the HO groups.[5]

5. Under pressure from host governments, who may want to use MNC subsidiaries to further national development goals, subsidiaries may diversify into businesses unfamiliar to the HO (e.g., Union Carbide's move into shrimp fishing in India).

As a result of these trends, the HO must depend on mechanisms other than control over strategic resources—capital, technology, management, or access to markets—as a basis for strategic control. The essential strategic control dilemma in an MNC can be summarized as follows:

1. The HO cannot rely exclusively on the use of strategic resources as a basis of control, especially in situations where the subsidiaries are more or less self-sufficient in such resources. This forces MNCs to re-examine the process of control where the relationship between the HO and subsidiaries is not based on a one-way dependence. Yet, in order for the HO to develop a global strategy, it has to gain the co-operation of subsidiaries who may be autonomous in their strategic resource requirements. This creates the need to formulate the strategic control process in the context of reciprocal dependence between the HO and subsidiaries.

2. The strategic control process has inherent tensions imposed on it by the economic and political imperatives of a global business. This means that responsiveness and flexibility in strategy must coexist with desires for global rationalization.

3. Since the strategy must be responsive to environmental demands, it can lead to unco-ordinated and fragmented resource commitments. However, in order to gain global competitive advantage, the MNC must be able to focus its resource commitments.

4. The strategic process must be more than just responsive to competitive pressures or host government demands in a reactive mode. It must support purposive, proactive changes in strategy.

5. Under competitive pressure or a profit crisis (a reactive situation), changes in strategy can be imposed. However, to implement proactive strategic changes, the HO and subsidiaries must perceive the legitimacy of these changes.

These five conditions, in our view, represent the key issues in the strategic control process for MNCs.

AN APPROACH TO STRATEGIC CONTROL

Dependence of a subsidiary on the HO for strategic resources allows the HO to control subsidiary strategy by controlling the flow of resources. However, the five dilemmas outlined above indicate that MNC managers should identify approaches other than the use of subsidiary 'dependence' as the basis for strategic control.

In our research, we find that MNCs in mature businesses increasingly have to depend on 'subtle mechanisms' for influencing the strategic direction of their subsidiaries. We suggest that the alternative to *substantive control*, i.e., restricting the flow of strategic resources, is the creation of an organizational context. This would facilitate the relationship between the HO and subsidiaries such that the HO can continue to influence and monitor subsidiary strategy.

The dynamics of the strategic control process as businesses mature may be illustrated schematically, as shown in Figure 1. In addition to the maturity of business, we ought to consider the size, the maturity, and the quality of subsidiary management. We should also consider the motivation of subsidiary managers to become independent of the HO with regard to strategic resources.

As illustrated in Figure 1, the ability of HO managers to use allocation of strategic resources as levers for control diminishes as the business and/or subsidiary matures. This declining role of substantive control is illustrated by the line SS1. On the other hand, for the HO to influence subsidiary strategy, a certain minimum level of control may be

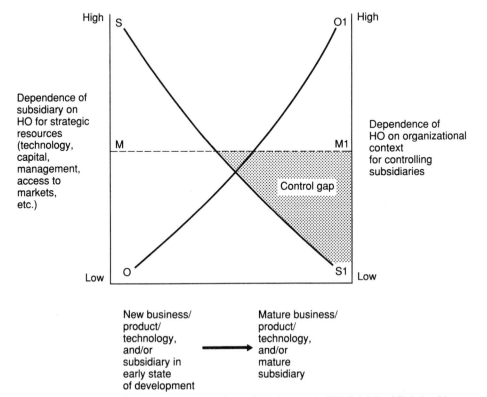

Figure 1. Schematic Representation of Shifts in Control Mechanisms in HO-Subsidiary Relationship.

needed. This is represented by the line MM1. If the MNC depends only on substantive control mechanisms to influence subsidiary strategy, then, as businesses and/or subsidiaries mature, a *control gap* will develop. The HO will not be able to influence subsidiary strategy.

Recognizing loss of control

Most often, HO managers who depend solely on substantive control mechanisms do not recognize the erosion of their ability to control subsidiaries. Typically, they recognize their inability to control subsidiary strategies only when competitive pressures call for a co-ordinated action and HO managers find that they cannot orchestrate such action.

Organizational context can be used as an effective substitute for substantive control. While the need for (and desire to create) a substitute for substantive control is highest when the control capability is at S1, there is no justification in waiting for a crisis. Furthermore, as the ability to use substantive control diminishes, the dependence of HO managers on the alternative—organizational context—to influence strategy of subsidiaries increases as shown by line OO1. Ideally, a *combination* of substantive control mechanisms and organizational context should provide an adequate basis for HO managers to stay above line MM1—and to avoid the problems caused by control gap.

CREATING AN APPROPRIATE ORGANIZATIONAL CONTEXT

The task of creating an appropriate organizational context for strategic control is built on two sets of concepts. First, we develop the notion that an organization is an aggregation of four orientations—cognitive, strategic, power, and administrative. Second, we identify the type of organizational mechanisms that managers can use to manipulate these four orientations. We will demonstrate that an ability to manipulate the four orientations provides managers with the alternative to substantive control.

The four orientations

Hierarchical notions have dominated our thinking about organizations. As a firm's overseas activities evolve, the organizational form also evolves.[6] Typically, the firm begins with an autonomous subsidiary system that is followed by an international division structure. As the scope of its overseas activities increases, the firm adopts a global structure integrated by area, product, or matrix.

These are three ideal modes of categorizing organizational structures used by MNCs. In most businesses, the strategic tensions created by balancing the economic and political imperatives force the MNC managers to work with a variety of hybrid structures.[7] Some businesses are organized by product, others by area, yet others by matrix structures. In a 'pure organizational form'—whether organized by area or product—the hierarchy dominates. The hierarchy determines:

1. The nature of information that managers collect and use, or their 'world view' (in an area of structure, information that is relevant to national portfolios of diverse businesses;

while in a product structure, information that is relevant to business portfolios consisting of diverse countries);

2. The way managers decide to compete—on a local for local basis (area organization) or by global rationalization (product organization);

3. The people who have the power to commit strategic resources (area managers or product managers); and

4. The basis for administrative procedures, such as career progression (across businesses in an area organization or within a business across area organizations).

In other words, in these pure organizational forms, if one knew 'who the boss was', or if one understood the hierarchy, one could understand the organization—its capabilities and limitations.

Complex strategies, complex structures

For a product organization to become sensitive to area needs (or vice versa), structural changes would be needed.[8] However, few MNCs have the privilege of adopting the simple strategic postures that a pure 'area' or 'product' mode indicates. Complex strategic postures that balance multiple and often conflicting goals (economic versus political imperatives) require complex structures. Hierarchical concepts applied to such an organization are of little use in helping managers to understand or manipulate the organization.

In a complex organizational form that seeks to balance national and global priorities flexibly from decision to decision, several orientations need to be managed explicitly. We consider a complex organizational form as the means to manage the four orientations:

1. *Cognitive orientation*, or the perception of the 'relevant environment' by individual managers within the organization. The relevant environment of a business is constructed of an understanding of the key competitors, the competitive structure, and the forces that are likely to mold the pattern of evolution of that business. We have to recognize that in a complex organization, different types of managers (area, product, and functional) and managers at different levels can have very different perceptions of the relevant environment. In other words, their cognitive orientations can be very different.

2. *Strategic orientation*, or the competitive posture and methods of competition that the various groups of managers are willing to adopt. If the various managers have different cognitive orientations, then they will have different perceptions of an appropriate strategic orientation to cope with the threats or to exploit the opportunities inherent in their different world views.

3. *Power orientation*, or the locus of power among managers in the organization to commit resources—financial, technological, and managerial—to pursue a strategy.

4. *Administrative orientation*, or the orientation of support systems such as the accounting system and the personnel system. Accounting data, for example, may be consolidated along product lines or along national subsidiary lines.

In a pure hierarchical organization, the four orientations tend to be aligned with the hierarchy. For example, in a pure product organization, the cognitive orientation of managers (the perception of competitive threats and opportunities) tends to be global; the strategic orientation tends to favour a rationalized global strategy; the power to commit resources is vested with product managers; and the support systems, such as accounting and personnel (the administrative orientation), we built to support it. However, in a complex organization that may have a hybrid or matrix structure, all four orientations need not be aligned.

HO managers who operate in hybrid or matrix structures should recognize that to gain and retain strategic control, they should influence the four orientations. By suitably modifying the four orientations, the strategic direction can be altered. In our research, we find that strategic change can be initiated by altering any one of the four orientations.

However, in order for the change process to be completed, the power orientation must be changed. What emerge as key findings are that HO managers must be sensitive to the distribution of power, and that they must manage the loci of power.

HO managers in the hybrid or matrix structures can use a variety of administrative mechanisms to influence the four orientations. These mechanisms can be classified as:

1. *Data Management Mechanisms.* Included in this category are mechanisms that generate and regulate the flow of information within the organization. Accounting systems, planning and budgeting systems, and management information systems belong in this category.

2. *Manager Management Mechanisms.* Included under this important category are power to assign managers to key positions, executive compensation plans, management development programmes, career progression, performance evaluation, and socialization patterns.

3. *Conflict Resolution Mechanisms.* Since conflict and tension are inherent in hybrid or matrix structures, mechanisms to resolve conflicts (such as task forces, planning committees, integrators, co-ordinating groups, and decision responsibility assignments) are some of the important elements of a manager's tool kit.

Managers can use a variety of these mechanisms to exercise influence selectively and to change the four orientations in an organization.

SUBSTANTIVE VERSUS ORGANIZATIONAL CONTEXT IN CONTROL

HO managers, in order to influence subsidiary strategy, should be sensitive to the use of both substantive controls, as well as to the use of organizational context as an approach to control. To retain substantive control, the HO managers must ensure that they continue to have strategic resource superiority over the subsidiaries—whether by technology, product design, marketing know-how or capital. This does not mean that the subsidiaries should be kept weak. (Very strong subsidiaries can be very dependent.)

For example, IBM's major subsidiaries in the UK, Germany, France, and Japan are large and technologically capable. While they operate significant manufacturing and R&D facilities, IBM ensures that no non-US subsidiary is self-sufficient in all key systems. Each subsidiary markets a total line of systems but can manufacture only some. As a result, all the subsidiaries are woven into a corporate network of product, resource, and competency flows that can be orchestrated by HO managers.[9]

On the other hand, the sophistication of managers in using the administrative tools to alter the four orientations can serve a similar end.

THE STRATEGIC CONTROL DILEMMA

The strategic control dilemma can now be redefined. We can classify MNCs and their various businesses. This is shown in Figure 2. The four categories of MNCs that result are:

1. *Fragmented*—where the possibilities of substantive control are low and the sophistication of HO managers in using organizational context is also low. In such a case, co-ordinating the strategies of subsidiaries or influencing subsidiary strategies are extremely difficult. In such situations, MNCs tend to move the subsidiary up to the status indicated in quadrants (B) or (D), or give up attempts at co-ordination, or divest the subsidiary altogether.[10]

2. *Dependent*—where the sophistication of the organizational context is low, but the subsidiaries continue to be dependent on the HO for strategic resources. Typically, this situation exists in technology intensive businesses (e.g. Westinghouse's nuclear power business in Europe during the early 1970s) or where the subsidiaries are small. As the technology matures and as subsidiaries grow, the tendency for the control capability to drift toward quadrant (C), a fragmented state, cannot be ruled out.

3. *Autonomous*—where the subsidiaries are self-sufficient in strategic resources and their dependence on HO is low. However, the sophistication of managers in using organizational context is high. While the subsidiaries are autonomous, HO managers can still exercise significant influence over subsidiary strategy.

For example, L. M. Ericsson, the Swedish telecommunications firm, has traditionally relied on a common corporate value system and patterns of socialization to influence subsidiary strategy.[11] MNCs in this category often attempt to move toward quadrant (A), the integrated state.

4. *Integrated*—where the MNC has built a high degree of substantive and organizational context control capability. IBM is an example.[12]

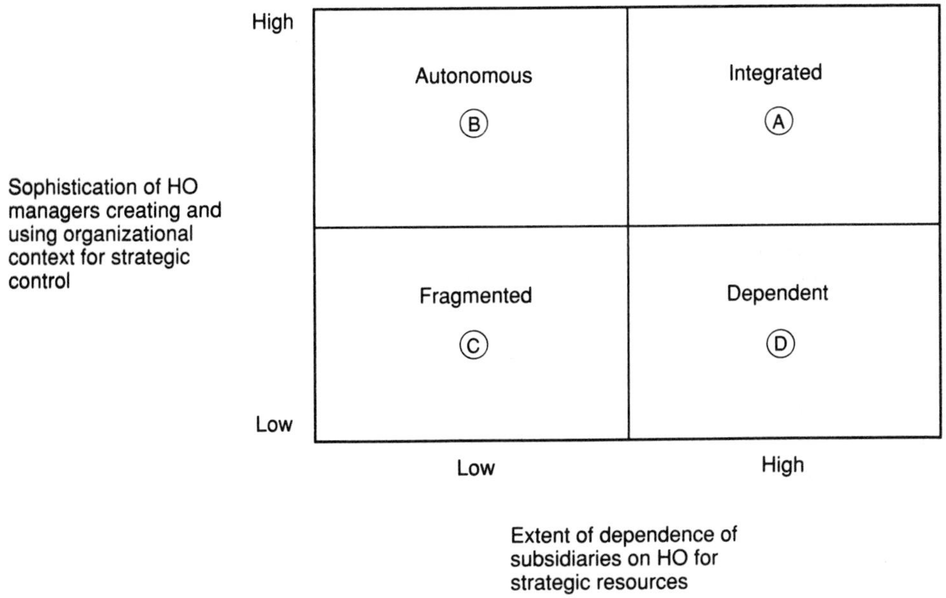

Figure 2. The Strategic Control Dilemma in MNCs.

We have found, in our research, firms who were attempting to move from (C) to (D), (C) to (B), and (B) to (A), as well as those who were unfortunate enough to move from (D) to (C) and (B) to (C). The most interesting challenge to top management is the move from (C) to (B) or (D) and then to (A).

A crisis may provide opportunities for top managers to intervene and introduce systems that can help the transition process. However, when there is no apparent profit crisis, the task is considerably more difficult.

CONCLUSION

We have argued in this article that the ability of HOs to influence subsidiary strategy cannot be taken for granted. With the maturing of subsidiaries and with the eroding of HO control over strategic resources, alternative approaches to strategic control become necessary. We have suggested that sophistication in using organizational context can offset the erosion of strategic control capability at the HO.

We have classified MNCs and the nature of their strategic control capabilities (using substantive control and organizational context control as the two basic approaches) into the four categories—fragmented, autonomous, dependent, and integrated. This scheme provides us with a basis for diagnosing the state of the HO control over subsidiary strategy in a multinational corporation. It is also useful in deciding a desirable future state and a basic approach—be it substantive control or organizational context—to develop control. The companion article will examine in-depth the process of moving from one quadrant to the other; that is, the process of increasing the sophistication of strategic control capability in a complex MNC.

APPENDIX

Research methodology

The research project on which this article was based lasted a total of six years. In 1974, following the pilot study of a diversified materials and chemicals company, a small sample of companies that were in the process of shifting from subsidiary autonomy to headquarters control and centralized strategy making was studied in detail. These companies were: L. M. Ericsson, Brown Boveri & Cie., General Telephone and Electronics, General Motors, Gamma (disguised European diversified MNC), Nippon (disguised Japanese multinational), Ford Motor Co., Corning Glass Works, IVECO, Alcan, and Massey Ferguson. Some of these companies were studied by doctoral students. The evolution of each company was documented through internal company documents and interviews with involved executives at headquarters and at subsidiaries. Interviews numbered between twenty and sixty per company. In some cases, such as GM, IVECO, or Corning, events were followed as they unfolded, since the researchers got involved before the shift was completed.

Detailed descriptions of the various evolutions were then written and checked with managers in the particular company for accuracy and completeness. Some of these descriptions have been published as cases; others will be as they are released by the companies.

From these descriptions were developed chronological protocols identifying the sequence and timing in the use of managerial mechanisms, their intent, and their results. In turn, the general propositions presented in these articles are the researchers' conceptualization of the data offered by the protocols and the company descriptions.

NOTES

1. See P. Abell, 'Parent Companies' Control of Subsidiaries: Evidence from the U.K.,' *Multinational Business*, 1974.

2. Several studies have demonstrated the extent of globalization of the competitive structure of industries. For example, see: (a) The Boston Consulting Group's study of *Strategy Alternatives for the British Motorcycle Industry*, HMSO, 1975;

(b) American Iron & Steel Institute, *Steel at the Crossroads: The American Steel Industry in the 1980s.* January 1980; American Iron & Steel Institute, *The Economic Implications of Foreign Steel Pricing Practices in the U.S. Market*, August 1978; American Iron & Steel Institute, *Economics of International Steel Trade: Policy Implications for the U.S.*, May 1977;

(c) Note on the watch industries in Switzerland, Japan, and the U.S., ICCH No. 9-373-090, Rev. 9/76; 'Japanese Heat on the Watch Industry,' *Business Week*, 5 May 1980; 'Digital Watches: Bringing Watchmaking Back to the U.S.,' *Business Week*, 27 October 1975.

(d) Volkswagen A.G., ICCH No. 9-376-108; Ford in Spain (A), No. 4-380-091; Ford in Spain (B), No. 380-092; Ford Bobcat (A), No. 4-380-093; Ford Bobcat (B), No. 9-380-100; Ford Bobcat (C), No. 4-380-101; Ford Bobcat (D), No. 4-380-102.

(e) The U.S. TV Set Market, Prewar to 1970, No. 1-380-180; The U.S. TV Set Market, 1970–1979, No. 1-380-181; The Television Set Industry in 1979: Japan and Europe, No. 1-380-191.

3. See Y. L. Doz and C. K. Prahalad, 'How MNCs Cope with Host Government Intervention,' *Harvard Business Review*, March–April 1980.

4. See L. G. Franko, *Joint Venture Survival in International Business* (New York: Praeger Publishers, 1971); Also see, 'Disinvestment-Corporate Strategy or Admission of Failure,' *Multinational Business*, 1975.

5. See the following case studies: Brown Boveri & Cie, ICCH No. 9-378-115; Corning Glass Works International (A), ICCH No. 9-379-051.

6. See J. Stopford and L. T. Wells, Jr., *Managing the Multinational Enterprise* (New York: Basic Books, 1972); L. G. Franko, *The European Multinationals* (Stamford, CT: Greylock, 1977).

7. See Y. L. Doz, C. A. Bartlett, and C. K. Prahalad, 'Global Competitive Pressure vs. Host Country Demands: Managing Tensions in MNCs,' *California Management Review*, Winter 1981.

8. For example, see E. P. Neufeld. *A Global Corporation: A History of the International Development of Massey Ferguson Ltd.* (Toronto, Canada: University of Toronto Press, 1969).

9. See R. Ronstadt, 'R and D Abroad: The Creation and Evolution of Foreign Research and Development Activities of U.S. Based Multinational Enterprise' (Boston, MA: D.B.A. dissertation, Harvard Business School, 1975).

10. Some tentative evidence on divestment patterns suggests that on a sample of MNCs operations in Europe, divestments occur more often in these situations. See N. Hood and S. Young, *European Development Strategies of U.S. Owned Manufacturing Companies* (Edinburgh: HMSO, 1980).

11. A description of L. M. Ericsson's approach is given in Y. L. Doz, *Government Control and Multinational Strategic Management* (New York: Praeger Publishers, 1979).

12. See A. Katz, 'Planning in the IBM Corporation' (paper submitted to the TIMS-ORSA Strategic Planning Conference, New Orleans, February 1977).

17

Multinational Structural Change: Evolution Versus Reorganization

Christopher A. Bartlett

For most of this century Westinghouse's international activities were managed through Westinghouse Electric International, a separate organization based in New York and maintaining only limited contact and interaction with the rest of the company.[1] In the 1960s, Westinghouse tried to build its overseas strength by acquiring strong national firms and linking them to the US parent through its international division. Difficulties arose not only in obtaining companies (de Gaulle personally vetoed one key acquisition) but also in integrating them into Westinghouse. Thus, in 1971 the separate international organization was disbanded and the company's 125 division managers were given worldwide responsibility for the businesses they had been managing in the domestic US market.

By 1978, however, top management was concerned that the company was gaining a reputation abroad for being internally disorganized with a total lack of co-ordination between divisions. Several of its overseas companies were in difficulty and had to be sold off. Furthermore, foreign customers and governments were complaining that the company was difficult to do business with because of its insensitivity to local situations and its inability to co-ordinate various businesses in a given country.

In early 1979 the vice-chairman's response was to reorganize once again. He gave one of his key executives 90 days to analyse Westinghouse's international operations and make recommendations for the organizational change required. The report recommended that the company supplement its worldwide product organization with a network of geographic managers reporting to a strong international chief. By July 1979 Westinghouse had begun installing a formal global matrix organization structure by overlaying the existing product organization with the new geographic organization. Newly appointed country managers reported to four regional presidents who, in turn, reported to an international president with a seat on the powerful corporate management committee. This reorganization, the company believed, would help it achieve the global integration it needed to remain efficient and competitive and the sensitivity to national environments it required to be effective locally.

The situation of Westinghouse provides a good illustration not only of the multiple

Harvard University Graduate School of Business Administration.

Reprinted with permission from *The Management of Headquarters Subsidiary Relationships in Multinational Corporations* by L. Otterbeck (ed)

strategic pressures that have confronted most companies as they have expanded abroad, but also of the typical structural responses in US based multinational corporations (MNCs).

Like Westinghouse, many MNCs found themselves confronted by multiple, and often conflicting strategic demands as they grew internationally. Most became aware quite early of the need to develop an understanding of the diverse characteristics of the various national environments in which they operated. However, as foreign operations grew they began to recognize the opportunity and the need to rationalize these diverse worldwide operations to capitalize on their potential global efficiencies. As global competition intensified and, at the same time, pressures from host countries grew, managers of MNCs were confronted with the simultaneous need to be globally competitive and nationally responsive.[2] Responding consistently and appropriately to the variety of diverse, changing, and often conflicting demands has provided, for many companies, the major administrative challenge of the past decade. Their decision processes had to adapt to the challenge of becoming multidimensional—able to respond simultaneously to the global and the national strategic imperatives.

For many companies, the need for the decision making process to respond to these diverse and growing pressures led to a series of reorganizations similar to those undertaken by Westinghouse. So familiar did the pattern become that various 'stages theories' of organizational development became widely recognized.[3] Some academics, consultants and managers began to think of this series of reorganizations in normative rather than descriptive terms, and for some MNCs it seemed that organization structure followed fashion as much as it related to strategy.[4] Reorganizations from international divisions to global product or area organizations, or from global structures to matrix forms, became widespread. This, after all, was the classic organizational sequence described in the 'stages theories'.

Yet many companies that had expected such changes to provide them with the strategy-structure fit to meet the new pressures were disappointed. Developing a multidimensional decision making process that was able to balance the conflicting global and national needs was a subtle and time consuming process not necessarily achieved by redrawing the lines on a chart. Examples of failed or abandoned multinational organizations abound.[5]

While there were many companies, like Westinghouse, that appeared to concentrate largely on changes in the formal organization structure as a means to achieve the desired changes in their administrative processes, there were others that appeared to have developed successful multidimensional decision making processes without resorting to major changes in their formal organizations. Most notable was the substantial number of companies that had built large, complex and successful foreign operations while retaining their supposedly embryonic international division structures.[6] If these companies had been successful in achieving a strategy-structure 'fit', they had done so without resorting to the sequence of traumatic reorganizations as described in the stages theories and as experienced by Westinghouse.

To understand why this substantial group of MNCs had not followed the stages model of organizational change, a detailed clinical study of nine of these companies was undertaken.[7] It was hypothesized that either the parameters of the generally accepted stages models were inappropriate, or there were alternative means of structural response that were not revealed in a simple classification of formal organization.

The companies studied were selected from two industries with diverse strategic characteristics: four from the food processing industry, and five from the health care industry (ethical and proprietary drugs, hospital supplies). In trying to understand why these companies had not evolved through the series of reorganizations described in the stages models, two quite different explanations emerged.

The companies in the food processing industry had retained their international division structure for a very simple reason: the key strategic demands of their operations were perceived as being unidimensional. The nature of the business resulted in the key tasks being focused at the national level, with little long-term advantage to be gained by global operations. Product development, manufacturing, and marketing were all national rather than global tasks for a variety of cultural as well as economic reasons.[8] The conclusion reached was that increasing size and complexity did not cause these companies to abandon the 'federal' organization structure needed to manage this business.

This paper concentrates on the findings relating to the five companies in the health care industry (ethical and proprietary drugs, hospital supplies). The administrative challenges confronting managers in these companies were more interesting, since they clearly did face the diversity of global and national demands and environmental conditions that had forced many other companies to follow the traditional stages of reorganization into global then matrix forms of organization. The companies studied, however, seemed to achieve their state of strategy-structure fit by a different process. Rather than focusing on 'anatomical' changes, these companies seemed to spend more time modifying the 'physiological' characteristics of their organizations. They appeared to view the required change from unidimensional to multidimensional organization as an adaptive, evolutionary process rather than as a series of powerful, yet perhaps traumatic, reorganizations. In contrast to companies such as Westinghouse and others which followed the 'strategic crisis–structural reorganization' route, these companies developed, adjusted and integrated the required new skills, structures and processes gradually but continuously. It is this alternative process of adaptation from unidimensional to multidimensional organization that will be described in the remainder of this paper.

THE STRATEGIC DEMAND: MULTIDIMENSIONAL TASKS

Before describing the structural and administrative changes made by the various companies, it may be helpful to have an understanding of the overall task demands that provoked the changes. What were the strategic issues facing companies in the health care industry that prevented them from retaining the simple unidimensional 'federal' organization structure that proved adequate for the food processing companies?

The task complexity facing the health care companies could be described briefly along three dimensions: The need to be simultaneously responsive at the national level yet efficient globally; the need to develop multiple functional expertise at multiple organization levels; and the need to be flexible in the way all of these demands were managed. Each will be described briefly.

— As they expanded abroad, these companies needed to understand and respond to the variety of local national demands that affected their success in each national market. They had to understand the structure and operation of national health delivery systems, the nature of government product registration processes, the formal and informal demands for local sourcing of critical products, and a variety of other such national pressures. However, they also had to recognize that if they were to be effective global competitors, their research efforts, manufacturing capacity, product policy and a variety of other tasks had to be co-ordinated and perhaps integrated on a worldwide basis. In short, they were faced with the challenge of being simultaneously responsive and flexible at the national level while maintaining the competitive efficiency that comes from global co-ordination.

— Unlike the food processing industry where the marketing function was the dominant success factor, in the health care industry the marketing, research, and manufacturing functions were all regarded as key success factors. Furthermore, in the food industry all the key tasks were concentrated at the national level (e.g., products developed to meet national tastes, local manufacturing due to freshness and transportation limitations, etc.). Key tasks in the drug industry, however, needed to be managed at multiple organizational levels (e.g., for economic and quality control reasons active ingredients for most drugs were prepared centrally, while tablet and capsule plants could be operated efficiently on a regional or national basis; basic research obviously needed global co-ordination, yet product development was often handled on a regional basis, and local clinical trials were needed for national product registration).

— Unlike the food processing industry where the markets, the technology and the products were typically mature, the health care industry tended to present a much more dynamic operating environment. Particularly in the areas of new product development and government controls and regulations, changes were occurring at a very rapid rate in the 1960s and 1970s. Furthermore the stage of maturity and rate of change varied substantially by market.

THE STRUCTURAL RESPONSE: MULTIDIMENSIONAL ORGANIZATION

Clearly companies could not hope to manage this set of complex, diverse, and changing demands through their simple, unidimensional 'federal' organization structures. They were faced with the major challenge of developing complex, multidimensional 'global' organizations. As stated previously, in the companies studied, such organization structures were developed not through the series of reorganizations described by the stages theories, but through a more gradual evolutionary process. This process appeared to involve three distinct yet closely interrelated changes, and although there was considerable overlap, these changes tended to occur sequentially. First, new *management skills and perspectives* were gradually developed to reflect and respond to the growing range of task demands facing these companies; next, subtle modifications were made to the *organization structures and systems* to allow better interaction between the newly developed range of management perspectives; and finally, conscious efforts were made to change the *organization 'climate'* in attempt to institutionalize the relationships required in an effective decision making process in a complex and uncertain multidimensional organization environment.

The purpose of these changes in the formal and informal structures and systems was to allow the organization's decision making process to evolve from a unidimensional to a multidimensional focus. Associated with each stage of the structural development was a change in what can be termed the predominant 'management mode'. *Substantive decision management* by senior management in the first phase tended to evolve towards a *temporary coalition management* mode, which in turn gave way to *decision context management* in the final phase. Each will be explained and illustrated in the following sections.

The nature of these structural developments and the changes in the decision making process that accompanied them will provide the focus for the remainder of this paper. Only one additional note needs to be added at this stage. Although each of the companies studied had made adaptions to skills, structure and 'climate', it was also clear that they were not all at the same stage of development in creating their multidimensional organization structures and management processes. One had concentrated mainly on developing the range of management skills and perspectives required to respond to the diversity of task demands it faced and continued to utilize the substantive decision management mode. Others had supplemented such changes with varying degrees of change in their structures, systems, and basic administrative processes, and had broadened their repertoire of 'management modes' in decision making. To illustrate the description of each of these modes however, examples are provided from the companies that most closely correspond to the phase of multidimensional development being described. It should be recognized, however, that none of the companies fitted neatly into such convenient categories: in effect, there were as many structural and administrative solutions as there were companies studied.

DEVELOPING NEW MANAGEMENT PERSPECTIVES

Organizational changes

In their early stages of overseas expansion, all five of the health care companies studied had developed networks of strong independent country subsidiaries. The key strategic tasks were perceived as being first, to develop an understanding of the various national operating environments, and second, to use that knowledge to build strong initial market positions. Thus, country subsidiary managers with local expertise were granted considerable autonomy and independence to perform these tasks.

The organization structure that resulted could best be described as a 'federal' structure in which the country managers' knowledge of their national operating environments gave them a dominant role in key decisions. Their power was formally recognized by the fact that geographic managers were line managers in organizations in which line authority was rarely challenged. Product and functional managers filled staff roles that were primarily defined as support functions for the country managers. Headquarters intervention into subsidiary operations was limited and infrequent, and the country managers' view dominated the strategic decision process.

As a consequence, even decisions with global implications were frequently made on the largely unchallenged recommendation of country subsidiary managers. For example, in each of the companies studied, this early period of development was marked by the proliferation of manufacturing operations worldwide as country managers argued that a local plant was essential for the success of the national subsidiary. There was little resistance to such demands for two reasons. First, nobody in the organization had sufficient knowledge of the various national environments to challenge country managers' claims of customer demands or government pressures, and second, little if any analysis was being done to determine the global costs and efficiency of this multiple plant 'strategy'.

Although this 'federal system' proved adequate for the early stages of establishing foreign subsidiaries, it became clear that a company's global strategy could not be defined by the simple sum of its various national strategies. Geographic-based demands had to be supplemented with product and functional views; national perspectives had to be counterbalanced by regional and global perspectives.

The major impediment to the goal of adding new perspectives to the decision process was that the product and functional managers who should have been able to provide such input were unable to do so. The dominance of the geographic perspective in the past had resulted in the development of product and functional managers whose major task was to service the needs of country subsidiary managers and act as headquarters links and information conduits. They had neither the expertise nor the organizational credibility to counter the country managers' proposals with arguments that took a more integrated global viewpoint. The first challenge in building a more multidimensional organization therefore was to develop managers who could represent these additional perspectives.

In all five health care companies, the process of developing the broader product and functional management skills and viewpoints followed a remarkably similar pattern. It began with the growth of a regional office and culminated with the establishment of management groups at the divisional level that had a substantial input to all major strategic decisions.

Ironically, it was the demands of the geographic line managers for more support at the regional level that gave product and functional managers an opportunity to develop their information access, their control role, and their co-ordination responsibilities. Through these changes their power and influence in the ongoing decision process increased substantially. In response to subsidiary criticism that the staff groups at division headquarters were too distant and often of too little experience to provide the required level of support, regional offices were established in all five companies studied. By working closer to the various markets, product and functional managers made important developmental advances as they gained greater understanding of and credibility in the subsidiary operations.

The next phase that was critical in the development of the product and functional managers occurred during the control period that tended to follow the initial rapid growth abroad. As foreign sales and overseas investment levels grew to a level of corporate importance, senior management began demanding better information about and control over the largely autonomous subsidiaries. The product and functional management groups with their close contact with operations began to be seen as appropriate sources of information and means of control. Increasingly, their visits to subsidiaries were at the instruction of top management to report on a problem rather than at the request of the country manager to provide technical information or support.

With increased market knowledge, access to regular, current, reliable data, and power gained through their new control responsibility, it was inevitable that the product and functional managers eventually would move to the third important phase in their development within the organization. In each of the companies observed, these more sophisticated, more powerful management groups began to recognize opportunities to co-ordinate and integrate activities being managed separately by the various country operations. While initial projects tended to concentrate on the provision of regional services to subsidiaries (e.g., EDP systems and facilities, intercompany payments netting), as soon as their credibility was established, these managers often began to take on major co-ordination and integration responsibilities such as regional manufacturing rationalization or regional product management co-ordination.

The increased credibility that grew out of their greater access to operations, the new influence that derived from their control role, and the upgraded power that flowed from their new co-ordination responsibilities, all provided the regional product and functional managers with considerably greater impact on the decision process. Their increasing importance and power was symbolized by the growth of the regional office that took place during this period in each of the companies observed. Country managers were particularly conscious of this change in influence of product and functional managers, and in numerous instances tensions and even open conflict developed between staff and line.

Nevertheless, senior management found the additional information, services, and advice helpful in counterbalancing the previously unidimensional analyses and recommendations they had been receiving. To better develop global perspectives and to obtain improved access to the newly developed expertise, senior management typically began to build the product and functional management groups at the division headquarters level. Many of the stronger managers developed at the regional level were transferred to the division level as part of this process.

This development resulted in the power and influence of product and functional managers being developed even more. First, their proximity to senior management enhanced their access to and influence in key decision making processes. Equally important, however, was the role these managers began to play in linking the international division to the rest of the corporation. Their product or functional expertise gave them credibility in other parts of the organization, while their greatly improved understanding of country level operations made them knowlegeable spokesmen on international issues. Typically these managers became international representatives to corporate bodies responsible for product policy, research priorities, capacity decisions, and other such global issues.

In all five health care companies studied the development of strong, credible product and functional management groups appeared to be the first major sted in supplementing the country level geographically dominated decision process. The pattern of building a strong regional office then developing strong division level management groups was remarkably consistent, and seemed to provide a means to educate and legitimize the product and functional managers close to country level questions before bringing them to headquarters where they could input more directly into major decisions.

Management process change

Prior to the development of managers who could represent the global product and functional perspectives, country managers' analyses and proposals to senior managers went largely unchallenged. Even if a staff manager did question the country manager's views, his protests often went unheeded due to his low status and credibility in the organization. Clearly in these companies, decision influence was dominated by the geographic line managers.

As the new management skills and perspectives were developed, however, the decision process on key issues became more complex. Arguments for national responsiveness faced strong counter proposals for global integration, and the only means of resolving the inherent conflict was to elevate it to the senior management level. This mode of management can be termed *substantive decision management* because senior management's key role is as arbitrator on the merits of issues in dispute.

This process arose largely due to the lack of any other organizational means to resolve the inevitable differences in opinions and recommendations. However, it was also a process that seemed to suit senior management, at least temporarily. By retaining the integrator and arbitrator role, these managers were able to develop a fuller understanding of the global issues being raised by the newly developed product and functional groups, and to appreciate the nature and extent of the tradeoffs required between national and global perspectives.

All of the sample companies found the substantive decision management mode a convenient and simple way to integrate new perspectives into the management process in their early stages of multidimensional development. Not only did it provide a means for the newly developed global skills and perspectives to be integrated into the decision process, it also represented a process of education for senior management, allowing them to form judgements on the relative importance of the various perspectives on different issues. Eventually, however, most of them found it a cumbersome administrative system to maintain as the prime decision making process.

There were three major classes of problems that these companies seemed to encounter after using this management process over a period of time. The first related to the reliability of the inputs to key decisions. By having advocacy groups take frequently opposing positions on issues, the analysis and recommendations being fed to senior management risked being less than objective. Analyses were often based on incomplete, conflicting or even biased data, and decisions frequently had to be made from the limited and sometimes extreme set of alternatives generated.

The second type of problem encountered in this decision mode related to top management overload. As the only source of integration and resolution, senior management soon became overburdened. The inevitable slowdown in the decision-making process that followed had the effect of dampening the generation of proposals from within the organization, or of leading middle managers to short-circuit the system by making decisions without referral to others.

The third problem area was related to implementation. Disputed issues resolved by senior management often had to be implemented by managers who had fought hard for an opposite outcome. Without the uncompromising support of those responsible, implementation effectiveness often suffered.

While these problems caused most companies eventually to abandon the substantive decision management mode, one of the sample group retained this as a key part of its decision-making process. Having developed extremely strong functional management to counterbalance its geographic line managers, Merck and Company had used a substantive decision management style for many years and continued to use it as its dominant decision process in 1979.

The main reason for the continued use of this management mode appeared to be that such a process was neither unfamiliar nor uncomfortable in a company with a historical origin rooted in the fine chemicals business. Since this industry was characterized by large scale centralized manufacturing and research and a few big customers, centralized decision making was the norm, and Merck followed the pattern.

The acquisition of Sharp and Dohm took Merck into the international pharmaceutical business, and while its traditional management style did not appear to restrict the growth of foreign subsidiaries with substantial autonomy, senior management at Merck recognized very early the need to control their activities and counterbalance their strong national perspectives with more integrated global views. The division level functional staffs that were developed in this company were substantially larger than equivalent groups in similar companies studied. The international division marketing staff, for example, numbered over one hundred and its manufacturing staff over seventy—four to ten times the size of other similar sized drug companies studied.

These functionally organized division staff groups quickly established credibility with senior management and began to act as a filter and a control on subsidiary proposals, elevating those with which they did not agree for arbitration. A weekly international executive committee meeting, consisting of the division president and his geographic and functional vice presidents, was the centre of major decisions. From the different perspectives presented on key issues, senior management felt it was able to obtain a broader appreciation of implications than any of the middle managers alone. They felt this put them in a better position to resolve differences in opinions. The strength of their division staff groups allowed extensive analyses to be made at senior management's request to help reach final decisions.

Yet despite its strong tradition of centralized decision making, even Merck seemed to be moving away from the substantive decision management mode as its primary administrative process. The senior vice president responsible for Europe said: 'We centralize many more decisions than we should. Personally, I am trying to change this practice, primarily through my emphasis on grass roots profit planning.' His expectations were that alternative structures and systems would be developed to allow more views to be integrated and trade offs to be made below the senior management level. This certainly had been the path followed by the other companies in the sample.

DEVELOPING NEW STRUCTURES AND SYSTEMS

Organizational change

The process of developing appropriate and credible new management skills and perspectives clearly had implications for and impact on existing organization structures and systems. Regional offices were established, division level staff groups were strengthened in both quality and size, and management information and control systems became more sophisticated. These changes to the formal organization structure and systems provided the means by which the newly developed staff groups could enter the existing strategy decision making process. The regional and division offices gave them the legitimate power base, and the new systems provided them with the information flow and the communication channels they required to exercise their new skills and perspectives.

While these changes in formal structure increased the new product and functional managers' access to and credibility with senior management, the existing organizational structure and decision processes ensured that 'geographic' managers retained the power implicit in their line positions. Thus, although the new formal structures allowed the product and functional managers to influence the decision process, it required them to do so through the existing formal hierarchy. While most senior managements found this process helpful in educating themselves to the new perspectives being developed, in many situations the administrative burden of consolidating and resolving the conflicts generated by an evolving multidimensional organization created difficulties.

Most of the companies studied tried to alleviate some of these problems by developing additional structures and systems that would allow the required integration of divergent points of view to take place within the organization, rather than at the senior management level. Through the use of temporary structures and systems, many of them were able to bring together managers with different perspectives to review complex issues before automatically elevating any problems or conflicts for resolution.

As senior management became more familiar with the implications of the multiple management perspectives, they became more willing to delegate the responsibility of resolving the implicit conflict. Rather than asking a product manager to critique a subsidiary manager's proposal for example, a product-subsidiary project team might be created to make a joint recommendation on the particular issue. Ongoing decisions that required continual balancing of input were often passed through a standing committee that incorporated managers representing the various relevant points of view.

In four of the companies observed, there was a proliferation of such temporary structures and ad hoc groups soon after the newly established management perspectives were in place in the organization. It was through such task forces, joint teams, and committees that the variety of management perspectives could be engaged selectively into various decision processes. The key attribute of all of the devices used was that they were flexible, allowing management to continually shift the composition of the inputs to various decisions and issues.

In the global recession of 1974/1975 Baxter Travenol used a series of task forces to reorient subsidiary managers from their traditional focus on the income statement (and particularly on sales volume) to a greater concern for the balance sheet. Corporate or regional finance managers worked with subsidiary managers to set targets, and often assisted in the implementation. The new status of these staff managers was reinforced by the power they derived by being appointed to this high visibility task force by senior management. Their influence and achievements were very impressive, and senior management was relieved of the task of continually resolving arguments about the impact inventory reduction would have on budgeted sales levels, for example.

Bristol Myers' senior management found itself getting involved in product development disputes between country managers with priorities and modifications derived from their various market situations, and division product staff, whose priorities usually derived from existing corporate expertise and other constraints. A pharmaceutical council was formed with senior geographic line managers and business development staff managers as members. Debate in this forum allowed a jointly agreed set of priorities to be developed.

New plant capacity decisions were inevitably difficult ones in all companies, with various management perspectives justifying vastly different manufacturing configurations. For example, country managers typically promoted the need for local plants, finance managers argued to maximize the use of tax sheltered operations, and manufacturing staff groups pushed for large specialized plants as regional or global sources. Warner Lambert found one useful solution was to create a joint task force of regional geographic managers, together with manufacturing, finance, materials and marketing staff representatives to develop recommendations on worldwide capacity needs.

Management process change

Through the use of such teams, task forces and committees, senior management was able to ensure that the diverse recommendations generated by the development of multiple management skills and perspectives were reconciled, or at least more focused, before being escalated. As such devices began to be used more extensively, managers with different perspectives on the same problem developed an ability to work together to find solutions. Senior management found itself having to intervene directly in the substance of key decisions far less frequently. Yet its control of the decision process remained strong. By being able to decide the agenda, the focus, the composition, the leadership and the power of the particular overlaid structure, senior management could not only ensure that a particular issue was dealt with from a multidimensional perspective, but could also influence the direction of the resulting analysis, recommendations or decisions. This mode of management can be termed *temporary coalition management*.

The development of a variety of integrative structures and systems was a necessary phase for most of the sample companies in assimilating the new skills and perspectives that had been established. The use of such means of integration had an important impact on the interactions between managers with different perspectives and responsibilities. If the interventionist style of the 'substantive decision management' phase served to raise senior management's awareness and understanding of key issues from a variety of viewpoints, the 'temporary coalition management' phase tended to broaden the perspectives of the middle management group. Not only was this phase important in exposing managers throughout the organization to the complex trade offs required in most decisions, but it also served to develop the interrelationships and communications necessary in a multi-dimensional decision making process.

Of the sample companies, Bristol Myers and Warner Lambert seemed to have evolved to this stage. Not only had they developed managers with the skills and perspectives necessary to supplement and counterbalance the predominantly local national view, but they had supplemented the traditional structure with a variety of temporarily overlaid devices that allowed these new perspectives to be integrated into the decision process lower in the organization. In effect, these companies had increased their decision-making repertoire by supplementing the substantive resolution made with a coalition management approach.

In both companies the increased use of task force teams and committees provided the vehicles by which product and functional managers could become involved in the decision process at an earlier stage. Yet as the use of those temporary structures increased, country managers felt that corporate level understanding of local needs was being increasingly threatened. Their concerns derived not only from the fact that product and functional groups were being upgraded in size and status, but also because they were positioned organizationally to leverage their point of view. On the latter point, two factors were important. First, they had the substantial advantage of physical proximity to senior management; and second, they had strong well-established product and functional counterparts elsewhere in the organization with whom they could form powerful alliances. The country managers expressed the concern that because they were so distant from corporate headquarters and because they had no geographic counterparts there to defend their point of view, the proposals for global co-ordination and integration presented by the product and functional managers could easily swamp their arguments for local flexibility and responsiveness.

Senior management at both Bristol Myers and Warner Lambert were conscious that such concerns could be well founded. Therefore, while the product and functional managers were given greater access to the decision making process through their appointment to task forces and committees simultaneous efforts were made to reassert the role and power of the country manager and to ensure that his point of view was not overwhelmed by these changes.

Although the reality clearly was that there was a narrowing power and influence gap between product and functional staff managers and geographic line managers, in both companies a vigorous defence of the key role of the country manager was undertaken. At Bristol Myers management continually emphasized that the country manager was 'king in his country' and that the growing product and functional staff influence was to help him supplement his entrepreneurial skills with technical and administrative capabilities. Warner Lambert's senior management also talked about the increasing role of staff managers as being 'to help build rounded managers at the country level'.

In the two companies that were using the temporary coalition mode to supplement their substantive decision management process, senior management seemed to concentrate on two key tasks: maintaining the legitimacy of the groups and individuals representing each of the decision perspectives, and ensuring the appropriate influence of each of these perspectives in key decisions. The achievement of the first objective led senior management in Bristol Myers and Warner Lambert to spend considerable time supporting and emphasizing the continuing key role of country managers, while simultaneously creating the temporary structures that allowed product and functional staff to input to important issues. In both companies, all groups of managers felt their influence and responsibility had increased—an impression that was probably well founded given their prior roles in a more 'substantive decision management' process. It was this widespread sense of legitimacy and influence in the decision process that appeared to be a prerequisite for the successful operations of the temporary coalition mode of management. In the words of Bristol Myers International president, 'As all managers began to be perceived as having legitimate points of view and viable influence on decisions the absolute distinction that has historically been drawn between line and staff managers is starting to have less meaning.'

The second prerequisite of this mode of management was to ensure that the various management perspectives were appropriately represented in each of the many key decisions. It was here that companies experienced greatest difficulty.

Despite the clear advantage the 'coalition management' process offered over the 'substantive decision intervention' stage, demands on senior management were still substantial in forming, restructuring, and dissolving coalitions to manage the growing number of multidimensional problems. Furthermore, the mere creation of various coalitions did not ensure that the resulting decision process would be co-operative, and stress and divisiveness seemed an inevitable part of the operation of many teams and committees. In some cases the result was paralysis as opposing views became locked in impasse; in other instances decision making deteriorated to 'horse trading' rather than open interchange of views that was expected.

Thus, while task forces, teams, and committees often did provide useful means by which solutions to multidimensional issues could be found without continual intervention by senior management, they were limited when they degenerated into forced alliances between reluctant colleagues. Some companies that had perceived the coalition management mode as being the solution to the bottleneck problems of their earlier substantive decision management process, began to recognize the need for further organizational adaptation. The open communication, co-operation and understanding that is required between managers in multidimensional decisions could not be legislated by changes in the formal organization alone.

Developing a new organizational 'climate': decision context management

Just as they had recognized the difficulty of having senior management intervening in the content of key decisions, some companies began to recognize that to have them continually involved in structuring and controlling a large number of complex, variable decision making processes was also very limiting. In the judgment of many managers a process that often depended on forced alliances between reluctant colleagues, each protective of his turf probably would not be effective in the long run.

Having developed the appropriate management perspectives, then created viable structures and systems through which they could interact, the next major challenge for the developing multidimensional organization was to build an appropriate decision-making environment. The goal was to create an organizational climate in which flexible, constructive and co-operative interaction between managers with different perspectives was institutionalized. Rather than having individual decisions being arbitrated or regulated from above, the objective was to achieve a more self regulating decision process in which managers themselves could negotiate the appropriate balance of views in multidimensional decisions.

In order to achieve this kind of environment, the managers had to supplement their ability and willingness to represent a particular viewpoint with an overall understanding of the corporation's broad objectives and a willingness to adapt, co-operate, and compromise to achieve those larger goals. Such changes could not be achieved overnight and required top management to focus on three major tasks:

1. To broaden managers' perspectives and open multiple channels of communication through the creative use and control of manager movement and interaction within the organization;
2. To change formal systems so as to facilitate and reinforce the desired co-operative and flexible decision making climate; and
3. To create a value system that provided the organizational security required to encourage managers to take the risk involved in such flexible, broad perspective decision making.

Of the companies studied, Eli Lilly and Baxter Travenol appeared to be the most conscious of creating this type of flexible, co-operative decision environment. Examples of the changes made will be drawn from these companies.

Management of both companies seemed to realize that flexible co-operative interactions would be difficult to develop solely through the limited channels and hierachical relationships provided by the formal organization. Management's considerable control over individual's movements and interactions in the organization gave it a powerful tool to impact two separate aspects of the decision environment. First, managers' understanding and appreciation of different organizational issues could be influenced; and second, interpersonal relationships and informal communications channels could be developed. For example, a subsidiary marketing manager transferred to a headquarters staff is likely to develop a far greater appreciation for both the local and the global issues involved in key marketing decisions. Furthermore, the personal relationships he develops in each assignment facilitate communications and co-operation on issues involving national and global marketing input.

Eli Lilly had a well established career development system in which managers were transferred throughout their careers from line positions to staff, from country operations to headquarters, from product to functional or geographic responsibility. Several managers attributed the good contacts and co-operative working relationships that were the norm at Lilly, largely to this strongly institutionalized career development track. While less well developed, Baxter had also consciously begun to engage in a similar use of temporary assignments and long term transfers.

Both companies also created forums in which multidimensional issues could be explored openly, without the pressures or competitiveness that often existed in task forces. Baxter, for instance, modified its annual country general managers meeting to become a senior management conference to which staff and line managers were invited. For one week each year common management problems were confronted by the entire group, and joint recommendations and action plans agreed to. The president explained that his objectives were twofold; to broaden the identification of his top management from their parochial geographic or functional views to a company-wide perspective, and to create an environment in which they could co-operate on key multidimensional problems.

By consciously focusing on transfers, assignments, career paths, forums and meetings, senior management was shifting its means of influence from the formal to the informal organization structures and systems.

This conscious subtle use of transfers, assignments, and meetings provided senior management with a means of influencing the organization's informal structure and systems rather than the formal channels that had previously been their main focus. Their ability to influence the informal structure was strengthened by the fact that in a multinational corporation there were considerable barriers of distance, language and culture that tended to limit contacts and interactions between individuals. Managements' control of the nature, frequency and composition of interpersonal interactions therefore could have a very strong influence on the development of an informal structure.

In both Lilly and Baxter, senior management were conscious of this important influence and used it continuously. They also recognized that the behaviours and relationships that could be developed through the informal systems needed to be reinforced through the formal organization. Existing management systems had to be changed to recognize the need for co-operative flexible decision-making behaviour.

In Eli Lilly, for example, the formal evaluation process was changed so that a manager would be evaluated not only by his immediate line superior, but also by managers in other parts of the company with whom he had regular working relationships. Baxter also began broadening its evaluation process to allow product and functional managers to input into the evaluation of country managers and vice versa.

At Lilly, career path management had become highly formalized. There were personnel directors for each major function, product and geographic area who met frequently with senior management to review all actual and potential openings and all possible candidates. Managers were counselled on the importance of developing contacts and expertise in multiple responsibilities, and the broad career development histories of the senior management provided models for younger managers.

However, the process of influencing the informal system to develop co-operation and mutual understanding and realigning formal systems to reinforce such behaviour could only be successful if undertaken in an operating environment that was extremely supportive. Asking a manager to abandon the simple certainty of defending his clear point of view from his defined position of organizational responsibility is asking him to take substantive personal and organizational risk. To foster the desired flexible compromising decision-making process, an organization needs a strong, well-established value system that provides the stability and security to allow an individual to take such risks.

Eli Lilly had an internal value system that not only had its roots in the founders' objectives, but also was continually reinforced by current management. In the words of the late Mr Eli Lilly, 'Values are, quite simply the core of both men and institutions. By combining our thoughts and helping one another, we are able to merge the parts of the corporation into a rational, workable management system.' The values he spoke of were also referred to frequently in the organization, and included openness, honesty in dealings with others, and the need for mutual trust. With strongly held corporate values such as these, the development of the desired co-operative, flexible interaction between managers was more easily achieved.

Although Baxter's corporate value system had tended to be more competitive and less supportive, over a number of years the international division president had been working to modify some of the accepted organizational norms. At every gathering of managers, his speeches and private remarks emphasized the need for co-operation and joint action between managers. He tried to make his own behaviour and management style a model for the organization. He publicly applauded appropriate co-operative problem solving and decision making among management groups with diverse interests and perspectives. Gradually the adversary relationship that existed between country managers and headquarters staff gave way to a co-operative mutual respect.

Management process change

There was a noticeable cumulative effect of helping to build a network of co-operative informal relationships, reinforcing such co-operation through the formal systems, and institutionalizing the resulting decision-making behaviour in a set of organizational values that strongly supported a flexible and co-operative management style. The companies that consciously worked on these changes began to develop an organizational climate in which managers recognized the broad corporate goals and worked co-operatively to help achieve them, even when this meant compromising some more parochial concerns. This management mode can be labelled *decision context management*.

Senior management's role in this mode was twofold: to support the organizational values, the informal structure and the formal systems that created the co-operative flexible decision process; and to communicate clearly and frequently the broad corporate objectives towards which such decisions should be directed. This represented a subtle and a delicate task, but less all-consuming than an involvement with individual decision outcomes or even with coalition building and management.

In the decision context management mode, the middle management level showed a much greater willingness to take multidimensional approach on key issues. In Baxter, for example, when the general manager of the Brazilian subsidiary wanted to build a local plant, he first discussed the matter at length with both the manufacturing manager and the product marketing manager at division headquarters, and with the corporate financial staff. When all views had been fully discussed, a mutually agreed set of alternatives and a recommended approach was submitted to top management.

It should be noted again that decision making in companies that pursued the decision context management mode were not all so easily self-regulated. On sensitive issues, senior mangement still had to intervene either by defining the coalition that was to make the analysis, recommendation, or decision, or by actually resolving specific issues where resolution by co-operation and compromise had not been possible. Like the other modes, this one simply broadened the repertoire of decision processes available to help resolve complex multidimensional issues.

CONCLUSION

The strategic challenges faced by the five health care companies are typical of the situations confronting many MNCs. Increasing pressure from host governments and global competitors increasingly force companies to develop and integrate its management capabilities at the local *and* the global levels; accelerating change in both arenas require that these multiple skills and perspectives interact flexibly.

While change in the formal organization has been thought of by many managers as the principal means of adapting the decision processes, the subtlety and complexity of a flexible multidimensional decision-making process appears difficult to achieve solely (or even primarily) through formal organizational change. By retaining their simple international division structures, the five companies observed maintained a stability in their formal organization that allowed gradual changes in people, relationships, and processes to be introduced through more informal and less traumatic means. Rather than focusing their attention on the structure per se, managers of these companies seemed to be more concerned with the nature of decision process that the change was designed to achieve.

While their formal organization structures seemed to belie the fact, each of these companies had developed the flexible multidimensional decision process that its strategic environment demanded. Westinghouse's hope was that its newly installed matrix structure might take five years 'to force product managers to interact with geographic specialists'. Managers in the health care companies studied believed that their evolutionary approach achieved the same ends with less trauma.

NOTES

1. This account of Westinghouse's growth abroad is based largely on the article 'Westinghouse Takes Aim at the World', *Fortune*, January 14, 1980, pp. 48–53.

2. Yves Doz has written extensively on the nature of these demands. See, for example, 'Strategic Management in Multinational Companies', *Sloan Management Review*.

3. Perhaps the best known of the 'stages theories' of multinational organization development was developed by John Stopford. See, for example, John M. Stopford and Louis T. Wells, *Managing the Multinational Enterprise*, New York: Basic Books, 1972. The first half of the book describes the patterns of organization structure evolution based on a study of 170 companies. The typical 'stages' evolution is described as follows. A structure in which autonomous foreign subsidiaries are loosely linked to the parent company, is replaced by one in which subsidiaries are consolidated under an international division. Then a 'global' product or area organization is typically installed, which, in turn, is replaced by a multidimensional (or 'grid') organization structure.

4. Richard Rumelt noted a tendency for strategy to follow fashion in his study of Fortune 500 companies. See Richard P. Rumelt, *Strategy, Structure, and Economic Performance*, Boston: Division of Research, Harvard Business School, 1974, p. 149.

5. Perhaps the two most widely cited examples of multinational matrix organizations apparently have pulled back from their original structure. Davis and Lawrence describe the demise of Dow Chemical's global matrix, but point to the emergence of a more recent multinational matrix success: Citibank (Stanley M. Davis and Paul R. Lawrence, *Matrix*, Addison Wesley, Reading, MA, 1977, pp. 206–222). Recent reports indicate that Citibank has now abandoned its global matrix (see 'Its a Stronger Bank that David Rockefeller is Passing to his Successor', *Fortune*, Vol. 101, No. 1, Jan. 14, 1980, p. 44).

6. A follow-up study of the original Stopford sample of companies is planned. A preliminary estimate indicates that well over 30% of the companies classified as having international divisions in 1967 retained them twelve years later despite their growth and the changing environmental demands.

7. See Christopher A. Bartlett, *Multinational Structural Evolution: The Changing Decision Environment in International Divisions*, unpublished doctoral dissertation, Harvard Business School, 1979.

8. For a full exploration of the strategic demands in the food industry, see Ulrich E. Wiechmann, *Marketing Management in Multinational Firms*, New York: Praeger, 1976.

18

Emergence of New Structures in Swedish Multinationals

Pervez N. Ghauri

INTRODUCTION

Much of the literature on multinationals deals with the structural development of MNCs—from domestic to global structure. This paper addresses an evolutionary phenomenon where the foreign subsidiaries become more prominent than the parent firm. Using a network approach, it is assumed that a foreign subsidiary has a three-dimensional relationship: (1) with the head office, (2) with local authorities, and (3) with the local network. Data on Swedish firms operating in Southeast Asia support the assumption that a new form of MNC structure is emerging: foreign subsidiaries are becoming more influential and independent than the parent firm. Furthermore, the emergence of a 'centre-centre' relationship suggests that some regional subsidiaries become the centre for a number of subsidiaries around them.

INVOLVEMENT OF SWEDISH FIRMS

The involvement of Swedish firms in international markets dates as far back as the 1870s. By the 1890s, several firms such as AGA, Alfa Laval, Nitroglycerin, and Ericsson, had their manufacturing operations abroad. The decades immediately after World War II were, however, the golden era for the Swedish international business activities and by the 1960s most of the larger Swedish firms were involved in international marketing. Innovation capabilities and a well-established network of relationships have been important factors for this success.

Literature on multinational firms tends to focus on traditional firms from large countries such as the United States (Franko, 1976; Kindleberg, 1979; Aggarwal, 1988). Research on Swedish firms and their international marketing activities is rather limited, however, a number of studies have dealt with the internationalization process (Johanson

Pervez N. Ghauri, University of Oslo and University of Maastricht.
This reading is taken from (1990) *Advances in International Comparative Management*. JAI Press Inc.: Greenwich, CT.

and Wiedersheim-Paul, 1975) and on the export behaviour of these firms (Kaynak and Ghauri, 1987). Some studies have also been undertaken to study the Swedish firms and their activities in Western Europe (Jagren and Horwitz, 1984). In some studies it has been suggested that subsidiaries of major European multinationals (e.g., Siemens, Philips, Nestlé) tended to overwhelm their parent firms (Eliasson, 1988).

The phenomenon of subsidiaries becoming more influential and independent has, however, not been systematically studied. In the early 1980s, a government committee report (1983) on the impact of inward and outward foreign direct investments was submitted. Hedlund and Aman (1984) following Stopford and Wells (1972) and Franko (1976) delineated the structural development of multinational companies and explained how the structure of these firms developed from domestic to global structure. Hedlund and Aman (1984) presented a 'Swedish model' of managing foreign subsidiaries, containing the following key strategic structural components:

- The Swedish firms have been competing on the basis of advanced technology, superior products, and premium prices.
- Primarily, these firms have been producing for industrial buyers.
- Early internationalization.
- Low product diversity, expansion only in related areas.
- International expansion through 'green-field' investments.
- Mother–daughter structure, with subsidiaries reporting directly to the president of the parent company.
- More autonomy for subsidiary managers as compared to subsidiaries from other countries.
- Extended personal networks of close contacts between headquarters, and important foreign subsidiaries.
- Informal personalized control through information sharing and common experience.
- Strong position of managers with a technical/manufacturing background.

THE NETWORK APPROACH

In this paper, the operating characteristics and the recent evolution of Swedish MNCs are examined using a framework based on the network approach. According to this approach a firm has to develop various relationships to acquire raw material, components, and other factors of production. The firm also has to sell and distribute its products. These relationships have to be developed and nurtured, both before and after the firm operates in the production chain, with sub-contractors, suppliers, distributors, and wholesalers. Moreover, the firm has to develop relationships (liaison) with other actors in the same network, such as competitors, local authorities and other third parties working in the same industry (Ghauri, 1988).

In the existing literature, multinationals (MNCs) are portrayed as working with a strong head office that controls and co-ordinates its subsidiaries around the globe (Swedenborg, 1982). Top management in these firms is, therefore, assumed to formulate an overall strategy and control for all the units. According to this view the MNC functions with a strong head office, 'centre', and a number of subsidiaries, 'peripheries', as illustrated by Figure 1.

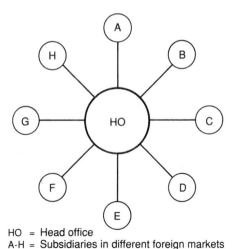

HO = Head office
A-H = Subsidiaries in different foreign markets

Figure 1. Traditional Head Office Subsidiary Relationship.

It is assumed that a new stage of multinational structure is emerging after the global stage, as noted by Stopford and Wells (1972), and that a new phenomenon is emerging: the head office/subsidiary relationship is changing. This changing relationship is a step further in the internationalization process of the firm. This concept was introduced earlier by Aggarwal and Ghauri (1989), and we can see the emergence of a number of centres within the same firm. Due to their size and importance some regional subsidiaries have started functioning as centres, however, this picture is also changing as illustrated by Figure 2.

This phenomenon is somewhat different from regional headquarters, where the head office itself delegates some of its decision making to some regional headquarters to encourage better co-ordination (Eliasson, 1988). This is a further step in the internationalization process, which may not be initiated according to the policies of head-quarters.

Here, a number of subsidiaries such as A, B, and C, are functioning as centres for other subsidiaries. In some cases the subsidiaries may or may not have contacts with the head office. As a result, a 'centre-centre' structure is emerging. Hedlund and Aman (1984) also concluded that interdependencies vary among the head office and its subsidiaries, depending upon the degree and experience of different markets. The subsidiaries, through adaptation to local markets, acquire a prominent position in the local network.

In the case of MNCs, the subsidiaries in the foreign markets are a part of the parent company's network as long as they have their own network in the local market. These subsidiaries have to function and survive in the local market and must comply with the demands of the local network. At times, these demands may be counter to the policies of the parent company. Subsidiaries thus come to have a three-dimensional relationship: (1) there is the hierarchical relationship with the head office; (2) their activities are limited by the rules and regulations of the local government, and (3) they have to comply with the demands of other actors of the local network. This is illustrated in Figure 3.

As shown, the traditional head office/subsidiary relationship is very strong, while the local network is rather weak. In the early stages of establishing the subsidiary, the head office directs the subsidiary in all matters, such as how it would handle its relationship

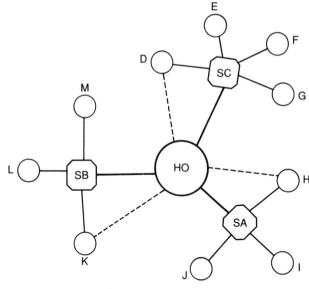

—— = Strong relationship

---- = Moderate relationship

HO = Head office

SA = Subsidiary A in a foreign market

SB = Subsidiary B in a foreign market

SC = Subsidiary C in a foreign market

D-M = Different subsidiaries in foreign markets

Figure 2. 'Centre-Centre' Relationship in Multinational Firms.

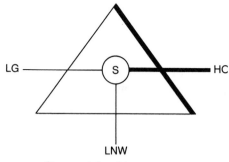

■■■ = Strong relationship

—— = Moderate relationship

HO = Head office

S = Subsidiary in a foreign market

LG = Local government in a foreign market

LNW = Local network in a foreign market

Figure 3. The Three Dimensional Relationship for a Foreign Subsidiary.

with the local government and the local network. However, as the subsidiary gains more experience in the local market, it may acquire a stronger position in the local network. It also may be resourceful enough to cope with the rules and regulations of the local government, and eventually, its relationship priorities tend to change as illustrated by Figure 4.

As can be noted, the most important relationship for the subsidiary at this stage, is with other actors of the local network, and, it has to abide by the rules and regulations of the local government. The relationship with the head office thus becomes less important at this stage.

According to the network approach described earlier, the most important relationship for the subsidiary is the local network in which it has to operate. In that case it is interesting to see how these firms are dealing with the issues and policies of the head office which conflict with the demands of the local network. This study assumes that the subsidiary would take care of its own interests (i.e., the demands of the local network) and could act contrary to the policies of the head office. This, of course, depends upon several factors such as the size of the local market and the position of the subsidiary in the local network. The stronger the position, the more inclined it is to have its own policies, and not consider itself dependent on the head office. Similarly, the bigger the size of the market (bigger than the parent company's market) the greater the chances are that the subsidiary becomes independent.

These inferences are based on data gathered from Swedish firms having wholly- or partly-owned subsidiaries in Thailand, Philippines, and Indonesia. The data collection was done through personal interviews with the area managers at the head office of each firm in Sweden and with the managing director of each subsidiary in the respective

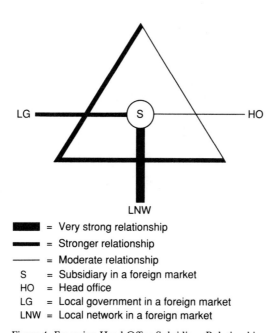

LNW

■■■■ = Very strong relationship
■■■ = Stronger relationship
—— = Moderate relationship
S = Subsidiary in a foreign market
HO = Head office
LG = Local government in a foreign market
LNW = Local network in a foreign market

Figure 4. Emerging Head Office Subsidiary Relationship.

foreign country. In some cases, the marketing managers of the subsidiaries were also interviewed.

INTERNATIONAL GROWTH OF SWEDISH FIRMS

Since Sweden was not involved in World War II, and was rich in raw material, it could develop its international trade and investment. Swedish firms initially found an easy market in Europe where countries needed Swedish raw materials and other products to rebuild their infrastructure after the war. This was, however, not the only factor for the success of Swedish firms abroad. The great demand in the European market and abolition of trade restrictions after World War II, helped Swedish firms expand internationally.

In 1965, 82 Swedish firms had 800 overseas manufacturing and sales subsidiaries with 170,000 employees. However, in the growth of Swedish multinationals, the 1970s and 1980s were critical. The Swedish firms' ability to serve foreign markets through exports alone declined and had to increase activities involving FDI to protect markets developed with exports from Sweden. In terms of expansion, one could identify two groups of firms: (1) those that started international activity long before the two World Wars, such as AGA, Alfa Laval, SKF, ASEA, and Swedish Match, (Johanson and Wiedersheim-Paul, 1975), and (2) those firms which began after World War II, such as Volvo, Electrolux, and Saab.

However, most of the Swedish firms, such as ASEA, Atlas Copco, Sandvik, Nitro Nobel, and Volvo, have gone international in the traditional way. They started their activities first in the adjacent markets of Europe and later on went to Southeast Asia. They then followed the traditional modes of internationalization, starting first with an agent that was then converted into a sales subsidiary and only later into a manufacturing subsidiary. Swedish firms are generally among the world leaders in their product areas. Evidence from our study reveals that the firms' knowledge of the market and relationship with all the actors are the more important elements of competitive strategies rather than low cost production.

The foreign operation of larger Swedish firms, even as of 1970, are good examples to illustrate the above point. Table 1 provides a list of the 30 largest Swedish firms ranked in terms of their total sales and the part/percentage of sales derived from foreign markets.

These firms are quite large by themselves and compared to other international firms. Most of these firms work on special products for relatively small international market niches where a network of relationships is more important than the price.

The major part of Swedish FDI is undertaken by the larger firms with more than 500 employees abroad. The 30 largest firms have between 2,000 and 60,000 employees outside of Sweden. According to Swedenborg (1982), approximately one-third of the 118 Swedish firms having manufacturing abroad, accounted for 90% of the employees of these firms outside of Sweden. Table 2 shows the 1965–1985 trend in employment by Swedish affiliates abroad.

As indicated by the above discussion, there has been considerable growth in Swedish FDI. Not only have these firms expanded their activities abroad but have also grown in their home market. Table 3 illustrates both inward and outward Swedish foreign direct investments between 1975 and 1987.

Table 1. Largest Swedish firms in terms of 1986 sales (millions of SEK)

Rank	Name	Sales	Foreign Sales	%FS
1	Volvo	84,090	70,604	84
2	Electrolux	53,090	43,434	82
3	Asea	46,031	33,447	73
4	Saab-Scania	35,222	23,247	66
5	Ericsson	32,278	25,177	78
6	KF	29,476	4,185	14
7	ICA	28,469	na	—
8	Televerket	26,340	na	—
9	Carnegie	20,411	na	—
10	SKF	20,232	19,220	95
11	SJ	16,431	na	—
12	Skanska	16,103	2,632	16
13	SCA	15,303	10,406	68
14	Procordia	15,299	4,950	32
15	Nordstjernan	15,251	7,000	46
16	Vattenfall	15,207	na	—
17	Stora	13,238	6,863	52
18	SSAB	13,010	5,204	40
19	Sandvik	12,721	11,652	92
20	Boliden	12,384	6,232	50
21	Postverket	11,956	na	—
22	Systembolaget	11,922	na	—
23	A Johanson & Co.	11,543	na	—
24	Nobel Industries	11,535	6,865	60
25	Esselte	11,251	7,421	66
26	Swedish Match	10,912	7,976	73
27	Flakt (Asea)	10,352	8,075	78
28	Atlas Copco	10,351	na	—
29	Alfa-Laval	10,300	na	—
30	ABV	9,661	1,700	18

na: not available.
%FS: Foreign Sales as a Per cent of Total Sales.
SEK: Swedish krona.
Source: Veckans Affarer nr. 38/17 (September 1987 and Company Annual Reports)

Table 2. Employment abroad in foreign subsidiaries of Swedish firms

Year	1965	1970	1978	1981	1985
Number of employees (thousands)	171	222	301	326	329
Percent of employment in manufacturing industry in Sweden	18	24	33	39	43

Source: Government Proposition 1986/1987, Central Bank of Sweden, 74, app. 3, p. 299

IMPORTANCE OF REINVESTMENTS

In an MIT project (1982), undertaken on behalf of STU Styrelsen (for Teknisk Utveckling), it was found that a typical newly established firm, after 10 years, has a turnover of around SEK 20 million, sells 80% of its production out of the country, and by this time has a turnover of SEK 80 million.

In recent years, however, reinvestment has become more important than new investments. Reinvestment in already existing markets and acquisition of suppliers, competitors, and distributors has become quite common in recent years. For example, Swedish Match has acquired its suppliers both in Thailand and the Philippines as it is very important to have a secure supply of raw material. Forgren (1990) concluded that most acquisitions by Swedish firms have taken place in the countries where these companies were already well established. A number of acquisitions by Electrolux in North America, Italy, and England are also good examples. Table 4 illustrates the increasing importance of acquisitions by Swedish firms, 1971–1985.

Table 3. Swedish foreign direct investment (in billions of SEK)

Year	Outflow	Inflow
1975	2.0	0.53
1976	2.8	0.47
1977	3.8	0.65
1978	2.6	0.74
1979	2.0	0.70
1980	3.0	1.29
1981	5.0	1.10
1982	6.9	1.78
1983	9.2	1.48
1984	10.6	2.76
1985	14.3	5.37
1986	25.1	6.06
1987*	10.5	1.87

* Up to June
SEK: Swedish krona
Source: Kredit och Valutaoversikt, Central Bank of Sweden, Stockholm, various issues

Table 4. Acquisitions of foreign production companies by Swedish companies (with more than 500 employees abroad in 1982)

Period	Number
1971–1973	39
1974–1976	55
1977–1979	64
1980–1982	101
1983–1985	113

Source: Forsgren, M. (1990), *Managing the Internationalization Process: The Swedish Case.* London Routledge.

HEAD OFFICE SUBSIDIARY RELATIONSHIP

Importance of regional centres

There are several examples available where the subsidiaries have become larger than the parent firm in terms of sales and number of employees. Considering the size of the home market, it appears to be rather natural in the case of Swedish firms. These subsidiaries now have their own R&D as well as product development programmes. In some cases, a number of subsidiaries have been grouped together into regional networks. This mode has been popular in the case of Swedish firms in Southeast Asia with Singapore being the regional headquarters. These regional offices work as independent firms which are many times more powerful than the head office.

Sandvik's subsidiary in the Philippines, although all the components emanate from Sweden, always sends its requisitions to Singapore. All the materials are thus channelled through Singapore. Some of the components used are not available from Sandvik group firms and hence are bought from other foreign firms; even so, these components are bought and delivered by the regional office in Singapore. Accordingly, the payments for all these components are also made to Singapore, not to the head office or the suppliers. Singapore thus has jurisdiction over the Southeast Asia region, that is, Sandvik subsidiaries in Thailand, Malaysia, Singapore, Indonesia, the Philippines, Hong Kong, and Taiwan. All the financial reports are also sent to the regional office which later on consolidates all the returns and reports to the head office. For the head office, it is the performance of the regional office that counts the most, not the individual subsidiary.

The growth of foreign operation that enables the subsidiary to become larger than the head office can be accompanied by many conflicts, as illustrated by the Danish producer of farm equipment. The largest company established ten sales subsidiaries in major overseas markets during the 1970s as outlets for its home production. Soon, however, these sales subsidiaries began to modify the parent company's products in order to adapt them to local demands. This eventually evolved into local production. In some cases, the production facility even led to facilities for the development and manufacturing of new products. Most of these subsidiaries also started buying parts and components from local suppliers in order to compete successfully with other international companies such as Massey Ferguson, John Deere, International Harvester, and Caterpillar. One subsidiary in England was buying 65% of its components and parts from local suppliers which was a clear violation of head office policy.

The developments eventually led to conflicts between the parent company and its overseas subsidiaries with regard to sourcing and the optimal product mix. The parent company believed that the affiliates should purchase from each other. Some of the products offered by competitors were in process and qualities that were harder to beat. Therefore, they wanted to focus resources and know-how on product lines with higher technological content. Thus, purchasing policies and product mix strategies of the subsidiaries were dictated by local networks.

The head office–subsidiary conflict is also illustrated by the Electrolux subsidiary in the Philippines. During 1979/1980, the subsidiary was importing all of its components from the parent company, and from affiliated sister companies around the world. As it gained more experience and a better position in the local network, it not only started buying from local suppliers but, in fact, it helped local suppliers develop their own technical competence so that they could supply to Electrolux's specification. As a result, in 1987, the local subsidiary was buying more than 85% of its components locally and the vacuum cleaner manufactured in Philippines was quite different from the one Electrolux was manufacturing at its subsidiaries in Europe. A further example of how the product was being adapted to the local market can be seen in the case of Philippine water purifiers that were not even sold in the home market.

The case is not too different from the Nobel Industries subsidiary in the Philippines. The local firm purchases almost all of its components and raw material from the local—Japanese and American—suppliers with only a small portion of the material being bought from Sweden. In 1984, the subsidiary even started its own Research and Development (R&D) department. As far as marketing is concerned, in 1984 when the market was shrinking in the Philippines, the subsidiary started exporting to nearby countries. This led to conflicts among the sister firms from the countries where the subsidiary wanted to export. Finally, the head office had to solve this conflict by establishing a common sales subsidiary which would sell to Indonesia and Thailand, the countries where Nobel did not have presence.

Another example is Tetra Pak which sells machines and raw material for liquid packings. Its Philippine subsidiary imported all the machines and tools from Sweden and leased these machines to four different packers of milk and juices. Tetra Pak Philippines has a leasing contract for the service and maintenance of machines. The producers using their machines are not allowed to use any materials other than those supplied by Tetra Pak. The subsidiary is nonetheless importing all the material they sell in the Philippines from Singapore where Tetra Pak has a manufacturing subsidiary. In this case too we witness the emergence of a strong regional office—Tetra Pak, Singapore, supplying the material to all subsidiaries in Southeast Asia.

Swedish Match, wholly or partly owned 150 subsidiaries in about 40 countries, has 73% of its total sales and 55% of its production outside Sweden. Swedish Match started international production with manufacturing subsidiaries in markets as far as India, Thailand, and the Philippines as early as the 1920s and 1930s. Although these subsidiaries are wholly-owned by Swedish Match (except in India), they work autonomously. They purchase most of their material from local suppliers and even the imported material is not necessarily bought from parent or sister firms. Most of the imported material they purchase comes from Germany, Japan, China, and Finland. In the Philippines the subsidiary had two factories in two different locations, one in Cebu and one in Manila. In 1977, it sold one of its factories and bought 50% of the shares of one of the suppliers of raw material. It was considered more important to have a secure local supply of raw material than to have a greater market share, although this goal was clearly against the policy of the head office.

SUMMARY AND CONCLUSIONS

As the examples cited above show, it appears that the concept of centre and periphery, and the interdependence between the two are diminishing in importance in MNCs. In many cases, several centres in the same company have emerged. As in the case of Tetra Pak and Sandvik, the Singapore unit is emerging as a centre for subsidiaries in Southeast Asia. The 'Centre' or head office for these subsidiaries is Singapore, and not the parent company located in Sweden. The Electrolux subsidiary in the Philippines is working independently, has excellent manufacturing facilities, and exports to other Electrolux subsidiaries operating in the region—Thailand and Indonesia. Knowing the independent status of the Philippines subsidiary and also accepting the fact that it is one of the most successful subsidiaries for the whole concern, the parent company has chosen not to have any say in their business with other regional companies and in their purchasing policies. For Electrolux subsidiaries in the geographical area, the Philippines subsidiary is the resource 'centre'. The product manufactured in that subsidiary is more suitable for them than the products manufactured in Sweden, or in any other European subsidiary.

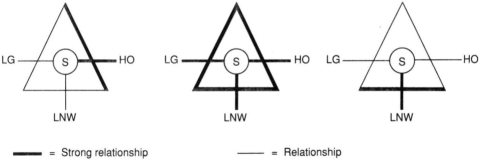

■■■■ = Strong relationship   ——— = Relationship

S   = Subsidiary in a foreign market

HO   = Head office

LG   = Local government in a foreign market

LNW = Local network in a foreign market

Figure 5. The Process of Changing Head Office Subsidiary Relationship.

We may conclude that changes in head office–subsidiary relationships are gradual. Our evidence suggests that this relationship changes with time and depends upon the position of the subsidiary in the local network. These changes can be hypothesized as going through three different stages as shown in Figure 5.

The first stage, is at the start of the internationalization which is the most important relationship with the head office. In the second stage, the subsidiary most likely gives equal importance to the head office, the local network, and the local government. Finally, in the third stage, the subsidiary gains more experience, knowledge, and a better stance in the local network and thus, that relationship becomes the most pivotal one. Moreover, in some cases, the subsidiary's relationship with the head office is replaced by its relationship with a regional office (centre).

This paper highlights the emerging concept of regional centres in MNCs based in small economies like Sweden. In such cases, foreign units are likely to become independent, or regional 'centre' oriented as they overtake the parent firm in size and influence. The Swedish cases from Southeast Asia are consistent with the recent developments regarding foreign direct investment. The results of our study are, however, difficult to generalize due to the limitations of empirical evidence. One hopes that this study would lead to further empirical studies of multinationals originating in Europe.

REFERENCES

Aggarwal, R. (1988). Multinationals of the South. *Journal of International Business Studies*, **19(1)**: 140–143.

Aggarwal, R., & Ghauri, P. N. (1989). *The Evolution of Multinationals from Small Economy: A Study of Swedish Firms in Asia*. Paper presented in UK meeting of Academy of International Business, University of Bath, Bath, England, April 7–8.

Doz, Y. L., Bartlett, C. A., & Prahalad, C. K. (1981). Global Competitive Pressures and Host Country Demands. *California Management Review*, **23**, 66.

Eliasson, G. (1988). *De utlandsetablerade foretagen och den svenska ekonomin, forskningsrapport.* no. 26, IUI. Stockholm: Almqvist & Wiksell.

Forsgren, M. (1989). *The International Process of Swedish Firms*. London: Routledge.

Forsgren, M. (1976). *Joint Venture Survival in Multinational Enterprise*. New York: Praeger.

Gates, S. R., & Egelhoff, W. G. (1986). Centralization in headquarters-subsidiary relationships. *Journal of International Business Studies*, **17**, 71–92.

Ghauri, P. N. (1988). Marketing Strategies: Swedish firms in South-East Asia. In R. Varaldo (Ed.), *International Marketing Cooperation*. Pica, Est.: Editirce.

Hedlund, G., & Aman, P. (1984). *Managing Relationships with Foreign Subsidiaries*. Vastervik: Sveriges Mekan Forbund.

Hornell, E., & Vahlne, J. E. (1986). *Multinationals: The Swedish Case*. London: Croom Helm.

Jagren, L., & Horwitz, E. C. (1984). *Svenska marknadsandelar* [Swedish marketing] (Working paper). Stockholm: IUI.

Johanson, J., & Wiedersheim-Paul, F. (1975). The Internationalization of the Firm: Four Swedish cases. *Journal of Management Studies*, October, 205–231.

Kaynak, E., & Ghauri, P. N. (1987). Export Behavior of Small Swedish firms. *Journal of Small Business Management*, **25(2)**: 26–32.

Kindleberger, C. P. (1979). *American Business Abroad*. New Haven, CT: Yale University Press.

Prahalad, C. H., & Doz, Y. L. (1981). An Approach to Strategic Controls in MNCs. *Sloan Management Review*, **22(4)**: 5–13.

Robock, S. H., & Simmonds, K. (1989). *International Business and Multinational Enterprises*. Homewood, IL: Irwin.

Stopford, J. M., & Wells, L. T. (1972). *Managing the Multinational Enterprise*. New York: Basic Books.

Swedenborg, B. (1982). *Svensk industri i utlandet* [Swedish industries abroad]. Stockholm: IUI.

19

Foreign Market Servicing by Multinationals: an Integrated Treatment

Peter J. Buckley, C. L. Pass and Kate Prescott

This article is an attempt to codify and integrate different approaches to the foreign market servicing strategies of multinational firms. It does so by widening the typical range of functions explicitly considered by the international business literature and by applying a uniform and unifying set of concepts to this enhanced range of functions carried out by the firm.

The orthodox theory of international business has paid far less attention to the non-production functions (stockholding, distribution, promotion, generating customers and transport) than to production itself. The marketing and transport functions are either ignored or are implicitly assumed to be governed by the same factors that determine production in the international business literature. The literature on international marketing, by contrast, concentrates on operational details of distribution and control of agents and tends to provide an arbitrary cut off, ignoring forms of doing business abroad other than exporting. An integration is long overdue. The article is exploratory and avoids detail on industry structure and company differences in an attempt to find regularities. The analysis relies on the two key choices for the firm for each function it performs: whether the function should be undertaken by the firm itself or subcontracted and where the function should be performed. These choices—the internationalization and location decision—are expanded later. The following section presents the key issues of our approach.

EXPANSION PATHS

Propositions

The argument of this article rests on four propositions.

Proposition 1: The whole channel must be considered in making market servicing decisions. Firms will be aiming at servicing their final customers with appropriate

Earlier versions of this paper were given at the Escula de Empresariales, Granada, Spain, in March 1989 and at the ESRC Competitiveness Workshop, Lancaster, in February 1989 and we are grateful to participants for their constructive comments. We also wish to acknowledge the comments of Stephen Young and two anonymous *IMR* referees.

products. This entails the necessity to meet customer needs. 'Closeness to the customer' entails the optimum mix of location and internalization decisions throughout the channel.

Proposition 2: Once a part of the channel is externalized, downstream activities (towards the consumer) will not be internalized.

Proposition 3: Once a part of the channel is located abroad, there will be a tendency for downstream activities also to be located abroad.

Proposition 4: Control and monitoring of information is vital to the success of international channel management. The control and direction of information will be a major reason for internalization of key functions.

Qualifications

The above propositions are fairly strong assertions on the pattern of international market servicing and channel management. Proposition 2 is particularly strong. It would be disproved if the pattern in Figure 1 occurred with any regularity. A similar disproof would apply to Proposition 3, although there are likely to be exceptions to this rule. The first exception applies to multi-product firms. The channel for one individual product within a given product portfolio may include downstream activities located at home after upstream activities are foreign based if that facility was fundamentally designed for a separate product. The channel system of one product taken separately can thus 'piggy back' on another product's channel. The second exception concerns the subcontracting ('putting out') of routine production abroad for cost reasons—this is often termed 'offshore production'. This basic production can then be reintegrated into a channel which may have a domestic location. Third, there are important complementarities between functions which do not exist as totally independent entities (see below).

Figure 1. Pattern Leading to the Disproof of Proportion 2: Market Servicing Channel.

Examples

Figure 2 shows possible market servicing modes highlighting potential downstream expansion paths. In general the location of production predetermines the location of stockholding. Consequently, only in the case of exporting can firms choose to locate their stockholding activities domestically. On the issue of internalization versus externalization, the choice of using independent organizations at a particular stage in the process generally determines that all activities further down the chain will also be externalized. This interdependence between functions suggests that firms must treat the channel as a *whole* rather than as a series of independent units when foreign market servicing strategies

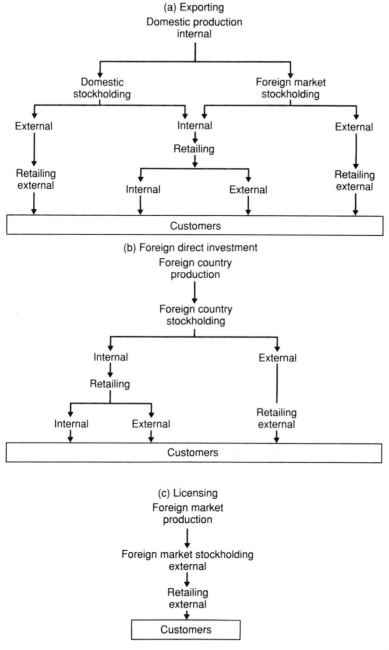

Figure 2. Schematic Diagrams of Typical Product Flows.

are developed. Although the diagrams in Figure 2 show decisions apparently emanating from the form of market servicing (i.e. exporting, licensing and foreign direct investment), important issues related to stockholding and retailing may, in turn, impinge on the location of production, determining the mode to be employed. It should be noted that particular factors specific to the firm and the market may result in certain levels of the channel being bypassed. What follows is an attempt to distinguish the factors which determine the decisions of location and internalization at the various stages in the process.

AN EXPOSITION OF BASIC CONCEPTS

Internalization

We can begin by envisaging the firm as an internalized bundle of resources which can be allocated (1) between product groups (changes in which are identified as conglomerate diversification) and (2) between national markets (expansion in this direction is multi-national diversification). The growth of the firm *relative to markets* is determined by its internalization decisions. The firm grows by replacing or creating neighbouring markets according to the (positive) balance between the benefits of internalization versus the costs in each instance. The growth of the firm, in this analysis, is determined by the superiority of the firm over the market (Buckley and Casson, 1976, 1981; Buckley, 1983a, 1988; Casson, 1987). In a shorter run, strategic context, internalization can be a weapon. Internalizing the market in key inputs (including technology) can represent a significant barrier to entry into the industry. The ability to use discriminatory pricing in an internal market allows a firm to cross-subsidize highly competitive markets where there is a fear of entry. Elimination of bilateral bargaining may further strengthen a firm relative to others faced with bargaining instability.

Further, internalization of markets across international frontiers allows the reduction of the firm's overall tax bill relative to firms which trade at arm's length. Consequently, internalization decisions can be a strategic weapon versus other firms in certain contexts. It is undeniable that certain managements will see internalization opportunities faster than others and may be more skilled at the evaluation of such opportunities. This will create differentials in the relative scope of firms with cost penalties for those with non-optimal scope (at a given point in time).

Location theory

Standard location theory assumes constant returns to scale, freely available and standardized technology, and that firms are price takers in all factor markets. Given such assumptions, firms choose their optimal location for each stage of production by evaluating regional production costs and choosing the set of locations for which the overall average cost of production is minimized. Regional production costs vary only according to regional differentials in non-tradeable goods (as the price of tradeables is standardized by trade), the relative prices of tradeables and non-tradeables and elasticities of substitution between pairs of non-tradeables and between tradeables and non-tradeables. Overall average production costs are minimized by the correct choice of the least cost 'route' from the location of raw materials through to the final market (Buckley and Casson, 1976, 1979).

For the purpose of explaining market servicing policies, the location of marketing services is crucial. Marketing may be considered to have four main constituents:

stockholding, distribution, generating new customers and promotion. The location of stockholding depends on the balance between the better quality of service provided by decentralized stockholding and the declining cost per unit of large, centralized ware-houses. Only above a certain market size is local stockholding efficient. Routine advertising and distribution are usually located in the final market. However, there is growing emphasis, in theory at least, on global advertising. Here, as elsewhere, there is a balance in the cost advantages of standardization versus the revenue advantages of adaptation to individual markets.

PRODUCTION

The location of production

At its most simple, exporting can be differentiated from licensing and foreign direct investment by the location effect. As with exports, the bulk of value adding activity takes place in the home country, whilst the other two methods transfer much of value adding activity to the host country. Arising out of standard location theory, much of the literature on choice of foreign market servicing mode (which is generally biased towards the location of production) is predominantly cost based. A number of theoretical models of the foreign market servicing strategy of firms are extant. They are almost entirely concerned with the switch from exporting to a foreign market to investing in it including the Product Cycle Approach (Vernon, 1966, 1974, 1979; see also Hirsch, 1976; Horst, 1971, 1972, 1974).

Internal versus external production

Licensing can be differentiated from exporting and foreign direct investment by the externalization effect (Davies, 1977; Buckley and Davies, 1980). Licensing represents a market sale of intermediate goods or corporate assets by the firm. In licensing the firm sells rights and the use of assets to a licensee. In exporting and foreign investment such activities are internalized (Buckley and Casson, 1976, 1985). Licensing generally takes place when firms possessing transferable competition advantages are unable to exploit the technology themselves—either due to limited available assets for foreign investment, or limited capacity to produce domestically for export, or a combination of both these factors. Alternatively, licensing may be the only available strategy where markets are protected by high tariffs, and limitations on investment.

Subcontracting of production is a clearly defined market relationship covering an agreement of one firm to purchase from another. Although such arrangements are, in ideal type, purely market based (externalized), linking purchaser to producer, in practice there is often an input from the purchaser to ensure that quality standards meet specification and often advice on methods of production is given. The factor means that violations to Proposition 2 are not absolute. Such 'production sharing' agreements usually involve sales in the purchasing firm's home market. Often, these arrangements are related to the tariff regulations in developed countries where producers from less developed countries, often located in free trade zones, carry out externalized production (Buckley, 1983b; Watanabe, 1971, 1972). Examples of international externalized production exist in textiles and electronic equipment including computers.

Foreign production: a summary

The simple differentiations between location effect and internalization are in practice highly complex. First, comparative costs are not easily calculable or obvious. In multi-product, process and functional firms, the internal division of labour and the costs associated with each activity are difficult to assess accurately. Further, there are many complex interactions between the activities involved. Location abroad of some activities will have effects on home costs and those of third countries within the firm's international network. Location decisions in the long run are examined by Dunning (1972), Casson (1985) and Buckley and Artisien (1987).

Second, the costs and benefits of internalization are nebulous and difficult to measure. Both sets of complications are entirely contingent on circumstances. The difficulty of these calculations is that the situation is dynamic and the determinants of choice of optimal market servicing strategies are continually shifting. Third, a major complicating factor in the analysis of foreign market servicing policies is that the forms are often complements, not substitutes. This fact means that a careful analysis of the relationship between modes is essential.

WHOLESALER/DISTRIBUTOR FUNCTIONS

The need for wholesaler/distributor functions in the channel

In international markets the need to include stockholding and physical distribution in the channel is generally perceived to be a result of manufacturer remoteness from the target market, both in physical and cultural terms, in addition to the more generally accepted functions of building bulk/breaking bulk which characterize domestic channel issues. The international perspective tends to suggest location of stockholding in a proximate location to the target market in order to minimize lead times and promote more efficient monitoring of demand through operating within the market where information gathering is facilitated. The latter point relates to product and target market characteristics widely discussed in channel management literature (for an example, see Christopher, 1972).

The location of wholesaler/distributor functions

The location of wholesaling/distributing, like that of production, is discussed in the international business literature in relation to costs.

The optimum *location* of inventory is dependent on (1) the ratio of stock to sales required to maintain a given quality of service to the customer (e.g. the time taken for a delivery from stock) is likely to decline as the warehouse turnover increases and (2) the technology of warehouse design favours the larger warehouse (e.g. the ratio of cubic capacity to surface area increases with size). These factors encourage the concentration of stockholding at just one location. Against these factors must be set the additional costs of distributing to the customer from a location remote from the market. The interplay of inventory and distribution costs will make local stockholding optimal for any volume of sales above a given critical level (Buckley and Casson, 1976).

A critical assumption of this analysis is that the quality of service to the customer is fixed. In certain circumstances of product/market conditions such an assumption cannot be justified. Remoteness may mean being out of touch with market needs. This may also be a factor in choosing a local stockholder who may be more in touch with local stockholding regulations and market needs. An alternative formulation of this problem is that of Berg (1971) who maps cost against time of delivery to give a total cost function including cost of lost sales, which is an increasing function of time.

The location of stockholding activities is inextricably interlinked with the location of production. Where foreign direct investment and licensing strategies are followed, then stockholding will necessarily be located in the host market. However, where exporting strategies are followed (i.e. production is based in the domestic market), the choice of location is not predetermined. The firm may choose to ship goods from domestically held stock, wherein the wholesaling/retailing function is internalized in the case of direct exporting (where the firm controls the exporting tasks) or, perhaps, externalized when indirect exporting modes are employed (stock being held by trading companies, joint export associations or the 'carrier' in piggyback exporting ventures) (Terpstra, 1983). Alternatively the firm may export goods to their own wholesaler/distributor in the host market, which may be tied in with a sales/marketing investment.

This is not to say, however, that the choice of production location is made independently of that of wholesaling/distributor location. Where competitive success relies on rapid delivery or 'just in time' delivery to retailers, the essential decision to stock goods abroad may have repercussions on the choice of production location.

It is dangerous to assume that the multinational firm has an unrestricted choice of mode and location of its wholesaler/dealer functions. Such activities face entry barriers such as the existence of established networks of dealers, the capital costs of establishments and external (including governmental) restriction on entry.

Internalization versus externalization of wholesaler/distribution functions

Like production, stock can be held internally or externalized to an independent wholesaler, distributor or stockholder. The choice of which form to follow depends primarily on five factors: (1) the relative costs of operation; (2) importance of market intelligence; (3) the perceived needs of the manufacturer to control operations; (4) host market infrastructure; (5) distinct competencies of the firm.

Relative costs

The balance between internalizing wholesaler/distributor functions rests on the heavy investment required to set up such functions versus the problems of constant renegotiation on price with existing external wholesalers. This can be resolved by examining the relative fixed and variable costs of each type of arrangement. The heavy fixed costs may deter firms from fully internalizing the function, particularly those firms sensitive to share price maintenance demands. However, a quasi-internalized channel may be a viable alternative when transaction costs can be reduced by the exercise of power within an administered channel by a dominant member (Brown, 1984; Diamantopoulos, 1987).

Market intelligence

In international operations, sensitivity to cultural and business differences in host markets is generally considered to be a key factor for success. An ability to understand and plan for these differences stems from the quality of market intelligence available to firms and the success with which it flows back to the decision-making locus within the manufacturing organization. Alternatively, successful implementation of business plans relies on forward information flows through the channel concerning strategic direction and product (differential advantages both actual and perceived). The wholesaler may then be seen as either a facilitator or a bottleneck for the flow of information through the channel, providing a link between the retailer/dealer and the manufacturer and indirectly between consumers and manufacturers. Information on demand fluctuations, retailer buyer behaviour, packaging, pricing and competitor activity may be directly available to wholesalers and information on consumer behaviour, reactions to promotion and product adaptation indirectly gathered through retailers. In addition the linkage between the manufacturer and wholesaler should allow the effective organization of inventory and production schedules.

Host country management who have experience in the particular foreign market may better understand the scope of information pertinent to decision making within their sector. There are three options facing manufacturers in this respect: (1) buying up this expertise through forward integration; (2) buying in this knowledge from outside in the event of greenfield operations; (3) utilizing the expertise of independents in relation to cultural and market understanding, perhaps at the expense of high quality information.

Manufacturer control

The major advantage of operating through an independent wholesaler is that the management of inventories and distribution is passed on, thus lowering manufacturer management costs (although costs will be incurred using this system in relation to monitoring of activities). One of the fundamental disadvantages is that the producer, in passing on the responsibility of these activities, also passes on control over them. Thus the producer must rely on the wholesaler/distributor stocking enough volume to serve retail demand, maintaining the quality of products in transit and storage, and also selling to the right retailers/dealers, that is, those who serve the market to whom the manufacturer's product is targeted. To some extent these problems may be overcome by the drawing up of contracts and agreements although others, often those arising from cultural distance and differences in management approach, may require the provision of additional support services which Munro and Beamish (1987) perceive as being a preferable alternative to increased compensation or threats. The expense incurred through providing support to intermediaries may diminish the cost-saving advantages of operating in this way.

Other factors may also impinge on the desire of manufacturers to control their own distribution operations. Firms may be more likely to invest resources when the product is a major contributor to their overall sales in order to enhance contact with clients/customers in the pursuit of additional sales (Davidson and McFetridge, 1985). Alternatively, where firms wish to protect patents in order to sustain a competitive advantage through technology or differentiation, they may be reluctant to operate via independent wholesalers, perceiving them as a potential source of 'leakage' (Anderson and Coughlan, 1987). Such issues are not, however, specific to international operations.

Host market infrastructure

The nature of the host market, particularly political and economic stability, may predetermine the form of channel to be employed. Government pressure on multinational firms to use indigenous channels, and legal restrictions on foreign direct investment, may diminish the choice of options available to firms. Indeed, firms may have no choice, being compelled by host governments to employ available resources in the form of independent wholesalers/distributors.

Competencies of the firm

Established distribution channels tend to determine the mode of distribution employed for the introduction of new products, i.e. if an integrated channel is already in place, the product will be sold through the existing arrangement, and independents will continue to be used where they are traditionally employed (Davidson and McFetridge, 1985). This also applies, to some extent, across borders. This is due to the management skills and competencies of head office personnel who, through their experience in managing either integrated or independent wholesale/distribution operations, will tend towards similar operations elsewhere in order to exploit existing skills.

RETAILING

The need for retailing in the channel

In consumer markets the need for retailing operations is generally determined by the wide geographic spread of consumers and the low value/high volume nature of purchases. In certain industrial markets, the need for a dealer network is determined by similar issues. In the case of high value 'big ticket' manufacturers, however, this level of channel intermediary may be bypassed in favour of selling directly to customers or shipping straight to customers ex-wholesale stock. These issues apply equally at both domestic and international levels. In an international context the important consideration is the form of channel traditionally employed in various overseas markets which tends to determine buyer behaviour. Where products are traditionally sold through a retailer/dealer network, bypassing this stage in the channel will necessitate customer 're-education' and specific benefits of purchasing offered by the alternative mode. This can prove a costly exercise, although it may prove preferable to competing head-on in highly competitive retail markets.

Internal versus external retail operations

The large number of outlets and the wide geographic spread necessary to serve retail demand make internalization of such operations costly and difficult to manage centrally. In addition the growing trend towards 'one-stop-shopping' in the consumer goods sector that originated in the USA but that is now spreading throughout the developed world, means that single manufacturers cannot provide the breadth of product range necessary to cater to this kind of buyer behaviour. In this respect, ownership of retail activities is rare in the area of consumer goods. In industrial markets, specialist dealers are perhaps more easily integrated by manufacturers, particularly those who manufacture a complementary range of products. Geographic dispersal of outlets may be less important for goods, as consumers are prepared to travel further for specialist equipment.

The level of product differentiation may affect the decision to internalize retail activities. It raises the need for specialized sales/marketing and servicing capabilities best served through integrated retail outlets. Anderson and Coughlan (1987) suggest that products which are highly differentiated and not perceived as substitutes by the consumer should be internalized, as alternative products do not compete directly: 'In contrast, non-differentiated products do compete directly, creating price-wars that drain the manufacturers' profits in integrated channels' (Anderson and Coughlan, 1987, p. 73).

Franchising retail distribution is a separate case, being an alternative mode of tying retailers to the manufacturer particularly where perceived differentiation is important to success. Here, ownership relates to patents, know-how, management style, brand-name, form and decor of retail outlets, etc. It permits manufacturers a certain degree of control over their franchisees, who are bound to work for the benefit of the producer, whilst minimizing investment outlay. The franchisor's compensation—a one-off fee, royalty on sales, rental/lease on equipment and fixtures, regular licence fee or share of profits (Kotler, 1984)—may mean that income per unit sale is lower than if they were to operate through alternative forms of market servicing. However, the opportunity to maximize the number and regional spread of their operations means that a wider market can be served, and thus the volume of sales compensates for low unit value. One of the major problems of operating a franchise system is that it relies on independent organizations to maintain the standards and quality designated by the manufacturer or service organization.

Another alternative way of tying 'retail' operations to the manufacturer is through catalogue sales. This is growing in importance in both consumer and industrial markets. In international markets this relies on establishing regional wholesalers or employing independents with a well-dispersed wholesale network, and the availability of, or resources to establish, a transport operation to ensure rapid delivery.

The flow of information through the channel may be greatly assisted through integrating retail operations. As manufacturers are provided with an opportunity to interface directly with their customers, detailed information on the specific needs and wants of the market, and scope for segmentation and adaptation, becomes easier to gather and assess. In the case of franchising these benefits will be diluted, as the successful flow of information depends on the adeptness of franchise managers to gather relevant information and pass it on to the manufacturer. With catalogue sales, although manufacturers may deal directly with consumers, the lack of face-to-face contact may similarly dilute the amount and quality of information. To what extent this factor determines the decision to integrate retail operations is not clear, although it would appear a secondary issue in the light of the limited number of manufacturers who have integrated forwards into retailing in the consumer sector, which is traditionally motivated by market research.

ASSOCIATED CHANNEL FUNCTIONS

Agents' functions, promotion and transport traverse the integrated model, feeding directly into the strategic decisions facing firms at different levels in the channel.

Agent functions

In most marketing channel systems there is a need, at some stage in the channel, for agents, whose primary function is to generate new business contacts. Typically agents and other similar intermediaries do not take title to the goods, they simply generate contacts. They may be used at the stage of the wholesaler/distributor to generate new retail customers or end-users or at the level of the manufacturer contacting end-users direct or finding new wholesalers to handle their products.

Internalization versus externalization of agents

The relative advantages/disadvantages of using independent agents as opposed to a company-controlled salesforce are well documented in the literature. In terms of cost: 'The fixed costs of engaging a sales agency are lower than those of establishing a company sales office. But costs rise faster through a sales agency because sales agents get a larger commission than company sales people' (Kotler, 1984).

The decision to use company-employed salesmen/agents may be influenced by the problems associated with dealing with agents. The problem of control of agents is a classic dilemma in economics, leading to the whole of the literature on principal-agent problems and agency theory, which is capable of a wide range of applications. (For a review see Thompson, 1988; the most influential model is that of Jensen and Meckling, 1976.)

The monitoring of the performance of salesmanship is fraught with difficulties (Nicholas, 1983, 1986). Ways of bonding the agent to the principal, through exclusive contracts, reward systems, etc., are measured as incentive systems against internal direction and provide a classic instance of contracts versus the market as the most efficient motivation. Means of holding hostages against good performance and systems for punishing bad performance in an external market must be set against internal systems of control (performance, special increments, etc.).

In an international context, the International Product Life Cycle proposes that as firms gain experience from operating abroad through using independent intermediaries, they are likely to invest in overseas facilities including sales and marketing functions (Vernon, 1966). This argument is derived from an assumed lack of knowledge on the part of manufacturers relating to cultural and business practices in the foreign market. However, independent agencies will have (often location-specific) skills and contacts with key purchasers. Local knowledge may not be available by buying in key individuals who may already be selling their services packaged into an agency. The reward for these individuals may be greater in selling their services to a number of principals rather than tied to the internal market of one (multinational) firm. In the long term, then, continuing to operate via independent firms may prove the optimal mode of generating new customers.

Promotion

Like the function of agents/salesmen, promotion can take place at different levels in the channel, and by different channel members. It is often assumed that promotion is only directed at consumers at the end of the channel. Within standard marketing systems, where channel functions are externalized, manufacturers operating through two stage channels (i.e. giving title to wholesalers who sell on to retailers who in turn sell to final customers) may find the need to target four different sets of promotional literature:

- information directed at wholesalers aimed at persuading them to stock their products;
- information for wholesalers to use in their agents'/salesforce's sales to retailers;
- promotional literature for retail outlets designed to persuade end-users to purchase their goods (as opposed to substitute products);
- direct advertising to end-users designed to generate demand.

The second and third elements in the list may be passed on to wholesalers and retailers in the transfer of title. The decision to pass on such responsibility may depend on the need to promote a standardized brand image, or the need to convey specialist information on technology or differential advantages to all members of the channel and the final customer. The co-ordination of promotion with the performance of other functions is crucial to competitive success. This process is highly information-intensive, and gathering relevant information on which promotional campaigns may be based is often perceived as facilitated by internalizing functions (i.e. production, wholesaling, retailing and sales/marketing).

Transport

The management of the transport function requires great skill and sensitivity because, uniquely, at some point it involves the transnational transfer of goods and usually of rights (see, in another context, Buckley, 1987). This may be when the final product is transferred to a foreign warehouse or where a domestic (central) warehouse exports to a foreign distributor or else where a direct distribution sale is made from home. The national boundary can impinge at any of these stages, as can the change of ownership (see also Graham, 1972).

Information flow is also of great importance to the planning of transportation modes: information on the modes of transport available, relative costings, feedback from drivers and shippers, and also consumers concerning their level of satisfaction with quality and delivery schedules. Once again, this kind of information is perhaps easier to collect where certain areas of the transport functions are internalized. The propensity of firms to integrate their transport functions will be influenced by the transport infrastructure available. In some less developed countries poor indigenous transport facilities may determine manufacturers establishing some kind of network of their own.

SYNTHESIS

Figure 3 is an attempt to encompass the key elements of the market servicing decision. The key functions are shown: production, which may be a multi-stage process, stockholding, distribution control, promotion, generating customers, transport and retailing. The flow of physical product runs through the production stages, distribution control and (possibly) retailing to the customer. These functions are linked therefore by flows of physical product but equally crucial are the flows of information between the functions which also tie in promotion and the generation of customers. These flows are difficult to ensure and secure in an externalized environment. Worries about secrecy, creating competitors, and misinformation argue for internalization. However, the local knowledge of agents (and their contacts) performing the role of generating customers and of external promotional agencies may counterbalance these arguments. Moreover agents and promoters may have specialized skills unavailable to (foreign) entrants. Consequently the internal/external decision must be taken on a case by case basis. It is, however, crucial to recognize the interdependence between the various functions shown in Figure 3. It is also the case that imperfect competition (monopoly, monopsony, bilateral monopoly) at one stage of production induces price distortions in this multi-stage process and creates an incentive for backward or forward integration (Buckley and Casson, 1976; Casson, 1985).

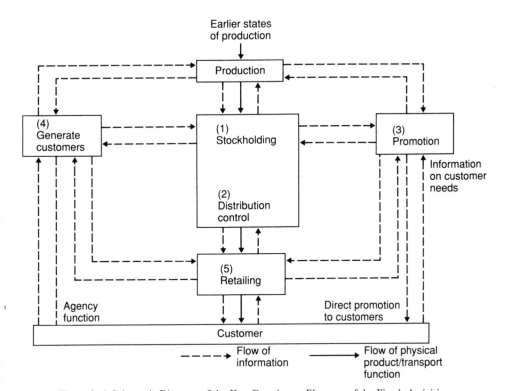

Figure 3. A Schematic Diagram of the Key Constituent Elements of the Firm's Activities.

Flows of information

The flows of information in Figure 3 are vital sources of competitive advantage. For instance, the flow of information from the retailer/customer interface can be the source of data on consumer tastes, preferences and selection between closely competing products. The retailer, then, may act as a facilitator or bottleneck for the flow of such information. His willingness to gather and forward relevant data depends, in part, on the importance of the manufacturer's brand within the product range he offers and the contribution it makes to turnover. Information feedback from the interface with the customer to distribution control, stockholding and eventually production is also a fundamental input into a marketing information system.

Consequently any analysis of the foreign market servicing decision must consider all the activities listed and the key elements determining their location and internal versus external performance. The activities cannot and should not be considered in isolation. It is the interrelationships and interdependencies between the activities which make the market servicing decision so complex. Because of the many factors affecting the configuration of activities, policies should be constantly under review.

CONCLUSION

The view expressed in this article is that the categorization of foreign market servicing strategies into exporting, licensing and foreign investment is too crude a division because it ignores the crucial role of channel management. Marketing costs cannot simply be aggregated as a lump: costs of distribution, stockholding, transport, promotion, retailing and generating new customers are radically different. The location and internalize/externalize (do or buy) decisions are as crucial for each of these functions as they are for production. An integrated treatment recognizing the interdependencies and cost implications of each function is essential for a complete conceptualization of the foreign market servicing decision. This necessitates an analysis of the crucial role of information flows between and among channel members, be they internal or external, foreign or domestic, and to possibilities of information blockage in the channel. This article has made a start in this important area. Grafting detail and regularities by type of firm and industry should enable empirical advances to take place in the field of foreign market servicing, sourcing and internationalization strategies.

REFERENCES

Anderson, E. and Coughlan, A. T. (1987). 'International Market Entry and Expansion via Independent or Integrated Channels of Distribution', *Journal of Marketing*, Vol. 51, January, pp. 71–82.

Berg, T. L. (1971), 'Designing the Distribution System', in Stevens, W. D. (Ed.), *The Social Responsibility of Marketing*, American Marketing Association, Chicago.

Brown, W. (1984), 'Firm-like Behaviour in Markets: The Administered Channel', *International Journal of Industrial Organisation*, Vol. 2, pp. 263–76.

Buckley, P. J. (1983a), 'New Theories of International Business: Some Unresolved Issues', in Casson, M. (Ed.), *The Growth of International Business*, George Allen & Unwin, London.

Buckley, P. J. (1983b), 'New Forms of International Co-operation: A Survey of the Literature', *Aussenwirtschaft*, Vol. 38 No. 2, June, pp. 195–222. Reprinted in Buckley and Casson (1985).

Buckley, P. J. (1987), 'An Economic Transactions Analysis of Tourism', *Tourism Management*, Vol. 8 No. 3, September, pp. 190–4.

Buckley, P. J. (1988), 'The Limits of Explanation: Testing the Internalisation Theory of the Multinational Enterprise', *Journal of International Business Studies*, Vol. XIX No. 2, Summer, pp. 181–93.

Buckley, P. J. and Artisien, P. F. R. (1987), *North-South Direct Investment in the European Communities*, Macmillan, London.

Buckley, P. J. and Casson, M. (1976), *The Future of the Multinational Enterprise*, Macmillan, London.

Buckley, P. J. and Casson, M. (1979), 'A Theory of International Operations', in Leontiades, J. and Ghertman, M. (Eds.), *European Research in International Business*, North Holland, Amsterdam.

Buckley, P. J. and Casson, M. (1981), 'The Optimal Timing of a Foreign Direct Investment', *Economic Journal*, Vol. 92 No. 361, March, pp. 75–81. Reprinted in Buckley and Casson (1985).

Buckley, P. J. and Casson, M. (1985), *The Economic Theory of the Multinational Enterprise: Selected Readings*, Macmillan, London.

Buckley, P. J. and Davies, H. (1980), 'Foreign Licensing in Overseas Operations: Theory and Evidence from the UK', *Technology Transfer and Economic Development*, JAI Press, Greenwich, Conn.

Casson, M. (1985), 'Multinationals and Intermediate Product Table', in Buckley, P. J. and Casson, M. (Eds.), *The Economic Theory of the Multinational Enterprise*, Macmillan, London.

Casson, M. (1987), *The Firm and the Market: Studies in Multinational Enterprise and the Scope of the Firm*, George Allen & Unwin, London.

Christopher, M. (1972), 'The Marketing Channel', in Christopher, M. and Wills, G. (Eds.), *Marketing Logistics and Distribution Planning*, George Allen & Unwin, London.

Davidson, W. H. and McFetridge, D. G. (1985), 'Key Characteristics in the Choice of International Technology Transfer Mode', *Journal of International Business Studies*, Vol. 11, Summer, pp. 5–21.

Davies, H. (1977), 'Technology Transfer through Commercial Transactions', *Journal of Industrial Economics*, Vol. 26 No. 4, pp. 161–75.

Diamantopoulos, A. (1987), Vertical Quasi-integration Revisited: The Role of Power', *Managerial and Decision Economics*, Vol. 8, pp. 185–94.

Dunning, J. H. (1972), *The Location of International Firms in an Enlarged EEC: An Exploratory Paper*, Manchester Statistical Society, Manchester.

Graham, M. G. (1972), 'The Through Transport Concept', in Christopher, M. and Wills, G. (Eds.), *Marketing Logistics and Distribution Planning*, George Allen & Unwin, London.

Hirsch, S. (1976), 'An International Trade and Investment Theory of the Firm', *Oxford Economic Papers*, Vol. 28, pp. 258–70.

Horst, T. D. (1971), 'The Theory of the Multinational Firm—Optimal Behaviour under Different Tariff and Tax Rates', *Journal of Political Economy*, Vol. 79, pp. 1059–72.

Horst, T. O. (1972), 'Firm and Industry Determinants of the Decision to Investment Abroad: An Empirical Study', *Review of Economics and Statistics*, Vol. 54, pp. 258–66.

Horst, T. O. (1974), 'The Theory of the Firm', in Dunning, J. H. (Ed.), *Economic Analysis and the Multinational Enterprise*, George Allen & Unwin, London.

Jensen, M. C. and Meckling, W. H. (1976), 'The Theory of the Firm: Managerial Behaviour, Agency Costs and Ownership Structure', *Journal of Financial Economics*, Vol. 3, pp. 305–60.

Kotler, P. (1984), *Marketing Management: Analysis, Planning and Control*, 5th ed., Prentice-Hall, Englewood Cliffs, NJ.

Munro, H. J. and Beamish, P. W. (1987), 'Distribution Methods and Export Performance', in Rosson, P. J. and Reid, S. D. (Eds.), *Managing Export Entry and Expansion*, Praeger, New York.

Nicholas, S. J. (1983), 'Agency Contracts, Institutional Modes and the Transition to Foreign Direct Investment by British Manufacturing Multinationals Before 1939', *Journal of Economic History*, Vol. 43, pp. 675–86.

Nicholas, S. J. (1986), *Multinationals, Transaction Costs and Choice of Institutional Form*, University of Reading Discussion Papers in International Investment and Business Studies, No. 97, December.

Terpstra, V. (1983), *International Marketing*, 3rd ed., Dryden Press, Chicago.

Thompson, S. (1988), 'Agency Costs of Internal Organisation', in Thompson, S. and Wright, M. (Eds.), *Internal Organisation, Efficiency and Profit*, Philip Allan, Oxford.

Vernon, R. (1966), 'International Investment and International Trade in the Product Cycle', *Quarterly Journal of Economics*, Vol. 80, pp. 190–207.

Vernon, R. (1974), 'The Location of Economic Activity', in Dunning, J. H. (Ed.), *Economic Analysis and the Multinational Enterprise*, George Allen & Unwin, London.

Vernon, R. (1979), 'The Product Cycle in a New International Environment', *Oxford Bulletin of Economics and Statistics*, Vol. 41, pp. 255–67.

Watanabe, S. (1971), 'Subcontracting, Industrialisation and Employment Creation', *International Labour Review*, Vol. 104, pp. 51–76.

Watanabe, S. (1972), 'International Subcontracting: Employment and Skill Promotion', *International Labour Review*, Vol. 106, pp. 425–49.

Part V

Scandinavian Applications

CONTENTS

20

Psychic Distance and Buyer–Seller Interaction

Lars Hallén and Finn Wiedersheim-Paul

1. INTRODUCTION

There is always a distance between a selling and a buying organization, both in a geographical and in a mental sense. There are distances in both these dimensions also between actors in the same organization. These distances will cause difficulties for the different types of flows between buyer and seller: flows like information, products, and money. Disturbances in the flows of products and money have been discussed by several authors, but less so factors disturbing or preventing the flows of information. In this article we will formulate definitions of different types of psychic distance and also state a dynamic model of psychic distance and its development.

Psychic distance is particularly important in the interaction approach to the study of marketing exchanges, where the creation and maintenance of long lasting links between buyer and seller are basic assumptions.

Below we will discuss some aspects of this distance or closeness between buyers and sellers. The idea of closeness in industrial markets is seen as connected with the situation (or 'atmosphere') within specific buyer-seller dyads. The concept has also been analysed and defined on more general levels, however. Our discussion therefore will be focused on distance at different levels of specificity, i.e. with respect to the degree of individualization of the identification of the parties.

2. PSYCHIC DISTANCE—DEFINITION AND EXAMPLES

The internationalization of firms often takes place gradually. When the need to go beyond the local market develops, expansion is often initiated by selling to customers that are situated closely to the local market. Initially the growth is a type of 'internationalization at home', i.e. a domestic expansion process. Later on exports will occur.

As mentioned above, it is not just the geographical distance but also other factors that are of importance when measuring distance. On an inter-country level concepts and

Lars Hallén, member of the IM Group, is a Ph.D. candidate in marketing and Lecturer at the Department of Business Administration at the University of Uppsala.

Finn Wiedersheim-Paul, member of the IM Group, is a Ph.D. in international business where he also currently is doing research. He is Chairman of the Centre for International Business Studies at the Department of Business Administration, University of Uppsala.

Lars Hallén og Finn Wiedersheim-Paul: *Organisasjon, Marked og Samfund*, Vol 16, No 5, pp 308–324, reprinted with permission
Copyright © 1979 Organisasjon, Marked og Samfund

measurements have been developed by Vahlne and Wiedersheim-Paul (1973, Chs 3 and 4). They use the term 'psychic distance' to denote those factors which inhibit trade between countries in a wide sense. As indicators they have used the level of development and its difference to the selling country, the level of education and its difference to the selling country and the difference in business and everyday languages. These factors have been selected due to the observation that the levels of development and education must have reached a certain minimum level in order to allow trade to take place. Furthermore it has been observed that trade is favoured between countries of roughly the same level of development (Burenstam-Linder, 1961), i.e. the difference between them should not be too big, and this is also the case regarding the effects of the language differences. By means of statistical analysis a great number of countries have been ranked with respect to this psychic distance from Sweden.

So far we have not made a strict definition of psychic distance. In order to do so we first need a definition of marketing. We define marketing in a general sense as the activities used for 'bridging the gap' between buyer and seller. This gap can be defined in several ways. We have chosen to utilize *different perceptions*:

(1) the buyer's perception of his own need (i.e. his 'ideal solution');
(2) the buyer's perception of the seller's offer;
(3) the seller's perception of his own offer;
(4) the seller's perception of the buyer's need.

In these definitions we have assumed that the different perceptions do exist, i.e. the seller has a perception (a picture) of the buyer's need in a specific situation. The 'perception' is really a package of perceptions in different dimensions such as product quality, service, price, and ability to deliver.

We have not assumed that the buyer's and the seller's perception packages will contain the same dimensions. Rather incongruity between the packages will be an important feature of the gaps discussed below.

This means that Figure 1 (below) only is intended as a very simple illustration of the rare case when the perceptions only exist in one common dimension or when it has been possible to translate them to one dimension.

Using the four definitions of perceptions given above we can now define two types of gaps:

—marketing gaps
—psychic distance.

These gaps are illustrated in Figure 1.

As indicated in Figure 1 there are two types of marketing gaps

—*marketing gap* (S) which denotes the difference between perceptions 3 and 4 above and indicates the gap between buyer and seller as perceived by the seller.
—*marketing gap* (B) which denotes the difference between perceptions 1 and 2 above and indicates the gap between buyer and seller as perceived by the buyer.

Marketing gap (S) will form the basis for the seller's marketing behaviour. It is not a correct basis, because the buyer's buying behaviour will be influenced by marketing gap (B).

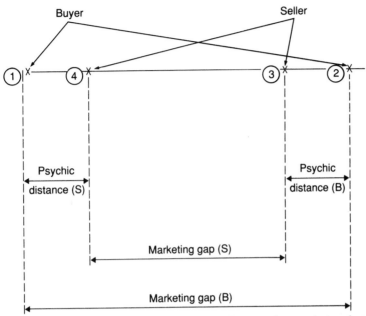

This figure illustrates the very specific situation where the perceptions can be transformed to one dimension. In all real situations a multidimensional illustration would be necessary. The numbers refer to the four different perceptions defined in the text.

Figure 1. Illustration of Gaps Between Perceptions.

In this article we are not going to discuss these marketing gaps and their consequences for marketing behaviour in any detail. Instead we will concentrate on the 'marketing disturbance component' labelled psychic distance. The difference between the two marketing gaps is explained by the psychic distance which is defined as consisting of two components:

A. Different perception of needs

The difference between the seller's perception of the buyer's need and the buyer's perception of his own need (4 and 1).
This is psychic distance with particular relevance for the seller, *psychic distance (S)*.

B. Different perception of offers

—The difference between the buyer's perception of the seller's offer and the seller's perception of his own offer (2 and 3).
This is psychic distance with particular relevance for the buyer, *psychic distance (B)*.

It will be obvious from these definitions that psychic distance is a measure of the difficulty a seller has to perceive or estimate the needs of a buyer or the corresponding difficulty a buyer experiences in perceiving the seller's offer.

Psychic distance (S) and psychic distance (B) will be labelled *inter-firm distances*. On the analogy of their definition we will also create two other measures:

—*inter-country distances*, which will denote the psychic distance between two countries, i.e. the difference between the perceptions of an average firm in one country as seen by foreign and by domestic businessmen.

—*intra-firm distances* which will denote the psychic distances between any two actors in each of the organizations, i.e. the difference between the perceptions of a counterpart as seen by different people in the same firm.

It should be observed, that psychic distances will occur within organizations as well as between organizations. This follows from the fact that we have defined psychic distance as a difference in perceptions.

These three definitions of psychic distance will later in this article form the basis for a dynamic model of psychic distance. But let us first give some more examples of psychic distance 'in action', which will indicate the type of factors causing psychic distances to occur. Also, some examples of such factors were mentioned on page 292 of the article.

Inter-country and inter-firm distances—an example

Within the framework of established international buyer-seller relationships there is not necessarily a correspondence between the intercountry psychic distance and the distance or closeness that characterizes the inter-firm relationship. The relationship between a Swedish equipment producing firm and its French supplier of a certain quality of steel may exemplify this. Compared to other major countries in Western Europe France is perceived by many Swedish businessmen as a country which it is difficult to deal with. There are not only language difficulties (Swedes seldom speak French, and Frenchmen often give the impression of just reluctantly accepting other languages than their own), but there are also differences in business culture (e.g. Frenchmen are believed to favour centralized and formal procedures, whereas Swedes are seen to be more flexible and informal). Furthermore, both Swedes and Frenchmen sometimes have a tendency of considering their own technical standards self-evidently superior to foreign ones and consequently mistrusting other solutions. (See Hallén 1980.)

The Swedish firm of our example has bought its raw material from the French supplier—one of the major French steel works—since the mid 60's. On the average one third of the Swedish firm's needs has been covered by deliveries from the French steel works, but lately it has expanded its share of the Swedish firm's needs to 100%. This is against the will of the French firm—they want to reduce their share to 50% in order not to make the Swedish firm too dependent. The relationship runs extremely smoothly: the Swedes have almost never made any complaints, deliveries arrive regularly every month, and there are good personal contacts both between the marketers and purchasers and between the technical and laboratory personnel of the two firms. There is a long-term contract between the firms since 1974, but previously there were no contracts. The purchasing manager of the Swedish firm considers this contract unnecessary and means that the situation could be handled as well also before the contract was concluded. 'Contracts', he said, 'are papers that are intended for people who are not honest. Instead of legal procedures we rely upon common sense.' The inter-firm atmosphere thus renders the cultural differences unimportant. 'We do not speak French', the Swedish purchasing manager said. 'We can just say, "je t'aime", and that is sufficient.'

Inter-country distance: the firm-to-country difference

The method of analysis used by Vahlne and Wiedersheim-Paul (1973) implies that the study focuses on the impact on company behaviour of conditions on the national level. This approach is of special interest when the analysis is concerned with processes that cover long time spans, e.g. the internationalization process of Swedish firms in the 20th century. The inter-firm differences are suppressed in the analysis, and this may be a correct way of handling the problem given that no crucial inter-firm differences are present. This is in a way so: looking at a long perspective it is clear that once a firm had e.g. no exporting experience, which makes it comparable to other inexperienced firms in that respect.

Utilizing the measures developed by Vahlne and Wiedersheim-Paul (1973), the internationalization process of individual firms, i.e. the order in which establishments of selling and producing subsidiaries have taken place in various countries, has been compared to the computed values of psychic distance to the countries in question. Similarities and dissimilarities in the internationalization process of individual firms were observed and analysed (see Johanson and Wiedersheim-Paul, 1975).

Håkansson and Wootz (1975) have examined the selection of suppliers in an international context. Purchasers have chosen suppliers for certain products in a quasi-experimental situation. The suppliers have been identified with information about size and address etc, and based on the purchasers' decisions conclusions have been made regarding the tendency to select suppliers from countries at different psychic distances when certain variations in price and quality separate the offers from each other. The psychic distance between the purchasing firms in Sweden and their foreign suppliers is analysed on the company level, but it is only the buying firms, i.e. the firms where the participants of the experiment are to be found, that are actual ones: the counterpart is an abstraction, with whom the buyers thus have no personal experience. The analysis of the psychic distance is inferred from the purchasers' reactions to the relative importance of price and quality differences when buying from abroad. Their behaviour is considered to be based upon their general experience of foreign suppliers. It can thus be argued that the analysis is made on the company level as seen from the buying side but on the country level as seen from the selling side.

The conclusions of the study by Håkansson and Wootz are compatible with Vahlne and Wiedersheim-Paul's results insofar as the domestic market and Britain/Germany were considered to be closer to Sweden than France/Italy. This is what might have been expected, as the counterpart is defined abstractly, although using different indicators.

Inter-firm distances and total image

The interaction approach to the study of buyer-seller relationships in industrial markets implies that there is an interaction process between individual identified parties. This forms the buying and the selling behaviour. The trust that may have developed between the parties within a specific relationship due to previous contacts in connection with deliveries or other activities before or after earlier transactions has a profound influence on behaviour. These processes have been studied in an international setting by the researchers participating in the IMP Project (see Håkansson, 1980). The distance between sellers and buyers are here studied at two different levels. Firstly, the opinions of counterparts in general in five Western European countries are mapped. Secondly, the relation to one specific supplier or purchaser is investigated. The number of relationships mapped in this way exceeds 900.

An analysis of distance between buyers and sellers based on the first of the two approaches that are used in the IMP Project is reported by Hallén (1980). In contrast to the mentioned studies by Vahlne and Wiedersheim-Paul (1973) and Håkansson and

Wootz (1975) the analysis here deals with actual firms on the perceiving as well as on the perceived side. But as the respondents have expressed their opinions of their actual suppliers or customers in general, total images are obtained. The experience of incidents and episodes within one specific buyer-seller relationship, which certainly has formed the opinion to a high extent, still cannot be observed directly. The counterpart is an aggregate, although an aggregate of actual firms.

A rather crude measure has been applied in the determination of the psychic distance in this context. The respondent's opinions of difficulties in communication due to language problems, of difficulties to make friends with the personnel in the other firm, and their feeling of being understood by their customers/suppliers in the other country were expressed on a five-point scale and added with each other into an index. The five-country design of the study gives the opportunity to analyse this distance also from other viewpoints than Sweden. This analysis shows that some countries seem to be more 'distant' than others both according to their own opinions and according to the opinion of their foreign business partners. Thus Italy seems to be the most isolated country of the group of five countries (Sweden, W. Germany, Britain, France, and Italy), and Sweden actually seems to be most integrated in the group, although the other four are members of the European Communities and Sweden is not. Another observation from the analysis is that purchasers generally consider the distance to be shorter than the marketers. A possible reason for this is that marketers more often take upon them the task to bridge the gap between buyer and seller than purchasers do, which might make the marketers more aware of the distance that may exist. Also, the observation stresses the important fact that psychic distance between two parties is asymmetrical.

Inter-firm distance and atmosphere

For a deeper understanding of the psychic distance in an international setting it is probably necessary to conduct the analysis on a firm-to-firm level. The interaction between buyer and seller leads to the development of an 'atmosphere', which can be described in terms of closeness/distance, conflict/co-operation, and power/dependence. The closeness or distance between the parties in a buyer-seller dyad is conditioned by characteristics of the interacting firms and the interaction processes as well as environmental factors. In the approaches described above these environmental factors have played quite a dominating role, but their importance in the company specific analysis is reduced to one factor group amongst others. Its importance for the development of an atmosphere characterized by 'closeness' between the parties is often secondary to the effects of the interaction processes, e.g. the adaptations and the role institutionalization that takes place within an ongoing relationship. A Swedish firm may experience a greater distance to another Swedish firm than to an established British supplier, in spite of the language and spatial gaps between Sweden and Britain. The access to informal communication channels to the foreign firm may be an indication of such 'closeness'.

Interaction processes between marketers and purchasers of the two firms in a buyer-seller dyad may bring these individuals together in a way that makes them feel as representatives of a common buying-selling organization rather than of their respective firms. Thus, the inter-firm distance, i.e. the distance between the two firms, in certain situations is shorter than the intra-firm distance between the selling or buying function and other involved functions of the concerned firms. The phenomenon of 'side-changing' mentioned by Ford (1979) where employees of one company in a buyer-seller dyad act in the interest of the other company may be seen as an extreme example of short inter-firm distance coupled with certain intra-firm distances.

Inter-firm and intra-firm distances—an example

In order to further clarify the various concepts of distance we will use a case description of the relations between a Swedish firm ('Nya Mekaniska Verkstaden', NMV) and a large French mining company, which we may call 'Union des Montagnes Métallifères', UMM. The Swedish firm is rather small and is specialized in the production of capital equipment for use in the mining industry. In 1962 the first drilling equipment was sold by NMV to UMM as a result of an ambitious campaign by NMV to establish itself as a company with world-wide sales. Based on advertising in professional journals all over the world NMV wanted to create a basis for expanded production by means of acquiring sales in other countries than the domestic market, to which most of its sales had gone before. This general approach to export marketing turned out to be too resource demanding, and therefore NMV decided to concentrate its marketing efforts to some ten countries. One of these countries was France, where a sales subsidiary was established in order to take care of contacts with prospective buyers of NMV's products. As the number of mining companies in France is rather limited (NMV believes that there are about 50 firms) contacts have been established with almost all of them, and about 20 firms in France more or less regularly buy NMV's drilling equipment. But a very large share of NMV's total sales to the French firms is bought by its largest French customer: UMM. Between 25 and 50 per cent of NMV's French sales have during the last years gone to UMM.

From the very beginning NMV tried to get into contact with technicians and production managers in UMM rather than to negotiate through UMM's purchasing department. NMV considers its product to have two major advantages compared to competing equipment: it considerably improves the working environment for the miners, and it increases the speed of the operations. Both these arguments impress upon production managers, NMV believes.

During the period between 1962 and 1975 NMV thus established what they considered to be a strong position as a supplier of mining equipment and spare parts to UMM. But during 1975 and 1976 production costs rose in Sweden, and NMV raised their prices with more than 80% during the three years 1975/77. This did not at all please the purchasing department at UMM. As far as NMV was able to find out, a decision was made centrally by the top management at UMM that NMV should be 'black-listed', i.e. nothing was to be bought from NMV, neither complete units nor spare parts.

This decision created problems for two of the involved parties. First of all it naturally worried the marketers at NMV. But it also annoyed the production department at UMM. They needed spare parts from NMV for their equipment, and they did not want to change from NMV's equipment to substitutes as UMM's technicians considered those inferior. Therefore, they continued to order from NMV, and after some time they also resumed purchasing new equipment. The black-listing may still formally be in force, but it seems to have turned into a dead letter. At present, UMM buys two or three units of equipment every year from NMV, and there are good relations between the firms, particularly between NMV's marketers and UMM's technicians. NMV tries to obtain a situation where decisions are made at the purchasing department in UMM, but as a NMV marketer put it: 'We would not make any extreme efforts in order to get hold of one of their purchasers.'

An analysis of this mini-case shows us that factors relating to 'distance' have been of importance in several instances. Firstly, there is the inter-country distance. The Swedish firm NMV did not inform UMM in advance of their plans to raise prices, and they also let these prices rise so as to compensate Swedish cost increases fully. It did not occur to the Swedes to negotiate this with the French purchasing unit, probably because they felt that the 'real' decision-makers in the French firm were not the purchasers but the production engineers. The Swedish marketers characterized the French purchasers of UMM as 'very French Frenchmen', and by this they meant that they found them aloof and secretive. Thus, there are clear differences in behaviour and expectations between the Swedes and the Frenchmen, and this may have been one of the major reasons to the development that led up to the black-listing.

Secondly, there is the inter-firm distance—the state of the inter-firm relationship in terms of conflict/co-operation, closeness/distance, and power/dependence. The production engineers of UMM seemed to consider themselves to have interests that were compatible with NMV's, and they were also dependent on NMV for spare parts for uninterrupted production.

In terms of closeness/distance UMM's production unit can be said to be rather close to NMV, as five of roughly ten persons from UMM with regular contacts with NMV were technicians. Only one regular contact came from UMM's purchasing unit. The total atmosphere of the relationship was thus characterized not only by cultural differences but also by similarities in terms of perceived needs of co-operation and of dependence. The inter-firm distance was shorter than the inter-country distance.

Thirdly, the case gives an example of the difference between intra-firm and inter-firm distances. As seen from NMV (which is the source of information) the purchasing department of UMM had not very good contacts with their own production people, although the purchasing unit was believed to have a high status in the French firm. The outcome of the crisis seems to indicate that the purchasing unit of UMM with its 'black-listing' were more distant from the actual decision-making and actions of their own organization than NMV's marketers were.

3. A DYNAMIC MODEL OF PSYCHIC DISTANCE

We are now in a position to develop a model of psychic distance and its implications for firms, based on the definitions given earlier and the different examples presented above. In this model we will study the changing impact of psychic distance in the development process of a buyer-seller relation where the parties are located in different environments. In order to simplify the discussion we assume that these environments are two different countries. The development of different types of psychic distance is of course a continuous process but in order to simplify the discussion below we have chosen to identify the following three stages:

pre-contact stage
initial interaction stage
maturing interaction stage.

During the first stage the seller has not yet any contacts with the buyer. In the extreme case when the seller is in the position to enter the export market for the first time the inter-country distance will be the relevant measure of psychic distance. This means that the difference between the buyer's and the seller's perception of the relevant need of the buyer (psychic distance (S)) will mainly be determined by factors on a national level, e.g. differences in language, level of development and level of education between the countries in question.

The same would be true for a potential buyer; his perception of the unknown seller's offer would be determined by his perception of the seller's country of origin (unless the buyer has some previous experience of other sellers in this country).

In those cases where the seller has exported to the specific country or to other countries the psychic distance will consist not only of the intercountry component but also to some extent of distance more on the interfirm level. Two cases would be rather common:

— The seller has other customers in the specific country. In this situation a kind of *halo* effect will occur; the new customer belongs to the same family, as it were.
— The seller has a representative/agent selling to the specific country. In this case much of the psychic distance between seller and potential customer will consist of the inter-firm distance between seller and representative/agent.

This latter case contains a number of sub-cases: the representative/agent is located in the same country as the seller or the representative/agent is located in the specific foreign market. These situations will reflect a choice, intentional or unintentional, in locating the psychic distance. In the first situation most of the psychic distance will occur between representative/agent and the market, in the second situation most of the distance will occur between seller and representative/agent. It is of course impossible to state *the* best solution, but the discussion in Johanson (1972) will give some indication.

A related case is when the seller uses a representative in a third country for marketing in a specific country. An example would be the use of trading houses in London for approaching present or former Commonwealth countries. It is to be expected that this deviation via third country would result in a shorter psychic distance than if a representative in the seller's or the buyer's country were chosen.

In the initial interaction phase there has been a first contact between seller and buyer and this contact has resulted in a purchase. The psychic distance between the two firms will consist of a mixture of inter-country and inter-firm distances. The impact of the inter-country distance will still be comparatively strong but the importance will gradually shift to the inter-firm distance at the same time as this factor changes. The process is illustrated in Figure 2.

According to this illustration the interaction between buyer and seller may start with any of the factors purchase, information or trust. A 'normal' course of events would perhaps start with information, leading to trust, leading to purchase. The psychic distance plays different roles in this process. Apart from disturbing or preventing the start of the process, it slows down or prevents information from resulting in trust and trust in leading to purchase. But if the barrier between information and trust or between trust and purchase has been passed it will in itself be changed.

In some cases the psychic distance will increase, causing the interaction process to end. In other cases it will decrease leading to a more intensive interaction process. The development of the inter-firm psychic distance will also have an impact on the inter-country distance; the 'image' of a country will improve if there are improving relations with a firm in that country.

If the initial contacts between two firms will develop into an interaction process (and if so at what speed) also depends on the buyer's perception of the initial state and the subsequent changes of the uncertainty variables: need uncertainty, market uncertainty, and transaction uncertainty (Håkansson, Johanson and Wootz, 1977). High need uncertainty, indicating a considerable perceived difficulty for the buyer to interpret the

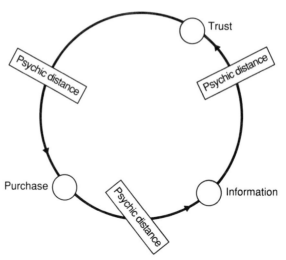

Figure 2. Interaction and Psychic Distance.

exact nature of the need for which a functional solution is required, would thus mean a large initial inter-firm psychic distance and a slow decrease in this distance. We will not penetrate these problems here, however.

If the relations between buyer and seller continue we will gradually move into the maturing interaction stage. In this phase, it is assumed that the elements that are exchanged within the transaction episodes (the product and/or service, the information, the means of payment, the social elements) eventually will lead to adaptations between the parties in terms of e.g. product modifications, special inventories, changed administration routines or the establishment of informal communication channels and the development of liking and trust between individuals of the concerned firms. This development will cause the inter-firm distance between buyer and seller to decrease but other effects will also occur. The informal contacts and the trust that may be present within well established relations often have the effect of raising barriers to entry against new partners, i.e. the inter-firm distances towards these potential sellers will increase.

The close relation between buyer and seller may result in the intra-firm distances becoming important, e.g. employees in the selling firm working in close contact with the buying firm may feel split loyalties between the two parties. In this maturing interaction stage the different perceptions illustrated in Figure 1 tend to be close together but not totally coinciding. A coincidence would be impossible due to differences between individuals and the continuous change in the problem situation.

4. CONCLUDING REMARKS

Our discussion of the different 'levels' or 'approaches' to the concept of inter-country and inter-firm psychic distance and degree of closeness in the interaction atmosphere is intended to illuminate when these differently defined concepts are applicable. In this concluding section we will focus upon two categories of marketing situations, viz. (1) the differences between the marketing of consumer goods and the marketing of industrial goods and (2) the difference between the initiation and the continuation of buyer-seller relationships in markets for producer goods.

The inter-country differences are likely to be more important in consumer goods marketing than in industrial marketing, whereas the inter-firm distance to a higher extent affects industrial marketing. Cultural idiosyncracies probably are of considerable import-ance for the purchasing decisions of households and other end-consumers. Here subtle aspects of marketing such as design, ways of distribution and 'image' may mean the difference between success and failure, and thus it may be difficult to operate in a culturally distant market. As mass marketing is the norm for consumer goods the necessary 'feeling' for the right approach to the market cannot be replaced by the development of special relations to selected customers. For an analysis of consumer goods situations the concept of 'psychic distance' on the intercountry level thus may prove useful.

It is an over-simplification, however, to state that the dividing line between the applicability of the 'general' level of distance as opposed to the 'specific' distance within the framework of a buyer-seller dyad coincides with the dividing line between marketing to individual end consumers and marketing to organizations. The interaction approach to marketing deals primarily with the development of existing customer relations; the initiation of a relationship is seen as a 'special case'. Before there is any relation between the firms, there is not either any 'atmosphere' that may act to compensate for cultural differences between the seller and his prospective buyer. Thus, the general concept of 'psychic distance' also is applicable for the analysis of the industrial marketing problem in new markets. The studies of the internationalization process of Swedish firms mentioned above take as a starting point the situation when most firms were domestically oriented and the gradual penetration of foreign markets is analysed against the background of inter-country differences. This first phase of future interaction processes with customers abroad is often approached with marketing tools that can be classified as belonging to the marketing mix 'tool kit'. The Swedish firm NMV of our final example above approached the French market with advertisements in professional journals. Here the psychic distance in a general sense may affect the outcome of the attempts to market entry. But in later stages of buyer-seller relationships the inter-firm aspects may turn into the dominant feature of the distance/closeness question. Here an analysis of the marketing problems may better be conducted using the interaction approach.

The ongoing discussion in Sweden whether Swedes are bad international marketers or not is to a large extent a question of psychic distance between Swedish marketers and their foreign customers. Consequently, the discussion would improve if a distinction was made between the ability to create a new relation and the ability to maintain a stable relation. According to recent studies (Phillips-Martinsson, 1979 and Hallén, 1980) the first mentioned ability is perhaps inferior to the second one. If this is correct it may cause considerable difficulties in the long run, as the ability to create new relations may become comparatively more important. This is one aspect of the domain problem of the firm, i.e. the problem to select the directions of future expansion: new customers, new knowledge, new products or what? (Wiedersheim-Paul and Erland, 1979; Wiedersheim-Paul, 1979).

There may also develop new types of distance problems, viz. the perception of possible internal distances within each firm. The institutionalization of roles, e.g. the boundary-spanning roles of the purchasers and marketers of the two organizations involved in a transaction, may create a feeling that they represent their common 'buyer-seller unit' rather than their respective firms. A reduction of inter-company distance may be obtained at the expense of intra-firm distances.

REFERENCES

Burenstam-Linder, S. (1961), *An Essay on Trade and Transformation.* Almqvist and Wiksell, Uppsala.

Ford, D. (1980), Developing Buyer-Seller Relationships in Export Marketing. *Organisation,* Marknad och Samhälle, vol. 16, No. 5.

Håkansson, H., (ed.), 1980, *Industrial Marketing and Purchasing in Europe. An Interaction Approach.* Forthcoming.

Håkansson, H. and Wootz, B. (1975), Supplier Selection in an International Environment. *Journal of Marketing Research,* Vol. XII (Feb), pp. 46–51.

Håkansson, H., Johanson, J. and Wootz, B. (1977), Influence Tactics in Buyer-Seller Processes. *Industrial Marketing Management,* Vol. 5, pp. 319–332.

Hallén, L. (1980), Sverige på Europamarknaden. *Studentlitteratur,* Lund.

Johanson, J. (1972), Fasta affärsförbindelser vid export. En jämförelse mellan olika exportkanaler. In: Johanson, J. (ed), *Exportstrategiska problem.* Stockholm.

Johanson, J. and Wiedersheim-Paul, F. (1975), The Internationalization of the Firm—Four Swedish Cases. *Journal of Management Studies,* October.

Phillips-Martinsson, J. (1979), *Cross-Cultural Relations in International Marketing.* Stockholm.

Vahlne, J.-E. and Wiedersheim-Paul, F. (1973), Ekonomiskt avstånd—modell och empirisk undersökning. In: Hörnell, E., Vahlne, J.-E. and Wiedersheim-Paul, F. *Export och utlandsetableringar.* Almqvist and Wiksell, Stockholm.

Wiedersheim-Paul, F. (1979), Towards a Model of International Marketing. In: Ståhl, I. (ed.), *Forskning, utbildning, praxis.* EFI, Stockholm.

Wiedersheim-Paul, F. and Erland, O. (1979), Technological Strategies and Internationalization. In: Mattsson, L.-G. and Wiedersheim-Paul, F. (eds.), *Recent Research on the Internationalization of Business.* Almqvist and Wiksell, Uppsala.

21

Internationalization in Industrial Systems—A Network Approach

Jan Johanson and Lars-Gunnar Mattsson

1. INTRODUCTION

The theme of the book suggests that international interdependence between firms and within industries is of great and increasing importance. Analyses of international trade, international investments, industrial organization and international business behaviour attempt to describe, explain and give advice about these interdependencies. The theoretical bases and the level of aggregation of such analyses are naturally quite varied.

In this chapter we discuss explanations of internationalization of industrial firms with the aid of a model that describes industrial markets as networks of relationships between firms. The reason for this exercise is a belief that the network model, being superior to some other models of 'markets', makes it possible to consider some important interdependencies and development processes on international markets. The models that we have selected for some comparative analyses are the transaction cost based 'theory of internationalization' for multinational enterprise and the 'Uppsala Internationalization Process Model' emphasizing experiential learning and gradual commitments. While the former is a dominating theoretical explanation of multinational enterprise (Buckley and Casson, 1976), the latter seems to be the most cited explanation of a firm's foreign market selection and mode of international resource transfer over time (Bilkey, 1978; Johanson and Vahlne, 1977).

We will first present some empirical data in support of some basic assumptions of the network model. We will then describe this model, commenting especially on the investment nature of marketing activities. Internationalization of the firm and of the network is also given a conceptual interpretation. We are then in a position to analyse four cases concerning internationalization of the firm and of the network. The Early Starter, The Lonely International, The Later Starter and The International Among Others. Finally, we will comment on some research issues raised by our analysis.

2. CUSTOMER-SUPPLIER RELATIONSHIPS IN INDUSTRIAL MARKETS: SOME EMPIRICAL FINDINGS

A number of studies in industrial marketing and purchasing have demonstrated the existence of long-term relationships between suppliers and customers in industrial markets (e.g. Blois, 1972; Ford, 1978; Guillet de Monthoux, 1975; Håkansson and Östberg, 1975; Levitt, 1983; Wind, 1970). It has also been emphasized by a leading marketing scholar that 'for strategic purposes, the central focus of industrial marketing should not be on products or on markets, broadly defined, but on buyer-seller relationships' (Webster, 1979, p. 50). Such relationships have also been noted in studies of contractual relations (Macneil, 1978; Williamson, 1979) and in studies of technical development (von Hippel, 1978).

In an extensive international research project, industrial customer-supplier relationships were investigated. Interviews were made with industrial suppliers in Germany, France, Britain, and Sweden about the relations to their most important customers in the four countries and in Italy. Interviews were conducted with managers who had personal experience of the customers (Håkansson, 1982). Business transactions with important customers generally took place within well-established relationships. The average age of the 300 relations investigated was around 13 years (Hallén, 1986). The relationships were important to the two parties involved. In export relationships the suppliers were 'main supplier'—in the sense that they provided at least half of the customer's needs for the products concerned—in about half of the cases. In the domestic relationships the suppliers were more often main suppliers—in around 80% of the relationships.

The customers were also important to the suppliers. In the German sub-sample in which data about the customer's share of the supplier's sales are available, the average share of the customers investigated was 5.5%. If we (somewhat arbitrarily) define a relationship as important to the customer if the supplier provides at least half of the need, and important to the supplier if the customer purchases at least 1% of the supplier's sales, then 35% of the relationships are classified as mutually important, 25% as important to the supplier only, 18% as important to the customer only, and 22% as not important.

One of the reasons for the existence of long-term relationships is that suppliers and customers need extensive knowledge about each other if they are to carry on important business with each other. They need knowledge not only about price and quality, which may be very complex and difficult to determine; they also need knowledge about deliveries and a number of services before, during and after delivery. Much of that knowledge can in fact only be gained after transactions have taken place. Besides, they need knowledge about each others' resources, organization and development possibilities. Knowledge about all these issues is seldom concentrated in one person in the firms. Not only marketers and purchasers, but also specialists in manufacturing, design, development, quality control, service, finance, and so on may take part in the information exchange between the companies. Contacts on several levels in the organizational hierarchies may be required. Such contacts may include personnel on the shop floor, top management and, of course, middle and lower management. The average total number of interacting persons in the relationships is between seven and eight from each party. Such contacts take time to establish: it takes time to learn which persons in a company possess certain types of knowledge, and which have the potentiality to influence certain conditions. On many occasions direct experience is the only possible way to learn so much about each other that the information exchange between the parties works efficiently. Such experiences certainly take time to acquire, and the parties invest in knowledge about each other.

Around 40% of the relationships include contacts on the general management level. Specialists from manufacturing are involved on the customer side in 60–70% of the relationships. Specialists on design and development take part in about 50% of the relationships, and in both cases the supplier side is most involved. On the whole there are quite complex contact and interaction patterns in the relationships between the firms. Another aspect of the relationships is that significant business transactions require that the parties have confidence in each others' ability and willingness to fulfil their commitments. It takes time and effort to build such levels of confidence. The perceived social distance to the customers indicates the investments in confidence in the relationships. In 60–70% of the relationships the respondent considered the relation as involving 'close personal relations' or 'friendly business relations' rather than more 'formal business relations'. Evidently these important relationships are also usually rather close, implying that they result from investments in the relationships.

Suppliers and customers are also often linked to each other through various types of technical and administrative arrangements. They may adapt products, processes, scheduling, delivery routines and logistical systems to the needs and capabilities of the specific counterpart. In the German sub-sample some data are available about this type of investment in customer-supplier relationships. In the eight German customer relationships investigated, on average 2.5 inter-firm production system adaptations were made. In almost every relationship some adaptation of this kind was made. The adaptations were somewhat more common in domestic than they were in export relationships.

Against the background of this type of evidence, we assume that firms in industrial markets are linked to each other through long-lasting relationships. The parties in the relationships are important to each other; they establish and develop complex, inter-firm information channels, and they also develop social and technical bonds with each other. Generally, domestic relationships seem to be more developed and stronger than export relationships. However, many export relationships are also important and long-lasting. We assume that the relationships are important for the functioning of industrial markets and for the market strategies of industrial firms.

3. MARKETS AS NETWORKS—A GENERAL DESCRIPTION

The network approach in the form described in this section has been developed by a group of Swedish researchers whose background is research on distribution *systems*, internationalization *processes* of industrial firms, and industrial purchasing and marketing behaviour as *interaction* between firms (Mattsson (1985) describes this background). The approach is developed in a general way in Hägg and Johanson (1982) and Hammarkvist, Håkansson and Mattsson (1982). This section builds on those publications, and on Johanson and Mattsson (1985, 1986).

The industrial system is composed of firms engaged in production, distribution and use of goods and services. We describe this system as a network of relationships between the firms. There is a division of work in the network which means that the firms are dependent on each other, and their activities therefore need to be co-ordinated. Co-ordination is not brought about through a central plan or an organizational hierarchy, nor does it take place through the price mechanism as in the traditional market model. Instead, co-ordination occurs through interaction between firms in the network, where price is just one of several influencing conditions (cf. Lindblom, 1977). The firms are free to choose counterparts and thus 'market forces' are at play. To gain access to external resources and make it possible to sell products, however, exchange *relationships* have to be established with other firms. Such relationships take time and effort to establish and develop, processes which constrain the firms' possibilities to change counterparts. The need for adjustments between the interdependent firms in terms of the quantity and quality of goods and services exchanged, and the timing of such exchange, call for more or less explicit co-ordination through joint planning, or through power exercised by one party over the other. Each firm in the network has relationships with customers, distributors, suppliers, and so on (and sometimes also directly with competitors), as well as indirect relations via those firms with suppliers' suppliers, customers' customers, competitors, and so on.

The networks are stable and changing. Individual business transactions between firms usually take place within the framework of established relationships. Evidently, some new relationships are occasionally established and some old relationships are disrupted for some reason (e.g. competitive activities), but most exchanges take place within earlier existing relationships. However, those existing relationships are continually changing through activities in connection with transactions made within the relationship. Efforts are made to maintain, develop, change and sometimes disrupt the relationships. As an aspect of those relationships, *bonds* of various kinds are developed between the firms. We distinguish here between technical, planning, knowledge, social, economic, and legal bonds. These bonds can be exemplified by, respectively, product and process adjustments, logistical co-ordination, knowledge about the counterpart, personal confidence and liking, special credit agreements, and long-term contracts.

We stress complementarity in the network. Of course, there are also important competitive relations. Other firms want to obtain access to specific exchange possibilities either as sellers or as buyers, and co-operating firms also have partially conflicting objectives. The relationships imply that there are *specific inter-firm dependence relations* which are of a different character compared with the general dependence relations to the market in the traditional market model. A firm has direct and specific dependence relations to those firms with which it has exchange relationships. It has indirect and specific dependence relations with those firms with which its direct counterparts have exchange relationships—that is, the other firms operating in the network in which it is engaged. Because of the network of relationships the firms operate in a complex system of specific dependence relations which is difficult to survey.

To become established in a new market—that is, a network which is new to the firm—it has to build relationships which are new both to itself and its counterparts. This is sometimes done by breaking old, existing relationships, and sometimes by adding a relationship to already existing ones. Initiatives can be taken both by the seller and by the buyer. A supplier can become established in a network which is new to the firm, because a buying firm takes the initiative.

This model of industrial markets implies that the firm's activities in industrial markets are *cumulative processes* in which relationships are continually established, maintained, developed, and broken in order to give satisfactory, short-term economic return, and to create positions in the network, securing the long-term survival and development of the firm. Through the activities in the network, the firm develops relationships which secure its access to important resources and the sale of its products and services.

Because of the cumulative nature of the market activities, the market *position* is an important concept. At each point in time the firm has certain positions in the network which characterize its relations to other firms. These positions are a result of earlier activities in the network both by the firm and by other firms, and constitute the base which defines the development possibilities and constraints of the firm in the network (see Mattsson (1985) for an analysis of the position concept and its use in a discussion of market strategies.) We distinguish here between *micro-positions* and *macro-positions*. A micro-position refers to the relationship with a specific individual counterpart: A macro-position refers in the relations to a network as a whole or to a specific section of it. A micro-position is characterized by:

(1) the role the firm has for the other firm;
(2) its importance to the other firm; and
(3) the strength of the relationship with the other firm.

A macro-position is characterized by:

(1) the identity of the other firms with which the firm has direct relationships and indirect relations in the network;
(2) the role of the firm in the network;
(3) the importance of the firm in the network; and
(4) the strength of the relationships with the other firms.

The macro-positions are also affected by the interdependencies in the whole network as well as by the complementarity of the micro-positions in the network. Thus, in the context of the whole network, the macro-position is not an aggregation of micro-positions.

Example: Firm A's micro-position in relation to firm B. (1) It is a secondary supplier of fine paper and of knowhow about printing processes. (2) The sales volume is 100, A's share of B's purchases of fine paper is 30% and A is an important source of technical information. (3) The knowledge bonds are strong, but social bonds are rather weak due to recent changes in personnel in both A and B.

Example: Firm A's macro-position. (1) Lists exist of suppliers, customers, competitors and other firms in the network to whom the firm is directly or indirectly related. (2) It has the role as a full line distributor of fine paper in southern Sweden. (3) Its market share is 50%, making it the market leader. (4) It enjoys strong knowledge, planning and social bonds to its major customers, and strong economic and legal bonds to its suppliers.

The positions describe the firm's relations to its industrial environment and thereby some important strategic possibilities and restrictions. All the other firms in the network have their own positions and likewise have future objectives regarding those positions. Desired changes or defence of positions thus describe important aspects of the firm's strategy. The strategies of firms can be complementary to each other, or competitive, or both. Important dimensions of the network structure are related to the set of positions of the organizations that are established there. The *degree of structuring* of the network is the extent to which positions of the organizations are interdependent. In tightly structured networks, the interdependence is high, the bonds are strong, and the positions of the firms are well defined. In loosely structured networks, the bonds are weak and the positions are less well defined.

The global industrial network can be partitioned in various ways. Delimitations can be made concerning geographical areas, products, techniques, and so on. We use the term 'net' for specifically defined sections of the total network. When the grouping is made according to national borders we distinguish between different 'national nets'. Correspondingly we refer to 'production nets' when the grouping is made on the basis of product areas. A production net contains relationships between those firms whose activities are linked to a specific product area. Thus, it is possible to distinguish a 'heavy truck net' including firms manufacturing, distributing, repairing and using heavy trucks. This heavy truck net differs from the corresponding 'industrial branch' as it also comprises firms with complementary activities, whereas the individual branch comprises firms with similar, mostly competing, activities. The firms in the net are linked to each other and have specific dependence relations to each other.

Within the framework of a product area with its production nets, different national production nets can be distinguished. Thus, in the heavy truck field we can speak of a Swedish, a Danish, a West German, an Italian, etc. heavy truck net, comprising the firms or operations in each country engaged in manufacture, distribution service and use of heavy trucks.

To sum up: we have described markets as networks of relationships between firms. The networks are stable *and* changing. Change and development processes in the networks are cumulative and take time. Individual firms have positions in the networks, and those positions are developed through activities in the network and define important possibilities and constraints for present and future activities. Marketing activities in networks serve to establish, maintain, develop and sometimes break relationships, to determine exchange conditions and to handle the actual exchange. Thus, important aspects of market analyses have to do with the present characteristics of the positions, the relations and their development patterns, in relevant networks for the firm. Important marketing problems for both management and for researchers are related to *investments*, since activities are cumulative; to *timing* of activities, because of interdependencies in the network; to *internal co-ordination* of activities, since 'all' the firm's resources are involved in the exchange and since the micro-positions are interdependent; and to *co-operation* with counterparts, since activities are complementary.

4. INVESTMENTS IN NETWORKS

Investments are processes in which resources are committed to create, build or acquire assets which can be used in the future, assets which can be tangible or intangible. Examples of the former are plants and machinery, while examples of the latter are production and marketing knowledge, and proprietary rights to brand names. We call these assets *internal assets*: they are controlled by the firm and are used to carry out production, marketing, development and other activities.

A basic assumption in the network model is that the individual firm is dependent on resources controlled by other firms. The firm gets access to these external resources through its network positions. Since the development of positions takes time and effort, and since the present positions define opportunities and restrictions for the future strategic development of the firm, we look at the firm's positions in the network as partially controlled, intangible *'market assets'*. Market assets generate revenues for the firm and serve to give the firm access to other firms' internal assets. Because of the interdependencies between firms, the use of the asset in one firm is dependent on the use of other firms' assets. Thus, in addition the investment processes, including their consequences, are interdependent in the network. (The reasoning in this section is developed at greater length in Johanson and Mattsson, 1985.)

5. INTERNATIONALIZATION ACCORDING TO THE NETWORK APPROACH

According to the network model, the internationalization of the firm means that the firm establishes and develops positions in relation to counterparts in foreign networks. This can be achieved (1) through establishment of positions in relation to counterparts in national nets that are new to the firm, i.e. *international extension*; (2) by developing the positions and increasing resource commitments in those nets abroad in which the firm already has positions, i.e. *penetration*; and (3) by increasing co-ordination between positions in different national nets, i.e. *international integration*. The firm's degree of internationalization informs about the extent to which the firm occupies certain positions in different national nets, and how important and integrated are those positions. International integration is an aspect of internationalization which it seems motivated to add to the traditional extension and penetration concepts, against the background of the specific dependence relations of the network model. Since position changes mean, by definition, that relationships with other firms are changed, internationalization will according to the network model direct attention analytically to the investments in internal assets and market assets used for exchange activities. Furthermore, the firm's positions before the internationalization process begins are of great interest, since they indicate market assets that might influence the process.

The network model also has consequences for the meaning of internationalization of the market (network). A production net can be more or less internationalized. A high degree of internationalization of a production net implies that there are many and strong relationships between the different national sections of the global production net. A low degree of internationalization, on the other hand, means that the national nets have few relationships with each other. Internationalization means that the number and strength of the relationships between the different parts of the global production network increase.

It can also be fruitful to distinguish between the internationalization of production nets, implying more and stronger links between the national sections of the global production net; and the internationalization of national nets, implying that they are becoming increasingly interconnected with other national nets. The difference is a matter of perspective: in the former case, attention is focused on a production net, in the latter on a national net. The distinction is interesting, because there may be important differences between the degree of internationalization of different national nets. In one country the production net may be highly internationalized, whereas the corresponding net may not be very internationalized in another country. The distinction is also interesting, because in some situations internationalization of the global production affects all the national sections of the global production net. In other situations only some specific national nets

		Degree of internationalization of the market (the production net)	
		Low	High
Degree of internationalization of the firm	Low	The Early Starter	The Late Starter
	High	The Lonely International	The International Among Others

Figure 1. Internationalization and the Network Model: The Situations to be Analyzed

with their production nets are internationalized. This may be the case when two or more national economies are integrated.

6. AN APPLICATION OF THE NETWORK MODEL TO ANALYSES OF THE INTERNATIONALIZATION OF INDUSTRIAL FIRMS

What are the reasons explaining why firms internationalize their activities? Let us assume that the driving forces for increased internationalization are that the firm wants to utilize and develop its resources in such a way that its long-run economic objectives are served. Firms then internationalize if that strategy increases the probability of reaching the general objectives. According to the network model, the firm's development is to an important extent dependent on its positions: it use its market assets in its further development. Thus, the internationalization characteristics of both the firm and of the market influence the process. The firm's market assets have a different structure if the firm is highly internationalized than they do if it is not. Furthermore, the market assets of the other firms in the network have a different structure if the market has a high or low degree of internationalization. We will therefore make a comparative analysis of four different situations, as set out in Figure 1.

The analysis of the four situations thus concerns internationalization processes in the three dimensions, extension, penetration and integration, and how these processes can at least partially be explained by reference to the network model. After this exercise we will make a comparison with what the internalization model and the internationalization model offer in the same types of situations.

6.1 The Early Starter

The firm has few and rather unimportant relationships with firms abroad. The same holds for other firms in the production net. Competitors, suppliers and other firms in the domestic market, as well as in foreign markets, have few important international relationships. In this situation the firm has little knowledge about foreign markets and it cannot count upon utilizing relationships in the domestic market to gain such knowledge. As ventures abroad demand resources for knowledge development and for quantitative and qualitative adjustments to counterparts in the foreign markets, the size and resourcefulness of the firm can be assumed to play an important role. The strategy, often found in empirical studies, that internationalization begins in nearby markets using agents rather than subsidiaries can be interpreted as (1) minimization of the need for knowledge development; (2) minimization of the demands for adjustments and (3) utilization of the positions in the market occupied by already established firms. The firm can utilize the market investments that the agent in the foreign market has made earlier, thereby reducing the need for its own investment and risk taking. As the volume sold in the foreign market increases, the increase in the market assets may justify investment in production facilities in the foreign market.

The alternative strategy, to start with an acquisition or greenfield investment, would require a greater investment in the short run, but might perhaps enhance the long-term possibilities for knowledge development and penetration in the market. This is a strategy which is possible mainly for firms which have already become large and resourceful in the home market before internationalization.

The importance of agents and other middle men is reinforced by the presumptive buyers' lack of experience of international operations. If those buyers happened to be at all conscious of foreign supply alternatives, they would probably be somewhat reluctant. This means that the supplier must let some third party—an agent—guarantee the firm's delivery capability, or itself invest in confidence-creating activities—for example, getting 'reference customers', keeping local stocks, building a service organization or even a manufacturing plant in the foreign market. This means further market investments.

Initiatives in the early internationalization of the firm are often taken by counter-parts—that is, distributors or users in the foreign market. Thus, the foreign counterpart uses its own market assets to establish a new firm within its own network. Whether the firm, with this introduction as base, can develop its position in the market is very uncertain, and may depend on the degree of structuring of the network and on the positions of the 'introducer'. If the 'introducer' is a leading distributor in a tightly structured network, the conditions are favourable for rapid penetration by the firm, given that the adjustments to the network are made. An obstacle may be that the demands for quantities become so high that the production capacity of the firm is too small. This may require increased engagement in the market through the establishment of production units. To reduce the risk of overcapacity, the parties may have to enter into long-term supply contracts, a process which is quite consistent with a tightly structured network.

As already discussed, the need for resource adjustment may become quite heavy in connection with a first step abroad. Such adjustments can be assumed to imply investments and it must be important to minimize the resource adjustment requirement in connection with early steps abroad. This holds for quantitative resource adjustments in connection with the capacity increases which the added market may demand, and it also holds for qualitative resource adjustments which may be required because of the possibility of new market needs deviating from earlier ones. Obviously, it may be possible to complement the resources through external sources. To the extent that such resource completions are made in the domestic market, they probably imply the same type of problems. They mean commitments which may be difficult to fulfil if the foreign engagement is a failure. On the other hand, they are probably risk reductions if they can be made in the actual foreign market. It is, however, not likely that a firm which has no experience of foreign operations would have qualifications for organizing resource completions in the foreign market—that is, to establish positions in relation to local suppliers.

Another problem is that some resource adjustments can be made possible by giving up control over the operations in exchange for the flexibility needed to reduce risk taking in connection with foreign ventures. Such ventures may be carried out if the old owner transfers control of the firm to someone who is able to complement the firm's resources. In the absence of internationalization of the environment, the extension to additional foreign markets will also be determined in general by the need for knowledge development and the need to create, or use already existing, market assets. If conditions in markets which are new to the firm are similar to the conditions in the home market (and/ or in the foreign markets in which the firm began its internationalization), then there is a greater likelihood that these markets will be the next ones. If, however, the network is tightly structured, or if there is a lack of effective 'introducers' on the foreign market that is 'next in line', from a knowledge and adjustment point of view we expect to find extension patterns with other characteristics.

As the firm becomes more internationalized, it changes from an Early Starter situation to becoming a Lonely International.

6.2. The Lonely International

How is the situation changed if the firm is highly internationalized while its market environment is not? To start with, in this situation the firm has experience of relationships with and in foreign countries. It has acquired knowledge and means to handle environments which differ with respect to culture, institutions, and so on, and failures are therefore less likely. The knowledge situation is more favourable when establishing the firm in a new national net.

The second advantage is that the international firm probably has a wider repertoire of resource adjustments. The need for resource adjustments is likely to be more marginal and less difficult to handle. This holds for both quantitative and qualitative adjustments even if the former are perhaps more strongly affected by the greater size which attends internationalization than they are by the internationalization *per se*. In particular it is easier for the international firm to make various types of resource completions in the foreign markets. This is a special case of the general advantage of international firms, because of much greater resource combination possibilities. Note that resource combinations also include those external resources to which the positions give access. The firm which is highly internationalized may also use its market investments to get a rapid diffusion of its new products. It may use its positions partially to control the internationalization moves of competitors, but may also involuntarily stimulate such moves (see below).

With regard to the structuring of the national nets, it can be assumed that the international firm will experience less difficulties than others in entering tightly structured nets. It already possesses good knowledge about many kinds of national markets. Further extension is not so dependent on similarities between markets as it is for the Early Starter. Experience and resources give the firm a repertoire which allows it to make the heavy market investments which are required to enter a tighly structured production net. It also has better possibilities for taking over firms with positions in the structured net or establishing relationships with such firms. It can also give its counterparts access to other national nets: for example, the international firm has greater possibilities than others to engage in barter trade.

Initiatives for furthering internationalization do not come from other parties in the production nets, since the firm's suppliers, customers and competitors are not internationalized. On the contrary, the Lonely International has the qualifications to promote internationalization of its production net, and consequently of the firms engaged in it. The firm's relationships both with and in other national nets may function as bridges to those nets for that firm's suppliers and customers. Perhaps they have a similar effect on competitors (cf. Knickerbocker, 1973). Firms which are internationalized before their competitors are forerunners in the internationalization process and may enjoy advantages for that reason, in particular in tightly structured nets, because they have developed network positions before the competitors.

To exploit the advantages of being a Lonely International, the firm has to co-ordinate activities in the different national nets. International integration is therefore an important feature in the development of the highly internationalized firm. However, the need to co-ordinate is probably less than for the International Among Others.

6.3. The Late Starter

If the suppliers, customers and competitors of the firm are international, even the purely domestic firm has a number of indirect relations with foreign networks. Relationships in the domestic market may be driving forces to enter foreign markets. The firm can be 'pulled out' by customers or suppliers, and in particular by complementary suppliers, e.g. 'big projects'. Thus, market investments in the domestic market are assets which can be utilized when going abroad. In that case it is not necessary to go from the nearby market to more distant markets and the step abroad can already be rather large in the beginning. In addition, nearby markets may be tightly structured and already 'occupied' by competitors. Thus, the extension pattern will be partly explained by the international character of indirect relations and the existence of entry opportunities.

Is the market penetration process of the firm affected by the degree of internationalization of the production network where it is operating? The need for co-ordination is greater in a highly internationalized production net, which implies that establishment of sales subsidiaries should be made earlier if the firm is a Late Starter than if it is an Early Starter. The size of the firm is probably important: for example, a small firm going abroad in an internationalized world probably has to be highly specialized and adjusted to problem solutions in specific sections of the production nets. Starting production abroad probably is a matter of what bonds to the customers are important. If joint planning with customers is essential it may be necessary to start local production early. Similarly, if technical development requires close contacts with the customers, it may be advantageous to manufacture locally. On the other hand, it may be better to use relationships with customers in the domestic market for development purposes, especially if these customers are internationalized (as they to some extent are, by definition, in the Late Starter case). However, such customers also have access to alternative, internationally based counterparts for their own development processes which might reduce the importance of their domestic suppliers.

The situation is different for large firms. As firms which have become large in the domestic market often are less specialized than small firms, their situation is often more complex than in the case of the small firm. One possibility is that of becoming established in a foreign production net through acquisition or joint venture. Of course, this is associated with great risks to a firm without experience of foreign acquisitions or joint ventures, particularly if other firms in the production net are internationalized. In general, it is probably more difficult for a firm which has become large at home to find a niche in highly internationalized nets. Unlike the small firm, it cannot adjust in a way which is necessary in such a net, nor has it the same ability as the small firm to react on the initiatives of other firms—which is probably the main road to internationalization in a net in which other firms are already international.

The Late Starter has a comparative disadvantage in terms of its lesser market knowledge as compared with its competitors. Furthermore, as suggested above, it is often difficult to establish new positions in a tightly structured net. The best distributors are, for example, already linked to competitors. More or less legally, competitors can make the late newcomer unprofitable, by means of predatory pricing. In addition in comparison with the Early Starter, the Late Starter probably has a less difficult task with regard to trust. Firms in the foreign markets already have experience of suppliers from abroad.

In a highly internationalized world the firms are probably more specialized. Consequently, a firm which is a Late Starter has to have a greater customer adaptation ability or a greater ability to influence the need specifications of the customers. However, the influence ability of a Late Starter is probably rather limited. The comparison between the Early Starter and the Late Starter illustrates the importance of timing as a basic issue in the analysis of strategies in networks.

6.4. The International Among Others

In this case both the firm and its environment are highly internationalized. A further internationalization of the firm only means marginal changes in extension and penetration, which, on the whole, do not imply any qualitative changes in the firm. It is probable, however, that international integration of the firm can lead to radical internationalization changes.

Both with regard to extension and penetration the firm has possibilities to use positions in one net for bridging over to other nets. A necessary condition for such bridging is that the lateral relations within the firm are quite strong. Some kind of international integration is required, not only in the 'vertical', hierarchical sense, but also in the lateral, decentralized sense (Galbraith, 1973). As extension takes place in a globally interdependent network, the driving forces and the obstacles to this extension are closely related to this interdependence. Models of global oligopolies fit the argument here. Entries are made in those sections of the global production net which the competitors consider their main markets in order to discourage the competitor from making threatening competitive moves in other markets. In such a situation the entry may meet some resistance, but it is difficult for the competitors to use predatory pricing.

For the Early Starter, penetration through production in a foreign market was mainly a result of a need to bring about a balance between internal resources and external demands and possibilities in the specific market. For the International Among Others, the situation is different. The operations in one market may make it possible to utilize production capacity for sales in other markets. This may lead to production co-ordination by specialization and increased volumes of intra-firm international trade. When the markets are expanding, it is possible in that case to put off capacity increases in one market, while capacity increases are made in another market before the positions in that market motivated such expansion. The surplus capacity could be linked to the wider international network, and this requires strong international integration of the firm.

Establishment of sales subsidiaries is probably speeded up by high internationalization, as the international knowledge level is higher and there is a stronger need to co-ordinate activities in different markets. The need for co-ordination places heavy demand on the organization. The competitors can utilize weaknesses in one market if they are not likely to meet counter-attacks in markets in which the firm is strong. Co-ordination gains in procurement, production and R&D are more likely than if the internationalization of the firm and of the network is low. National differences are smaller, innovations are diffused more rapidly, and indirect business relations via the 'third country' become more important to utilize. The market investments in one country will probably be more important as the external resources to which the relationships give access are more dispersed internationally.

The many positions which the International Among Others occupies in internationally linked networks give it access to, and some influence over, external resources. This means that the possibility for 'externalization' increases. The international manufacturing firm may thus increasingly tend to purchase components, sub-assemblies, etc. rather than do the manufacturing itself. Such subcontracting is sometimes required by host governments, but may also be a way to make the multinational enterprise more effective. Since important customers or joint-venture partners in one country are also by definition international, the International Among Others is faced with opportunities for further extension or penetration in 'third countries'. Thus a Swedish firm might increase its penetration in a South American market because of its relationship in Japan with an internationalizing Japanese firm. Other examples of such international interdependence are 'big projects' in which design, equipment supply, construction, ownership and operation can all be allocated to firms of different national origin, but with internationally more or less dispersed activities. In such production nets, further internationalization is probably predominantly dependent on the firm's configuration of network positions and on its ability not only to co-ordinate its own resources in different parts of the world, but also to influence, through its market assets, the use of resources owned by other firms.

The advantage of being able to co-ordinate operations in international networks is still more evident when changes take place in the environment. Assume that such changes spread from country to country: the international firm is then likely to have better possibilities to discover such changes as well as better opportunities to take advantage of them. A third advantage may be that the international firm can dominate and influence the international diffusion process and thus affect the development—but this probably requires size as well. Changes also occur in the localization of economic activity. The internationally co-ordinated firm has better opportunities to detect and adjust to such changes. It can, for example, use its earlier established positions in an expanding national market to increase its penetration in that market and perhaps also its extension to other national markets within an expanding region of such markets. A driving force for further internationalization by the International Among Others is to increase its ability to adjust to (or perhaps to influence) the geographical reallocation of activities in the production net.

The International Among Others predominantly faces counterparts and competitors who are themselves internationally active and markets that are rather tightly structured. This means that major position changes in this situation will increasingly take place through joint ventures, acquisitions and mergers, in contrast with the other three cases that we have analysed. If, finally, we compare with the Early Starter situation, internationalization for the International Among Others will be much less explicable by reference to the need for knowledge development and the similarities between the foreign markets and the home market. Instead, the driving forces and the restrictions are related to the strategic use of network positions.

7. THE NETWORK APPROACH COMPARED WITH TWO OTHER MODELS

7.1. The theory of internalization

The theory of internalization (Buckley and Casson, 1976; Rugman, 1982) currently seems to be generally accepted as an explanation of multinational enterprise. The theory assumes that a multinational enterprise has somehow developed a firm-specific advantage in its home market. This is usually in the form of internally developed, intangible assets giving the firm some superior production, product, marketing and/or management knowledge. If this asset cannot be exploited and safe-guarded effectively through market (or contractual) transactions, an 'internal market' has to be created. Expansions outside the firm's domestic market, given that local production is advantageous, will then take place through horizontal and/or vertical integration. The firm either establishes or buys manufacturing plants outside its home market. Thus, the multinational enterprise exists because of 'market failures' or high 'contracting costs'. The firm wants to protect its intangible assets and to be able to control the price others pay for the use of these assets. There are, however, also costs of internalizing in the form of internal administrative systems and risk-taking. These costs of internalization will be lower, the less different the foreign market is from the home market. Thus, the internalization model will predict that internalization starts in 'nearby' markets (Caves, 1982; chapter 1). It should be noted that the internalization model is not intended to explain processes; rather, it tries to explain a specific economic institution, the multinational enterprise. It does say something, however, about the driving forces for internalization and the modes of international resource transfer.

   We believe that the explanatory power of the internalization model is greater in the situations in which the environment is not internationalized. The application of the model to the Early Starter situation is somewhat less than straightforward, though, since in the beginning the Early Starter is not a multinational enterprise and it exports products rather than manufacturing them abroad. However, we might extend the reasoning underlying the internalization model to include not only manufacturing, but also marketing activities. Given such an interpretation, if the advantages of local manufacturing are small, then it seems reasonable to expect the firm to export its intangible assets 'embedded in products,' and that the marketing activities in the foreign market are carried out by a sales subsidiary rather than by an independent agent (unless the contracting costs are less than the cost of internalizing). The internalization model could be used to explain why firms enter a market using a sales subsidiary and not an independent agent, while the internalization model discussed below could be used to explain why agents precede sales subsidiaries. While the first model emphasizes the need for exploiting and protecting internally created intangible assets, the second model emphasizes the need for gradual development of market knowledge and the need to learn from interaction with other firms during the process.

In addition, the further expansion into the Lonely International case seems to fit with basic assumptions in the internalization approach. The intangible assets constitute a firm-specific advantage that can be exploited in many markets through the operations of a multinational enterprise. However, if it takes a long time from the beginning of the internationalization process to the status of Lonely International, the question arises as to how the firm can further develop its firm-specific advantage and not merely preserve and exploit it. It seems to be an implicit assumption in the internalization approach that the firm's development activities are 'internal'. In the network approach, development activities are to an important extent dependent on the relationships with other firms, and thus on the network positions of the firm. Since internationalization is a process by which network positions are established and changed, internationalization as such influences the further development of the products, production processes, marketing behaviour, etc.

We said earlier that firms in networks invest in relationships with other firms. The positions thus created are in this chapter regarded as market investments, or in other words, as a form of intangible assets. These assets give partial access to external resources. Thus, the multinational enterprise increasingly enjoys direct relationships with customers and users in foreign markets rather than the indirect relations through agents or licensees enjoyed by the less internationalized firm, operating only in its home market. This leads to a further observation linked to the network model. The highly internationalized firm may use its network positions effectively to 'externalize' some of its activities, without losing control of its crucial intangible assets. The manufacturing value added by multinational industrial firms might decrease because of increased 'subcontracting'. We believe that this is especially true in the International Among Others case.

If both the firm and its environment are highly internationalized, it seems that a model which aims to explain multinational enterprise loses some of its relevance for analysis of further internationalization. We might, of course, still be helped by the transaction cost approach in our attempts to understand just what institutional form penetration, expansion and integration actually take. However, the approach does not consider the cumulative nature of activities, the use of external assets, the development potential of network relationships, or the interdependence between national markets.

7.2. The (Uppsala) internationalization model

The internationalization process described as a gradual step-by-step commitment to sell and to manufacture internationally as part of a growth and experimental learning process is a model that is associated with the research on the internationalization of Swedish manufacturing industry that has been carried out at the University of Uppsala (see, for example, Hörnell et al, 1973; Johanson and Wiedersheim-Paul, 1974; and Johanson and Vahlne, 1977). Focusing especially on export behaviour Bilkey (1978) conceptualized, and found evidence for, the exporting process as a sequential learning process by which the firm goes through stages of increasing commitment to foreign markets. This 'stage model' has lately come under some criticism, even if its general acceptance in the research community as a valid description seems to be high. Reid (1983) argues that the model is too deterministic and general; according to him, the firm's choice of entry and expansion modes are more selective and context-specific, and can be explained by heterogeneous resource patterns and market opportunities. Firms will therefore use multiple modes of international transfers. Reid suggests that a transaction cost approach is superior to the experiential learning model. Hedlund and Kverneland (1984; 77) also criticize the model, concluding that the 'experiences of Swedish firms in Japan suggest that establishment and growth strategies on foreign markets are changing towards more direct and rapid entry modes than those implied by theories of gradual and slow internationalization processes'.

We believe that the internationalization model is less valid in situations in which both the market and the firm are highly internationalized. The firms which started their internationalization during the early twentieth century were usually in the Early Starter situation. The studies of Swedish industrial firms, on which the Uppsala model is based, describe and explain this situation and its transition to the Lonely International stage. There is no explicit consideration in the model of the internationalization of the firm's environment. We would therefore expect the internationalization model to be most valid in the Early Starter case and least valid in the International Among Others stage. Both the network approach and the internationalization model stress the cumulative nature of the firm's activities. The latter, however, is a model focusing on the internal development of the firm's knowledge and other resources, while the network approach also offers a model of the market and the firm's relations to that market.

In the Late Starter situation, we therefore expect the internationalization model to be less valid than the network model because of the importance of indirect international relations in the home market and because of the probably quite heterogeneous pattern of entry opportunities when foreign markets are compared. In the International Among Others case, the internationalization model seems to lose much of its relevance. Reid's, and Hedlund and Kverneland's arguments seem to be valid. Since by definition the firm and its counterparts and competitors have positions in a large number of markets, penetration and integration aspects of internationalization seem to be more important strategic moves than further extension. In such a global perspective, specific national market differences will likely have less explanatory power.

To sum up: we believe that both the internalization and the internationalization models leave out characteristics of the firm and the market which seem especially important in the case of 'global competition' and co-operation in industrial systems.

8. SOME CONCLUDING REMARKS CONCERNING RESEARCH ISSUES

Against the background of the above discussion, we believe that more research in two, closely related, fields will serve to increase knowledge about the internationalization of business: firstly, network internationalization processes; and secondly, use of markets assets in international competition.

8.1. Network internationalization

Studies of network internationalization may focus on internationalization of national nets or of production nets. Such studies should describe and analyse the roles of different types of industrial actors in the process. They should also investigate the implications of the cumulative nature of network processes. More specifically, we advocate research into foreign market entry strategies in different situations with regard to network internationalization. According to the network we can distinguish entry strategies which differ with regard to the character and number of relationships the entry firm seeks to establish with other firms in the network. We can also study which of the actors in the network take initiative in different entry processes and in networks which are more or less internationalized. Furthermore, the entry strategies may differ with regard to the ambitions of the entry firm in adopting or influencing the network structure in the entry market.

The network approach also implies that the strategic discretion is constrained by the character of the network in which the firm is operating or into which it intends to enter. This indicates that during the internationalization of a network, the timing of the operations of a firm is important. It can also be expected that, because of the cumulative nature of network processes, the sequential order of activities in international markets is important and should be given more attention in research. Perhaps, however, the problem of timing is next to impossible to solve. From a strategic point of view the most interesting research issue, then, is that of analysing how to build preparedness for action when the time is ripe. Presumably, preparedness is largely a matter of having relationships with other parties.

This view on industrial markets implies that there are strong interdependencies between different sections, i.e. national nets, of the global networks: hence, integration of operations is important. At the same time, the view implies that action has to be taken close to other actors in the market, often in response to their actions. Strategies can probably not be planned and designed by remote headquarters, and their implementation requires some kind of lateral relation between organizational units operating in different national nets. Research about the organization problem of integrating operations in international networks is required.

8.2. Use of market assets in international competition

We have emphasized the strategic importance of market assets and suggest research about their use in international competition. In particular, there is scope for work on the use of the market assets of one country as they affect competition with other countries. We think it would be interesting to study how market assets in one country are used when entering other country markets. Such studies should concern not only the use of domestic market assets in the first step abroad, but also the use of foreign market assets when entering third-country markets. They could focus on different types of market assets, or the country of the assets utilized—in terms of networks—or the target markets.

Another interesting research issue is the use of market assets in global competition. Such research could focus on the use of relationships with more or less multinational companies in global competition. Relationships with suppliers, customers, distributors or consultants are of different importance when competing in various types of production nets and national nets.

Finally, the strategic importance of market assets implies that fruitful research can be made about control of foreign market assets. Whereas internal assets are usually controlled hierarchically with ownership as the base, control of market assets must have other bases. Research has demonstrated that such factors as access to critical resources, information or legitimacy are often important as bases of control. The significance of those factors may differ considerably in different contexts. Both conceptual and empirical research is required.

REFERENCES

Bilkey, W. J. (1978) An Attempted Integration of Literature on the Export Behavior of Firms. *Journal of International Business Studies*, Spring, 93–8.

Blois, K. J. (1972) Vertical Quasi-Integration. *Journal of Industrial Economics*, **20**(3): 253–72.

Buckley, R. J. and Casson, M. C. (1976) *The Future of Multinational Enterprise*. Macmillan: London.

Caves, R. E. (1982) *Multinational Enterprise and Economic Analysis*. Cambridge University Press: Cambridge.

Ford, J. D. (1978) Stability Factors in Industrial Marketing Channels. *Industrial Marketing Management*, **7**(6): 410–22.

Galbraith, J. (1973) *Designing Complex Organizations*. Addison-Wesley: MA.

Guillet de Monthoux, P. (1975) Organizational Mating and Industrial Marketing Conservatism— Some Reasons why Industrial Marketing Managers Resist Marketing Theory. *Industrial Marketing Management*, **4**(1): 25–36.

Hågg, I. and Johanson, J. (eds) (1982) *Företag i nätverk*. SNS: Stockholm.

Håkansson, H. (ed.) (1982) *International Marketing and Purchasing of Industrial Goods: an Interaction Approach*. Wiley: Chichester.

—— and Östberg, C. (1975) Industrial Marketing—an Organizational Problem? *Industrial Marketing Management* **4**: 113–23.

Hallén, L. (1986) A Comparison of Strategic Marketing Approach. In P. W. Turnbull, and J. P. Valla (eds), *Strategies for International Industrial Marketing: a Comparative Analysis*. Croom Helm: London.

Hammarkvist, K.-O., Håkansson, H. and Mattson, L.-G. *Marknadsföring för konkurrenskraft*. Liber: Malmö.

Hedlund, G. and Kverneland, A. *Investing in Japan—the Experience of Swedish Firms*. Institute of International Business, Stockholm School of Economics.

Hörnell, E., Vahlne, J.-E. and Wiedersheim-Paul, F. (1973) *Export och utlandsestableringar*. Almqvist and Wiksell: Uppsala.

Johanson, J. and Mattsson, L.-G. Marketing Investments and Market Investments in Industrial Networks. *International Journal of Research in Marketing* **2**(3): 185–95.

—— and —— (1986) International Marketing and Internationalization Processes—A Network Approach. In S. Paliwoda and P. N. Turnbull (eds), *Research in International Marketing*. Croom Helm: London.

Johanson, J. and Vahlne, J.-E. (1977) The Internationalization Process of the Firm—a Model of Knowledge Development and Increasing Foreign Market Commitments. *Journal of International Business* **8** (Spring-Summer), 23–32.

—— and Wiedersheim-Paul, F. (1974) The internationalization of the firm—four Swedish case studies. *Journal of Management Studies* **3** (October), 305–22.

Knickerbocker, F. T. (1973) *Oligopolistic Reaction and Multinational Enterprise*. Division of Research, Harvard Graduate School of Business Administration: Cambridge, MA.

Levitt, T. (1983) *The Marketing Imagination*. The Free Press: New York.

Lindblom, C.-E. (1977) *Politics and Markets*. Basic Books: New York.

Macneil, I. R. (1978) Contracts: Adjustment of Long-term Economic Relations under Classical, Neoclassical, and Relational Contract Law, *Northwestern University Lay Review*, **72**(6): 854–905.

Mattsson, L.-G. (1985) An Application of a Network Approach to Marketing: Defending and Changing Market Positions. In N. Dholakia and J. Arndt (eds), *Alternative Paradigms for Widening Marketing Theory*. JAI Press: Greenwich CT.

Reid, S. (1983) Firm Internationalization, Transaction Costs and Strategic Choice. *International Marketing Review*, Winter, 44–56.

Rugman, A. M. (ed.) (1982) *New Theories of the Multinational Enterprise*. Croom Helm: London.

Webster, Jr., F. E. (1979) *Industrial Marketing Strategy*. Wiley: New York.

Von Hippel, E. (1978) Successful Industrial Products from Customer Ideas. *Journal of Marketing*, **42:** 39–49.

Williamson, O. E. (1979) Transaction Cost Economics: the Governance of Contractual Relations. *Journal of Law and Economics*, 233–61.

Wind, Y. (1970) Industrial Source Loyalty. *Journal of Marketing Research* **8:** 433–6.

22

Joint Venture Relationship between Swedish Firms and Developing Countries: a Longitudinal Study

Syed Akmal Hyder and Pervez N. Ghauri

Joint ventures have become more and more important in recent decades, both as technology-transfer projects in less developed countries (LDCs) demanded by host governments, and as a mode of foreign investment by multinational firms (MNCs). This pattern of co-operation has received a considerable importance by the researchers and there are a number of studies available on joint venture (JV) relationships between MNCs and LDCs (see for example Vernon, 1972; Ahn, 1980; Walmsley, 1982; Beamish, 1985). The relationship is, however, still facing great problems and the parties involved face difficulties in resolving their differences. The resources brought in by different partners, their organizations, the role of their social and cultural backgrounds and the environment in which JVs are to operate are more or less unknown to each other. The management of this relationship thus cannot succeed unless these differences are perceived and overcome. The available literature put forward several such management problems to discern and analyse the immediate conflict (see for example Wright, 1979; Simiar, 1983). Most of these works do not however investigate and explain ways of solving current problems, but rather concentrate on providing suggestions to avoid future problems. Questions remain as to why partners need to form JVs, what resources they contribute over time, why conflicts arise and how these are settled.

As mentioned earlier one reason for increasing interest in JV is that it is a very attractive form of foreign investment where the MNCs can overcome the uncertainties and share the risk with others; the rate of failure in JV is however, very high (Simiar, 1983; Beamish, 1985). One of the reasons for this high rate of failure is that MNCs are most probably not aware of the dynamism in the JV relationships—that co-operation and conflict can change over time. We argue that a JV is a dynamic process and the problems and advantages related to it should be treated in a process perspective.

The present study has a longitudinal approach to investigate reasons and consequences of partners' interactions in order to describe the development of the JV relationship over

Syed Akmal Hyder is Economist and Researcher, Swedish University of Agricultural Sciences, Uppsala. Pervez N. Ghauri is Associate Professor, Department of Business Studies, University of Uppsala.

Reprinted with permission from *Journal of Global Marketing*, Vol 2, No 4, pp 25–47 time. We expect that this work will be helpful to practitioners in understanding day-to-day problems in JVs. Researchers in the field will benefit by the view of considering a JV as a historical process. Two case studies are presented on the basis of two JVs between Indian and Swedish partners.

In this study the following questions are addressed:

—What role does exchange of resources play in the development of a JV relationship?
—How is control exercised in a JV?
—How and when do conflicts arise between the partners and how are these resolved?

BACKGROUND

Using a sample of 166 American domestic JVs, Pfeffer and Nowak (1976) assumed that firms would engage in JV to manage interorganizational interdependence. Unlike Pfeffer and Nowak, Aiken and Hage (1968) found the formation of joint activities a reason to create interdependence in order to satisfy different resource needs. We argue that JVs are formed both to manage interorganizational interdependence and to create inter-dependence. In our view, firms need to co-operate in solving many problems and if this co-operation extends to a stable relationship, the firms will be more dependent on each other than ever.

In general, the reason to form a JV is to gain complementary resources from each other and an important characteristic of resource exchange is its dynamic nature (see Bivens and Lovell, 1966; Otterbeck, 1979; Berg and Friedman, 1980; Connolly, 1984). Franko (1971) criticized the view of partners' contributions as a static bundle of skills or input; instead he argued that they were subject to change. Killing (1982, 1983), who studied JV success, also considered the change in the need for resources from one another due to the presence of continuous learning. Koot (1986) and Harrigan (1986) also observed the divergence of business interests among the partners over time.

Tomlinson (1970) and Friedmann and Béguin (1971) were in agreement that foreign firms who desired to have control required majority ownership in the JV. Gullander (1976, p. 110) argued that control of critical decisions is not always determined by management control. He asserted, 'For example, a parent who can control the supply of raw materials to the JV possesses power that could reach in decision areas other than those directly related to his immediate area of control, i.e. raw materials.' Abdul (1979), Ahn (1980), Otterbeck (1979, 1980) and Dunning (1978) also found critical resources as the sources of control. We recognize that survival of an organization depends on the supply of critical resources, which confer more effective control than ownership.

As far as conflict is concerned, 'lack of goal congruence' has been cited by many authors as a major reason for JV conflict (see Reynolds, 1984; Edström, 1975 and Simiar, 1983). Barlew (1984, p. 50) commented in this connection, 'The partners' business objectives may differ so radically that agreement on how to operate, fund, and benefit from the venture may be difficult to reach.' Beamish and Lane (1982) and Raveed and Renforth (1983) recognized cultural differences as a source of problems in JVs, especially in the developing countries. Understanding about conflicts is not enough, we feel it is also important to try to solve the problems in time before they get out of control.

Unfortunately, most studies are not concerned with resolution of the problems, and the reasons for JV failures remain more or less unexplored.

METHODOLOGY

As already mentioned, in contrast to most work on JVs, this study seeks to examine the relationship over time. In this longitudinal study, all major happenings over time are duly investigated, discussed and finally analysed. Due to the extensive nature of this work, it was possible to follow the exchange of resources, the origin of conflicts, and the gradual development of the relationship.

The data were collected from face-to-face and telephone interviews, correspondence and printed materials.[1] Face-to-face interviews, which were conducted between 1982–1985 provided valuable information. A questionnaire was prepared on the basis of the initial research problem after a review of previous JV studies, which were conducted for a similar purpose. The interviews were semi-structured, the interviewees were free to talk and the interviewer could ask additional questions. The duration of each interview varied from two to four hours depending on the depth and requirement of the discussions. One of the two local partners, foreign firms' representatives and chief executives of both the JVs were interviewed.

In the case analysis, exchange of resources is discussed from the point of expectation and actual contribution by the partners in order to observe differences between them. Other variables of the model, which are presented further in this section, are also described in both the cases. Finally, in conclusion, cases are compared and the results of the study are reported.

The model used for the analysis consists of partners' interests, exchange of resources, control, co-operation/conflict and performance (Figure 1). 'Partners' interests' explain why partners enter into a JV, what benefit they derive from it and finally, what interests they attach to it over time. Partners prefer to set up a JV when they have extensive needs,

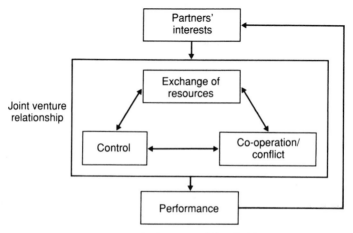

Figure 1. The Structure of the Model.

and consequently, are not satisfied with short term contracts or agreements. Interaction between organizations takes place through the 'exchange of resources', which are mostly complementary in nature. In a JV, five resource factors are of importance, i.e. input, capital, manpower, technology and market. Input material is necessary to ensure production. The sources of capital to a JV are equity from both partners in cash or kind, trade credits and loans from local or foreign capital markets. In every organization there is the need for manpower to carry out the operational activities according to the programmes reached. Baranson (1978, p. 13) defines technology as a package of product designs, production and process techniques and managerial systems which are used to manufacture particular industrial products. The market is often a vital resource area for a JV, especially for the foreign partner.

'Control' is important because partners put in capital, administrative efforts and reputation, so they want to safeguard their interests. Control can be divided into formal and informal depending on the pattern of application. Formal control is well defined because it is directly related to ownership. Informal control is wide and complicated, and access to scarce and essential resources is its power base. Co-operation/conflict is present in every negotiation, and in a JV many such negotiations continuously take place (Ghauri, 1983). Measurement of performance is essential because partners have certain expectations, and the outcome from the operation may need a capable partner to exercise more control or raise new conflicts or force the partners to co-operate.

As shown in Figure 1, a JV relationship is a process which develops over time by the interaction of exchange of resources, control and co-operation/conflict. The relationship is supposed to change if the pattern of interaction among the varibles changes. Partners' interests affect the relationship, which in turn largely determines the level of performance. Partners' interests also vary because owners are eager to know about the performance, both financial and non-financial, which is significant for their future attachment to the JV.

THE CASE OF ERICSSON INDIA

The foreign partner Ericsson is one of the few giant Swedish multinationals having a leading position in the telecommunications industry of the world. Its total net sales amounted to 15.2 billion SEK (1\$ = 6.30 SEK) during the first half of 1987. Technology transfer is an essential activity of Ericsson. It pursues no rigid policy regarding the form of investment. It has a large number of wholly-owned subsidiaries and both majority and minority JVs. The local partner is a well-established businessman in India and has been in the business for more than 30 years. His total investment in different businesses approaches 5M Rs (1\$ = 14 Rs).

Ericsson had been working in the Indian market with a wholly-owned subsidiary for 10–15 years before the JV was formed. This subsidiary was basically a trading house and had difficulty in competing with the other foreign companies, which had local production facilities. Personal liking played a major role in Ericsson's choice of the local associate. Ericsson's representative, who met his counterpart for the first time at the Swedish Embassy in India, found him charming. The local partner was approached by Ericsson and accepted the offer to set up a JV in January 1971.

Mutual resource expectation

At the initial stage, a significant proportion of the input material was expected to be obtained from external sources, not necessarily from Sweden.[2] Since the required input material for the JV was of an older type, Ericsson was put in a position to supply much of it from its own sources. Ericsson was expected to provide information about the foreign suppliers and negotiate with them on behalf of the JV until the latter could import its own material. Ericsson was not required to invest any cash during the time of JV formation, since its assets from Ericsson Telephone Sales Corporation sufficed to make up the share capital. Ericsson obtained major ownership while the local partner became the minority shareholder by making a cash investment. It was expected that the local partner would subsequently raise his share capital to comply with the government regulations.

Extensive training of the local people both in Sweden and in India was planned. It was also expected that Ericsson would provide technological assistance to the JV in manufacturing and marketing complex products through participation in the local tenders. As skilled and semi-skilled people were available in India, it was expected that the local partner would be able to recruit efficient manpower from the local market.

During the establishment of the JV, the local partner had no technical competence in the field and was wholly dependent on Ericsson where technology was concerned. It was decided by both sides that the full technological responsibility would be handed over to the local people as early as possible. It was a prime expectation that Ericsson's marketing experience from the wholly-owned subsidiary and knowledge of the products would be of great significance in respect to marketing. However, the role of the local partner was not underestimated due to his long marketing experience and contacts with the government authorities.

Exchange of resources over time

Ericsson had both information and legitimacy in the eyes of the prospective suppliers. In the host country and abroad, Ericsson had the exclusive responsibility for the procurement of input material in the first two to three years. The JV gradually learned to handle this task alone while Ericsson's contribution remained important over the years to facilitate import of new items and supply some useful input material from its own sources. At the time of the JV formation, the initial shareholding of Ericsson was 74% while the rest was in the possession of the local partner. During the next seven years, the share capital ratio was progressively increased in favour of the local partner to comply with the government regulations. In 1978, the local shareholding reached 60.4% while Ericsson had 39.6%. To set up the second factory, the JV had been granted a loan by a local bank. Besides this, the JV had also obtained credit facilities from two foreign banks located in Calcutta during 1979–1980. Both the loans were secured but the reputation and influence of the local partner were very helpful.

Recruitment was a primary responsibility of the local partner, since he had information and a close link with the local labour market. As the local partner was pre-occupied with other business and the JV became institutionalized, the task of recruitment was gradually passed on to the general manager (GM), who was the chief executive of the company. However, the local partner was always consulted if some important appointments were to be made. There were altogether four top ranking executives including the GM in the JV at the end of 1985. Each was well qualified and none was related to any of the directors.

The purpose of the JV formation was to make certain specialized communications equipment, namely, portable magnetor telephone switch boards for the Ministry of Defence. This product had been made for the last 15 years. During 1971 to 1973 Ericsson offered extensive training to the local technicians, both in the host country and in Sweden. According to the plan, technological responsibility was handed over to the local staff already at the end of 1974.

In marketing, the JV had two functions. One function was related to receiving orders from the buyers and delivering the goods after manufacture. The other was to act as liaison office for Ericsson to market the latter's products in the host country through the participation in international bids. For this second function, the JV maintained both formal and informal contacts with the buyers, supplied complementary information, and finally attended the opening of the tenders. Ericsson's work consisted of preparing offers, arranging for the requisite products and passing information to the buyers. The local partner often visited main customers and also provided legitimacy by his participation in the JV.

Control

Gradual change of share structure in favour of the local partner did not conflict with the interests of the foreign partner.[3] The formal control is shown in Table 1. There were four directors on the board. Two were nominated by Ericsson, while the other two were local shareholders. The local partner was chairman of the JV and the post of the GM was always left to a local professional executive in order to emphasize efficiency and effectiveness in the company. This attitude of the owners enabled the JV to have formal control in many important areas. Competence was the major criterion in appointing plant managers.

Table 1. Formal control

Determinants of control	Local partner	Ericsson	JV	Criticality
Shares 1971–75 1975–78 1978–85	(a) 26% (b) 40% (c) 60%	(a) 74% (b) 60% (c) 40%	—	Not critical
Board	2	2		Not critical
Chairman	The local partner throughout	—		Critical to exercise formal control
MD	—	—	A local executive	Critical for the development of the JV
Plant manager	—	—	·Local people	Critical for the development of the JV

The control through resources is illustrated in Table 2. As a buyer and a famous manufacturer of telecommunication equipment, Ericsson had enjoyed legitimacy for a great many years and could exercise some control through the procurement of input material. However, this control was short-lived, since the JV could meet all its requirements from both local and external sources after a certain period.

The local partner had both formal and informal control over the financial activities of the JV. He worked as managing partner and had day-to-day contact with the venture. The GM often required to consult with the local partner on financial matters. With a very few exceptions, all financial decisions were taken by the local partner during the last 15 years and his decisions were never challenged by the foreign partner.

The local partner could exercise control through the appointment of higher officials in the JV. However, the GM and the plant managers were also responsible for many appointments. Ericsson had no intention of retaining control in the technical area because the technology used in the JV was comparatively old. The JV succeeded in managing production, developing some new products and establishing an R&D department in the latter part of the operation.

From the beginning the JV had complete control over the marketing of its own products. It made contacts with the buyers, obtained orders, and finally supplied them on its own initiative. However, for the trading business, the JV had shared control with Ericsson, since it had to depend largely on Ericsson for offers, suggestions and technological information. Even the local partner enjoyed some control in marketing Ericsson's products, since he offered useful legitimacy and access to the many government buyers, which was essential in this context.

Co-operation/conflict

In the JV the partners were very co-operative over the years. Ericsson always extended a helping hand to the local people, so the transfer of technology was possible within a very

Table 2. Control through resources

Resources	Local partner	Ericsson	JV	Criticality
Input material	—	Control until the end of 1973	Responsibility during 1974 to 1985	Not critical as a source of control
Capital	Financial responsibility	—	—	Very critical source of control
Manpower	Control in major appointments	—	Responsible for ordinary appointments	Not critical to exercise control
Technology	—	Responsible until the end of 1973	Operations during 1974 to 1985	Critical for the JV's own control
Market	Meeting with the buyers	Supply technical information to the buyers	Marketing own products and trading activity	Main control with the JV

short time. No substantial conflict could arise in the JV due to the candour of the partners. Ericsson's main representative and the local partner had been personal friends since the end of the 60s and they could easily solve most of the problems.

Some implicit conflicts were, however, identified in the JV. There was a basic difference in opinion between the partners as to what would be its major area of interest. Ericsson was mainly interested in the trading business of the JV. The local partner's goal was always to produce more items locally and to gain recognition as a leading manufacturer of telecommunications components in the particular market. The local partner was somewhat suspicious of Ericsson's sincerity concerning the procurement of information. The JV needed information when selecting new products because it sought the rapid expansion of business through the increase of local production. It generally happened that such information arrived late or sometimes not at all. Another area of implicit conflict arose from the slow success of the JV in securing big local contracts.

On several occasions, the JV needed some concessions from Ericsson, because it faced real problems and expected favours from the foreign partner. The local management tried to explain the situation and Ericsson could understand the problem.

Performance

From 1980 to 1985 the turnover of the JV was between 10 and 15m SEK, while the profit after taxes was 15% thereof. The main representative of Ericsson found the local management to be efficient and the collaboration between the partners excellent, but could not understand why the JV could not do more trading business. The local partner and the GM asserted that local products were doing very well in the Indian market.

Besides manufacturing and initiating direct sale from Sweden, the JV had also arranged transfer of know-how from Ericsson to the government firms in recent years, which the GM regarded as a case of adaptation. The participation of both the partners was important for the JV but neither needed to interfere in the day-to-day activities. The JV had survived for 15 years in which no major crisis had arisen which could threaten its existence.[4] The JV was exposed to some external threats, since it could not find more products for local manufacturing due to legal restrictions on many attractive items.

The local partner's interest in the JV increased over time. He raised his share of capital to become the main owner and also devoted more time and energy to the success of the company. To Ericsson, the income from the JV had always been negligible compared with its other investments. But its interest in the JV was growing as it succeeded in signing some big technological contracts with the local government.

THE CASE OF KANTHAL INDIA

Kanthal, the foreign partner, is a medium-sized company compared with other Swedish multinationals, having sales of 1,671m SEK at the end of 1985. Its major area of production consists of electrical resistance materials and precision castings. Kanthal has now 20 foreign subsidiaries with both sales and manufacturing facilities in eight countries. The local partner has been in the business for a considerably long time and directly associated with Kanthal as the latter's representative in the Indian market for more than four decades.

Kanthal had been selling resistance materials in India since the 20s and succeeded in capturing 50% of the market during the late 50s and early 60s. As the demand for the resistance materials increased significantly, it became necessary to weigh the possibility of local production, inasmuch as the requirement could no longer be met by export from Sweden. Kanthal found the local agent as a suitable candidate for local partnership in order to start indigenous production. It was essential for a foreign investor to share equity with local interest to start manufacturing. After repeated negotiations, the JV was formed in 1965, having its head office in Calcutta, West Bengal. The JV has two manufacturing plants, one producing resistance wires (RW) while the other makes precision castings (PCG).

Mutual resource expectation

When the RW plant was established, it was decided that all the input materials would be supplied by Kanthal, as there was no local production. For the PCG plant, the situation was different, because many of its input materials were locally available. However, it was decided that expatriates would play a significant role in establishing contact with the local suppliers in the early years of the operation. During the establishment of the JV, the share capital was the same for both partners. When the PCG plant was set up, external finance was necessary and it was expected that local financial institutions would meet the requirement.

For the RW plant, no foreign recruitment was essential but the other factory needed help from expatriates due to the complex nature of production. The local partner had been given responsibility for all local recruitment. Under the agreement, Kanthal was to supply technology to the JV. The technology for the RW plant was simple and could easily be handed over to the local people. As far as the PCG plant was concerned, the technology was relatively modern and there was a need to serve foreign subsidiaries in India. Kanthal was expected to undertake the whole responsibility for the operation of the plant during the first years. The previous sales activity of the local partner was satisfactory and he was expected to contribute considerably in the marketing of the RW products. As the local partner had no experience of selling PCGs, Kanthal was expected to play a major role in approaching buyers unless the local agent could assume the full responsibility. The local partner was made sole distributor for both the products.

Exchange of resources over time

Kanthal supplied 95% of the input materials to the RW plant, while the rest were bought on the local market. In the PCG plant, Kanthal's contribution was at first 100% of the input materials. But due to the availability of indigenous substitutes, import was stopped already in 1974 but Kanthal still played a significant role in assessing the JV's needs and discovering the best possible alternatives from the local market. Contribution of the JV became important in this connection. Kanthal offered a credit facility all along to buy resistance materials, which solved a problem of working capital in the JV. The partners agreed to invest more but it was never realized. The local partner was directly involved with the major appointments in both the plants until the end of 1980. Kanthal played an important role by engaging expatriates and helping to select the right people for the PCG plant. In both the plants, the JV itself was to some extent responsible for personnel management.

Due to the simple nature of the technology, the JV personnel could perform all operational activities in the RW plant after two years of the JV's establishment. But in the PCG plant, Kanthal carried out the major task of production and other related activities until the expatriates left in 1979. Kanthal resumed its technical contribution to the plant after the signing of a new agreement between the partners in 1983. The local partner and the JV itself carried out the selling activity of both the products. The responsibility of the local partner was greater in this area as he was the sole agent for marketing the JV's products; he was, however, incapable of carrying out the function properly.

Control

During the formation of the JV, Kanthal and the local partner had equal ownership, which changed afterward with the signing of a new agreement in 1983. Due to change in the ownership, Kanthal lost 9% of its share to another local partner, and could finally retain only 40%. The formal control is shown in Table 3. There were altogether six members on the board of directors, three from each major partner. The local partner was MD until the end of 1980 and a new permanent MD came from Kanthal in 1983 as a part of the new agreement reached.

Kanthal had continuously carried sole responsibility for the procurement of input materials for the RW plant, since the JV had neither sufficient information nor legitimacy with the suppliers. Control through resources is illustrated in Table 4. There was production of PCG materials in the country and most of the raw materials were available locally. The JV was on good terms with the local suppliers and Kanthal's role in the procurement of precision materials became insignificant. From the beginning, the local partner had absolute financial control of the JV. The financial manager was sitting at the head office in Calcutta and dealt with most of the financial matters at both manufacturing plants. This executive was also responsible for finances at other companies of the local partner and had day-to-day contact with him. However, continuity of the credit facility

Table 3. Formal control

Determinants of control	Local partner	Kanthal	JV	Criticality
Shares	50%	40% to Kanthal and 10% to a selected local partner	—	Critical for equal formal control
Board	3	3	—	Critical for the balance of power
Chairman	Alternate chairman	Alternate chairman	—	Not critical
MD	—	Expatriate loyal to Kanthal	—	Very critical for Kanthal's control
Plant manager	Managers loyal to the local partner	—	—	Critical source of control for the local partner

Table 4. Control through resources

Resources	Local partner	Kanthal	JV	Criticality
Input material	—	Supply of RW materials from Sweden	Procurement of the PCG materials	Very critical for Kanthal's control
Capital	Control of financial resources	Credit facility	—	Critical source of control for the local partner
Manpower	Appointment of executives till 1980	Assisting the JV	Management of people after 1980	The local partner's control in the early days
Technology	—	Development work in the PCG plant	Operating activity in both plants	Very critical for Kanthal to have control in the PCG plant
Market	Sole selling agent	—	Significant performance	Not critical

gave some financial control to Kanthal. By appointing relatives and close associates to key positions, the local partner succeeded in exercising control of the JV.

In the PCG plant Kanthal exercised technological control through expatriates until 1979. This control pertained to development, testing and quality control of the products and overall maintenance of the machinery. The JV later had full control of technology and production. Due to the new agreement, Kanthal's control increased significantly with the adoption of relatively modern techniques and the establishment of a direct link with the JV.

Marketing was always the sole responsibility of the local partner and the MD had no authority to influence this activity. Kanthal and the local partner had different opinions as to how to carry out the marketing function. However, the JV had some control over sales, since its own staff used to market a significant proportion of both products. The JV was not entitled to compose an independent sales programme.

Co-operation/conflict

Both the partners were very co-operative at the beginning, inasmuch as they had known each other for many years and had a common goal, to increase their market share in India. But a major conflict emerged in 1980 when Kanthal was asked by the local government to sell 9% of its share to a local interest as the JV failed to fulfil the export target. The local partner was interested in acquiring those shares, which Kanthal did not accept. The local partner regarded the act by Kanthal as an insult and consequently filed a case against the latter at the Calcutta High Court in 1980. Besides the main grievance, other sources of dissatisfaction contributed to the damage of the relationship. One such was the death of the chairman of the JV in May 1980, because he acted as a bridge between the two major partners. The relationship deteriorated when Kanthal tried to appoint a new MD in the JV by its own initiative. One dissatisfaction from Kanthal's side consisted in the appointments of the local partner's relatives to the key positions of the JV.

Another conflicting issue was concerned with the selling performance of the local partner, because he was the sole selling agent for the JV products and Kanthal found him both inefficient and incapable of doing the job.

The partners signed a 'memorandum of understanding' on November 27th, 1983 to conclude the unfortunate crisis in order to create a favourable atmosphere for fruitful co-operation. The partners decided to respect their long-lasting relationship and forget the bitterness which had developed during the critical period.

Performance

During this long operational period, the profits of the JV were more or less satisfactory but unstable. In 1975, the JV earned a profit of Rs 2.35m which was the highest in its whole operating life. The total number of employees exceeded 170 by the end of 1986. As regards adaptation, the performance of the JV was satisfactory, since it could operate in the local market for such a long time. Kanthal continued to support the JV with the RW materials. Expatriates' participation in the PCG plant was related to the supervision of the day-to-day activity, technological upgrading and the establishment of relationships with the foreign buyers in India.

The JV has been in operation for more than two decades and recently survived from a dissolution. There was a great change in the share structure as Kanthal lost 9% of its original ownership to a third local partner. During this long period, the intensity of the relationship varied but both partners wanted the relationship to continue.

Both the partners realized the importance of the JV, and were thus unwilling to be detached from it. However, their interests diverged on some major issues. First of all, Kanthal considered it very important to leave the marketing responsibility to the JV for the latter's efficiency and future development, which the local partner could hardly accept. Secondly, Kanthal wanted formal and effective control over the JV, which the local partner had always opposed. Finally, the local partner was interested in immediate profits while Kanthal saw the opportunity from a long-term perspective.

CONCLUSION

At the outset, the foreign partners had absolute responsibility to procure input materials in both cases. For the RW plant in the case of Kanthal India, the foreign firm continued to supply input materials since it was a manufacturer of them and did not want to lose a reliable customer. Additional investment was required in both cases but only the partners in the case of Ericsson India could meet the requirement. Lack of financial resources greatly affected the relationship if the investment was acute and a partner failed to fulfil his commitment. One major difference between the cases was the policy of recruitment; in the case of Kanthal India emphasis was given to loyalty and relationship on one hand, and to efficiency and competence on the other. Change in technical responsibility was a common factor over time but foreign personnel were required to extend extensive support to improve the technical standard of the PCG plant in the case of Kanthal India. Marketing gradually became an important function of the JVs although the local partner was the sole selling agent in the case of Kanthal India.

The local partner in the case of Kanthal India found control necessary because he had difficulty in exercising control through the supply of critical resources. In the other case the local partner was well aware of his competence and was satisfied with keeping close contact with the JV. In this case the local government was the only buyer of the products, which ensured a stronger position for the local partner due to his ability in providing legitimacy. In the case of Kanthal India, the local partner was engaged to recruit his own people while efficient manpower were hired in the other case. This difference in attitude created suspicion and conflict between the partners in the case of Kanthal India but ensured understanding and co-operation in the other.

This study suggests that in developing mutual understanding, a foreign partner needs to expedite the transfer of technology to local hands if the technology concerned is not so complicated and modern, and also supply technical information whenever necessary. Major findings of the study are presented in Figure 2. A common problem in a JV can be avoided if a local partner avoids nepotism in recruiting local employees. This study asserts that the local partner's professional attitude in the case of Ericsson India creates reliance with the foreign partner while the opposite happens in the other, where blood relationship was stressed. A local partner can try to have a long-term perspective to match with the goal of the other partner. This is also positive for developing a relationship over time. The present study emphasizes that the difference between formal control and control through resources leads to conflict.

When a partner has formal control but lacks a corresponding resource, or when a partner provides a resource, even critical, but without formal control, can equally cause conflict. It is observed that control exercised by mutual agreement results in co-operation.

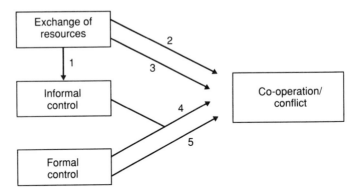

Explanations:

1 = Exchange of resources leading to informal control

2 = Exchange of resources on mutual understanding leading to co-operation

3 = Exchange of resources without understanding leading to conflict

4 = Conformity between formal and informal control leading to co-operation

5 = Formal control not properly backed by scarce resources leading to conflict

Figure 2. Co-operation/Conflict in Relation to Exchange of Resources and Control.

It is vital that a local partner is on good terms with the local government officials, but too much involvement with them may create suspicion. A local partner can openly discuss with the foreign partner about his contact with the authority, and also the purpose, if the topic is related with the JV's interests. In the case of Ericsson India, the local partner tried to understand the needs of the foreign partner and also kept the latter informed about what was going on in the JV, but it hardly occurred in the other case.

NOTES

1. This data was actually collected in connection with Syed Akmal Hyder's thesis, 'The Development of International Joint Venture Relationships: A Longitudinal Study of Exchange of Resources, Control and Conflicts' (1988).

2. Input materials were mainly different kinds of components to produce specialized communication equipments.

3. One executive of Ericsson commented, 'Our aim is to build up an organization in a right way so that it can represent Ericsson satisfactorily. There are many companies around the world who need either majority ownership or no ownership at all. But our case is different. We have government as our main customer, so we must be flexible concerning ownership and comply with the desires of the host country.'

4. Fifteen years have been calculated from 1971 to 1985. The JV was also operating at the end of 1987 but the present discussion covers the period up to 1985.

REFERENCES

Abdul, A. R. (1979). The Mixed Enterprises in Malaysia: A Study of Joint Ventures Between Malaysian Public Corporations and Foreign Enterprises, *Dissertation* (Katholicke Universiteit te Leuven, No. 36).

Ahn, D-S. (1980). Joint Ventures in the ASEAN Countries, *Intereconomics*, July–August, 193–198.

Aiken, M. and Hage, J. (1968). Organizational Interdependence and Interorganizational Structure, *American Sociological Review* **63**: 912–930.

Baranson, J. (1978). *Technology and the Multinationals: Corporate Strategies in a Changing World Economy*, MA: Lexington Books.

Barlew, F. K. (1984). The Joint Venture—A Way into Foreign Markets, *Harvard Business Review*, July–August **62**: 48–54.

Beamish, P. W. (1985). The Characteristics of Joint Ventures in Developed and Developing Countries, *Columbia Journal of World Business* **20** Fall, 13–19.

Beamish, P. and Lane, H. W. (1982). *Joint Venture Performance in Developing Countries*, Paper presented at the ASAC conference, Ottawa University.

Berg, S. V. and Friedman, P. (1980). Corporate Courtship and Successful Joint Ventures, *California Management Review* **22(2)**: 85–91.

Bivens, K. K. and Lovell, E. B. (1966). *Joint Ventures with Foreign Partners*, National Industrial Conference Board, Inc., New York.

Connolly, S. G. (1984). Joint Ventures with Third World Multinationals: A New Form of Entry to International Markets, *Columbia Journal of World Business*, (Summer) **19**: 18–22.

Dunning, J. (1978). *Eclectic Theory of International Production, Organizational Forms and Ownership Patterns*, Working paper, University of Reading.

Edström, A. (1975). *The Stability of Joint Ventures*, Re-Rapport, Företagsekonomiska Institutionen, Göteborgs Universitet, Sweden.

Franko, L. G. (1971). *Joint Venture Survival in Multinational Corporations*, New York: Praeger Publishers.

Friedmann, W. and Béguin, J-P. (1971). *Joint International Business Ventures in Developing Countries*, New York: Columbia University Press.

Ghauri, P. N. (1983). *Negotiating International Package Deals*, Stockholm: Almqvist and Wiksell International.

Gullander, S. (1976). Joint Ventures and Corporate Strategy, *Columbia Journal of World Business*, (Spring) **11**: 104–114.

Harrigan, K. R. (1986). *Managing for Joint Venture Success*, Lexington: Lexington Books.

Hyder, S. A. (1988). The Development of International Joint Venture Relationships: A Longitudinal Study of Exchange of Resources, Control and Conflicts, *Dissertation*, University of Uppsala, Sweden.

Killing, J. P. (1982). How to Make a Global Joint Venture Work, *Harvard Busines Review*, (May–June) **60**: 120–127.

Killing, J. P. (1983). *Strategies for Joint Venture Success*, Kent: Croom Helm Ltd.

Koot, W. T. M. (1986). *Underlying Dilemmas in the Management of International Joint Ventures*, Paper presented at the Conference of Co-operation Strategies in International Business held in October, The Wharton School and Rutgers Graduate School of Management.

Otterbeck, L. (1979). *Joint Ventures in Foreign Markets*, Stockholm School of Economics.

Otterbeck, L. (1980). *Management of Joint Ventures*, RP 80/10, Institute of International Business, Stockholm School of Economics.

Pfeffer, J. and Nowak, P. (1976). Joint Ventures and Interorganizational Interdependence, *Administrative Science Quarterly* **21**(3): 398–418.

Raveed, S. R. and Renforth, W. (1983). State Enterprise-Multinational Corporation Joint Ventures: How Well Do They Meet Partners' Needs?, *Management International Review* **23**(1): 47–57.

Reynolds, J. I. (1984). The 'Pinched Shoe' Effect of International Joint Ventures, *Columbia Journal of World Business* **19**(2): 23–29.

Simiar, F. (1983). Major Causes of Joint Venture Failures in the Middle East: The Case of Iran, *Management International Review* **23**(1): 58–68.

Tomlinson, J. W. C. (1970). *The Joint Venture Process in International Business: India and Pakistan*, Cambridge, Mass: MIT Press.

Vernon, R. (1972). *Restrictive Business Practices. The Operations of Multinational United States Enterprises in Developing Countries. Their Role in Trade and Development*, UN, New York.

Walmsley, J. (1982). *Handbook of International Joint Venture*, London: Graham and Trotman.

Wright, R. W. (1979). Joint Venture Problems in Japan, *Columbia Journal of World Business*, (Spring) **14**: 25–31.

23

Internationalization of Management—Dominance and Distance

Mats Forsgren and Ulf Holm

1. Divisionalization and Location of the Division Management

There has been a great deal of research into how the management of the big international company can handle more and more complex situations. One answer to this question since Chandler's study has been 'divisionalization' (Chandler, 1962; Stopford and Wells, 1972). By separating the company into 'quasi-firms' with their own management responsible for day-to-day operations the top management is able to concentrate on the overall strategic questions without being overloaded (Williamson, 1971; Franko, 1974; Hedlund and Åman, 1983; Fligstein, 1985; Palmer et al, 1987).

Divisionalization is expected to solve three basic management problems at the same time; size, operational diversity and geographical dispersion. One main theme behind this expectation is that the larger and more complex the firm the greater the difficulty faced by the top management in processing all the necessary information effectively to control the company (Galbraith, 1973; Galbraith and Nathanson, 1978; Egelhoff, 1988). Another main theme is that the top management has to stand aloof from all the special interests linked to the different operational units in order to be effective (Williamson, 1971). The distance, physical and psychic, between the different units and the headquarters becomes too large for the management to handle compared to the situation in the smaller, more homogeneous and geographically concentrated firm. It is assumed that by separating the company into several divisions, each having full responsibility for production and marketing within a certain field, and by making a sharp distinction between operational and strategic questions, these problems can be resolved.

In the divisionalized firm the managers of the divisions are especially important. Through these managers the group executive is expected to obtain the necessary strategic information about markets and products. The basic idea of divisionalization seems to be derived from confident (but unbiased) contacts between these two levels, even if very little has been said about how these contacts should be carried out. It is through the division

Department of Business Studies, Uppsala University
The project has been partly financed by The Swedish Council for Management and Work life Issues.

managers that the information between the operational level and the top management is mediated. On the one hand this role necessitates full-fledged contacts with the division's operations in order to achieve effective control thereof. On the other hand there is a need for intensive contacts between the division managers and headquarters in order to provide the latter with appropriate, strategic information.

This article focuses the problem of the physical location of the division management. It stresses the need for proximity between the headquarters and the division management on the one hand, as well as a corresponding physical contact between the division management and the operational level. When important subsidiaries, controlling great resources, are at a long distance from the corresponding division management a force is created that competes with the headquarter about nearness to the division management. The relation between the three management levels are here discussed in terms of dominance and distance. This idea is used to explain the internationalization of division management.

The following sections discuss the main components of this idea. First there is a discussion about divisionalization and psychic distance within the international firm. Then we discuss the concept of 'dominance and distance' and follow up with some structural data about the occurrence of foreign dominant centres in Swedish international firms and their dispersion in five different regions with increasing psychic distance from Sweden. The same analysis is then made for division managements. The chapter ends with some concluding remarks about the performance of the study, the results, and a short discussion about the concept of dominance and distance and its relation to the internationalization of management.

2. DIVISIONALIZATION AND PSYCHIC DISTANCE

In the literature about divisionalization it is difficult to find any profound discussion of the psychic distance between these three levels, notwithstanding its importance for the whole theory. This is more remarkable the more one considers the incongruity; on the one hand the importance of solid connections between the division managers and the divisions' operations, on the other the importance of links between the top management and the division managers. By psychic distance we mean all those factors which hinder information flows between two units (Johanson and Wiedersheim-Paul, 1975; Hallén and Wiedersheim-Paul, 1984; Sandström, 1990). If one considers knowledge as a critical resource, the importance of nearness becomes obvious. The more important the foreign operations of a division, the greater the problem created by the psychic distance between the division manager and the foreign operation. If the division managers fail to maintain good contacts with their divisions it will be impossible to control the different units' operation from that level, partly because of the lack of knowledge about the operational core of the units.

But the top management also needs frequent, confident contacts with the division managers in order to combine pieces of information and make strategic decisions, e.g. extension or shut down of operations. There is no reason to expect that this will decrease as a consequence of the growing importance of the divisions' foreign operations. There is also no a priori statement telling us which of the two couplings is the more important. When considerable psychic distance exists between the home-based and the foreign-based parts of the international firm priority cannot be given to the one without seriously obstructing the other.

One possible reason for not having analysed this problem more extensively is the concentration in the literature on size and operational diversity rather than on geographical dispersion, even though divisionalization is alleged to solve the management problem within international firms also (see e.g. Stopford and Wells, 1972). Distance between people and operations has not been a major problem in the analysis. After all, in a geographically concentrated firm, the location of division managers in relation to the operational units and headquarters respectively is not a profound issue.

In the international firm this problem becomes more obvious. The more the firm invests abroad and moves out from its former centre the more important it will be for the division managers to consider their physical location. At the same time there is no reason to assume that the top management's need of information links to the division level will decrease during the internationalization process. If we assume that distance is a real problem even in a world with better communication technology a serious dilemma will arise in the international firm because of these opposite requirements of connectedness. As illustrated in Figure 1 this dilemma is less obvious in the beginning of the internationalization process as long as the international part of the division is limited (t_1). But when investment in production and marketing abroad increases and the foreign subsidiaries become more and more important, absolutely and relatively, a certain point will be reached where it is no longer obvious that the head of the divisions will be placed in the home country (t_2). A significant force is created that is attracting the division management. When the subsidiary's activities and resource base increases, at the operational level, the division

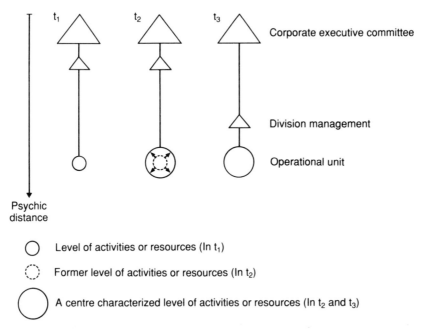

Figure 1. Internationalization of Division Management as a Consequence of Long Distance and Increasing Foreign Activities.

management is internationalized and placed in the vicinity of the subsidiary (t_3). The new location will be challenged in the future by forces from other units within the division which may become important in a corresponding way. This includes the option of moving back into the vicinity of the corporate executive committee.

Another reason for the limited concern with the physical location of division managers may also be the perspective used. In most studies a hierarchical perspective is applied which means that the headquarters is thought to design the formal organization in an optimal way considering the information processing requirements and capabilities at different levels (see e.g. Galbraith and Nathanson, 1978; Goehle, 1980; Hedlund, 1981; Egelhoff, 1988). A basic concept related to divisionalization then is decentralization, by which these requirements and capabilities are handled. But it seems obvious that in this context decentralization is above all related to the decision structure, not the physical location. In the divisionalized firm, international or national, the top management and the division managers are expected to work in each other's vicinity. The decisions, not the physical presence, are moved out from the headquarters. On the whole the locational aspects play a minor role in the analysis, which is surprising considering the importance of distance between units for the possibility to exchange information and co-operate. But a reasonable hypothesis from the traditional hierarchical perspective would be that the headquarters is unwilling to move the division management to the operational level, if this level is far away. This action would seriously harm the top management's possibilities for using the division manager as intended, even if a location nearer the most important subsidiaries would be an advantage from the division manager's point of view.

This conclusion is valid even when using an interorganizational framework (Pfeffer and Salancik, 1978). Such a framework implies that a divisionalized firm is described as a 'mandated federation' instead of a unitary organization (Provan, 1983, p. 83). The concept of federation means that a power structure related to the different operational units coexists with the hierarchical authority. A federation can be analysed as an organization-set in which the different units, e.g. divisions or subsidiaries within divisions, are embedded in local networks. Depending on the unit's position within the network and how this network is related to the whole organization the unit can exercise influence over its own and other units' strategy and structure, sometimes in opposition to the formal hierarchy (Forsgren, 1989; Ghoshal and Bartlett, 1990). A political rather than a hierarchical perspective lies at the heart of such a framework (Pfeffer, 1981).

Even if we use an interorganizational framework the top management is still prone to keep the division management in its neighbourhood due to the great importance of close contact between these two levels for the top management's position in a divisionalized organization. But the crucial difference between this and the hierarchical perspective appears in the possibility of top management hindering an internationalization of the division management. Within the hierarchical perspective the headquarters has the power to make the final decision on where to place the divisions as well as their management. Within the political perspective the existing formal organization, including the division structure and the location of management, is very much influenced by a continuing struggle between different interests, of which the top manager represents only one among many other interests with different powers (Fligstein, 1985). Therefore an expectation would be that the greater the power the foreign-based part of the international firm can execute because of the resources it controls the higher the possibility for attracting the management of the division to which it belongs, more so if this is in accordance with the interests of the division managers. Or expressed otherwise, the more important a foreign unit, e.g. a subsidiary, in relation to the whole group, the higher the probability that this unit will constitute a division with its management placed abroad.

3. DOMINANCE AND DISTANCE IN INTERNATIONAL MULTI-CENTRE FIRMS

From a political perspective there are two consequences of a foreign unit becoming a dominant part of a division. First, it will exert a stronger influence over the division's operations. Second, the division management will experience a greater need to gain access to the unit's local, critical resources, e.g. information, to be able to influence its activities. The larger a unit's share of a division's operations the more likely that the unit controls or has access to resources which are critical for the whole division. The more critical the resources the greater the division management's need for a local base, at least if it wants to have a significant influence on the unit's operations.

The dominance of a unit in the division is not, however, the only factor influencing the location of the division manager. As long as the psychic distance between the unit and the management is relatively small, e.g. between two neighbouring countries, the need to locate the management in the absolute vicinity is less even if the unit dominates the division's operations. But when the distance increases, the need to change the location in favour of the dominant unit also increases. The management's location near a specific foreign unit should therefore be regarded as a consequence of the concurrent combination of dominance and distance.

This background implies that particular attention should be paid to the character of the firms' foreign operational units. An international firm contains different foreign units, some having a very subordinate character, highly dependent on the parent company or other units in the group. Other foreign units have characteristics which give them a more dominant position in the firm. We call these latter units 'centres'.

The existence of foreign centre units in the international firm can roughly be connected to its internationalization process. Early in the process the foreign subsidiaries more or less constitute the parent company's long arm and are very dependent on the parent company for products and knowledge. As the subsidiaries develop and adjust their operations to the local national markets they will gradually disengage from the operations of the mother company. They become more independent relative to the parent company than before, but their influence on the corporate strategy of the whole group is limited.

A further internationalization implies that some firms and subsidiaries grow in a way which gives them a dominant position above the local level. The former periphery develops into new centres of power which compete with the top and division managements for influence on the corporate strategy of the firm. The earlier centre-periphery structure with the centre in the home country has changed to a structure with centres in several different countries (Forsgren, 1989, compare the concept of heterarchy in Hedlund, 1986). The multi-centre structure can be especially prominent in highly internationalized firms where there are several geographically separated subsidiaries, more or less interdependent through their respective business networks in which they are embedded (Forsgren et al, 1990).

In the multi-centre firm it is expected that different centres 'pull' in different directions with different power. The firm's continuing development will result from the positions the centres have in their markets, their interests and the resources they can mobilize to implement their interests, and how they in different ways are dependent on each other and the top management. In an earlier article we have labelled this development of international firms into multi-centre structures 'internationalization of the second degree' (Forsgren et al, 1991).

In this context a centre in an international firm is defined as a foreign unit—preferably a subsidiary—which has a significant influence on the firm's operations. Such centres may have different characteristics and functions but have in common that other units in the firm are more or less dependent on them. The relative size is of importance to the extent that a large unit, *ceteris paribus*, can be assumed to be of greater importance than a small one. If the unit also has operations in several countries and is involved in product- or process-development the character of a centre is stressed.

An important aspect is the operational connections and the conditions of dependency these connections constitute. A unit's competence and capacity can be crucial for other units' possibilities to compete and develop their business. A function, e.g. production, marketing, or R&D, which refers to other parts of the firm, gives the unit an importance disproportionate to its relative size in the firm. The concept of centre therefore contains both a size-dimension and a dimension which mirrors the conditions of operational dependencies between the units in a firm.

These characteristics indicate the difficulties inherent in unequivocally deciding how a centre should be identified and delimited. It will be rather a matter of distinguishing centre-characteristics and finding different indicators of the phenomenon. The theoretical base, however, would be on one hand the consequences for the rest of the firm of the removal of the unit from the firm and on the other hand the consequences of such a removal for the unit itself. If the firm's dependence on the unit is high substantial consequences will ensue which should be compared with those arising for the single unit. The part which would experience the least consequences can be assumed to be in a better position to influence the other and consequently the activities which are carried out. Figure 2 illustrates how an activity with a character of centre creates a centre unit. The unit belongs to a division which sometimes consists of other units which also can be classified as centres.

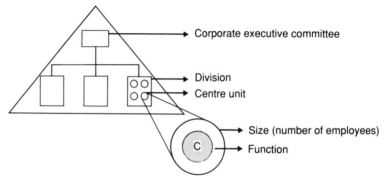

Figure 2. Size and Function as Indicators of a Unit's Centre Characteristics.

4. MULTI-CENTRE STRUCTURES AND THE INTERNATIONALIZATION OF DIVISION MANAGEMENT

To what extent can we see traces of multi-centre structures in Swedish international companies and how can we relate these traces to the internationalization of the division management? A partial answer is given in a study of 22 of the most internationalized firms in 1989 (Forsgren et al, 1991). Four indicators were employed in that study in order to find foreign-based centres, related to production, marketing, purchasing and R&D respectively.

A production centre was defined as a foreign subsidiary manufacturing and selling a product to at least five countries except the local market. These sales must account for at least 25% of the subsidiary's turnover. To be a production centre the subsidiary must also have product development of its own. Correspondingly, a marketing centre and a purchasing centre signified a foreign subsidiary with full responsibility for marketing and purchasing respectively of the products within a business area and encompassing at least five countries. If a foreign subsidiary independently carried out R&D aiming at fulfilling the requirements of the group as a whole (or a large part thereof) it qualified as a research centre.

The level of five countries except the local market is of course crucial for identifying centres. This requirement is arbitrary but is motivated to the extent that the level should be more than two countries in order not to include local units with a certain amount of cross-border selling. At the same time the level can not be set too high since a whole continent consist of relatively few countries. (The US has because of its size and significance of the market been excluded from the rule of the 'five countries level'. For units placed in North America which do not fulfil this rule an additional criterion has been applied saying that the unit shall have at least 10% of the corresponding division's turnover.) The level of five countries mirrors two aspects of the criteria for a centre. These are on the one hand the size of the unit and on the other hand the internationalization on the operational level.

The indicators used are not unobjectionable. They could have been defined in another way or other indicators could have been used as well. There are for example large subsidiaries not covered by the definitions because their operations are not directed to as many countries as are stipulated. Nevertheless the indicators have been used primarily as a crude measure of the existence of the phenomenon as such rather than as an attempt to determine the exact number of centres within every single firm.

All the data were collected via extensive interviews, which entailed possibilities of explaining the meaning of the concept of a centre and the indicators used. A certain amount of arbitrariness is unavoidable when deciding whether a subsidiary qualifies as a centre according to a certain indicator. Sometimes there has been a matter of judgment, e.g., whether a product accounts for more than 25% of a subsidiary's sales or whether a research activity is directed to the group as a whole or not (see Holm (1991) for a more detailed discussion of methodological problems).

5. EXISTENCE OF CENTRES

The existence of centres in different firms is described in Table 1. In the 22 firms there were altogether 265 overseas centres in 1989. Production centres are most common, 206,

Table 1. Number of centres in different firms

Firm	Production	Centre functions Marketing	Purchasing	R&D	Total
AGA	0	0	0	0	0
Alfa Laval	29	1	0	0	30
ASSI	0	0	0	0	0
Astra	0	4	0	2	6
Atlas Copco	8	1	0	1	10
Dynapac	6	4	0	1	11
Electrolux	65	1	0	0	66
Ericsson	5	5	0	0	10
ESAB	5	1	0	0	6
Esselte	9	6	0	0	15
Euroc	3	0	0	0	3
Gambro	8	4	0	2	14
MoDo	0	1	0	0	1
NCB	1	0	0	0	1
Nobel	10	0	0	1	11
Perstorp	7	2	0	0	9
Pharmacia	3	2	0	1	6
Saab	3	2	0	0	5
Sandvik	8	3	0	0	11
SCA	3	3	0	2	8
SKF	26	1	0	8	35
Volvo	7	0	0	0	7
Total	206	41	0	18	265

followed by marketing centres, 41. Research centres are less common, only 18, with eight in SKF. Purchasing centres were non-existent.

Table 1 also indicates that there are great differences in the occurrence of centres between firms, with Electrolux, SKF and Alfa Laval at the one extreme and AGA and ASSI at the other.

Table 2 depicts the geographical spread of the centres into five different regions, according to the psychic distance from Sweden. For the definition of psychic distance to each country see Johanson and Wiedershiem-Paul (1975). A recent study made by Nordström (1991) shows that the rank of different countries' psychic distance from Sweden are about the same as in the study made by Johanson and Wiedersheim-Paul (1975).

The centre structure seems to be most frequent in Europe 1, North America and Europe 2 with 69, 60 and 87 centres respectively. In total, there is a concentration of centres in Europe and North America of 82% which to a certain extent mirrors the geographical distribution of the firms' business activities in general. This pattern is also evident at the firm level although Alfa Laval, Electrolux, Ericsson and Esselte have centres in the Nordic countries and/or the world outside Europe and North America.

Table 2. Number of centres in different regions with increasing psychic distance from Sweden[1]

Firm	Nordic countries[2]	Europe 1[3]	North America	Europe 2[4]	RoW[5]	Total
AGA	0	0	0	0	0	0
Alfa Laval	5	11	4	7	3	30
ASSI	0	0	0	0	0	0
Atlas Copco	0	6	3	1	0	10
Astra	1	3	0	0	2	6
Dynapac	0	5	2	2	2	11
Electrolux	10	9	21	24	2	66
Ericsson	0	2	0	3	5	10
ESAB	0	2	2	2	0	6
Esselte	0	8	3	1	3	15
Euroc	0	0	2	1	0	3
Gambro	0	3	2	7	2	14
MoDo	0	0	1	0	0	1
NCB	0	1	0	0	0	1
Nobel	1	2	2	6	0	11
Perstorp	0	0	2	6	1	9
Pharmacia	2	0	4	0	0	6
Saab Scania	1	2	2	0	0	5
Sandvik	0	4	3	1	3	11
SCA	1	1	0	6	0	8
SKF	0	10	6	18	1	35
Volvo	0	2	1	2	2	7
Total	21	71	60	87	26	265

[1] Africa has no centres and is therefore excluded from the table
[2] Except Sweden
[3] Great Britain, Holland, Belgium and Germany
[4] Countries in the rest of Europe
[5] Rest of the world
Source: Interview material

6. INTERNATIONALIZATION OF DIVISION MANAGEMENT

The main organizational structure of the studied firms is the global product organization in which operations are divided according to product areas, each unit responsible for international as well as domestic operations. These units constitute the first organizational level beneath the corporate executive officer and the usual name is division or business area. Here we will use the former expression. Legally they can be either a company or an organizational unit within the corporation. In some countries foreign subsidiaries are shared by several divisions but to a large extent the divisions have their own subsidiaries. Sometimes this organization is supplemented by a regional or functionally oriented structure into a matrix, but typical for the investigated firms is the dominance of the product area dimension.

By the term division management we mean the executive officer for the global division and his staff, often consisting of only a few people. The criteria for a division management to be internationalized are that it be located abroad and have a direct responsibility for reporting on the division's operations to the parent company. The degree of a firm's internationalization of division management then is a matter of the number of its division managers stationed abroad.

Table 3 depicts the number of internationalized division managements in the same firms as Tables 1 and 2.

Division management was internationalized in 31 cases concentrated in companies with an internationalization degree of about 50% or more (Forsgren et al, 1991). On the whole, there seems to be a concentration in Europe and North America on about the same level as in the case of the centres. Europe 1 is the most important region for placing divisional headquarters. It should be observed, however, that five of the 14 headquarters in this region belong to just one company, namely Esselte. Only one firm, Astra, has a division management in the Nordic countries (outside Sweden).

The extent to which these divisional headquarters abroad are connected to divisions with corresponding centres is shown in Table 4. The connection between foreign centres in a division and the existence of division management abroad is evident here.

Three of the firms, however, have divisions with management abroad without corresponding foreign centres. Esselte has located the management for two of their

Table 3. Internationalization of division management in different regions with increasing psychic distance from Sweden[1]

Firm	Nordic countries[2]	Europe 1[3]	North America	Europe 2[4]	RoW[5]	Total
AGA	0	0	0	0	0	0
Alfa Laval	0	2	0	0	0	2
ASSI	0	0	0	0	0	0
Atlas Copco	0	0	0	0	0	0
Astra	1	2	0	0	1	4
Dynapac	0	2	0	0	1	3
Electrolux	0	0	2	3	0	5
Ericsson	0	0	0	0	0	0
ESAB	0	0	1	0	0	1
Esselte	0	5	1	0	0	6
Euroc	0	2	0	1	0	3
Gambro	0	0	1	0	1	2
MoDo	0	0	0	0	0	0
NCB	0	1	0	0	0	0
Nobel	0	0	0	0	0	0
Perstorp	0	0	0	2	0	2
Pharmacia	0	0	0	0	0	0
Saab Scania	0	0	0	0	0	0
Sandvik	0	0	0	0	1	1
SCA	0	0	0	0	0	0
SKF	0	0	1	0	0	1
Volvo	0	0	0	0	0	0
Total	1	14	6	6	4	31

[1] Africa has no centres and is therefore excluded from the table
[2] Except Sweden
[3] Great Britain, Holland, Belgium and Germany
[4] Countries in the rest of Europe
[5] Rest of the world
Source: Interview material

Table 4. Close co-existence of internationalized division management and centre units

Firm	Division management	Centre units	Country
Astra	4	4	Denmark, Germany, England, Australia
Alfa Laval	2	2	Germany, Belgium
Atlas Copco	1	1	Belgium
Dynapac	3	3	Germany, England, Brazil
Electrolux	5	4	USA, Italy
Esselte	6	2	England, USA
ESAB	1	1	USA
Euroc	3	0	England, Holland, Austria
Gambro	2	2	USA, Japan
Perstorp	2	2	France, Austria
Sandvik	1	1	Germany
SKF	1	1	USA
Total	31	23	

Source: Interview material

divisions in England and in Belgium respectively, while the corresponding centre has the opposite location. Nevertheless one of Esselte's divisions has its management in Europe but the two corresponding centres in Asia. In the case of Euroc at least two out of three division managements are placed in the vicinity of the corresponding units which are claimed to be central for the division's operations. These units have, however, because of their operational character, been excluded from the centre definition as they basically produce cement which is not exported and are consequently considered as national rather than international business according to the five-country criteria.

The extent to which the internationalization of division management is connected to dominance of foreign centres can be analysed further by comparing the significance of these centres between those with and those without division management abroad. The underlying hypothesis is that the greater the dominance of a centre within its corresponding division the stronger the forces which lead to a placement of the division management in the vicinity of the centre. This analysis is illustrated in Table 5, which contains the centres' average share of the corresponding division in both groups.

Table 5. Difference in relative size between production centres in divisions with 'Foreign' or 'Swedish' placed management

	'Foreign' division managements	'Swedish' Division managements
Number of Divisions ...	25	117
... number of corresponding production centres	18	106
Production centres' average[1] share of division	41%	14%
Divisional share of total firm	10%	16%

[1] The centres' average share is based on the relative number of employees. For foreign division managements only 10 out of the 18 units characterized as centres have been included because of difficulties in gaining access to numbers of employees in every single centre unit

Source: Interview material

Table 5 shows that the majority, 117 out of 148 of the firms' divisions still have their management located in Sweden. Moreover, for the subsidiaries analysed the average share of the divisions is three times as high for divisions with an internationalized management, 41%, than for divisions with the management in Sweden, 14%. This supports the hypothesis the more dominant the centre is in the division the higher the probability that the division management will be located abroad.

7. CONCLUDING REMARKS

For a causal analysis of firms' multi-centre structures versus internationalization of management a longitudinal study would have been preferable. The analysis above, however, indicates that the existence of functional centres of gravity abroad can be an important factor behind the internationalization of the management structure in Swedish firms. When the dominance of such units within the division has reached a certain level the interests behind the internationalization of management have become strong enough to enforce the relocalization.

A relocalization, however, seems also to be dependent on the psychic distance between the division headquarters and the centre unit. A centre unit, e.g. in the Nordic countries, does not seem to attract division headquarters even if it is highly dominant in the division. The distance between the two levels must be great enough to cause management problems for the division headquarters before a move out to the centre will be considered. A certain combination of dominance and distance is therefore needed.

In some firms, despite the combination of dominance and distance, the division management has not yet been relocated abroad. Insofar as the distance between the division management and the foreign units is great there is a potential 'force' creating an expectation for a further internationalization of the division management. A consequence of our analysis is that such a development is expected when the firms' centre structures in the world outside the Nordic countries have reached a certain magnitude, including dominating centres. Based on our material we would expect that managements for some divisions in firms such as Atlas Copco, Dynapac, Perstorp, Pharmacia, SCA and Volvo are more likely to be internationalized than managements of divisions without any centres of corresponding significance.

The development of firms into multi-centre structures creates foreign bases of substantial resources on the operative level. These bases constitute influence structures which more or less deviate from the formal organization structure. The firms' internationalization of division management can be seen as a gradual adaptation of the formal organization to such influence structures. The theoretical conclusion then is: the higher the significance of a multi-centre structure, the higher the probability of an internationalization of management and consequently a gradual relocalization of the governance structure in the firms. According to the political perspective on the divisionalized firm the headquarter's loss of vicinity to the division management will change the power balance between the top level and the division mangement level in favour of the latter.

REFERENCES

Chandler, A. (1962) *Strategy and Structure: Chapters in the History of the American Industrial Enterprise.* MIT Press: Cambridge, MA.

Egelhoff, W. (1988) *Organizing the Multinational Enterprise: An Information-Processing Perspective.* Ballinger Publishing Company: Cambridge, MA.

Fligstein, N. (1985) The Spread of the Multinational Form among Large Firms, 1919–1979. *American Sociological Review* **50:** 377–391.

Forsgren, M. (1989) *Managing the Internationalization Process, The Swedish Case,* Routledge: London.

Forsgren, M., Holm, U., Johanson, J. (1991) The Internationalization of the Second Degree. In Young, S. (ed) *Europe and the Multinationals: Issues and Responses for the 1990s,* Edwar Elgar: Cheltenham.

Franko, L. (1974) The Move toward a Multinational Structure in European Organizations, *Administrative Science Quarterly* **19:** 493–506.

Galbraith, J. (1973) *Designing Complex Organizations.* Addison Wesley: Reading, MA.

Galbraith, J., Nathanson, D. (1978) *Strategy Implementation: The Role of Structure and Process.* West Publishing Company: St Paul, MN.

Ghoshal, S., Bartlett, C. A. (1990) The Multinational Corporation as an Interorganizational Network. *Academy of Management Review* **15:** 603–625.

Goehle, D. (1980) *Decision Making in International Corporations.* UMI Research Press: Ann Arbor, MI.

Hallén, L., Wiedersheim-Paul, F. (1984) The Evolution of Psychic Distance in International Business Relations. In Hägg, J., Wiedersheim-Paul, F. (eds) *Between Market and Hierarchy.* Department of Business Studies: Uppsala.

Hedlund, G. (1981) Autonomy of subsidiaries and formalization of headquarter-subsidiary relationships in Swedish multinational enterprises. In Otterbeck (ed) *The Management of Headquarter-Subsidiary Relationships in Multinational Corporations.* Gover: Stockholm.

Hedlund, G. (1986) The Hypermodern MNC—a Heterarchy? *Human Resource Management* 25(1): 9–35.

Hedlund, G., Åman, P. (1984) *The Foreign Subsidiaries Headquarter Relationship.* Sveriges Mekanför-bund: Stockholm.

Holm, U. (1991) *Internationalisering av Andra Graden—En Studie av Svenska Företags Internationella Centrumstruktur* (Internationalization of the Second Degree—A Study of Swedish Companies Foreign Structures). Department of Business Studies: Uppsala.

Johanson, J., Wiedersheim-Paul, F. (1975) The Internationalization of the firm—four Swedish case studies, *Journal of Management Studies* 12(3).

Nordström, K., (1991) *The Internationalization Process of the Firm—Searching for New Patterns and Explanations,* Institute of International Business, Stockholm School of Economics.

Palmer, D., Friedland, R., Jennings, P. D., Powers, M. E. (1987) The Economics and Politics of Structure: The Multinational Form and the Large US Corporation. *Administrative Science Quarterly* **32:** 25–48.

Pfeffer, J. (1981) *Power in Organizations.* Pitman Books Ltd: Marchfield, MA.

Pfeffer, J., Salancik, G. (1978) *The External Control of Organizations.* New York: Harper & Row: New York.

Provan, K. G. (1983) The Federation as an Interorganizational Linkage Network. *Academy of Management Review* 8(1): 78–79.

Sandström, M. (1990) The Cultural Influence on Business Relationships. In Forsgren, M., Johanson, J. (eds) *Managing Networks in International Business.* Gordon & Breach Inc: Philadelphia (forthcoming).

Stopford, J. M., Wells, L. T. (1972) *Managing the Multinational Enterprise.* London: Longman Groups Ltd: London.

Williamson, O. E. (1971) Managerial discretion, organization form and the multidivision hypothesis. In Marris, R., Wood, A. (eds) *The Corporate Economy Growth, Competition and Innovative Power.* Macmillan: London, pp. 343–386.

24

International Strategy: A Study of Norwegian Companies

Pat Joynt

INTRODUCTION

During the recent past, there has been a growing interest in the international activities of nation-states, as well as business activity and industrial organizations. The focal point of major research associated with business activity has been foreign direct investment (FDI) and the multinational corporation. Delving into the dynamic aspects, some Scandinavian researchers in the 1970s placed an emphasis on outlining patterns as well as key dynamic factors in the internationalization process (e.g. Johanson and Wiedersheim-Paul, 1975; Johanson and Vahlne, 1977).

Norway, with a population of slightly over four million people and a land area larger than its counterparts in West Germany or Britain, provides an interesting Scandinavian setting to probe the internationalizing process. At the turn of the century the country was the poorest in Europe; however, industrial development, first fuelled by hydro-power and, later, by North Sea oil, has made Norway a highly prosperous country. Exports and imports now account for over 70% of Norway's GNP, yet the top 30 firms in the country employ no more. than a total of 150,000 people. (As a small country with small organizations by international standards, Norway has to partake in open and free competition on the international scene.) There are 3,000 companies in Norway engaged in exporting; the ten largest account for 34% of the nation's total export. Only two of the companies. *Norsk Hydro* and *Statoil*, are among the 500 largest in the world, both are partly owned by the government.

The focus of this paper is on 100 of these Norwegian companies and their dynamic (longitudinal) behaviour in the international environment. It has been common for these firms to use some type of niche strategy. In order to capture the salient aspects of this behaviour, we have relied heavily on Porter's (1985) model.

Porter used a model to analyse international competition at the organizational and national levels. The model, consisting of some nine basic activities and their associated co-ordination and integration, has formed the basis for the analysis in this paper. In addition to Porter's work, the works of Scandinavian researchers, notably from Sweden, are also integrated.

CAPTURING THE BROADER CONCEPT OF THE INTERNATIONALIZATION PROCESS

According to Ansoff (1987), scientific interest in strategic behaviour of purposive organizations dates back to the early 1950s. He defines strategy as the 'loop which guides the process by which an organization adapts to its external environment.' While one can debate the nature of this process (as a problem of policy formulation, a problem of strategy formulation, an action involving top management, or an organic unmanaged process), there is little disagreement about strategy being one of the key organizational processes in contemporary organization life.

It is impossible to do justice to the plethora of literature on the process of internationalization; the concept itself tends to be used with different meanings by different researchers. For our purposes, the concept of *internationalization* is taken to mean the process by which international business activities are developed at the level of a firm, industry, or even, nation-state. While this process may apply to inward, as well as outward, activities, our emphasis is on internationalization as an external development using an inner functional orientation. Of course, inward and outward behaviour of firms is becoming increasingly intertwined.

A further problem in delineating the internationalization concept arises from determining exactly what it means for a firm to be involved in international business. Simplistically, one might use a measure such as the proportion of international sales to total company sales. However, this does not capture the broad dimensions of international involvement such as the investment aspects. To capture the broader perspective of internationalization, and, ultimately, to explain the process, it is appropriate to consider (1) the level of organizational commitment to international operations (resources allocated, organizational arrangements, personnel aspects), (2) the range of markets serviced, and (3) the objective of international marketing operations (Luostarinen, 1979).

From a research perspective two areas seem to be of particular importance in understanding the internationalization process. First, there has been a focus on the particular decisions, or stages, which make up part of the internationalization process. Consider, for example, the initial decision to enter and then develop export operations (Welch and Wiedersheim-Paul, 1980). Second, there is the initial foreign investment decision (Buckley et al, 1979). When one attempts to identify the key determinants of decisions taken at a particular point in time (or over a limited phase of the internationalization process), it can be seen that such research does contribute to an overall understanding of what happens and why.

However, a vital question remains unanswered: *What ties the overall process together?* Because of the time perspective, a complete analysis of a firm's internationalization process is a demanding exercise. In tracing the internationalization of Swedish and Finnish companies through time, Johanson and Vahlne (1977) discerned an evolutionary pattern of development with a variation in operative influences at different stages; but with an underlying importance of the learning process as a basis for forward momentum. Perceptions of risk and uncertainty, and control, were correlated with knowledge of growth in the phases in international development. Often both risk and control were high during the initial phases of the firms' internationalization process. Also, Walters (1985) in an analysis of the Norwegian experience in the UK, pointed out that the obvious starting point for studies of this type was the large body of research already done on patterns of internationalization, especially those using work involving other Scandinavian firms.

Fundamental to internationalization are the ideas of learning and a feedback process. Uncertainty and risk are minimized by following strategies which direct initial overseas operations to those foreign markets where the firm is most experienced, and where the barriers to the retrieval and interpretation of information are perceived to be low. Penetration of foreign markets is hypothesized to proceed in a gradual, carefully orchestrated manner; extensive resource commitments are only initiated when significant experimental knowledge has been acquired by the organization.

Gandemo and Mattsson (1984) examined internationalization strategies of Swedish firms. Their findings point to a pattern of step-wise market penetration, and the importance of cultural factors when selecting initial overseas markets to enter. There is also considerable empirical support to the step-wise model outside a Scandinavian context. Cavusgil and Godiwalla (1982) have commented that studies of British, Australian, Swedish, French and American firms all support a gradual pattern in internationalization. However, Hedlund and Kverneland (1983), Turnbull, (1985) and others caution against such a tacit acceptance of evolutionary pattern as a definitive pattern; it should not be the sole reflection of a firm's strategy.

Much research work remains to be done in unravelling the key elements of processes at work in internationalization. The investigation described here seeks to contribute to this end. The research, given the nature of internationalization has a longitudinal bias: as Mintzberg and McHugh (1985) have noted, 'to teach strategies . . . requires a longitudinal approach.' Other disciplinary dimensions should also be included in the analysis of an organization's strategy concerning the internationalization process. Differential advantages and disadvantages are part of a large body of economic theory which has often formed the basis for the concept of internationalization. Also, work in the area of technology (Thompson, 1967) and environment (Joynt, 1981) as well as work in production and materials-handling theory bring these issues close to the topic we now call internationalization. Another important dimension includes such demographics of the firm as size, ownership, location and years of export or other international experience. At this stage, the present research model followed Welch (1979) and comprised the following six axes:

1. Production methods
2. Sales objectives
3. Organization structure
4. Market servicing methods
5. Markets
6. Personnel

Each axis is described in a longitudinal fashion as shown in Figure 1. The axes along with the activities identified on each axis, formed the first phase of the research involved.

There is a substantial amount of literature on international competition which dates back to the days of Adam Smith. Porter (1986) points out that this literature is limited when it comes to the choice of a firm's international competition strategy. Porter also points out that while the appropriate unit of analysis is 'industry', international strategy for the firm often 'collapses' to a series of domestic strategies. Taking the Norwegian perspective, it seems natural to accept the organization as the basic unit of analysis. From a practical point of view, the main arguments involve the small size of the typical international-oriented company in Norway. From a research point of view, the orientation is toward cases. This study, therefore, departs somewhat from the traditional industry bias, from one that Porter often uses, toward the single case study of a Norwegian firm. However, the results presented here are an aggregate conclusion based on many individual company cases involving many different branches.

The two key concepts in Porter's (1985) 'value chain model' are internal and external organizational activities and integration. Each firm is a collection of some nine generic and discrete activities, according to Porter, which add to or detract from the firm's total

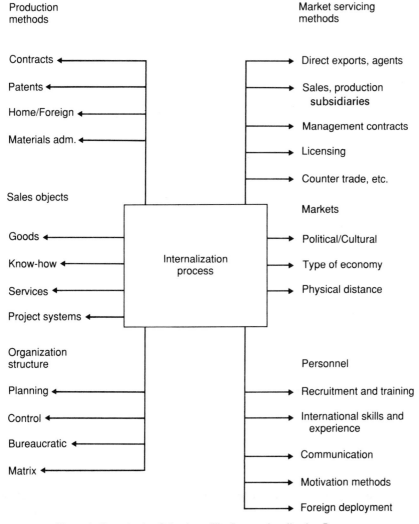

Figure 1. Organization Behaviour: The Internationalization Process.

value. Porter divides these activities into two broad groups which are called primary activities and support activities. The four support activities include:

- Procurement, which is the obtaining of purchased inputs;
- Technology Development, which encompasses design of product activities, basically Research and Development;
- Human Resource Management, which is the recruiting, training, organizing and development of personnel; and,
- Infrastructure, which encompasses activities such as management, accounting, legal, and strategic planning.

The primary activities are those involved in the physical creation of a product or service and its delivery to the market: service after the sale is also included. Porter uses five typical firm functions in his model; we have added a sixth based on the results obtained from the Norwegian research reported.

Porter's five are:

1. Inbound logistics
2. Operations
3. Outbound logistics
4. Marketing and Sales
5. Service
6. The one we have added as the sixth is *internationalization*.

In an international organization, strategy often involves deciding how to spread these activities above among countries. Secondly, co-ordination is required so that the activities from the different countries are integrated with each other. In this area, management faces an array of strategic options. Such factors as economies of scale, product/market learning curves and comparative advantages are important here. Co-ordination also allows a firm to react to a dynamic world of shifting comparative advantages. Co-ordination strategies also give the firm the flexibility of responding to both competitors and markets.

Porter (1985) also suggests that a firm must make the strategic decision as to whether to emphasize price, focus or differentiation as a means of gaining a competitive advantage from the world market place. The above aspects of Porter's theory were used along with the Welch model (Figure 1) as the basic theoretical framework for this study.

THE ACTION RESEARCH METHODOLOGY

Action-learning and the associated action-research processes have received considerable attention in the recent literature. Common expressions such as 'learning from our mistakes', 'the only constant thing is change', 'history always repeats itself', 'live and learn' all are part of the action learning and research processes. Learning is often defined in terms of gaining knowledge, of being informed, or of retention in the memory. Research, which should be closely associated with the learning process, involves the traditional goals of understanding, prediction and control. Linking research and learning together offers us, (as students of organizational behaviour), an opportunity to study, document, and share our findings with interested readers. Feedback is central to both the learning and research processes and can be studied in two ways: theoretical (for example, cybernetics); or concrete (for example, an export contract). In a behavioural context, feedback involves two types of reactions and one can classify them as positive and negative at this point. Often, the concept of learning loops is introduced at this point as an initial loop that may involve the immediate experience and the consequences from feedback. The model for both loops is an essential part of the behaviour methodology literature and can be shown as a *Single Loop Action Learning Process:*

Situation Now > Behavioural Action > Response > Consequence(s) of Action which is an Error, or *non-essential.*

The error can be corrected by maintaining the central features of the organization theory-in-use, or one can look at learning as a *Double Loop Learning Process:*

Situation now > Behavioural Action > Response > Consequence of the Action is Conflict where New Norms and New Learning are Necessary

In this last example, the action, or episode, cannot be corrected using in-use-theories; rather, inquiry will take the form of the restructuring of organizational norms and, thus, new strategies. Conflict is resolved through the process of inquiry and new solutions (Argyris and Schon, 1978).

A single human act (management in the context of this project) is usually regarded as the basic element of an organization. This element includes the individual involved in a situation and requires purposeful action (Pearsons, 1937). Organizational structure is created by repeated actions (Weick, 1969) or loops of learning. The network of activities which emerges from these action loops are often called Formal Organization context. There is a great deal of literature which tells us that an international-oriented status system is necessary if a company is to succeed on the international scene. The same is also true with international communications, international growth, and understanding international conflict processes. An obvious conclusion is that we should be studying status, communications, growth and conflict by observing the actions of the managers who, in essence, are central actors in any (international) organization. We now turn to the essence of this section, namely 'action learning' as defined by Reg Revans.

Revans (1983) suggests that Learning (L) involves the acquisition of Programmed Knowledge (P) and Questioned Insight (Q), resulting in this learning equation: $L = P + Q$. The principal interest in this internationalization project is with Q. The (P) model of learning often involves a basic research phase followed by applied research. Theory is developed around the issues associated with each phase, and the research methodologies often involve a major emphasis on the validity and reliability of the concepts and models involved. The (P) model is often very descriptive in the basic research phase, and becomes normative in the applied research phase (e.g., a typical textbook on International Management). The descriptive model becomes normative as most of the actors involved will agree with it; it describes, from a theoretical point of view, the way the world ought to be. Using the (Q) orientation, the research team developed the project around groups of managers who represented, approximately, 100 Norwegian firms. Most of the managers had key middle and top management positions in their respective organizations; and the network framework used for the project was a one-year advanced university course in international management involving some 250 hours of direct contact with the group.

Early in this one-year course each manager was given a brief two-page summary of the purpose and scope of the research project. They were, also, given approximately 20 hours of instruction on research methodologies and the research process. They were then asked to prepare a 20-page report on their own organization. In summary the project involved:

Phase 1: Statement of the problem or opportunity (in this project, a summary of the internationalization process for their organization).
Phase 2: A course on research methodologies and processes.
Phase 3: A two to three month period to write their research report.
Phase 4: An emphasis on using the Welch and Porter models in writing the final report, using (Q) orientations.
Phase 5: Feedback on their report with respect to their own organization and the results of the other organizations.

In summary, the participants were asked to use the double or triple loop learning strategy as shown in Figure 2 in making their reports. They were also encouraged to triangulate, that is, use, a variety of methodologies such as the questionnaire, the interview and written reports. A suggested strategy for this type of action research methodology is shown in Figure 2. Those reports formed the background information base for this paper.

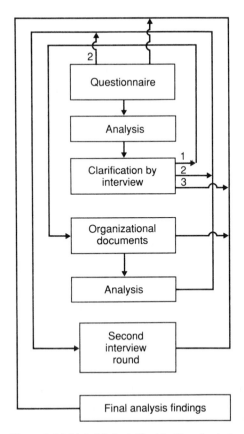

Figure 2. Multiple Methods Used in Firm Analysis.

RESULTS

Results are based on 100 reports from middle and top managers generated by use of the action learning/research methodology described in the previous section. In addition, some 20 of these companies were given questionnaires concerning Porter's value strategy with follow-up interviews conducted (Valeur, 1987). Finally, an aggregate model was constructed for Norway (Joynt, 1987) and was reviewed with 15 top managers. It was altered with only minor changes. It is of interest to note this study used the individual company as the main unit of analysis, rather than the branch which is common in other Porter model work. In this chapter we will concentrate on the aggregate model, generated from the 100 or so company studies mentioned above. We will also limit the analysis to value chain activities; thus, price, focus, and differentiation strategies, as well as co-ordinating and integrating mechanisms, will not be reviewed.

NORWEGIAN DATA AND PORTER'S PRIMARY ACTIVITIES

Inbound logistics is the first of a firm's activities involved in the physical creation of goods or services. Here, receiving, storing, and information concerning inputs are important factors, and, while Porter assumes the logistics function as discrete, it is closely related to the production function. Since Norway lies on the periphery of Europe, it is natural to assume that the inbound logistics activity will be costly; and, indeed it is. In addition, a clear majority of the firms sampled, especially through interviews, stated that this activity was often poorly administered. Warehouses were often too small or too big; inventory control was often done manually; material handling often involved manual rather than automatic operations; and, vehicle scheduling was often irregular or non-existent.

One notable factor to consider is the typical size of a Norwegian firm—often very small by international standards. This size factor plays a major role in the professionalization of logistics; the smaller the firm, the less professional. As a matter of fact, many of the smaller firms were unaware of the costs entailed.

Production, or operations, is the second primary activity and is associated with the transforming of inputs into the final product, or service, in many cases. Here we found that Norwegian companies tended to be very service-oriented with some 70% of the sample emphasizing service rather than a product as the major output. With high wages at the operative organizational level, it is difficult for an operation activity involving a product to be competitive. The large production-oriented companies that were not in a monopoly situation were, for the most part having serious competitive problems in this area, mainly because of high labour costs; poor management practices were also a factor. Several of the firms had become internationalized and had, therefore, moved these activities out of the country.

Outbound logistics is associated with the storage and physical distribution of the product to the customer. Again, many of the weaknesses found in the inbound logistics activity were found here. Also, the two activities were often combined because of the typically small size of the firm. An important thing to note is that top management, in most cases, did not consider the competitive aspects of logistics. The activities were there and, therefore, had to be dealt with. This was the typical response.

Marketing is, perhaps, the most interesting activity in the value chain for the average Norwegian company. In some respects the research results represent a paradox; on one hand marketing and sales are the major activities of many Norwegian firms, and on the other hand the competence and professional level of the marketing activity remains rather low. There are three generic strategies for achieving good performance in an industry: cost leadership; differentiation; and focus. Porter has used variants of these strategies. Cost focus and differentiation focus are examples. The important thing is that if it wishes to stay competitive, a firm must make a choice as it cannot 'be all things to all people'. No decision often means no competitive advantage; and, this was the situation of over 90% of the firms in the sample. Porter (1985) calls this situation 'stuck in the middle'.

The competence and professional level of the marketing activity is not a major problem with respect to the national markets; but it becomes the biggest problem Norwegian firms have in the international markets. Our results showed there is usually a major advantage, in terms of quality, when one can use the mark 'Made in Norway'. This advantage often disappears because not enough professional effort is used in making the final sale. This is a unique form of marketing myopia where the initial advantage of 'Made in Norway' is lost because of the incompetence involved in making the sale. In addition, since advertising and promotion techniques are limited by law in Norway, there are inherent experience disadvantages involved when behaving in the international market place for Norwegian firms.

Service is the final primary activity in Porter's theory. It involves providing service to maintain or enhance the product; this includes everything from repair to adjustment of a product, or some type of follow up associated with a service such as air transport. Our results showed that Norwegian firms score very high with international activities but have some problems with national activities. We will not dwell on this second issue for it is beyond the scope of this paper. We will, however, concentrate on the international aspects of service. SAS, Veritas, Unitor, Norsk Hydro and other companies are typical Norwegian firms which have formidable strength competitively because of their service image. Service Mangement is a popular concept in the Scandinavias; it is even sold by consultants in the international arena. The best example perhaps is SAS, which has benefited a great deal from its service image.

SUPPORT ACTIVITIES

The four support activities of infrastructure, human resource management, technological development, and procurement provide the inputs that allow the primary activities to take place on an ongoing basis. Infrastructure consists of such activities as management, finance, legal, or governmental contact. Infrastructure, or organizational structure in the Norwegian context, involves small organizations usually involved in the marketing activity abroad as far as international strategy is concerned. After the study done by Valeur (1987), the activity of 'internationalization' was 'added' to the 'Norwegian' Porter Model. The reasoning behind this will be explained; it is important to note that this change was made because of the concluding comments in many of the 100 studies, as well as in the interviews done by Valeur. Organizational structure, particularly bureaucracy, is an integral part of any Norwegian firm older than a couple of years. Possible explanations which are a central position of this activity might include: traditions—we always do it this way, that is, use some type of engineering education and, thus, a rational or bureaucratic bias; unemployment—the rate of unemployment is often around 1%, low by international standards as organizations are encouraged not to eliminate people during hard times; they often work with activities involving bureaucracy. This activity does not involve a bureaucracy with its many levels of management; rather, it is a flat organization with lots of people occupied with a variety of organizational structure activities. While very few of the firms in the sample had reduced their management positions, many did agree in the interviews there were many excesses in the administrative area. Because of the heavy emphasis on organizational structure activities in a national context, and an emphasis on marketing as the main international activity, the international activity is to be considered an additional primary activity in the Porter model (Joynt and Welch, 1988) as is shown in Figure 3. In conclusion, we found that there was a tendency towards a flat but excessive bureaucratic structure at home, with almost no emphasis on activities other than marketing abroad.

Human resources management is the second of the four support activities and involves recruitment, training, motivation, and development of personnel. Almost every activity

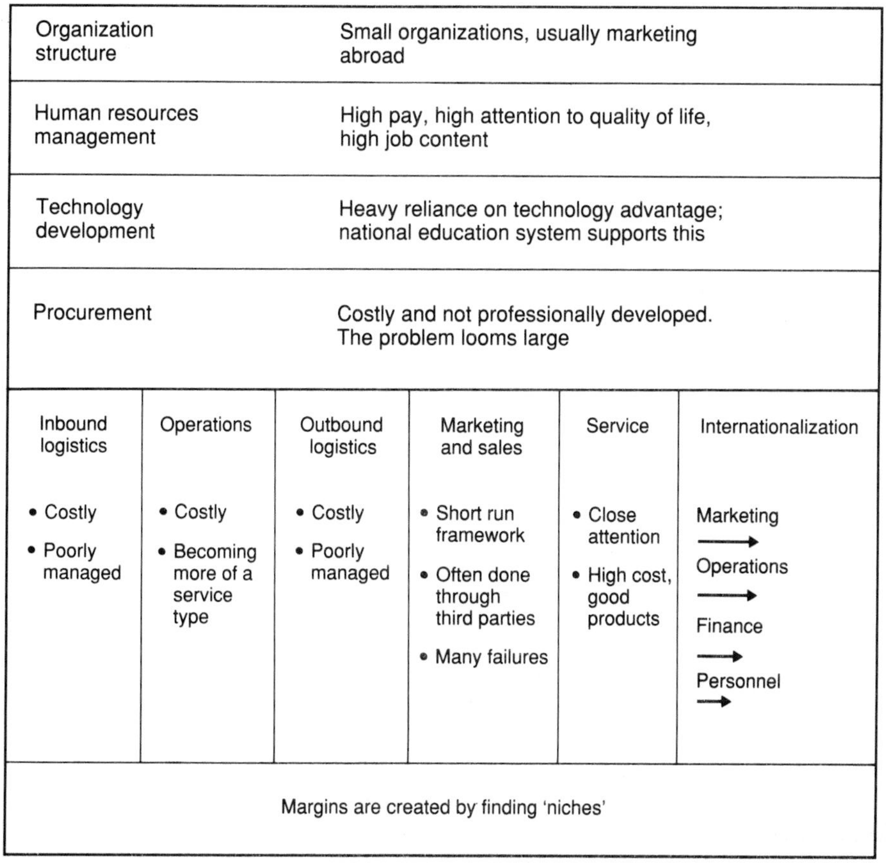

Organization structure	Small organizations, usually marketing abroad				
Human resources management	High pay, high attention to quality of life, high job content				
Technology development	Heavy reliance on technology advantage; national education system supports this				
Procurement	Costly and not professionally developed. The problem looms large				
Inbound logistics	Operations	Outbound logistics	Marketing and sales	Service	Internationalization
• Costly • Poorly managed	• Costly • Becoming more of a service type	• Costly • Poorly managed	• Short run framework • Often done through third parties • Many failures	• Close attention • High cost, good products	Marketing ——▶ Operations ——▶ Finance ——▶ Personnel ——▶
Margins are created by finding 'niches'					

Figure 3. Aggregate Model for Norwegian Internationalization Based on Earlier Empirical Work on 100 Firms.

involves human resource management; Norway is competitively very strong in this area as the typical employee usually has high job satisfaction, as well as a good education. Wages are high and the quality of work is also very high. These can be considered as uncompetitive activities as they cost money. National legislation concerning work environment laws, as well as flat organizations, (mentioned above) forms the framework for firms engaged in high technology or services. Johnson (1988) suggests a new philosophy of work may arise out of this major emphasis on industrial democracy. With a small firm, which is typical in Norway, this new technology may be easier to offer as a model for the rest of the world in providing an example of a clear competitive advantage.

With a very high level of education at the national level; technological development is one of the support activities where most Norwegian firms enjoy a competitive advantage. Since technology involves everything from preparing documents to product design, one has to analyse the work done in the typical firm. Norway is very advanced in robots, in computers, and in the use of new techniques to get things done faster and cheaper. With the high wages the country pays employees, it is important that each firm 'automate' as much as possible. The country with its mountains and lakes presents communications and transport challenges which can be transferred to other lands after a trial experience period in Norway. Water power, oil exploration, information technology, word processing, aluminium manufacture, ship building and aqua-farming are just a few examples. In conclusion, the technology factor is one of the strongest of the positive competitive advantage activities.

The final activity in the support part of the value chain involves procurement which can be defined as purchasing inputs for *all* the activities in the chain such as building, machinery, etc. Norway is one of the most expensive countries in the world, both because of its physical location and a rather high tax system which supports a highly social democratic form of government system. These costs have caused many firms to transfer their production activities to other parts of the globe where such costs are lower. This activity is possibly the major non-competitive activity in the value chain and in recent years it has caused the failure of many firms. In addition, the management of procurement in a small firm is not as professional as in larger firms, and is, therefore, an area often neglected by management.

CONCLUSION

In conclusion, the most competitive activities involve human resources management, service and technological development, while the activities involving procurement, marketing, and organization structure often are not competitive when compared with firms outside Norway. The aggregate model for the internationalization of the Norwegian firms is shown in Figure 3. Competitive advantage is at the heart of a firm's strategy and performance in competitive markets. A final comment is due with respect to the internationalization of the Norwegian firm.

Because of its small size, a Norwegian company's effort to find a niche in a large market has often been its typical strategy. This has been the source of a good deal of frustration and major problems as the firm initially is acting in a non-competitive area and can often fail when the niche becomes competitive.

IMPLICATIONS FOR FUTURE RESEARCH

Kohn (1987) states that the substance of social science comes from the process of speculation, testing, new speculation, new testing—the continuous process of using data to test ideas. This, he said, is a 'fundamental tenet of my scientific faith'. This study involves an initial analysis of data from some 100 Norwegian firms. They are, in many respects, on-going cases for an action-learning research methodology. Porter's model is especially appropriate for this type of research work for it involves a dynamic pragmatic framework practitioners can use in their day-to-day work with international strategy. The Welch model formed the first step in our research process. It formed the bridge between the scientific traditions of Scandinavian research in the area of internationalization as a *process* and Porter's emphasis on internationalization as a *strategy*.

The main implications for future research involve the use of Porter's model at the firm level of analysis in forming the background for national competitive strategy models such as the one generated in this study. The Porter model has to be modified to fit the national situation as we did by introducing a new dimension in the model, that of internationalization as a main primary activity for Norwegian firms. A second implication involves the move from descriptive research, often based on past actions, to a more action learning type of research where dynamic concepts such as strategy are considered. This research represents a first step in this direction. Many refinements are needed in the future.

Finally, there are important applications for the managers of international organizations. Competition is the 'name of the game'; the older descriptive approaches to international strategy need refinement. Perhaps, trial-error oriented learning at the firm and the national level is one approach which could be undertaken. With its limited base and high activity in the international scene, Norway provides an ideal situation for this type of thinking.

Overall, the concept of international strategy has yet to be developed as a research object; given its importance, research responsive to this dynamic character of the process is a high priority, perhaps in the regional-comparative context.

REFERENCES

Ansoff, I. (1987) The emerging paradigm of strategic behavior. *Strategic Management Journal*, **8**(6): 501–515.

Argyris, C., Schon, D. (1978) *Organization Learning: A Theory of Action Perspective*. Reading, MA: Addison-Wesley.

Bernard, C. (1938) *The Functions of the Executive*. Cambridge, MA: Harvard University Press.

Buckley, P. J., Newbold, G. D., Thurwell, J. (1979) Going international—The foreign direct investment behavior of smaller firms. In L. G. Mattsson and F. Wiedersheim-Paul (eds), *Recent Research on the Internationalization of Business*. Uppsala: Almqist & Wiksell.

Cavusgil, S. T. (1982) Some observations on the relevance of critical variables for internationalization stages. In M. Czinkota and G. Tesar (eds), *Export Management*. New York: Praeger.

Cavusgil, S. T., Godiwalla, Y. M. (1982) Decision making for international marketing: A comparative review. *Management Decision* **20**(4): 40.

Cooper, R. G., Kleinschmidt, E. J. (1985) The impact of export strategies on export sales performance. *Journal of International Business Studies* **16**(1): 37–56.

Daft, R. L. (1980) The evolution of organization analysis in ASQ, 1959–1970. *Administrative Science Quarterly* **25**: 623–636.

Gandemo, B., Mattsson, J. (1984) Internationalization of firms-patterns and strategies. *Bedrifts Okonom*, **6**(August), 314–17.

Hedlund, G., Kverneland, A. (1983) *Are Establishments and Growth Strategies for Foreign Markets Changing?* Paper presented at the 9th annual conference of EIBA, Oslo, Norway, December, 18–20.

Heller, F. (1985) Comparative Research. In P. Joynt and M. Warner (eds.), *Managing in Different Cultures*. Oslo: Universitetsforlaget.

Hornell, E., Vahlne, J. (1982) *Changing Structure of Foreign Investment by Swedish MNCs*. Paper presented at the 8th Annual Conference of EIBA, Fontainebleau, France, December.

Johanson, J., Wiedersheim-Paul, F. (1975) The internationalization of the firm: four Swedish cases. *Journal of Management Studies* **12**(3).

Johanson, J., Vahlne, J. (1977) The internationalization process of the firm. *Journal of International Business Studies*, **8**(1): 23–32.

Johnson, A. (1988) The democratization of the workplace: The Norwegian experiments. Norwegian School of Management, Institute for Management Research. No. 2, pp. 1–22.

Joynt, P. (1987) *International strategy: A Study of 100 Norwegian Firms*. Annual EIBA Meetings, Antwerp, Belgium, December.

Joynt, P., Welch, L. (1988) *The International Process of Norwegian Firms*. Norwegian School of Management.

Kohn, M. (1987) Cross-national research as an analytic strategy. *American Sociological Review* **52**(December).

Luostarinen, R. (1979) *Internationalization of the Firm*. Helsinki: Acta Academiae Oeconomicae Hewlsingiensis.

Masuch, M. (1985) Vicious circles in organizations. *Administrative Science Quarterly* **30**(2): 14–20.

Mintzberg, H., McHugh, A. (1985) Strategy formation in an adhocracy. *Administrative Science Quarterly* **30**(June).

Parsons, T. (1937) On the concept of power. In *The Social System*. Glencoe, IL: Free Press.

Porter, M. (1986) Changing patterns of international competition. *California Management Review* **18**(2).

Porter, M. (1985) *Competitive Advantage*, New York: The Free Press.

Susman, G. I., Evered, R. D. (1978) An assessment of the scientific merits of action research. *Administrative Science Quarterly*, **23**(4): 582–604.

Swedenborg, B. (1982) *The Multinational Operations of Swedish Firms*. Stockholm. Almquist & Wilksell.

Turnbull, P. (1985) *Internationalization of the Firm—A Stages Process or Not*. Paper presented at the Conference on Export Expansion and Modes of Export Market Entry, Halifax, October 15–16.

Thompson, J. D. (1967) *Organization in Action*. New York: McGraw-Hill.

Valeur, J. (1987) *Internasjonalisering, En Global Modell og Noen Empriske Observasjoner i Norsk Naeringsliv*. Oslo: BI-U-LF.

Walters, P. (1985) Study of planning for export operations. *International Marketing Review* **2**(3).

Weber, M. (1947) *The Theory of Social and Economic Organizations* (A. M. Henderson, trans. and Talcott Parsons, ed.).

Weick, K. E. (1979) *The Social Psychology of Organizing*. Reading, MA: Addison-Wesley.

Welch, L. S., Luostarinen, R. (1988) Internationalization: Evolution of a concept. *Journal of General Management* **14**(2): 32–55.

Welch, L. S., Wiedersheim-Paul, F. (1980) Initial exports—A marketing failure? *Journal of Management Studies* **17**(October), 333–44.

Index